Series: Of Islands and Women
Number 6

CW01426038

Isle of Wight

Also by Susanna Hoe

Lady in the Chamber (Collins 1971)

God Save the Tsar (Michael Joseph/St Martin's Press 1978)

The Man Who Gave His Company Away: A Biography of Ernest Bader, Founder of the Scott Bader Commonwealth (Heinemann 1978)

The Private Life of Old Hong Kong: Western Women in the British Colony 1841–1941 (Oxford University Press 1991)

Chinese Footprints: Exploring Women's History in China, Hong Kong and Macau (Roundhouse Publications Asia 1996)

Stories for Eva: A Reader for Chinese Women Learning English (Hong Kong Language Fund 1997)

The Taking of Hong Kong: Charles and Clara Elliot in China Waters (with Derek Roebuck) (Curzon Press 1999; Hong Kong University Press 2009)

Women at the Siege, Peking 1900 (HOLO Books 2000)

At Home in Paradise: A House and Garden in Papua New Guinea (HOLO Books 2003)

Madeira: Women, History, Books and Places (HOLO Books 2004)

Crete: Women, History, Books and Places (HOLO Books 2005)

Watching the Flag Come Down: An Englishwoman in Hong Kong 1987–97 (HOLO Books 2007)

Tasmania: Women, History, Books and Places (HOLO Books 2010)

Travels in Tandem: The Writing of Women and Men Who Travelled Together (HOLO Books 2012)

Malta: Women, History, Books and Places (HOLO Books 2015)

Women in Disputes: A History of European Women in Mediation and Arbitration (with Derek Roebuck) (HOLO Books 2018)

Sardinia: Women, History, Books and Places (HOLO Books 2022)

Isle of Wight

Women, History, Books and Places

Susanna Hoe

HOLO BOOKS
THE WOMEN'S HISTORY PRESS
OXFORD

First published 2024 by
HOLO Books: The Women's History Press
Clarendon House
52 Cornmarket
Oxford OX1 3HJ

email:holobooks@yahoo.co.uk
www.holobooks.co.uk
and www.centralbooks.com

British Cataloguing in Publication Data
A catalogue record for this book is available from the British Library

ISBN   978-1-9196318-5-1   (pbk)
ISBN   978-1-9196318-7-5   (e-book)
ISBN   978-1-9196318-6-8   (Kindle)

This book is printed on paper suitable for recycling and made from fully managed
and sustained forest sources. Logging, pulping and manufacturing processes are
expected to conform to the environmental regulations of the country of origin.

Produced and typeset for HOLO Books by
Stanford DTP Services, Northampton, England
Printed in the UK

For Jane
From 'last resort', through driver and guide, to friend.
With thanks.

Contents

Illustrations

Preface

How did I come to write about the Isle of Wight? There is usually some trigger, and so there was this time. 'We had a nice 5 days on the Isle of Wight a couple of weeks back', wrote a close friend. And she continued:

> We went to Osborne House and also to Carisbrooke Castle. We really enjoyed Carisbrooke and learned a bit about the history of the IoW. I thought of you and your women and islands when we read about Countess Isabella de Fortibus who ruled IoW in the 1290s. You probably know about her – but mentioning just in case you don't. There certainly weren't many prominent women back then.

In response, I had to chide her for forgetting the four pages about Isabella in *Women in Disputes: A History of European Women in Mediation and Arbitration* (2018) which my late husband, Derek Roebuck, and I wrote together. But she had got me thinking. Since Derek's death four years ago, and my inevitable ageing, I had rather gone off travelling to the sort of place we used to go in search of 'my women' for my series 'Of Islands and Women'. Not only could I not explore in the same way without his help, but neither was doing so the fun and excitement of the research chase we'd shared. But it was that remark, 'There certainly weren't many prominent women back then', that nagged at my mind. Really? Then there were the stories about frightful queues at airports when there were air transport problems, the rising cost of living that made flying less affordable, not to mention the cost of air travel to the environment. When I decided that writing about the Island was a good idea, I was taken aback by how many people I mentioned it to had been there.

Actually, Derek and I had been there too. Many years ago, Mummy broke a leg. Living alone, as she did in Spain, in a flat accessed by a stone staircase, she needed somewhere to convalesce, and she'd organised it at Osborne House. So we drove her over to the Island. During the First World War, one of the secondary wings of Victoria and Albert's Island retreat was used as an officers' convalescent home. Known as the King Edward VII Retirement Home for Officers, it later, until 2000, accommodated convalescents from military and civil backgrounds, including retired officers of the British armed services and, it turned out, their wives. We later went over to pick her up. But that is all we saw of the Island, and I have to confess I couldn't remember much about it, except that Mummy was made so welcome, and Derek met a retired judge before whom he'd appeared many years before and who, in his 90s, professed to remember him. There is no obvious sign of what had been when you visit Osborne House now; it is as it was in Victoria and Albert's day.

So, with my friend's prompt, I booked a room in Seaview where they had stayed – the Seaview Hotel – and the hotel booked my ferry passage from Portsmouth to Ryde, and off I went on my first research trip. And I did, indeed, find the Carisbrooke Castle a treasure trove. What is more, it revealed many women who required further exploration, and so the list of them began to grow, and grow, many of them 'prominent'; hence such chapters as 'Women of Property' which features Isabella, among others; and 'Women in a Man's World', the penultimate chapter of *The Isle of Wight: Women, History, Books and Places*. For my second research trip, I stayed again at that hotel, which has a good restaurant, and where the staff were interested in, and helpful about, my research.

On my third trip I took the ferry from Lymington to Yarmouth and stayed at the George Hotel, which went way back into history as a private house, where one of my women had enjoyed(?) trysts with a prominent man (and got pregnant), and which also had a good restaurant. Staying in Yarmouth allowed me to visit Freshwater, and you could hardly describe the pioneer photographer Julia Margaret Cameron as 'not prominent'.

My fourth trip took me from Southampton to West Cowes where I stayed at the Union Inn which not only is around the corner from where the French Impressionist Berthe Morisot painted the scene that appears on the cover of this book, but, in the eighteenth century, was run by a woman who aided and abetted smugglers, including her husband. One night she forgot to light the lamp at the top of the inn; now her ghost roams about it, though not in my room. Good cocktails and wonderful seafood, including lobster for which I hankered, are to be had at the Smoking Lobster. Cowes has also got an excellent bookshop – the Medina. I shall return.

As this preface suggests, the book itself is, perhaps, more personal than earlier books have been in the series 'Of Islands and Women'.

Oxford, June 2024

Acknowledgements

Jane Richter, to whom the book is dedicated, almost deserves the status of co-author, so much has she been involved in the creation of it – but then she would have to answer for any mistakes and infelicities. As the dedication suggests, from a small acorn, quite a hardy sapling has grown. From when I first contacted her – as a 'last resort' – and we agreed terms because I didn't want to be taken on the sort of grand, expensive tour I assumed from her website that she usually provided, she drove me round to wherever I needed to go during three research trips. During those drives and at the places we visited, she gave me the benefit of her knowledge. Later, with that knowledge of the Island's history, as well as its present places, she read the whole book, correcting the obvious errors. And, even when I disagreed with her opinions, as she did mine, we didn't fall out, and sometimes I accepted her suggestions, and took account of them, and sometimes I didn't!

That long thanks to Jane, should not detract from my gratitude to the others who have helped me. Many of them read chapters or sections in which they or the place connected with them, appeared; often they showed me around; once even driving me there as well. Sometimes it was answering a question, or providing information or photographs. They include, in alphabetical order: John Allen (3 Alexandra Gardens), Wendy Ball, Mary Beard, Cynthia Burek, Ian Calder, Alan Crockard (Athenaeum Photographic Group), Janet Dore (Classic Boat Museum Gallery, East Cowes), Vaudine England, Octavio Ferraz, Penrose Halson, Christina Hemmett (Athenaeum), Evie Hodgson, Bruce Huber, Janet Hurst, Megan Jacobs, Miranda Kaufman, Ashley Keen (St Augustine Villa), Mimi Khalvati, Emily Lyle, Suzie Marwood, Vivienne Monk, Judith Okely, James Rayner, Rebecca Redfern (Museum of London), Libby Rodger, Caroline Scallon, Kevin Shaw, Karolyn Shindler, Sue (Farringford), Lesley Telford, Hamo Thornycoft, Tim Wander, Trudie Wilson, Margaret Hopkinson Woolley and William Twining.

During my first couple of research trips I depended on several taxi drivers who entered into the spirit of my venture; they included James Brotherton, Sean Glassett (he of the useful contacts), Andrew Moore and Dennis. Where I first stayed, The Seaview Hotel, had an all-women staff who could not have been more helpful. And I'll never forget the woman staff member – Nicola – at The George in Yarmouth who (when I had already been drowned once in a rainstorm, and tried to dry all my soaked clothing in the cloakroom), sheltered me with an umbrella, without being asked, from the hotel to the ferry terminal. She will never know how much that gesture meant.

I am so grateful for the help I received from directors, curators and other staff and volunteers of Natural History Museums on the Island, in London and in Oxford which made possible my entrée into the world of dinosaurs and their fossils, previously one about which I knew nothing. They include Mike Day, Susie Maidment, Jenny McAuley, Martin Munt, Susan Newell, Kathryn Rooke

(Archivist, London) and Chloe Williams. Special thanks need to go to Neil Adams who not only showed me fossils, and then provided me with essential material pertinent to women, but also carefully scrutinised and suggested changes to the chapter written by a complete tyro. And Eliza Howlett, in Oxford, who put up with an awful lot of bother from me, and even re-wrote a section that was beyond me, lifting a stupidly heavy burden off my shoulders.

I would not like to forget those in other establishments who have helped me: staff in the British Library, particularly Elias Mazzucco in the Rare Books Room, Paula and David (Brading Roman Villa), Toby Ensch (Cambridge University Press), Jenny Courtney (Site Manager, Newtown Old Town Hall, National Trust), Caroline Hampton (Isle of Wight Heritage Service), The Lincoln Repository, Ruth Watson (Max Aitken Museum, West Cowes) and Corina Westwood (Curator Human History, Isle of Wight Heritage Service).

Thanks go, too, to those who have provided images, without charge, which makes such a difference. My contact in each place was so helpful, and pleasant about it. They include the Classic Boat Museum Gallery (East Cowes, Mark McNeill), The National Portrait Gallery (Bruna Laga Fazolo, Rights and Image Officer), The Royal Collection Trust (Lauren Stark) and the Tennyson Society (Ros Boyce).

On the subject of illustrations, being somewhat of an ageing Luddite, I could not for a moment manage to cope with uploading the images on to my computer without the unbelievably patient and kind competence of Bob McIntyre who, when extolling his virtues out of his hearing, I call my 'computer boffin'.

I think I may have run out of original words suitable to thank HOLO Books' Editor and, I hope I may now, after very many years of working together, call a dear friend, Susan Faircloth. My warm thanks too, yet again, to Dave Stanford who designs our covers, typesets our books, and sees them through the printing process while also replying by return and with grace to the most trivial request for help.

Last, but never least, I thank the memory of my husband, Derek Roebuck, who was part of the creation of every book I wrote while we were together, but who died four years ago. I wish he had been with me on the Isle of Wight, and could have read the draft of this book before I put it before any public gaze. It would have been so much better.

Author's Note

This series 'Of Islands and Women', with its sub-title 'Women, History, Books and Places', has developed its own style over the years. Some explanations may, therefore, be helpful. The names of historical women connected with the Isle of Wight are in bold on their first appearance, including in quotations. This is intended to make it clear when the details of a woman start, especially those whose stories are told in some detail. I tend to use first names after women are first introduced. I am more formal with my contemporaries, and they are not in bold. Women who feature substantially are included in the Index, though women mentioned only once, perhaps in passing, may not be there.

There are, as usual, intentionally no footnotes or endnotes, which may be irritating for a scholarly reader. Instead, I put sources within the text; this is intended to make the book accessible to the general reader, but I also hope that scholars or Isle of Wight readers will find those sources, together with the bibliography, sufficient. I hope they will also find what I have written to be as accurate as the facts and my understanding allow. Many alleged facts, it has to be said, are contradicted by other alleged facts. I have had to use my nous.

If a scholar conversant with a particular aspect of the Isle of Wight's history feels that something I have written is out of date, I can only apologise. So much material, new and old, becomes constantly, and more than ever, available, that I have had to leave a chapter to speak for itself at the time of writing. Exceptions are where a kind expert reading my draft has pointed out what should usefully be included or changed, or where something I came across later obviously demanded it.

If you are familiar with the usual format of the other five books in the series 'Of Islands and Women', you will know that the history is written in chronological chapters. This book is different: the chapters are ordered thematically – though within that theme the account can be chronological – and the dates relevant to the subheadings are given there and in the Contents. That is simply because that is how the material ordained it to be. Another difference is that there is not a separate section of the book devoted to itineraries. Instead, details about how to visit a particular place, as well as a description of a place concerning a particular woman, are incorporated into her history. The lack of itineraries also applied to *Sardinia*, for different reasons. (Anyone having acquired that book can look up on the publisher's website: www.holobooks. co.uk an account of a later trip I took around Sardinia; click on 'Updates'.)

The bibliography is rather extensive and may seem, at first sight, unduly complicated. It is split into several sections. If the author or title you seek is not immediately obvious, please persevere. By this system, I hope to guide the reader into the sort of book or article that best suits their purpose, as I have drawn on books of appeal to the general reader and books and articles by scholars indiscriminately in the text. The Internet, including Wikipedia, though to be used with discretion, is an invaluable hunting ground for information about women who still tend to be neglected in the re-creating of history; the Internet may be the only source. I do not apologise for sometimes relying on Wikipedia, but tend not to name it as a source – that is, in spite of the recent controversy about omitting to name sources. If a source is lacking in the text, it may well have been Wikipedia. As proliferation of Internet material increases over the years, that section of the bibliography is long. Many scholarly articles can also be found on the Internet, as can even some otherwise difficult to access historical travel accounts or histories.

Where historical sums of money are mentioned, sometimes someone has made a stab at its value today. If they haven't, the sum is left in the original.

This is not a guide book but there is a map of the Isle of Wight, with the main places marked – not necessarily with geographical accuracy, but simply to give an idea.

Map xvii

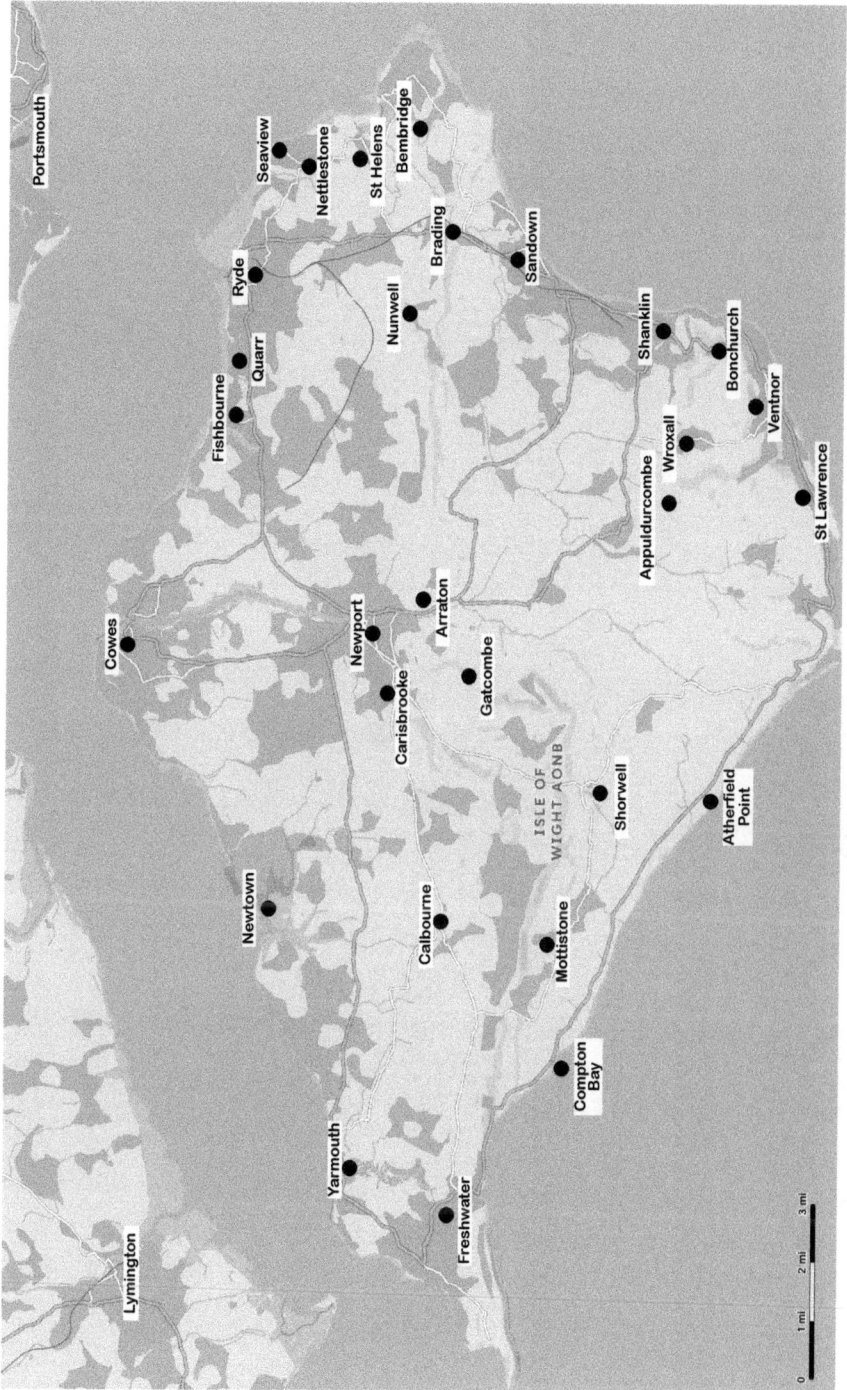

Introduction

The most obvious difference between islands and other lands is that they are surrounded by water. Though this is hardly worth mentioning, it is so obvious, for some islands this attribute has more importance than for others. I suggest that this is true of the Isle of Wight, at least that is how it seems to have emerged from the pages that follow.

I have, in the other volumes in this series 'Of Islands and Women' – *Madeira, Crete, Tasmania, Malta* and *Sardinia* – established what might be called a conceit: I have been able to start each of the island's stories with an early woman arriving on the island's shore, sometimes shipwrecked, sometimes in another way worth noting. There has been one exception, that was *Malta*, where I couldn't find such a woman. But that allowed me to take the conceit in another direction. I started the introduction to that book:

> Of the eight planets in the Solar System, Mercury is the smallest and closest to the sun. You can sometimes see it in the morning sky, or in the evening, though not at night. But what you cannot see with the naked eye are its craters. One of them is named after Maria de Dominici (1645–1703), the earliest known Maltese woman artist. Her existence is little spoken of, certainly outside Malta …

I cannot, either, find a named woman arriving on the shore of the Isle of Wight, so I have taken to the sky again. While Maria de Dominici might be little known, Dame Ellen MacArthur is known of and admired throughout the world, not only for sailing round it, and beating the record for doing it the fastest, but for many other exploits on the sea. To come across the existence of asteroid 20043 Ellenmacarthur should not, therefore, be surprising. Dame Ellen, her sailing and the work of the foundations she has set up in Cowes where she lives, appear in Chapter 12, 'Women in a Man's World'.

Women involved in professional sailing and powerboat racing are more obvious off the shores of the Isle of Wight, than perhaps off other islands, but the waters that surround it have been important throughout history, partly because of its physical closeness to the mainland of England, and the ease with which the inhabitants of both could exploit that. From earliest times, the Island acted as a trading hub between, the various peoples of the mainland, the short distance across the Solent, and those in Gaul, often members of the same tribes, the other side of what is now the English Channel. These links are described in chapter 2 – From Prehistory to the Coming of the Romans. Was the skeleton of a woman who lived 2,000 years ago, and found in the silt left when the tide goes out in Fishbourne, something to do with that trade? It seems she may be part of something more sinister. Slavery appears from time to time in these pages.

The Island's situation between mainland England and Gaul, when the whole of that more southern landmass was united as France, was not always a happy one. Chapter 4, 'Troubled Times', tells of the many times there were attacks across the channel, and how the French were beaten off, once it is said by women archers. But the attacks, even if confined to the coastal towns, caused misery among women and their families, particularly when their town was set fire to, or when their menfolk were killed.

Trade, particularly in luxury goods such as brandy, inevitably lent itself, to smuggling, in which women could play an essential part, described in chapter 6, 'Outsiders'. In that chapter is the story of Molly Downer who was not only seen as a witch within her community, but also involved in smuggling. And in chapter 5, 'Irregular Relations', Sophie Dawes, the ultimate social climber, undoubtedly learned the art of dissembling, and succeeding, from helping her smuggler father, the famous Dicky Dawes, ply his trade.

The art of smuggling and that of retrieving goods from the many ships wrecked near the Island, is nicely illustrated as early as the thirteenth century and Isabella de Fortibus, 'Lady of the Isle' who dominates chapter 3, 'Women of Property', as she did the Island. The English King, Edward I, did much to get his hands on the Island, and thought he had won the long game in every way when he sent envoys to Isabella on her deathbed to sign the necessary document. But she had the last laugh. It harked back to a court case concerning 'the right of wreck', which she fought and won. But some time after she died, the Island by then in the possession of the Crown, Edward III wondered why he was failing to receive the proceeds of that right of wreck. It transpired that the locals were going out in boats and capturing the property from the wrecked ship before it drifted onto shore and, thereby, became the king's.

The cover of this book, a watercolour painted by the French Impressionist Berthe Morisot on honeymoon in Cowes in 1875, wonderfully captures the Cowes seascape during the week of the annual Regatta. She was told that during that week, she and her husband 'saw the most fashionable society in England.' Berthe is further discussed in chapter 9 'Women Artists'

Knowing how, increasingly, during the nineteenth century people crossed the Solent to the Island, left me wondering how they got there; even though it was not more than five nautical miles, it had to be crossed. It is not something that is much discussed in the literature. Mention is made of the coach or carriage ride and later in the nineteenth century, the train, to and from the south coast, and once you were on the Island, but not about the crossing itself. During Cowes week, transport would have been laid on, indeed, there is a 1874 painting by Berthe's fellow French artist, Tissot, entitled 'The Ball on Shipboard' (now in the Tate Gallery) which was almost certainly enjoyed on the Solent. And large passenger boats making the journey across may well have been common by then.

But by what means would an ordinary family travel across the Solent earlier in the century? A neat clue is offered in the introduction to chapter 10, 'Women Writers'. All Jane Austen knew about the Island, when she mentioned it in *Mansfield Park* (1814), came from her niece, Fanny Knight. With her father, Fanny travelled to the south coast of England in a gig, and she wrote in a letter of 7 June 1813: 'Breakfasted at Portsmouth. Dined and saw the Dock Yard at Portsmouth, & took a wherry over to the Isle of Wight in the evening. We slept at Ride [Ryde]'. A wherry was a light rowing boat.

Poor Empress Eugénie of France, who appears in chapter 11 'Foreign Royalty and Elite Visitors'. She travelled to the Island when her husband was overthrown in 1870. Her small party arrived at Ryde after a terrible journey fleeing from Paris, and an even more terrifying one across the channel through a storm. Instead of a warm welcome for a refugee empress, her dishevelled appearance meant that the first hotel they approached refused her entrance. In later years, she was Queen Victoria's guest at her Island home, Osborne House, and a rather elegant pair of beach shoes made by Cowes's premier shoemakers, Jolliffes, run by Gladys Jollife in its later years, is now held in the Carisbrooke Island Museum. Gladys appears in chapter 12.

The Empress Elizabeth of Austria chose Ventnor as her Island retreat. In 1874, doctors advised her that what her ailing youngest daughter needed to recover was good sea air and good sea bathing. The empress and her suite took over Steephill Castle, with its private beach, for some months. Steephill gave way to a housing estate and now only exists in pictures, and books, but Ventnor's micro-climate continued to attract, particularly exiles from Russia and other revolution-troubled East European countries. The woman who looked after Alexander's Herzen's children, Malwida von Meysenbug, was an accomplished artist and left both a sketch of the cliffs looking east along the coast from Ventnor, and another where the family stayed looking out over the sea, with a sailing boat below. She and the Empress appear in chapter 11.

And so it's back to Ellen MacArthur's sailing, and a couple of pioneer power boat racing women of note. If you feel that chapter 1 'Dinosaur Isle' has been neglected in this overview, it is not so much about dinosaurs but about the women and girls who looked for, found, and collected their fossils, which almost all came from the prone-to-slipping cliffs above the sea shore, particularly on the south and east coasts of the Island. The women start with Barbara Rawdon-Hastings, Marchioness of Hastings. The fossils, examined, cared for, analysed and sometimes reconstructed either by women artists, or from piecing together their fossils, are to be found in Natural History Museums, for example, on the Island, in London and in Oxford.

Ellen MacArthur doesn't need me to secure her place in history; she's done that very effectively herself. But how many readers of these chapters had ever heard of the diva of mid-nineteenth-century fossilists, Barbara Hastings, until they saw her name in the paragraph above? Even among today's workers in that scientific field, she is probably little known of, unless they're a specialist. One of the purposes of this book, as well as the others in the series, if not already apparent, is to give many sorts of women who, otherwise, would be without their voice in history, their life and achievements un-recorded. Barbara opens the chapter that follows.

1 – 'Dinosaur Isle', 1840–2024

The living things in the world we have inherited did not start with dinosaurs millions of years ago, or even the small mammals upon which some of them feasted. That's what I assumed, not having given the matter much thought, until listening to a recent radio programme. More millions of years earlier, I learned, there were microbes and, within that group, bacteria, living here and, over eons, evolving into, for example, plants. Only eventually did dinosaurs come into existence.

Perhaps I should start with the women microbiologists who study them, or have studied them. But there would be nothing we could go and see and marvel at, as we can the remains of dinosaurs in natural history museums. Instead I am starting with the women and girls who have hunted for, and found, their fossils on the Isle of Wight, commonly known as 'Dinosaur Isle'. It is a pity that we cannot (yet) sex dinosaurs from their remains. Although there are some hints concerning females and pregnancy, they do not bear scientific scrutiny.

Given my level of ignorance, some of which is revealed here, I should confess that I have never been interested in dinosaurs. They have been beyond my ken as a human, and even previously beyond my scope as a re-creator of women's history. But I have had to become a bit interested in them and have, indeed, been privileged to have been shown fossils found on the Isle of Wight not usually on public display. Even now, I am by no means any sort of authority on them, as will surely be revealed in what follows, but I have become interested and acquired a smidgeon of understanding. And the passion of female fossil hunters, or accidental finders, has become of much interest. The women in this chapter include early illustrators who used the fossils to draw how particular dinosaurs might have looked, or illustrated reconstructed skeletons of dinosaurs. Some women illustrated the fossil finds of their husbands. Three girls have a section of their own in what follows. The first woman discussed here was not the first woman fossil finder; the focus below is on the connection with the Isle of Wight.

It is important to note, as one of my generous informants made clear in an email, and as will become clear in what follows, that not all the fossil finds on the Island are those of dinosaurs; as she added, 'It is much more diverse than the Cretaceous terrestrial deposits, there is actually so much here from later time periods too such as the Eocene/Oligocene which has an expansive fossil record in itself. Not to mention the vast array of ammonites found in our Cretaceous marine deposits.'

'The First Lady of Fossils' and the Isle of Wight

The first, and perhaps best known, if the quantity of material about her is anything to go by, was **Barbara Rawdon-Hastings** (Marchioness of Hastings, 20th Baroness Grey of Ruthyn; née Yelverton; 1810–1858). Born at Brandon

House in Warwickshire, Barbara was the only child of Henry Yelverton, 19th Baron Grey de Ruthyn, and his wife, Anna Maria Kellam. She was only seven months old when her father died, and she inherited his title. There is no evidence of a formal education, so that for all she achieved in later years, she was self-taught through sheer intelligence, application and enthusiasm.

In 1831, aged 21, the beautiful young Baroness Grey de Ruthyn married debt-ridden George Rawdon-Hastings, 2nd Marquess of Hastings. It is said that he was so passionate about hunting that the marriage was postponed until the summer, so as not to interrupt the season. Barbara's passion was for travelling and gambling, particularly in Paris, so that she acquired the sobriquet of 'jolly fast marchioness'. She would sometimes sit at the tables until 3am but then rise early after which, on one occasion, as her sister-in- law put it, the end would come 'in an hysteric cry from sheer exhaustion'. Somehow she found time and energy to produce five children; she was pregnant with the sixth when, in 1844, her husband died. Before that, as early as 1840, she is recorded as collecting fossils from the Isle of Wight.

1. Barbara Rawdon Hastings, © National Portrait Gallery, London

In April 1845, Barbara married her second husband, Captain Hastings Reginald Henry RN who, in 1849, by royal licence, took the surname Yelverton. With him Barbara had her seventh child. In 1846 they bought Efford House, between Milford-on-Sea and Lymington, most importantly, near Hordle Cliff – a prime Eocene spot for collecting 36-million-year-old fossils, and across the Solent opposite the north-west coast of the Isle of Wight. That is when she became a serious fossil hunter/collector, building an extension to the house in which to set up a museum for her fast-growing collection which, in the end, contained several thousand fossils.

This much-titled woman is most usefully known as Barbara Hastings; and, to me here, she is Barbara. Because the record of her finds is so extensive, for simplicity I'm drawing mainly on the articles/blogs/papers of three scholars. The title of Karolyn Shindler's 'Barbara Hastings: the first Lady of fossils' (2010) says it all. She also wrote a short piece for the 2011 Hogg Conference on Geological Collectors and Collecting – '"I have found wonders": the life, letters and passion for collecting of the 19th century fossilist, Barbara Yelverton, Marchioness of Hastings', which, again, says so much. I should add that, having sat in the archives that contain Barbara's 64 letters to Richard Owen – founder of the Natural History section of the British Museum – for some hours, anyone who has managed to read her handwriting deserves a medal. Two blogs by Nina Morgan appear on the nicely named Trowelblazers website: 'Barbara Hastings' (2014) and 'More than Equal' (2010). A more academic, more detailed, treatment of Barbara is Martina Kolbl-Ebert's 'Barbara Marchioness of Hastings (1810–1858) – Fossil Collector and "Lady Geologist"' (2004). Those works published in 2010 celebrated the centenary of Barbara's birth. It needs to be added that Martina Kolbl-Ebert wrote many more articles than that one; help from them, too, infuses what follows. They were provided for me by a most generous curator at the Natural History Museum in London.

There is some question over whether or not Barbara actually got her hands dirty in her search for fossils. Karolyn Shindler writes that she was:

> highly intelligent and a passionate fossil-hunter. Not that she often got too dirty herself – she would stand at the foot of the cliffs she was excavating, orchestrating the digging of her workmen.

However, Barbara wrote to Owen, 'I am enchanted my dear Mr Owen at my good fortune ... I brought home after a most arduous miry walk the other day two more iguanodon-like teeth.' And that 'orchestration' included making stratigraphical observations which she later published. Of these observations, although they were not of the Isle of Wight, Nicholas Edwards notes in 'The Hastings Collection ...' (1970), 'Hers were the first accurate stratigraphical accounts of Hordle and Beacon Cliffs published, and although other accounts have been published since, those by the Marchioness remain among the best.'

By no means all Barbara's fossils were found by her or her workmen, or a specific man whom she employed for four or five years to work on Hordle

Cliff: she also bought from other fossil finders – local women and children, whom she encouraged to help her, so they could also earn money, or from finders abroad. She made yachting excursions along the South Coast, to the Isle of Wight, Bournemouth, Lyme Regis and Torquay collecting all the time. What is certain is that, once they were in her possession, she knew how to treat them. She became skilled at what was termed a 'preparator' of her fossils: she spent a great deal of time carefully extracting the fossil from its matrix, then repairing her fragile brittle finds, many in hundreds of fragments, with an expertise publicly praised by Owen and other geologists. If she felt uncertain about any fossil, or simply wanted Owen to see it, it was sent off to him, with one of her scrawled notes.

What is rather attractive about Barbara is how she managed to mix fossils with professionals – famous palaeontologists and geologists – with friendship; they may have been invited to see her museum collection, but there was more to it than that. Geologist Edward Forbes, for example, wrote to a colleague:

I spent a few days very delightfully and very usefully with Lady Hastings, who is one of the most excellent (and without exception the cleverest) woman I have ever met. Her husband too, Captain Henry, is an exceeding nice person. He is an amateur chemist, she is a 'fossilist' and knows her work, and both are enthusiasts in music and drawing; both playing and singing, and painting admirably. There is not the slightest grain of nonsense or affectation in either so you may guess my pleasure in becoming intimate with such trumps, even though they be – only in name – aristocrats. Lady Hastings has the finest collection of Speeton clay fossils I have ever met with … I have carried away a new oolitic star-fish too, most conveniently for my report on the subject.

Barbara had more to offer Forbes than that: in her museum, she presided over a real hub for scholars and collectors; he wrote to another colleague:

Yesterday & today I have been hard at work at Lady Hastings tertiaries [a particular period]. The collection is really a wonderful one. I have gone over & named all her shells & she has laid aside for us a complete set of duplicates & promises to go on collecting for us. These will be very valuable, since with the exception of Edward's coin, I do not think any one equals hers in this department. In vertebrates she beats all the private collections. … when the Isle of Wight shall have to be done her stores will be valuable material to us.

But the most appealing relationship was with palaeontologist Richard Owen, who much admired her scholarship, but wrote to his sister in 1847 about a musical evening:

The Marchioness is an extraordinary vocalist – two octaves clear and more. Captain Henry, her husband plays the violoncello; I take the flute, Lady H the harp, and one of her daughters the piano ... too tired to write when I go to bed, and seldom awake earlier than in time for an hour's work in the museum before breakfast. It is chiefly of fossils, several thousands, and some of them the finest in the world. I described one at the Geological Society on Wednesday night.

Owen not only described her work at learned meetings, but also included it, together with illustrations, in several of the many papers he published. But he was difficult to persuade to visit her; she had to try and lure him, writing, for example 'I suspect you don't know what treasures I have got from the I[sle] of W[ight] & from Hordle, or yu would not quite relinquish pay'g us a visit.' It is difficult to know when to stop quoting passages from or about Barbara. This note shows how she had to mix domestic affairs with work; she wrote to Owen – always Dear Mr Owen, and often undated:

I have not a moment hardly my dear Mr Owen, having been busy every minute of the day till past 12 at night dressing a German Christmas tree for tomorrow, but I am anxious to tell you I have a beautifully perfect under jaw (The fellow to the upper one drawn by yr artist) wh I will send up by a private hand this week – if that will do ... There is nothing but a German Tree for you to see & Tea after, as it is simply a child's party.

The nicest story about the mixture of the personal and professional, took place during her only pregnancy with her second husband. She was trying her best to carry on with her work obligations when she wrote, perhaps rather revealingly for the period, 'Were I in travelling condition, I wd bring up my treasures myself but as in two months I am expecting my confinement, I am compelled to be quiet'. A few weeks later, she continued 'Of the hordle Tri[onyx] – I have a large series of bones & Carapaces for you. Pray call one Barbara, I shall be charmed & just now I move about very Tortoise like.' (The baby born of that pregnancy was the Hon Barbara Yelverton.)

To see one of the tortoise carapaces in the basement of the Natural History Museum in London, as I was privileged to do, brings that note from Barbara alive; this is my own photograph of it. Does this, or does this not, make you think of a pregnant Barbara Hastings? One most fascinating morning I was shown a series of fossils by several different curators, each with their specific area of expertise; they are thanked in the Acknowledgements for doing more than showing me the fossils: their enthusiasm in their work was infectious.

The *Trionyxbarbarae* was indeed named after Barbara, though its name is now *Tryonyx henrici*. Examples of those fossils held by her museum came from both the Isle of Wight and the Hordle Cliff. Owen wrote to a colleague in September 1847:

The zeal of Lady Hastings has supplied me with a new and highly inter-esting generic form of Pachyderm from the Isle-of-Wight Eocene, which I

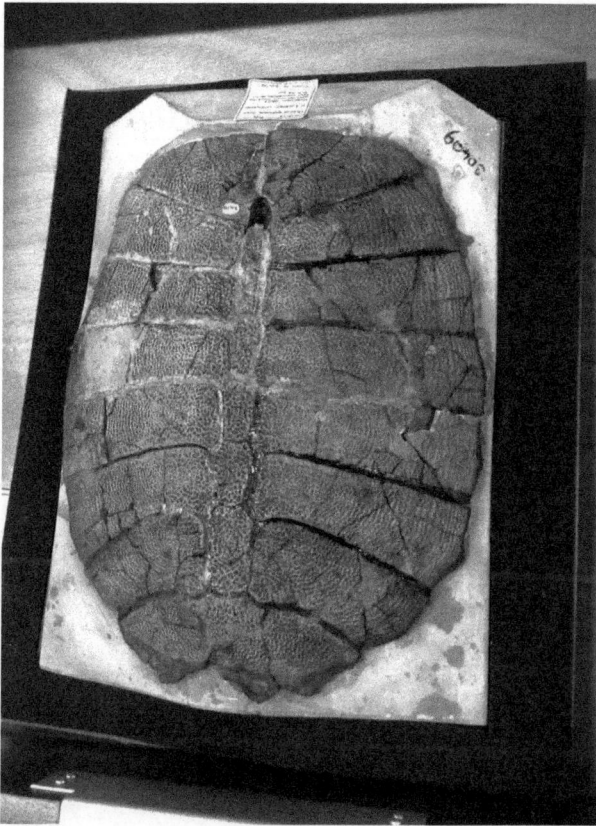

2. Turtle Shell, from the Natural History Museum in London,
photograph by the author

propose to make a subject for the next meeting of the Geological Society. This really important co-operation of her Ladyship in the common objects of the Society merits reciprocal attention and encouragement, which cannot be better manifested than by speedy and adequate illustration of the treasures, which she liberally lets out of her museum in our behoof; with, at the same time, a jealous appreciation of the specimens and that enhances the obligation.

'Her Ladyship' and elsewhere, in an Association report she is described as 'noble and accomplished': would her work have had the same reception if she had not been a wealthy aristocrat? One need only to go back to the earlier story of Mary Anning (1799–1847), significant fossil finder of Dorset's Jurassic Coast, and her struggle against the odds to gain recognition for her work to raise that question. Doing so takes nothing away from Barbara's work.

The 'Association' is the British Association for the Advancement of Science (BAAS). There is an occurrence that shows that Barbara was sometimes treated as a mere woman. She was able to present a short paper under her own name in the geology session of the 1847 Oxford meeting of the BAAS, but not read it out herself. Martina Kolbl-Ebert continued in 'Ladies with hammers – exploring a social paradox in early nineteenth-century Britain' (2023):

> However the paper had to be read by the session's secretary on her behalf, since it was considered inappropriate for a lady to exhibit herself in such a manner. She subsequently published the paper independently.

A piece Barbara wrote for the 1847 Report of the BAAS included,

> It is now eight years ago since I found in a locality between Cowes and Colwell bay, but little known, scales and teeth of the crocodiles, shell of Trionyx, the palate of the Prulis Hastingsii, then just named by M. Agassiz and a bone figured and described by Mr. Owen in his 'British Mammalia' as Lophiodon or Palaeotherium.

It's quite a long coastline from Cowes (north) to Colwell Bay, west (south of Yarmouth), and this provides an indication of where she made those finds. But with her exuberance that was as nothing.

Finally, in 1853, the first female members were admitted to the BAAS. Barbara wrote to Owen: 'I hope you know I am one of you now, being elected a Life member!!' She was, however, still excluded from the Geological Society of London. After a meeting of it, she had to write to Owen:

> I do so sadly want to know my dear Mr Owen how the introduction of my Hyopotamus went off – what Buckland said & …&…Do try & find a spare moment in wh to tell me.

I was also kindly shown among Barbara's finds a *Hyopotumus* (a mammal, known today as *Bothriodon*) by another curator during my morning in the basement of the Natural History Museum in London. It is worth noting that 'the Geological Society of London was officially founded on 13 November in 1807, but it was not until 21 May 1919 that the first female Fellow was elected.' 'Women and Geology in the 19th Century' (2022) a posting by the Society's library, continues,

> As in common with many of the other learned bodies, women were excluded from membership and attendance at the Society's lectures during the 19th century as they were believed to lack the intellectual rigour to engage in scientific study.

In spite of her continuing success, in the early 1850s Barbara's life took a turn away from her life as a fossilist: perhaps some personal tragedy took place. It is suggested that the death of her eldest son, Paulyn, the 3rd Marquess of

Hastings in a freak accident, aged 18, in 1851, may have been a factor. She did, though, publish two of her three papers after that, in 1852 and 1853. Perhaps she and her husband had simply decided to move away from Efford House, where Barbara had been tied by her passion for fossils, and wanted to spread her wings, as she had done in her youth. There is also some evidence for a significant theft by a steward, affecting the family fortune. By 1855, the couple had moved to London.

Barbara offered to sell her collection to the British Museum, but heard nothing back from them. She wrote again, threatening to sell 'the whole of my Tertiary fossils, crocodiles pachyderms, Tortoise and Birds' to the Paris Museum. Eventually the British Museum paid just £300 for the greater part of her collection – about 1,500 specimens – and then purchased a few more at her auction of the rest in June 1855. The Natural History Museum in London now holds a fair amount of her collection; she had promised Owen that her collection should become public property before or after her death. As for Barbara, in 1858, staying in Rome, on her way to meet her husband who was serving in Malta (he later became an admiral), she died of a stroke, aged only 48, and was buried in the English Cemetery there.

Museums of Natural History

Much has been said of the Natural History Museum in London but the Isle of Wight has its own Dinosaur Isle Museum, details of which will emerge below. Oxford University Museum of Natural History (OUMNH) also has connections with the Isle of Wight, some of which have been uncovered by Jenny McAuley, a volunteer researcher at the museum. And the woman she has unearthed is **Ada Scott** (1862–1932?), a collector of whom other writers on women and fossils seem to be unaware.

Jenny McAuley's work has been part of a project at OUMNH, the aim of which is similar to that which appears in chapter 10 'Women Writers', and may well be an increasingly prevalent area of exploration. The museum project, 'Coming Out of the Shadows', aimed 'to explore the often-hidden work of women in building, curating, and researching its collections, particularly in the 19th and early 20th centuries'. The purpose of the volunteers was to 'help … bring these women and their contributions out of the shadows and into the spotlight by creating brief biographies based on collections information and other online research', some of which would be published as blogs.

Ada Scott was a woman of independent means and amateur artist who was also involved in the Oxford University Extension Movement to enable access to higher education for non-University members (the forerunner of the present-day Oxford University Department of Continuing Education). She was born in Ryde, the second eldest of eight children of Alfred Scott, an ironmonger and his wife Anne Scott (née Ricketts). In about 1870, Scott purchased an ironmongers business at 4 High Street, in an increasingly fashionable Ventnor, as later chapters will show. In due course, he became a parish overseer and a director of the Ventnor Gas and Water Company as well as a high-ranking Freemason.

Census returns from 1871 to 1911 show Ada living continuously at the family home, and remaining there with her elder sister **Emily Maria Scott** (1861–?1933) after their father died. Both sisters seem to have remained unmarried and are described in 1911 as being of no occupation and living on 'private means'. Ada attended the Ventnor School of Art during the 1880s and early 1890s, passing examinations that qualified her for an art teachers' certificate from the Science and Art Department, South Kensington, which was by then a subdivision of the Board of Trade. She was also a keen exhibitor of her work during the 1890s, winning prizes in the Ventnor Photographic Exhibition in 1891, and showing work at the Royal Academy of Arts, London. Both Ada and her younger sister, **Dora Amy Scott** (b *c.*1890), attended a 'ladies' class' in elementary physiology in Ventnor in 1888.

There were also fortnightly Thursday evening lectures in Ventnor given by Edward Clarke Spicer, an Australian-born Anglican priest, then based in Oxford, who had studied geology at New College. Detailed reports on these lectures were published in the *Isle of Wight County Press*, beginning with 'The Isle of Wight, its form and History' at Sandown Higher-Grade School on 8 October 1903, and continuing with subjects including 'the protozoic or marine period' at the Literary Institution, Ventnor (29 October).

This is where Ada's interest in geology came to the fore. At the sixth of the lectures, held in Ventnor on 10 December 1903, the report noted that, 'A collection of fossils made by Miss Scott from the chalk in the locality came in for much favourable comment from the lecturer'. These may not have been the same as the specimens which she donated to OUMNH in 1904, described in the museum's annual report as 'a large collection of fossils from the Lower Greensand of Atherfield', but the praise may well have contributed to Ada's decision to donate fossils to Oxford the following year.

Fossils collected from the Atherfield Clay Formation (further west along the coast from Ventnor) include the pterosaur *Vectidraco*, which will feature under the sub-heading 'The Girl Fossil Finders', and which is to be found in the Natural History Museum in London, and the sandownid turtle *Sandownia*. These are Lower Cretaceous in age, so older than the Chalk fossils, which come from the Upper Cretaceous.

What is particularly attractive about Ada is that not only did she consume any learning available, but she also gave back: she was directly involved in administration. 'The Misses Scott' (i.e. Emily and Ada) sat on the general committee for the Oxford University Extension's 'Ventnor Centre' which met to discuss the success of the 1903–4 course on 30 March 1904, when Ada Scott was also re-elected to that committee and elected to the working committee for organising future courses.

Documentary evidence on Ada is limited and her story might well have ended there but Chloe Williams, another of the OUMNH project volunteers, has now catalogued Ada's fossil collection, uncovering additional information from the collection itself. To see it on a spreadsheet, specimen by specimen, is impressive. There are 85 specimens in all, including brachiopods, bivalves, gastropods, ammonites, crustaceans, echinoids and shark teeth. Seventy-three are from the Lower Greensand, as stated in the annual report, but 13 are from the Chalk, and five of these are from Ventnor. It seems that some of the fossils that came in for favourable comment from the lecturer may have been preserved after all.

There is one other woman with connections to OUMNH and a slightly elusive connection with the Isle of Wight. Although it is connected with her future husband, her part in his work was to be pivotal to much of its success. What is more, **Mary Buckland** (1797–1857) was already an accomplished naturalist and avid collector before she met William Buckland.

Barbara Hastings has introduced Buckland in a passing reference to him above, concerning a meeting that she was not allowed, as a woman, to attend; now, in 'Ladies with hammers', Martina Kolbl-Ebert puts some flesh on him. He was initially resistant to women attending meetings, writing to a fellow organiser of the BAAS conference held in Oxford in 1832:

> [I]f the meeting is to be of scientific utility, ladies ought not to attend the reading of the papers – especially in a place like Oxford – as it would at once turn the thing into a sort of Albermarle-dilettanti-meeting, instead of a serious philosophical union of working men.

(Buckland's reference to 'dilettanti' was intended as a putdown: the Dilettanti Club had been founded in London in 1734, and the best way of becoming a member was to have been on the Grand Tour.)

However, 15 years later, when the conference was next in Oxford, his attitude had changed:

> [B]y the end of the Oxford Conference, it was generally agreed that the presence of the ladies had probably contributed significantly to the high tone and dignified respectability which had distinguished the proceedings.

Buckland, having won a scholarship to Corpus Christi College, Oxford, in 1801, made a long and distinguished career there. After graduating, he worked initially as a college tutor, only developing his lifelong interest in geology from about 1809. He later achieved great success as the university's first joint Professor of Mineralogy and Geology. By 1824 his combined geological museum and lecture room occupied an entire floor of the Old Ashmolean. By 1825, when Mary Morland married him, he was Canon of Christ Church – one of the richest governmental rewards for academic distinction.

Mary Morland first met Buckland in 1819 or slightly before. Some biographical details posted on the Geological Society website include their daughter Elizabeth's version of the meeting, as well as further information below:

Dr Buckland was once travelling somewhere in Dorsetshire, and reading a new and weighty book of Cuvier's which he had just received from the publisher; a lady was also in the coach, and amongst her books was this identical one, which Cuvier had sent her. They got into conversation, the drift of which was so peculiar that Dr Buckland at last exclaimed, 'You must be Miss Morland to whom I am about to deliver a letter of introduction'.

Mary was the eldest daughter of solicitor Benjamin Morland and his wife Harriet Baster. Her father was the first to stimulate her interest in geology, but this was increased following her mother's death, when she spent much of her childhood with Sir Christopher Pegge, Regius Professor of Anatomy, Oxford, and his wife. Pegge, who also lectured in geology and mineralogy, encouraged Mary's scientific pursuits and, on his death in 1822, left her,

his mineral cabinets and all the minerals and fossils contained in them at the time of my decease and all my books of natural history and comparative anatomy as a mark of my esteem and regard for her.

The meeting on the coach and the books Mary had with her (which, Elizabeth recognised, may well be inaccurate given that Cuvier's book on fossil bones wasn't published until the early 1820s) are significant because, with the skills she had developed as a scientific illustrator, Mary had already done drawings for Georges Cuvier before her marriage to Buckland.

In 1825, Buckland was finally able financially to propose to Mary, and they were married that December. In the years that followed, Mary had nine children who probably slowed down her work, though she continued to offer invaluable support to Buckland's endeavours. Their eldest son, Frank, gives the following account, contained in the OUMNH posting 'William Buckland', of his mother and her contribution to her husband's work:

Not only was she a pious amiable and excellent helpmate to my father, but being naturally endowed with great mental powers, habits of perseverance and order, tempered by excellent judgement, she materially assisted her husband in his literary labours, and often gave to them a polish which added not a little to their merit. Not only with her pen did she render material assistance, but her natural talent in the use of her pencil enabled her to give accurate illustrations and finished drawings. She was also particularly clever and neat in mending broken fossils. It was her occupation also to label the specimens.

The couple's connection with the Isle of Wight is quite slight, but Mary's scientific life as the wife of a Georgian/Victorian scientist is an example of other wives, such as Charlotte Murchison, and Mary Lyell, and the married trajectory of their lives. In OUMNH there are three fossils with labels in Mary's hand:

Iguanodon phalanx (toe bone) found East of Sandown Fort, Sandown Bay, Isle of Wight;

Iguanodon femur (thigh bone) found Yaverland, East of Sandown Fort, Isle of Wight. Collected by John Smith, 1829;

Iguanodon vertebra (back bone) found Yaverland, East of Sandown Fort, Isle of Wight. Collected by John Smith, 1829.

Buckland, in his 1829 paper 'On the discovery of Fossil Bones of the Iguanodon, in the Iron Sand of the Wealden Formation in the Isle of Wight, and in the Isle of Purbeck', identifies and acknowledges John Smith as residing at Yaverland Farm. It seems likely that he was a farmer but not a farm owner, whom he would have referred to as 'John Smith, Esq'.

It is known that Mary Buckland accompanied her husband on field trips, continuing to be a practising geologist, making observations, illustrations and models, and assisting in specimen collection and the preparation of papers. But did she ever go to the Isle of Wight? That is the so-pertinent question. A positive answer is given in passing in a letter of 23 November 1821 from the American Martha Hare, aunt of a professor of natural history, to Buckland. She acted as a go-between her nephew and him. What she writes of relevance is:

My own summer's excursion was to that most interesting spot the Isle of Wight where I had the pleasure of Meeting Miss Moreland [sic]; and through her kindness that of looking through Sir H Englefield's work upon that Island. I have of course returned laden with Fossils and Clays though nothing new...

Sir Henry Englefield's book was *A Description of the Principal Picturesque Beauties, Antiquities and Geological Phoenomena of the Isle of Wight* (1816). The copy may have been one of those left to her by Pegge, or it may have belonged to Buckland. By then, they had known each other for a couple of years, and it appears that there was an understanding between them, but he was not yet in a financial position to marry her.

A connection worth highlighting is that between the various wives, often scientists in their own right, who were more known as 'helpmates' in their husband's scientific work. This is illustrated by this extract from an 1833 letter from Charlotte Murchison to Mary Somerville contained in 'Ladies with hammers':

My dear Mrs Somerville

I hear that my husband is going to send you a copy of his discourse, & I must add a mite of my compositions [...] Mrs Charl. Lyell is in the picture of health & happiness – I saw her last night at a soirée Babbage gave to his fair admirers (great and little) ... why will you not come over to the Cambridge party? ... Mrs Buckland not very well, quite overworked assisting at the birth of his essay – too bad with so many births of another description to endure.

More is to be learned about the work of Charlotte Murchison and Mary Lyell in Martina Kolbl-Ebert and Susan Turner's 'Towards a history of women in the geosciences'.

The Draughtswomen

Finding fossils and analysing, discussing, naming and cataloguing what they were is one thing, usually done by an educated finder or a scientist – palae- ontologist or geologist. But what did the living creature look like? That had to draw on physical details that the fossils suggested, guidance from the scientist and skilled imagination. Sometimes they drew from reconstructed creatures. At least two women – sisters – represent the profession of illustrator, or draughts- woman. Although they were particularly skilled in their craft, it seems that they did not aspire to any other role.

Regarding the Isle of Wight, **Alice Bolingbroke Woodward** (1862–1951), English artist and illustrator, was one of the most prolific illustrators at the turn of the twentieth century. She is perhaps mainly known for her illustration of children's literature, such as that in later editions of *Alice in Wonderland, Black Beauty* and *Peter Pan*. But, as far as the Isle of Wight dinosaurs are concerned, it is her scientific illustrations that are described here. Both sisters had a head start in this regard: their father was a well-known scientist and the Keeper of Geology at the Natural History Museum in London. Their mother was Ellen Sophia, née Page.

Alice and Gertrude, along with three other sisters and two brothers, were educated at home by governesses; all of them were encouraged to draw. All the girls became artists; the boys, scientists – it was relatively unusual then for women to become scientists, even if Barbara Hastings did. By her late teens, Alice was skilled enough to illustrate her father's scientific lectures and those of his colleagues; the illustrations had to be large enough to be shown in a lecture hall. She earned money for this and seems to have paid for her studies at South Kensington School of Art, then at the Westminster School of Art; and later at the Académie Julian in Paris. Initially that led to illustration commissions from publishers for books for children; nevertheless, she continued to illustrate scientific work throughout her career. The Archives of the Natural History Museum in London hold 22 of those drawings, contained in an envelope as postcards. They cost 1s each in 1925. I managed to buy on the Internet one of the postcards produced, relevant to the Isle of Wight, shown here. 'Forgotten Women in an extinct saurian (man's) world' (2010) by Susan Turner et al is the best source for Alice Woodward; the following passage from it is key:

> She based her illustrations on actual fossils, as is seen in the *Illustrated London News* (Woodward 1925) where it is noted that the restored figure of the *Iguanodon* was based upon fossils found in the Isle of Wight by Hulke J.W. (FRS)

3. *Iguanodon*, Alice Woodward postcard

RESTORATIONS OF EXTINCT REPTILES
IGUANODON
Height of shoulder about 10 feet
BRITISH MUSEUM (NATURAL HISTORY)
G 68
Produced by W. F. Sedgwick, Limited

That is not only the Alice illustration here, but it is also the same as the very large *Iguanodon* skeleton made up from fossils found, and somehow married up, that you see if you enter the Hintze Hall in the Natural History Museum in London. It really does give you an impression of the living creature's size and shape; close your eyes and you can put flesh and skin on it. Happily, it was herbivorous. I have learned subsequently that one of the curators who gave me so generously of her time, has, with her students, been re-examining the skeleton, confirming that it is distinct enough from the *Iguanodon* to merit a new name, *Mantellisaurus*.

John Hulke was a surgeon by training, and practised as such, but he also, at first in his spare time, became a geologist. His work on vertebrate palaeontology was mainly on the Isle of Wight, and fossils of the *Iguanodon* are of particular interest. After his death, his wife Julia Grace Hulke, née Ridley, donated his collection to the Natural History Museum in London. Down in the basement, the first curator to look after me showed me other *Iguanodon* fossils found by Hulke; though they are large (and heavy) one must wonder at the skill it took to put the pieces together to reconstruct a full dinosaur.

On the back of the sketch of Alice's early restoration of *Iguanodon*, which she sketched in 1895 when she was 33, and which may also have been used in the *Illustrated London News*, is written:

Animal is shown in the attitude in which it usually walked. The fore limbs are much shorter than the hind limbs, which are very powerful, having three toes to each foot and the same number of joints as in a bird's foot.

The ponderous tail no doubt gave support to the animal when in an erect position and was also used in swimming.

After Alice's death, her sister Katherine wrote to the Natural History Museum in London asking if they would like a collection of Alice's postcards, and the reply was positive. There are several letters quoted in the article, but what the authors wrote about Alice best describes her work, and why they might wish to write about it:

These exchanges illustrate the high esteem in which she was held both by members of the NHM and [by] the scientific and business world. Alice Bolingbroke Woodward is, perhaps, one of the foremost forgotten illustrators of the extinct saurians in a man's world. Her work reflected the reconstruction style of the day but sometimes she produced scenes that leap from the page and brighten the day for any palaeontologist, some of which have not been surpassed for recreating an environment 'feel'. She showed visually the Mesozoic settlings for dinosaurs and reconstructed them according to how she thought they would fit with the fossil remains. Without a doubt, her association with her father and his colleagues would have helped her but her skill and deductions must not be underestimated.

The Linda Hall Library (Science, Engineering, Technology) of Kansas City, made Alice 'Scientist of the Day' on 3 October 2016.

During the First World War Alice did some tutoring and worked for a short time for Naval Intelligence. She went to live in Bushey and occupied a studio there for the rest of her life.

Rather less is known about the work of Alice's elder sister, **Gertrude Mary Woodward** (1854–1939) who was also an illustrator of children's books, as well as scientific papers. The only connection with the Island is that she 'may be' the illustrator of two fossils found there in 1865 by the Reverend William Fox. The 'bird-hipped *Polacanthus foxii* was an armoured spiked and plant-eating dinosaur described by Hulke in 1881. Who named it for Fox is disputed, though it was probably Owen; but you did not name a fossil after yourself.'

Concerning the naming of fossils, leap forward to the twenty-first century. On the death of palaeontologist and long-established, and valued, curator at the Natural History Museum in London, Angela Milner, the *Riparovenator milnerae* (Milner's Riverbank Hunter) was named after her. It was to honour her and her work – not apparently on the Island – and her example to young women who followed her at the NHM. It turns out, however, that she visited her mother who lived on the Isle of Wight, and Angela died just before publication of the fossil find on the Island, though not found by her.

Alice and Gertrude Woodward engaged professionally as scientific draughtswomen of dinosaur fossils, and it has been possible to link their work to the Isle of Wight. But there was a cohort of other nineteenth-century women, sometimes scientists in their own right, though not recognised institutionally as such, sometimes fossil collectors themselves who had one other valuable skill which Martina Kolbl-Ebert describes in 'Drawing as a female Accomplishment in the service of Geology':

Many if not most of the wives, daughters, sisters, or other female relatives or acquaintances of prominent early British geologists had a more or less thorough education in drawing and painting, which made them well suited to fulfil the needs of these geologists. Female paintbrushes and pencils were engaged in the service of geology in several ways.

The Girl Fossil Finders

Sometimes it needs only enthusiasm, opportunity, sharp young eyes and luck, to find an important fossil on the Isle of Wight. Two girls vie for being the youngest to find a dinosaur fossil there; about one, aged five, plenty has been written; the other, apparently four, is more elusive. All that seems to have been recorded about four-year-old **Megan Brooks** is the 2015 newspaper (Reading-Berkshire) headline 'Caversham girl makes rare dinosaur bone discovery on the Isle of Wight'. A photograph shows a toothy Megan holding up her fossil find to the camera, and the caption reads, 'four-year-old Megan Brooks with the dinosaur bone she found on the Isle of Wight'. The short text under that reads:

A four year-old girl from Caversham has possibly become Britain's youngest palaeontologist after discovering a dinosaur bone on the Isle of Wight. Megan Brooks was on holiday with her parents Nigel and Rebecca when she unearthed part of the rib from an Iguanodon dinosaur on Compton Beach, on the west of the Island. Megan was on a fossil-hunting trip and guide Oliver Mattsson said, 'In over 20 years of fossil collecting on this beach I think Megan must be the youngest person to discover a dinosaur bone'.

An even shorter entry in the *Isle of Wight County Press* (8 June 2015) notes: 'Quick success for fossil hunter Megan'– 'Sharp-eyed Megan spotted what to the uninitiated would appear to be an ordinary stone – but which was part of the rib of an **Iguanodon**.'

Fortunately, more is known about Daisy Morris who, according to her mother, Sian Morris, started hunting for fossils aged three. Under a photograph of her – plump arms resting on her knees, curly hair above smiley eyes – is the strapline 'Daisy Morris had just turned five when she found the fossil, from the Lower Cretaceous period, on Atherton beach, Isle of Wight'. (Atherton Beach is on the south coast to the west of Ventnor, the area known as Back of the Wight.) That was in 2009. Fast forward to 2013, when Daisy was nine years old, and a BBC posting has the headline 'Isle of Wight "pterosaur girl" named tourism ambassador'. The time lag was the length of time it took to examine what Daisy had found, and identify and validate it as a *pterosaur* fossil. The family then donated it to the Natural History Museum in London. This was another fossil that I was shown there by the curator in charge of pterosaurs. I have to confess that, seeing what seemed a very small piece of bone, even insignificant, palaeontologists must be very good at their job to identify it, and what part of the creature it was. That was done in this case by those at the University of Southampton. More technical details are to be found on their website.

Not only was Daisy to be tourism ambassador but the fossil was named after her – *Vectidraco daisymorrisae*. *Vectidraco* means 'Isle of Wight dragon' (Vectis being the Roman name for the Island). And at that stage the Museum named the Isle of Wight the 'dinosaur capital of Great Britain'. The discovery was a completely new species and genus of pterosaur – the size of a large crow and toothless. Pterosaurs were flying reptiles that lived in the same time period as dinosaurs, and closely related to them, up to 220 million years ago. Pterosaurs came in astonishingly different sizes. The smallest had wingspans of under 25 centimetres, while the largest were as tall as giraffes and had wingspans over 10 metres! Pterosaurs probably occupied a variety of different environments from zipping through dense forests to soaring over open plains.

Sian Morris, a teaching assistant at the time, said of her daughter, 'She has a very good eye for tiny little fossils and found these tiny little black bones sticking out of the mud and decided to dig a bit further and scoop them all out. We are all very proud of her.'

There was so much interest in Daisy and her find that Martin Simpson wrote *Daisy and the Isle of Wight Dragon* (2013). This A5, slender, quirky and nicely illustrated booklet is aimed primarily at children, but offers no barrier to adults.

To hear Daisy's own voice, though, you need to look at her blog of 16 March 2014, when she was 10. It was the last thing I found about her, after I had completed my first draft, which I have not changed because it shows how a re-creation of history may always be corrected. The blog starts with a number of photographs of the fossil, one of her having a look at the drawers of fossils at the museum and one of Lorna Steel who, at the time, looked after all the pterosaur fossils at the Museum. I love the first couple of lines of her text. During the period of hoo-ha that followed her fossil find and its naming, it was said that she was aged five. But now she firmly corrected the record: 'in 2008 when I was 4 years and 7 months old'. (That is, the same age as Megan Brooks, the Caversham girl!) And it was Daisy who decided to donate the fossil, not her 'family'. And she elaborated on what followed her outing:

After the release of the new find everyone in the world wanted to know about how I had found it, about my collection of fossils and bones and wanted to speak to me abut it. I have been on Newsround, the One Show and Canadian news (by Skype video) and done loads of radio interviews, been in the newspapers in Britain, India and Hong Kong and children's magazines in Germany and Britain, spent the day with Barney and crew from Blue Peter and appearing on there as well. ... I have also been made the Children's

Ambassador for Visit the Isle of Wight and had a part in an advert for the Isle of Wight which was shown on ITV.

It looks as if Daisy admirably filled her ambassadorial role! But I have been unable to track her down and find out what became of her.

Trudie Wilson sent me two most enlightening emails in 2023 that sketched her life, from her childhood fossil interest to her adult years as an artist and palaeontologist. In my first draft of this chapter, I picked out relevant bits from both emails and chose the most relevant sequence of them. This chapter also ends with an insight into the relationship between art and science from someone practising both. Since then, a year later, a third email has brought her life and work up to date. Of her childhood she wrote in the second email:

As for my personal history with fossils – the earliest fossil in my collection [was found] when I was less than 10 but I can't remember exactly how old. I was also inspired when I was 11 at school and thought I would be a palae-ontologist when I grew up. Somehow I've ended up by circling back from a different route and working in palaeontology.

From Childhood to Grown-up Fossil Finding

Trudie Wilson's fossil life story email continued:

I didn't then properly get into palaeontology until 2017 between my degree and masters. I visited the museum [Dinosaur Isle Museum] and wanted to get involved in digs and asked about volunteering. That summer [I] re-dis-covered the place I had called home for 20 years. I was inspired by Victorian monographs initially when visiting the museum and this along with the fossils themselves completely changed my course of study and thus my practice in life.

She told me what she then intended, and, indeed, the path she pursued, writing in her first email:

I have lived on the Island for most of my life and have spent the past 5 [now 6] years really uncovering [its] many secrets. The history and prehistory here is fascinating. I am continually out in the landscape whether walking or fossil hunting, photographing, sketching etc.

I work here as an interdisciplinary artist – working between art and science. My work aims to build bridges both for my own practice and also others. I was recently given an artist residency exploring the biosphere reserve and the residency took place in a school where I shared my practice with hundreds of students.

In her third email she writes:

> My work … is inspired by the island, especially the geology, palaeontology
> as it is incredibly rich and diverse. I work closely with the museum and I
> also assist on digs – even being lucky enough to help excavate a new species
> of dinosaur. In the last year I've also found more of a new species whilst out
> field walking – these bones will be heading to the museum to join the rest
> of the dinosaur.

She emphasises that in her life as an artist, she works within palaeontology. She depicted the *Vectaerovenator inopinatus*, a new genus of theropod
dinosaur, fossils of which had been found over a period of weeks in 2019 and
taken to the museum by amateur fossil hunters, in this case more than one
family. There may well be more fossil parts of this dinosaur still to be found.
Here is a fascinating Trudie Wilson depiction of this long-tailed dinosaur lying
on its back as it floated downwards through the water to become a fossil in the
sands, parts of it later found on the Shanklin foreshore.

Trudie Wilson wrote to me about this find, 'I was lucky enough to illustrate it (working alongside Southampton University) when it was published as
a new species – the artwork that I produced being shared globally alongside
the press release.' Earlier, the first dinosaur that she actually helped excavate
on the Island, written up by Southampton University, was the *Riparovenator*,
a spinosaurid. She continues to work closely with the Museum, and assists on
digs – even being lucky enough to help excavate a new species of dinosaur. In

4. *Vectaeroventor inopinatus*, courtesy of Trudie Wilson

the last couple of years, she wrote, 'I've also found more of a new species whilst out field walking – these bones are with the local museum ready for scientific study before going on public display.'

It is well worth looking at her website to see photographs of her artwork. For all her involvement with palaeontology, 'I am a fine artist foremost'. She has recently undertaken a deep investigation into island pigments and transforming them into artist materials. This work was exhibited in a well received solo exhibition at Quay Arts (an arts centre/gallery holding events, courses and workshops, with a café bar and a theatre, at 15 Sea Street, Newport).

Another girl fossil finder who went on to become a palaeontologist, particularly interested in geology, is **Megan Jacobs**. In the first of the several emails we exchanged before we met, she wrote, using an expression that will be explained below for the uninitiated: 'I grew upon on the Island (born and bred caulkhead they call us), and spent my whole childhood collecting fossils with my dad!' She did not say at what date that started or give any details of their finds, but over the years she built up quite a fossil collection. At the age of 20, while a palaeontology student at the University of Portsmouth, she was in the news: the *Island Echo* reported in 2016: 'Largest known Eotryrannus tooth discovered on the Isle of Wight.' It continued:

Megan Jacobs, 20 was walking along Compton beach off [The] Military Road when she noticed something shiny and black sticking out of the grey mud at the base of the cliff. After carefully examining it she thought it looked like a meat eating dinosaur tooth. Megan took her tooth to the Dinosaur Expeditions Centre where palaeontologists identified her tooth as belonging to Eotyrannus Lengii.

The article went on to report that Megan had been collecting fossils on the island beaches since she was just five years old. The article quotes some of what the palaeontologist who examined the fossil pronounced:

Comparison with other Eotyrannus teeth that this is the largest [one] discovered to date and suggests that the dinosaur is bigger than previous estimated. From 4 metres (13 feet) long to over 6 metres (over 20 feet long)

Megan has made an exceptional, once-in-a lifetime discovery which saved the tooth from being damaged or lost forever.

A 1995 discovery in Brighstone Bay of that dinosaur's remains was, after many years of careful conservation, officially named in 2001, and identified as a small ancestor of the *Tyrannosaurus rex*, the name of dinosaurs perhaps best associated in the public's mind with the creatures. The article ended, 'Meanwhile Megan is on the beach almost daily in the hope that she will discover more fossil remains of Eotyrannus Lengii.'

Compton beach became Megan's favourite location to search, but it required not only experience, but also luck. In her 2015 paper 'Histology of a sauropod rib bone from the Wessex Formation, Hanover Point, Isle of Wight' she wrote:

In September 2015 I went to Compton Bay ... to hunt for dinosaur bones. It was equinox tides all week, so an ideal time to get out on the furthest rocks of the Wessex formation, dating from the Barremian stage of the early Cretaceous (about 130Ma) also famous for the bone debris beds, which are highly fossiliferous. Time passed and I hadn't had a great amount of luck. So deciding today was not my day, I decided to head home. As I turned, I glanced down to see a beautiful piece of rib bone with the most amazing internal structure I've ever seen before.

I took it to show my tutor ... at the University of Portsmouth. He was quick to identify it as being from a sauropod. ...He then followed the identification by: 'how'd you fancy cutting it in half for a thin section?

She goes on to explain the purpose of a thin section, and the result of her doing it.

Once a fully fledged palaeontologist, she became involved in identifying fossils, often found by amateurs, identifying them and writing up the findings, sometimes as leader, as she was with the 'first side-necked turtle ever discover[ed] in UK'. These turtles are so named because they fold their neck into their shell sideways when threatened. This means they can only see out with one eye. It was an almost complete shell (missing its skull), found on Brook Beach, in the south-west of the Island.

The technology for examining constantly advances; in this case cutting-edge micro CT scanning was used. Megan and her colleagues dissected minerals from inside the turtle shell and analysed them for uranium and lead. By measuring the ratio of lead to radioactive uranium, they established the turtle was from the Lower Cretaceous period, around 127 million years ago. The paper was published in the scientific journal *Crustaceous Research*. The finder donated the fossil to the Dinosaur Isle Museum. That find is only one of the many fossils that Megan has been involved with in one way or the other, too numerous to detail here.

As well as her scientific work with others in the field, and her own fossil hunting, in 2019 Megan was part of a team to establish 'a professional and bespoke guided fossil hunting and educational experience ...'. I don't think that is how I first made contact with her; I think it was through the museum. However it was, she offered to take me to Compton Beach without being part of a tour, but simply out of generosity; that afternoon we became friends. That is probably why I have slipped into calling her by her first name when my practice is to use such names only for women no longer living.

Megan picked me up from my hotel and drove me almost to the other end of the island, to Compton Bay. There you walk from one of two carparks at the top, and climb down some steps to the beach. Once there, and beginning to walk to the left, I soon realised that a sizzling day was not ideal for my advancing years, and struggled a bit to keep up. The first tranche of the walk took us to where dinosaur footprints are quite clearly indented in the rock. That is a most eerie experience, allowing you to throw your imagination back millions of years. Then the walk continued the other way, to the right past the steps down. There with a waft of the hand Megan showed me where she and her father are working on a major find, not yet completed and therefore not for publicising.

Adult Women and Fossils

Under one of the photographs on Daisy Morris's blog is the caption 'Lorna Steel looks after all the Pterosaur fossils at the museum.' I have been unable to ascertain whether or not Lorna Steel hunted for fossils in her childhood, in spite of unrelenting attempts to make contact to ask her. But in palaeontological circles at natural history museums, particularly in London, Radnor and the Isle of Wight, she is well known. From when she was appointed as a new curator at Radnor Museum, there is a rather nice photograph of her cuddling a large soft toy crocodile, presumably a replica of an ancient one. By then she had worked in museums for more than 20 years.

Between 1995 and 2003, fragments of an unknown pterosaur were found in the Yaverland area near Sandown. It was an anhanguerid Pterosaur which lived during the Early Cretaceous period, about 130 million years ago. In 2005, therefore, a new genus was named and described by Lorna Steel and colleagues – *Caulkicephalus trimicrodon* – kephale, Greek for head *trimicrodon* meaning 'three small teeth'. An example of the papers is Lorna Steel's 'A new pterodactyloid pterosaur from the Wessex Formation (Lower Cretaceous) of the Isle of Wight, England' (2005).

Someone with a sense of humour must have decided on the name of this beast, 'caulkheads' being the name given to, or taken by, those who have lived on the Island for several generations, going back to the days when Islanders were involved in caulking ships. It is traditionally used derogatorively by mainlanders and proudly by Islanders. A *Guardian* website letter – one of several on the subject – gives a neat, if lengthy, explanation:

Since asking this question, a new friend on the IOW has given me this answer: ships would call in to the Solent Ports to get stores, painted, de-barnacled and to have their leaky old seams in the hull repaired. This process was called caulking and it was really cotton wadding in long strips like thick boot laces that were hammered in with a sort of chisel-type tool then sealed with pitch. This would swell up when wet, giving a watertight seal between the ship's hull planking. The Islanders were particularly good at this and jolly chaps on the Mainland would poke fun that their rivals on the Island were stupid and their heads were full of cork (caulk-wadding).

When Lorna Steel worked for the Isle of Wight Council museums, at the beginning of her career, she helped to set up the new geological museum now called 'Dinosaur Isle Museum' on the outskirts of Sandown. At the end of my long, generous and fruitful meeting with the director, I was shown a fossil which he called Lorna Steel's *Pterosaurus* in its museum showcase. He also taught me that you don't pronounce the P.

I hope I have made it clear, without wanting the beaches of the Island where fossils have been found to be besieged by visitors to the Island, that amateurs coming across fossils sometimes make finds that turn out to be important. Thus it was that on 11 April 1994 a headline declared 'Major Find For Amateur Fossil Collector'. The text beneath read:

Mrs Lin Spearpoint, who has been collecting fossils for less that a year, has unearthed the bones of one of the world's rarest dinosaurs. The most complete skeleton of polacanthus was found at Brightsone [sic] on the Isle of Wight.

On finding the first bones, Mrs Spearpoint showed them to Mr Martin Simpson a respected amateur from Whitwell who recognised that they were of major importance and immediately set in motion a full-scale excavation. Only two partial skeletons of the armour plated herbivore have been found before, one in 1867 and the other in 1979, and both are in the British Museum.

On the Island, Simpson is not known as an amateur but, according to an informant, he is 'THE fossil man'. By chance the 1867 [1865?] find was made by the Reverend William Fox on the Isle of Wight, was named *Polacanthus foxii*, and a reconstruction was illustrated by Gertrude Woodward (written about in this chapter under the sub-heading, 'The Draughtswomen', above).

An appropriate and, indeed, moving end to this chapter, came in the second email sent to me by Trudie Wilson whose interest was first piqued when she was 10, and who is today a palaeontologist, artist and illustrator. She wrote:

A note on excavating and finding, there is a moment where your significance of the find connects you with the time and the sublime – no one in the whole of human history has ever seen that before. Alongside this the find itself predates all of human existence. Yet almost simultaneously you are reminded of your minuscule place in this universe. This connection I believe is what both in hunting and art, the discovery of the unknown and a quest of sorts.

Having said all this it's not just about the fossils but about experiencing the landscape itself and being present when discovering, whether a fossil or just a spectacular place, the island is full of them. The sublime is very relevant to this and my practice.

2 – From Prehistory to the Coming of the Normans

Prehistory

What is now the Isle of Wight separated from the British mainland about 7,000 years ago at the end of the last Ice Age (about 8,000–9,000 years ago) as sea levels rose and the land of southern Britain sank. This flooded the river valley of the Solent to the north, and the future English Channel to the south. Once open to the sea, scouring widened the Solent, which is, however, nowhere more than 5km wide.

The Palaeolithic Period

The Palaeolithic (Old Stone Age) people who then found themselves on the warming Island would have been hunter-gatherers. They were, indeed, the first Islanders. Of their presence, only some flints displayed in the Carisbrooke Castle Museum have so far been found. Mainly men would have hunted what animals were left stranded by the separation – deer, boar, wild cattle – while women would have gathered whatever plants they found to be edible, or useful for medicine, and probably fashioned coverings from animal skins. I think it important to suggest that there is no reason why women would not have been involved in hunting. Remains of wooden fish traps have been discovered in the silt in the north. They could have been in the care of women. Warmer weather encouraged the growth of trees, providing wood to make them.

The Neolithic Period

The Neolithic (New Stone Age) people have left more trace; perhaps the most surprising is the presence of wheat. It is speculated that wheat was traded from the Middle East 8,000 years ago; that is longer ago than it is known to have grown in northern Europe. There is evidence, therefore, that they started farming, and domesticating animals. More obvious is the creation some 6,000 years ago on the south-west of the island of what is now called the Longstone, the only megalithic monument in the Isle of Wight and, it seems, somewhat older than Stonehenge (2,000–3,000 years old). It consists of two roughly hewn slabs of local greensand stone, one upright (12ft [4m] tall and 6ft [2m] wide), the smaller flat, perhaps having fallen, near the village of Mottistone. The stones seem to guard the entrance to a 70-ft-long raised mound or barrow running east to west towards the stones, a presumed communal burial place, apparently where only parts of the body were interred. It is deduced that these Neolithic people worshipped at the stones facing east to catch the rising sun.

The first scholarly reference to the stones was in 1708. In 1856, Lord Dillon, the local landowner, arranged to have the fallen stone lifted, and the soil beneath the stone excavated, to see what could be found – as far as is recorded, there was nothing. But it was a hundred years later, in 1956, that **Jacquetta Hawkes** (1910–1996), an established archaeologist, started excavating the barrow. Daughter of the biochemist and Nobel laureate, Sir Frederick Gowland Hopkins, she studied the new subjects of archaeology and anthropology at Newnham College, Cambridge, the first woman to do so, graduating with first class honours. In her second year she took part in the excavation of a Roman site near Colchester; there she met and then married, in 1933, the archaeologist Charles Hawkes; they worked together thereafter. She published her first article in *Antiquity* in 1934. After the Second World War, she met and fell in love with JB Priestly. Eventually, in 1953, they married and they moved to Brook Hill House which adjoins the Mottistone Estate, part of Mottistone village to the west. (For his part, Jacquetta's former husband married the archaeologist, also of early England, Sonia Chadwick.)

According to legend, St Catherine and the Devil once held a competition to see who should control the Isle of Wight. St Catherine supposedly threw the long stone from the Down (now known as St Catherine's Down) in the east, beating the Devil and winning control of the Island. Like any number of other islands, the Isle of Wight is full of myths and legends but, those aside, the Longstone was to maintain its cultural and mystical significance to the many different peoples who were to inhabit the Island thereafter. The Saxons, for example, may well have used it as a meeting place, where judicial and administrative affairs were carried out. 'Moot' is Saxon for meeting place and it is possible that the name Mottistone, is a corruption of 'Moot stone'. Different sources suggest slightly different, though not contradictory derivations, the scholarly Jacquetta Hawkes proposing it is from the Old English *motere stan*, the speaker's or pleader's stone, which would be relevant to a Neolithic or Saxon meeting place. Even today gatherings take place there at the solstices and equinoxes.

What are the easily digestible facts of the archaeological dig that Jacquetta made with the help of her 21-year-old son, Nicholas, and the curator of the Carisbrooke Museum? However learned her article, she manages, sometimes through the use of language, to paint a real picture of such a dig. For example, she suggests that a 'bite in the mound about half way along' seems to have been the result of sand quarrying. Problems included the stumps of intrusive nearby pine trees and rabbit warrens and other results of their digging; but thankfully there was no mud. As Jacquetta was unconvinced by the first dig attempt, she tried again in another area, this time with more success:

> As I cleared down into the top of the vertical kerbstone, I found a well-made oval flint scraper, 1 1/2 in. in length, resting directly upon it ... and a small, plain, potsherd nearby. Another sherd was subsequently found beneath the tumble of stone outside the revetment [stone facing]. The sherds were unhappily indeterminate; the first, a grey gritty fragment could well be

Windmill Hill ware, while the second is reddish and could be likened to beaker fabrics.

Windmill Hill ware refers to Neolithic archaeological finds at that place, in Wiltshire, of handcrafted ceramic vessels for cooking and storing precious crops and food supplies. Beaker ware was named for an inverted-bell beaker drinking vessel made by the Beaker people who were widely dispersed at the very beginning of the European Bronze Age. That is helpful; but this paragraph, which ends Jacquetta's article, is the most instructive concerning her work:

> Only full excavation, that we never intended to undertake, could discover whether any internal structure or burial places survive. Nor is it at all certain that it would, for damage and erosion have been severe, and the conditions of work could hardly be more unrewarding. Meanwhile, I have expressed my confidence in the authenticity of the Longstone barrow by asking the Forestry Commission to clear away their trees.

No amount of Internet digging has informed me that any excavation took place after Jacquetta's. Without access to her article, I would have kept saying to myself, but where are the bones?

5. Jacquetta Hawkes, from 'The Longstone, Mottistone' by Jacquetta Hawkes

Unfortunately, largely because of their celebrity, the idyllic life that Jacquetta and Priestly enjoyed at Brook Hill House came to an end in the 1960s. That is indeed a pity, as the best image I have seen of the stones, and a lovely one of Jacquetta, as well as being the most appropriate to show here, is of her perched on the stone lying down. Where her feet reach indicates the thickness of the stone better than any measurement. The original photograph is to be found at the end of her difficult to access article, 'The Longstone, Mottistone' (1957).

I cannot help feeling annoyed that, when Internet searching for Brook House, which one source suggests is 'reputed to be the most haunted house on the island', I could find nothing about ghosts (suitable for a later chapter), but all the sources parade JB Priestly, the celebrated writer and broadcaster, and the other celebrities who flocked to visit him there, with no mention of Jacquetta, let alone her archaeological work, not only that at Longstone, and well-received writing (such as *Prehistoric Britain* (1943)). (The Professor Hawkes mentioned in some sources concerning archaeological excavation on the Island at Chillerton Down, refers to Jacquetta's former husband.)

The Iron Age, 800 BC–AD 43

As it happens, one of Charles Hawkes' areas of interest was Iron Age forts, and part of the hilltop earthworks, deemed to be the ramparts of one of those, is what was found at Chillerton Down. This neatly leads into the Island's pre-Roman history, into that era when its people are called Celts. In spite of the size of the Island (23 by 13 miles; 37 by 21km) they are not, however, seen as having been unified but as having consisted of several tribes and having links with others across the Solent and the Channel. That was partly because the river Medina neatly splits the Island in half, rising as it does at St Catherine's Down and wending its way to its mouth at East and West Cowes, tidal and traditionally navigable as far as Newport.

That navigation played a large part in the Island's Iron Age history is suggested by Kevin Trott and David Tomalin in their long and detailed article 'The Maritime Role of the Island of Vectis in the British pre-Roman Iron Age' (2003). I wish this article were more accessible to the general reader, for it opens a new vista into that period, of which it is practical here to give only a glimpse. Today the Island is surrounded by the sailing of yachts and the racing of power boats; There are also ships of all sizes making their way via the Solent to the mainland. But it seems that much the same, *mutatis mutandis*, was true in the Iron Age; indeed, there was three-pronged trade between the Island, the mainland and the north of Gaul (France), to the area called Amorica (between Paris and the Loire, including Brittany). Several tribes traded from there, including the Durotriges and the Lexovii, and evidence of their goods and coins are to be found on both the mainland and the Island.

On the Island, in 2009, detectorists searching near Shalfleet to the west found an Iron Age hoard, known now as the Shalfleet Hoard. It consisted of four large bowl-, or boat-shaped, silver ingots, six small silver fragments, and one gold

British stater (coin). Oyster fishing off Yarmouth has netted imported Iron Age pottery from Amorica and from Durotrigian territory in Dorset. In the east, in the valley of the river Yar, is an Iron Age gully in which a large quantity of carbonized emmer (durum wheat) and spelt wheat was found and examined. Similar evidence has been found a few miles away in two locations. As the authors suggest, 'these settlements offer a glimpse of a well-populated island, generously endowed with fertile soil'. It was likely that there was often a surplus of grain ready to be traded. It is also suggested that the aristocratic families of East Wight were foremost in grasping the opportunities offered. No evidence has been found that a surplus of the salt known to have been produced on the Island was traded.

It is not clear how women featured in any of this, but undoubtedly there would have been a part for them, particularly in agriculture, and perhaps the production of salt. I can see them, too, being involved in the trading process; they would have been good at haggling. I have to guess because no work seems to have been done on them during the Iron Age period, though there has been research on those that were soon to follow.

Trading brought Roman luxury goods from northern Gaul some time before the Roman invasion. Writing of the Veneti tribe towards the Atlantic coast, Caesar commented, 'the Veneti are much the most powerful tribe on this coast. They have the largest fleet of ships, in which they traffic with Britain.' The seafarers from Vectis – the Roman name for the Isle of Wight – were, it is proposed, involved in the redistribution of such goods to the British mainland. That the Vectuarii – as the Islanders by this time called themselves according to the early historian the Venerable Bede – also traded their own ware to Gaul where Vectis ware has been excavated. I posit that women may well have been involved in the making of this ware, as they were in other islands about which I have written. It is not clear when the wheel was invented in this area. The trade from Britain included grain, cattle, gold, silver and iron, along with hides, slaves and clever hunting dogs. There is something toe-curling to the modern reader to see slaves included thus, and there is no information as to who they may have been. In return goods imported northwards from Gaul included wine, walnuts, figs, cider, Calvados, and early fruit and vegetables.

I could not let the subject of exported slaves rest there. An Internet article, 'Slave Chains', with the subheading 'Staff Pick' was posted by the Maidstone Museum in 2016. It is illustrated by a set of chains, the first sight of iron in this Iron Age, and notes:

These Iron Age slave chains are evidence that one of the major exports from Britain to the Roman world were slaves during the 1st century AD. For those wearing them, living conditions would've been brutal and life expectancy shortened. However, during the Iron Age the slave trade was thriving. Can you believe that people sometimes even sold themselves or their children into slavery just to settle their debts. ... During this era, slaves would often be gathered by war lords during raids, and even be used as gift exchange.

In their conclusions, Trott and Tomalin write,

We cannot claim that the Iron Age communities of the Isle of Wight held sole control over the transportation of all of their imported Gallic goods, but we can now recognize a people who were capable of crossing and mastering the sea.

And, finally, some words that take the story further:

Scatters such as these [island anchorages] must prompt the realization that valuable archaeological resources are still concealed within the European seabed. Where these resources have been noted in this study there remains a pressing need to investigate their parent sub-tidal sediments.

Though that study was published in 2003, an earlier one shows that work had already been started and, indeed, David Tomalin was one of the authors, along with Isle of Wight archaeologist Rebecca Loader. 'An archaeological Survey of the Wootton-Quarr Coast' was first published in *Time and Tide* in 1997, and reprinted in 2002. It summarises, as the authors explain, five years of exploration and survey in the soft eroding intertidal muds on the north-east coast of the Isle of Wight. The importance of this study to my book will be revealed when I have described a few of their findings. Because of the nature of the prevailing conditions much archaeological material was preserved that could not have been saved on dry land. This included, for example, wood, leather, rope, and a wide range of environmental evidence such as pollen, suggesting the development of cereal cultivation, and trees, part of the forest dating from Neolithic times. At the time of the separation that created the Island, the main feature is what is known as the Solent river. 'This river was fed by the Medina, the Yar and in the project area by streams running out from Wootton Quarr and Binstead.'

On the east bank of Wootton Creek is the port town of Fishbourne, with its beach, integral to this project, to the right of the ferry terminal. But it could only be accessed at low tide, at particular times of the year (low-water Spring Tides), fortnightly, and in the early morning and evening. Imagine the logistics! Among the first examples noted are the well-preserved wooden trackways of Neolithic date at the low-water boundary. 'Where the peaty surface gave way to salt marsh, Islanders used stone axes to cut branches of oak, willow and hazel which they used to build wooden trackways leading towards the water's edge.' Wooden posts were associated with fish traps of the Neolithic and Bronze Ages (the latter age preceded the Iron Age). Remains of two salt-drying kilns of Late Iron Age/Early Roman date were found well below high water at Fishbourne and Quarr, and these must have been sited just above the high water. Most revealing of preservation was leather Roman footwear. Confirming the trading finds of the earlier study discussed, Iron Age pottery from France and Germany had found its way to the Island's north-east coast. Fishbourne was to continue to be a trading port during the Roman occupation of the Island. Many animal bones and skulls have been found, one skull radio carbon dated, indicating that animals were brought to the beach here to be slaughtered, and then traded to the mainland. With the first Viking raid of 897 and subsequent raids, port facilities were moved further up Wootton Creek. But Fishbourne was to become notable for shipbuilding in the post-medieval period.

In that 2003 maritime article, mostly abut the Iron Age, there is only one hint of women, but it does not seem to go anywhere that I can build on; it reads:

Once the families of the East Wight region had consolidated their short-haul links with the neighbouring communities around the natural harbours of Portsmouth, Langstone and Chichester, trade and marriage ties with the south eastern Atrebates or Regni would naturally ensue. The first sign of an Iron Age maritime community in this sector of the island seems to be on the eastern shore of the former great inlet known as Brading Haven.

The Atrebates were a Belgic tribe of the Iron Age and Roman period, originally dwelling in the Artois region of Gaul. In the mid-first century BC, an offshoot of the tribe lived in Britain, occupying a region stretching between the Thames, the Test and West Sussex. Regni was the name given to the tribe a little later.

The importance of this isolated remark within the article is that there seems to have been intermarriage between the various trading partners. At last there is something to work on.

On 9 March 2016, brothers Hubert and Graham Smyth discovered skeleton remains as they set a string of swinging boat moorings on Fishbourne Beach at low tide. The bones were in the silt which is under the waterline when the tide is in. Radiographer Graham Smyth gently lifted out one of the bones, confident that it was a human radius, so he left the rest of the skeleton in situ and called the police. Barrister and HM Senior Coroner for the Island, Caroline Sumeray, takes up the story:

A decision was made to recover as many of the bones as possible from the surface of the mud before the tide came in. The remains were lying on their left-hand side in a foetal position with the arms up against the chest and the legs bent at roughly 90 degrees to the body. There was no clothing or any other object attached or adjacent.

My first job was to establish if this was a recently deceased person or something a little older. … If the body was recently deceased, I needed to rule out an unnatural death.

The Home Office pathologist carried out a post mortem, and reported that the bones were ancient, the remains of an adult human female who died almost certainly beyond living memory. The cause of death could not be established but there was no evidence of injury or dismemberment. To be certain of the age of the bones, each one identified, radio-carbon dating was used. 'The results stunned me,' Caroline said. 'My lady is indeed a long time dead! The remains were dated to AD28–AD 90 – almost 2,000 years old and from the Late Iron Age.' You can imagine my interest when I read about this find. But who was she?

In my first draft that followed here about the female skeleton found on Fishbourne beach, I continued with the findings of the Home Office pathologist and then got carried away with my own imaginative reconstruction of who she might have been and how she might have got there, there being no information about that. I have now deleted that text in the light of an article thoughtfully brought to my attention by a contact attached to the Isle of Wight Heritage Centre whom I'd been plaguing with questions: 'Iron Age "predatory Landscapes": A bioarchaeological and Funerary Exploration of Captivity and Enslavement' (2020) by Dr Rebecca Redfern of the Museum of London. It was not easy to get my head around this detailed and technical article, particularly as it required me to go in a totally new direction, linking, with a whole page of boxes of technical findings, the Fishbourne woman to slavery, to which I had already devoted a paragraph earlier. I was so taken aback, as these findings seemed in many respects to contradict earlier ones that are in the public domain on the Internet, that I emailed Rebecca with several questions. More than generously, she replied by return and in detail to each of my questions.

Without criticising earlier examination of the skeleton upon which I'd depended, Rebecca explained that 'Pathologists are not used to seeing archaeological human remains, or the remains of prehistoric people'. In addition, 'Pathologists do not always employ the same ageing methods as bioarchaeologists.' So here I am: the evidence points to my Fishbourne woman having ended her life as a slave. Where she was from cannot be determined, given the shared geology of Hampshire, the Isle of Wight and Dorset. Rebecca explains in her email that,

the position and completeness of her body does not accord with her body being washed in to the beach or even washed-out of a grave in the past – I think that happened later, when the layers around her remains were removed by tidal action – that is why her lower legs and parts of her upper limbs are missing. I assumed (given her completeness, particularly of the bones with evidence for decapitation) that she had been buried in a crouched position inland, and over time, with coastal erosion, her burial became submerged and then more recently, was washed-out. Forensic taphonomy [the processes that lead to the preservation of biological remains] is very clear about this, and her remains do not conform to being put into the water and being washed-up on the beach.

As for determining her status as a slave, Rebecca directed me to another article, which I have not felt the need to read: her explanation, including evidence for the woman's decapitation and for labour etc, is enough. I had questioned her height, because she seems to have been taller than most women of the time. This can be ascribed to 'a combination of genetics and having a childhood whereby she did not experience food insecurity or poor health'. She seems, therefore, to have had a stable childhood, but was later enslaved in any of the ways I have described earlier.

I do not usually show the inner workings of my research so obviously, but I felt it necessary in this instance, if only to emphasise how earlier deductions can, and should, be challenged by careful later scholarship, and how one must be ready to delete hours of work in a more accurate re-creation of history. I was so excited to come across the finding of the woman's skeleton, and at least I can now be more confident about who she was, even if there are still many imponderables. Was she, for example, involved in any of the activities at Fishbourne, including on the beach, noted above?

The bones that make up her skeleton were donated to the Museum of Island History in Newport where such remains are ethically stored, in accordance with national guidelines for the treatment of human remains. They are only available to bona fide researchers. Throughout, I wanted her to have a name, but unfortunately, the only one she was given is 'Fishbourne skeleton' (PRN number 9356). The beach in Fishbourne where the woman's remains were found is surprisingly unspoilt, and peaceful, even with the ferry terminal in sight.

The Romans, AD 43–AD 410

The Romans made more than one failed attempt to invade Britain, starting with that by Julius Caesar in 55 BC. And even when they felt they had taken it, in AD 43, under the emperor Claudius, they still had to deal with indigenous uprisings, the last in AD 61 by Boudicca, Queen of the Iceni – an Iron Age Brittonic tribe of Eastern Britain. There does not appear to have been the same refusal to accept Roman rule by the Celtic tribes of the Isle of Wight. Vespasian, 34 years old, later emperor, commanding the 5,000 strong 2nd Legion, probably landing at Brading Haven, successfully took the Island in AD 44, the year after the final mainland invasion. It was Vespasian's biographer who refers to the Island as Vectem or Vecta. The word Vectis was used for the Island through nearly 400 years of apparently peaceful Roman occupation. The local bus company uses the name today.

Roman settlement on the Island does not seem to have been whole-hearted: no evidence of Roman roads has been found, nor Roman towns. Although there is said to be evidence of seven Roman villas, only two have been fully excavated, and it is suggested that the one south of Newport was probably a farm and house set up in the Roman style by an enterprising Celt; habitation of it lasted only 50 years. It is that villa, known as the Newport Roman Villa, and the Brading Roman Villa, that are explored here. Both are open to the public.

It is worth noting, however, that archaeological work continues. In August 2021, for example, a team from the Southampton City Council Archaeology

Unit started excavating the Hale Manor Quarry near Arreton. They found evidence of habitation and farming from the Bronze and Iron Ages and during Roman occupation. One of the finds was daub used for building material which led team member Emma Anderson to say that 'There must be a settlement still to be found here somewhere. I don't think it will be a Roman villa or anything like that but it could be quite significant … if and when it is found.'

The discovery of the Brading Roman Villa gives useful evidence of how the shape of the Island has developed. At the time of its existence, the villa lay close to the shore of a large natural harbour, later known as Brading Haven. But, by 1881, this harbour had been almost totally drained in order to create new farmland.

Two stories suggest the beginning of the Brading Villa find, which started in 1879. Cecil Aspinall Oglander starts it off in 'The Roman Villa at Brading' (1950). (I deduce that, after marrying into the Oglander family – his second wife was Joan Oglander – which had been powerful on the Island for 600 years, he appears to have thought it worth adding their name to his; he died at Nunwell, the Oglander family home.) Both stories begin with Captain Thorp(e), a retired merchant seaman interested in Roman antiquaries:

> In the Spring of 1879 this officer was strolling near the boundary of Morton Farm at a moment when a farmer named Munns, who owned the adjacent holding and lived in the house … 500 years away, was ploughing his field on the other side of the hedge. Two small children, the son and daughter of Mr Munns, were playing near the hedge.

> Suddenly these children began to quarrel for possession of something that had been turned up by the plough; and the argument became so heated that Captain Thorpe called to them to show him what they had found. He at once recognised it as a piece of 1st century Samian pottery. Crossing over the hedge, he approached Mr Munns, and showed him the 'find' excitedly.

> 'Have you ever seen any pieces like this in your field before?' he asked.

> 'Hundreds of 'em, drat 'em' answered the farmer. 'And stones and great tiles, too.'

> 'Then what do you do with them when you find them?'

> 'Do with 'em! Why, I throw 'em into the ditch.'

Here is the more sober, and a first-hand account, from the journal of Captain Thorp:

> 1st May 1879. During my research on Morton Farm, after probing many square yards of land, I hit upon broken Roman pottery in quantity on one

spot near a hedge which divides Lady Oglander's land from that of Morton Farm. Continuing my work, I found more tesserae in a loose state, but upon further search I found some in parts lay solid and evidently a pavement extending for some distance east and west. After making my work on the surface of the land all safe, I took bearings of the exact spot where I mediated [?] to excavate at some future time. ...

March 22 1880. The land now being free of crops, and with the sanction of the owner of the property, I exposed to view the first portion of the Roman pavement I had discovered on 1st May 1879 on Morton Farm.

The site of the villa at that time was owned by two different families. The southern half was owned by Mr Munns, the northern half by Lady Oglander of the Nunwell Estate. Before continuing with the excavating story, a pause is needed to introduce Lady Oglander because she is pivotal to it. **Louisa Oglander** (1822–1894), youngest daughter of Sir George William Leeds, 1st Baronet and his second wife, Eleanor Rowley, had, in 1845, married Sir Henry Oglander (1811–1874), 7th Baronet of Nunwell. By the time of her involvement in the excavation, she had been widowed for five years. The site now straddling the two properties, Louisa purchased Munns' farm and, over the succeeding years, provided whatever funds were needed. And, for the next 15 years the excavation was overseen by John Oglander FSA.

This Oglander was obviously not a son of the couple, who were childless, but was, I have discovered, born John Glynn. He was Sir Henry's heir, and there was a proviso in the latter's will that within a year of Louisa's death, John Glynn was to take the name and arms of Oglander. I've had to dig around for this fact. Looking at Sir Henry's will (which can be seen online but which is kept in the Wight Record Office), I noted that he left Louisa, not Nunwell, which was to go to trustees, but 'all watches, jewels, personal ornaments and wearing apparel, wines, liqueurs, Horses, carriages, saddlery and harness, stable furniture, tools, implements and utensils, either in my mansion house at Nunwell or that at Parnham Dorset, for her life and then the furniture at Nunwell to John Glynn.' And towards the end of clause 2 'to my wife for her life and after her death to convey the Isle of Wight estates of said John Glynn'. Letters between Louisa and John Glynn before her husband's death show friendliness and her updating him on local goings-on.

Presumably, with Nunwell hers for life, the money Louisa had available to spend on the excavation of the villa came from the proceeds of the estate which contained a farm, as well as the manor house; she may well also have had money from her own family. Whatever the source of her funds, Louisa Oglander enabled the Brading Roman Villa excavation of what we see today to progress. And the overseer of it, John Oglander FSA, took the surname after her death. In St Mary's Brading, there is a memorial tablet to John Henry Oglander (né Glynn) who died in 1924. One corner of the tablet commemorates Sir Henry Oglander, who restored the church in 1865, and his wife Louisa who died in 1894.

When exactly the Brading Villa was first built seems only to be guessed at from a collection of coins found there, starting in the reign of the Emperor Domitianus, AD 81–96. It was occupied until AD 395. It was then used for storing grain for an unknown period before, in the fifth century, it was destroyed by fire.

I had assumed the Roman villa was built soon after Roman occupation. But I discovered that, while evidence suggests that it was started in about AD 100, in its final and grandest manifestation, it probably dates to around AD 300. There has been speculation over who was responsible for the creation of that later version. It is assumed to have been a very rich and well-educated Roman, as shown not only by the extent and technical innovations, but also by the composition of the mosaics, particularly in the main state room. Details of these, especially of the females, such as goddesses, seasons of the year, and various other architectural features, are helpfully to be found in Cecil Aspinall Oglander's slender booklet *The Roman Villa at Brading* (1950). Only someone fully conversant with the richness of Roman culture could have commissioned the mosaics. As Cornelius Nicholson of Ashleigh Ventnor claims in 'A Descriptive Account of the Roman Villa Near Brading, Isle of Wight' (1880), when discussing the number and elegance of the mosaic pavements, 'There is nothing like this grouping, in England, if elsewhere'.

My eagerness to discover whose was the final creative imagination behind the villa stemmed from a desire to ascertain whether he had a wife and other female family members who could also have been behind the creation of the outstanding villa. An early suggestion seems to have been that it was a Roman responsible for running the Island but, given the lack of evidence of other Roman development, that might be mistaken. In any case, while the names of what one can loosely call the governors throughout the period of Roman Britain are well known, I can find no

6. Medusa, from Brading Roman Villa postcard

mention of such a person solely responsible for the governing of the Isle of Wight; it was more likely seen at that time as part of Britain.

A more recent suggestion is that the developer of the final villa was one of the high Roman officials exiled to Britain, not an infrequent punishment. And the name that is most often cited is Palladius. The reason for that suggestion is connected with an unusual mosaic character with the body of a man and the head of a rooster known as the Cock-Headed Man. The design is so extraordinary that as Neville Carr, retired curator of the villa, puts it in one of his posts, 'He or she must surely have been well educated and quite possibly with a sense of humour.' I couldn't help giving a wry smile of appreciation at the inclusion of 'she'. Carr tells the most accessible story of this possibility:

A likely candidate is an exiled high-ranking bureaucrat by the name of Palladius who served as Chief Marshall of the Court in Antioch. He appears to have got into hot water in AD 361, with the newly elected emperor, Julian. Julian … set up a tribunal to deal with outstanding proceedings against quite often falsely accused officials. Palladius was one such official who made complaints against a previous Emperor, Gallus, some time previously. Gallus in Latin also means 'cock' as in Cock-headed. Could Palladius, having been banished to Britain in AD 361, as the punishment for daring to complain that Gallus spent all his time in pleasure at the arena instead of governance as a Caesar, have parodied Gallus as our 'Cock-headed' man in the mosaic, hence no other such scene with its temple & fabulous animals being found yet in such a combination.

The Roman Solder Ammianus Marcellinus, better known as a historian who wrote the penultimate historical account surviving from antiquity, gives a little more information concerning Palladius, one of four men tried together. Their trial enabled Emperor Julian to fulfil his goal to show that the execution of Gallus was driven largely by individual words and passions instead of justice. Palladius was the former chief marshall of the court under Gallus, and was exiled because of the suspicion of defamation against Gallus, caesar (ruler), based in Antioch, of the eastern provinces from 351 until his execution in 354. While that throws a little more light on Palladius's apparent crime – though Julian excuses Gallus's Hippodrome enjoyment: it was probably to obtain popular support – it does not identify Palladius by a full name, but does help my story.

What is also annoying is that Ammianus lets us know about Gallus's wife, Constantina (AD 320–354). He was her second husband (m AD 351) and, it is said, the two of them brought a number of wealthy people to trial for magic, ending in the execution of innocents and in the confiscation of their wealth. With that information, just her name, following the link with her husband, it is possible to find out much more about Flavia Constantina, including that in the Middle Ages she was named a saint, apparently rather at variance with what was earlier known and said of her. (Assuming that her dates are correct, it is interesting that she died the year of her husband's execution, when she was only 34.)

If one accepts that Palladius was the rich and educated man responsible for the final Brading Villa, who were his wife, his mother, his sisters, his aunts, who might have lived there with him and, as well as playing a part in domestic arrangements, could have been involved in decorative decisions? Unfortunately, there were many Romans called Palladius with a public profile (at least 14) who might have fitted our bill, but the Antioch one sent into exile is hidden from my research. He is not Saint Palladius, a hermit in the Antioch desert. Frustration! Assuming Palladius had a wife, we can only imagine what it was like for her when he was on trial; the relief when he was exiled, not executed. What were her feelings about exile in advance, and in reality? She may well have made the most of her new life, perhaps partly responsible for the luxuriousness of her surroundings. One sign of a woman's presence that remains is in one of the display cases of findings – a baby's dummy.

Might there once, in the twentieth century, have been other woman-leaning finds on display? There is a strange – in that I have not seen it substantiated elsewhere – paragraph in Cecil Aspinall Oglander's 1950 booklet:

> The long table and showcases in the room contain many relics discovered during the excavation, though, unfortunately, some bronze ornaments and jewellery, which used to be on view in the centre case, did not survive the scrutiny of some of our gallant visitors from overseas who, during the recent war, when the Villa was closed to the public, begged to be allowed to see it, and were rather incautiously permitted to borrow the key.

That the Roman Villa was built in stages over the years is not surprising: as later chapters will touch on, the same thing happened to manor houses on the Island in the centuries that follow; Queen Victoria's Osborne House is an obvious example. As for Roman women, it would not be surprising to find them enterprising, if those I have written about in Sardinia are anything to go by, including those in exile.

I cannot leave the Brading Roman Villa without mentioning chickens. That head of a cock on the man's body introduces the subject. Traditionally, it is said that the Romans introduced chickens for food and, indeed, hares, to Britain, but Roman influence from Gaul and elsewhere had existed long before the Roman invasion. In April 2020, Alex Fox posted 'Hares and Chickens Were Revered as Gods – Not food in Ancient Britain'. He wrote,

> A team of researchers has discovered carefully buried Iron Age chicken and hare bones that show no signs of butchery … The skeletons corroborate other evidence indicating the animals were revered as deities by Iron Age Britons. As Julius Ceasar wrote in *Commentarii de Bello Gallico* 'The Britains consider it contrary to divine law to eat the hare, the chicken or the goose. They raise these, however, for their own amusement or pleasure.'

But the fact still remains that the Cock-headed Man could well have been intended as an insult, a figure of fun, by the Roman responsible for the villa's mosaics.

The building of the villa unearthed in 1926, and known as the Newport Roman Villa, is said to date from about AD 280. Evidence was to emerge, manifested by fragments of broken pottery and other household waste, of earlier Iron Age habitation on the site. The villa is located just south of Newport; indeed, it is in a suburb of the town, squashed between two modern houses. It was only discovered when Mr Cooper, a resident of Cypress Road, decided to build a garage. It was then that workmen uncovered some mosaic tiles. Not surprisingly, this villa gives a totally different impression to the visitor from the Brading Villa which sits in a wide open space.

The four-page information sheets helpfully handed to visitors suggest the sort of person who might have had the villa built and, for what purpose:

> ... the villa was a farm, the home of someone who worked the land and could afford to build a farm-house in the Roman style – probably a local landowner or chieftain who made the most of opportunities given by connections with Rome. Nearby would have been the barns, granaries, stabling and accommodation for the workforce.

The development of a new housing estate more recently meant that the outlying farm buildings are lost for good. Farming would have been a financially rewarding occupation, without too much hardship: fields were fertile for cattle, sheep and cereals, and the Island had been exporting a surplus of grain since at least the Iron Age. There is no evidence that the Romans disrupted the arteries, such as the River Medina, that previously facilitated trade.

As regards the dwelling itself, the discovery of fragments of glass on the site suggests that it had glazed windows, and remains of painted wall plaster during excavation show that at least some of the rooms had brightly coloured interior walls. Colours included red, grey, green, purple, brown and yellow. Did some woman with a hand in the decoration have an eye for colour? The roof consisted of massive slabs of Bembridge limestone supported by large roof timbers. It is obviously of Roman build, and it is likely that the owner was a person of some wealth. There is a well-preserved Roman bath suite with hypocaust underfloor heating. A servant (slave?) would have been responsible for feeding it with fuel. The hot air from the furnace passed through an arch at the base of the villa's back wall and circulated under the raised floors of three rooms. It should be said that such a furnace was environmentally destructive, leading as it did to the stripping of the Island's natural woodland.

Perhaps my favourite find, described in the villa's information sheet, comes in the reconstruction in the kitchen of a 'doormouse [sic] fattener'. By whom, and how, could this have been determined?

Why was such a comfortable villa used as a dwelling for only about 50 years? Early in the fourth century AD, the floors of some rooms were taken up, and the largest room was converted into a blacksmith's workspace. Perhaps the family who had been living in it fell on hard times. But there is even more of a mystery, perhaps most effectively described in a 2018 Internet posting by historian and classicist Rupert Willoughby:

> In the ensuing century, it is perhaps Saxon or Jutish raiders who were, literally, the death of the place, for the skull of a woman in her early thirties with two huge cracks in it, was found in the corner of one of the rooms, into which her decapitated head had been heartlessly tossed.

Nothing more seems to be known about the woman or the skull. But it is possible to see it in the History of the Isle of Wight Museum. And before this chapter moves on to the Jutes and Saxons, something needs to be said about the funding from the 1920s of the villa's excavation and its life thereafter.

A committee was formed. The *Isle of Wight County Press* inspired local interested residents to make generous donations. It was made worthwhile for Mr Cooper not to continue building his garage. Then, as further finds were made, Alderman John Curtis Millgate stepped in, saving the villa from being re-buried by purchasing the land. He suggested that the Town Council should take over the construction of a building to cover the villa's remains. They declined, so Millgate financed it himself. Writer of Roman villa history in England Derrick Napier's blog skips then to 1961, when the County Council took over responsibility. He makes no mention of how this came about, and the part played in it, following her father's death in 1956, by Millgate's daughter, **Grace Bessie Blanch Millgate** (1903–1988) who became the owner, with all the responsibility that entailed. In 1960, when the building site needed repairs, she offered it to the Newport Town Council; again the offer was declined. The Isle of Wight Council finally agreed to accept the gift of the site from Grace in December 1960, and the deeds were handed over in April 1961. That is not the end of the Millgate sisters, as will be seen when we meet Christabella in Chapter 12, 'Women in a Man's World'.

By AD 410 Roman occupation of the Isle of Wight and, indeed, of mainland Britain had come to an end, when the Western Roman empire was threatened with invasion and civil strife.

From Saxon Pirates to Queen Osburga, 286–856

As early as AD 286, according to Edward Boucher James in volume 1 of his *Letters Archaeological and Historical Relating to the Isle of Wight*, Saxon pirates began to ravage the coasts of Gaul and Britain. Indulge me for a moment to introduce another woman who could easily slip from history. James, an Oxford graduate, was vicar of Carisbrooke from 1858, and from 1883, chaplain to the governor of the Island. His two volumes were published in 1896; but he died in 1892. If you look carefully, you will see on the title page the words 'edited and collected by his wife'. If you are determined enough, you can discover that she was called Rachel. This would not be so interesting if the volumes were straightforwardly chronological, but they are not: they are like a dressing-up box from which anything might be pulled out. I can just imagine Rachel, determined that her husband's work be published, sitting on the floor surrounded by piles of material in no particular order, and trying to make sense of it – not altogether successfully. Nevertheless, it is possible to retrieve from it, in no particular chronology, some useful facts. **Rachel Boucher James** (1832–1898), having been widowed for six years, died aged 66, perhaps happy at a mammoth task completed, but surely exhausted.

Following invasion in about AD 530, the Isle of Wight was incorporated into a Jutish Kingdom – the Wihtwara – consisting of several different tribes originating from German-speaking lands. The Islanders had soon known where they were with the Romans and settled down, incorporating Roman ways; the Jutish takeover was one of violence. Boucher James maintains that the Roman conquest was less destructive than that of the Jutes, for the simple reason that there was less to destruct. What is more, Saxon piracy continued for many years. Barbara Yorke, historian of Anglo-Saxon England, provides reaction to the piracy. The three coastal regions of southern England formed a political confederation during the sixth century aimed at combating the threat of the pirates operating in the Channel who threatened the trade on which the prosperity of East Kent and the Isle of Wight depended. In those unsettled times, it does not take much imagination to picture what life was like for the Island's women, contending with marauding pirates and invading Jutes. There is perhaps a hint of what some endured in the decapitated skull found in the corner of a room in the Newport Roman Villa.

Little detail, though, is known about women's lives, let alone the identity of particular women; indeed, it is not easy to sort out a simple historical timeline, without getting bogged down in the comings and goings hinted at in various, often contradictory, sources about various leaders usually fighting each other. I have avoided that; I hope not to over-simplify. Arwald, we do know, was the last Jutish king of the Isle of Wight and the last pagan king in Anglo-Saxon England. He presided over 300 families which may have been only 1,200 people.

An Isle of Wight posting called 'Hidden Heroes' about Arwald's time describes how the people then lived in clearings surrounded by forest, in small hamlets of several families in thatched and wooden-tiled homes. They ground corn by hand and wove their own clothing. They made everyday items from wood, clay and iron. They were connected with nature and worshipped pagan gods such as Woden and Thor.

But Arwald died in 686, killed in battle when Caedwalla invaded the Island. He was a barbarian king from Mercia who was taken under the wing of a powerful evangelising bishop responsible, with support from the pope, for Christianising mainland Britain. It was under Caedwalla that the Islanders were forced to renounce their beliefs and convert to Christianity, many of them massacred in the process.

Boucher James cuts across this violent process of Christianisation with a vignette worth including because it gives a lively impression of how at least some of the Islander women saw it and, fancifully, I suspect Rachel did not feel able to omit it:

> The women thought it a miserable slavish existence for a man to glide in and out of houses clothed in a long robe like a woman, and instead of shouting out battle-songs, droning away at prayers or psalms. But they soon found out that these pale-faced men were no cowards.

They spoke to the people in 'their own Jutish tongue … or it was the chief or ealdorman, persuaded perhaps by his wife, who with his whole family and household went through the sacred rite [of baptism].'

We do know that Arwald had a sister and that she survived the massacre; but she is unnamed, no matter how hard one searches for a name. She is noted for becoming the wife of King Egbert of Kent (at the time ruling a Jutish kingdom besieged by Caedwalla) and she is a direct ancestor of Alfred the Great whose mother will in due course feature in the Island's story. It is maddening not to be able to find out anything more about Arwald's sister; how did she survive? How did she make her way to the mainland? She must have been a woman of some substance to have made the marriage she did, during the disjointed times in which she did, and become the matriarch of an important British dynasty.

The Mercian cemetery at Chessell Down pre-dates that violent Christian-isation time; and you will see why I appear to have taken a step backwards. The cemetery is now within a Forestry Commission conifer plantation in the parish of Shalfleet to the west of the Island. There were at least 110 graves in the cemetery, but it is best known for grave 45, the burial place of an obviously high-status woman, defined by the goods found with her remains. The details of the finds, and their significance, are best told by Sue Harrington in 'A Well-Married Landscape: Networks of Association and 6th Century Communities on the Isle of Wight', a chapter in *The Land of English Kin* (2020). The way she describes the excavation of the site in 1855 by antiquarian George Hillier shows a nice scholarly subtlety. She does not name him; she merely writes:

> The confused and piecemeal excavation of Chessell Down by antiquarian diggers in the 19th century need not be reprised here, suffice it to comment that this was a large and important site whose archive eventually found a secure home in the British Museum.

'Eventually' and 'secure' carry a bit of a load, for Hillier had a chequered career, one source telling how, following an earlier 'Hillier affair', 'Once more his good faith came into question, however, when artefacts for which he had agreed a sale with Lord Londesborough went to a pawnbroker.' Hillier died at Ryde in 1866.

The cist, or stone-built box, a precursor of a coffin, was about 8ft long, 5ft wide, and the skeleton, apparently whole, was found lying on its back. Sue Harrington adds,

The plan of grave 45 is an image used very frequently to illustrate a female burial in the sixth century, almost as an archetype, although in the context of her contemporaries she is clearly original … the extraordinary visual nature of her assemblage denotes her as exceptional rather than as representative of the sixth century.

'Assemblage' includes the goods found in the woman's grave, of which 15 are listed by material and provenance. One item not mentioned in what follows, but which is elsewhere, and which perhaps brings her closer to the modern woman, is a pair of tweezers. The list does include: a silver perforated spoon via Kent, a local iron knife, and an iron weaving batten, Kentish. A gold thread braided headband, 'Frankish', and a silver and iron buckle with the same provenance, added to suggestions of her status. Most of the jewellery consisted of garnets set in silver, but one of the rings was gold, provenance unknown. The Kentish and Frankish items confirmed continuing trading links. Sue Harrington has theories concerning the weaving batten:

The weaving batten has for many years been discussed as a tool for use on the warp weighted loom. It is now proposed that with its particular form, associated contexts and relatively short temporal span of use, it had a less utilitarian function and may rather relate to regulation of cloth widths for trade and tribute. This assertion would place this object on a par with weapon swords, if they themselves are seen as emblematic of a royal official such as a port reeve, charged with obtaining dues from trading activities along the coast.

Another source elaborates: 'The right hand was holding a weaving batten, which rested on the shoulder, and a massive gold ring was on the little finger. The batten is to be found in the British Museum, as is what is perhaps best known from the excavation of that site and that grave, the Chessell Down Brooch, which was actually one of three brooches.'

Sue Harrington suggests that while they are 'culturally Kentish, they are made of silver – a relatively rare raw material that could have come either from Francia or conceivably traded from on-going mine workings in the British West. No black and white photograph here could show the intricacies of each of the sections into which the 13.80 x 6.65cms brooch is divided – you could look at it on the internet or, much better, go and see it on display in the British Museum (G41/dc6/sB).'

The woman who wore that brooch, probably to pin her robe together, may have been of the highest status but there were eight other graves in that cemetery containing the remains of women who also had Frankish-style brooches. Sue Harrington poses the question,

> Does this group perhaps suggest an entourage of females, possibly an entire household or kin group? … such a grouping together of women may have strengthened the bonds of this outpost to the local community of traders and back to their Kentish and Frankish elites, as was the custom.

I have not seen a suggestion, a guess even, as to who the highest-status woman was. Could she have been Arwald's wife, who had died and been buried in more peaceful times? He certainly had a wife, because he had two sons who also survived the massacre in which he was killed. Like their sister, they fled to the mainland where, however, they were soon cut down. No wife is mentioned in anything I've read. I wait for my theory to be corrected!

Sue Harrington concluded by suggesting that not only did the women buried in the Chessell Down cemetery represent links between various trading partners 'but their presence does suggest parity with status of weapon bearing men'. They could be seen, too, as precursors of the role that elite women were to play in the early church in later centuries as powerful abbesses of convents. Some of these will have their time in the next chapter.

For this whole period, Ruth Waller of the Island's County Archaeology Service gives me a useful 'get-out' for any mistakes I make when she writes in 'Archaeological Resource Assessment of the Isle of Wight: Early Medieval Period' (2006):

> Conventional sequencing of Anglo-Saxon activity on the Isle of Wight is confused by the lack of cohesion concerning date and origins between two separate documentary sources and the archaeological evidence.

She goes on to give an example:

> The Anglo-Saxon Chronicle [says] that in AD 661 the Christian warlord Wulfhere laid the Island to waste and then sent priests to baptise the people, whilst Bede states that over 1200 families of heathen persuasion were exterminated when Caedwalla seized the Island in 686.

At least there is a named queen for me to latch on to, with parentage, well, a father, and provenance for the Saxon period that follows; but there are some names which, once written here, need not necessarily be committed to memory; and I'm not sure which is more difficult to grasp, the names or the politics of the time. Wulfhere (d.675) was the first Christian king of all Mercia, converted from Anglo-Saxon paganism. He went on to sponsor the baptism of Æthelwealh (fl *c.* 660–685), ruler of the still pagan ancient South Saxon Kingdom. Wulfhere, having advanced into Jutish southern Hampshire and the Isle of Wight in about 661, then gave Æthelwealh the territories of Meonwara, in the country of the West Saxons, and the Isle of Wight. Wulfhere then insisted that Æthelwealh marry **Eafe (Eabae, Ebba)** who had already been baptised in her own country, the province of Hwiccas (a tribal kingdom in Anglo-Saxon England). She was the daughter of Eanfrid, the brother of Aenhere, who were both probably kings and Christian, as were their people. Who her mother was, no one divulges, nor when she was born. But having been queen of the Isle of Wight, whatever that might have entailed, she was widowed in about 686 when her husband, too, was slain by Caedwalla. What all this meant to the Isle of Wight is unclear, though it was now a Christian Island.

In 787, the Isle of Wight was the first recorded place for a Danish attack on England; it was successfully repelled. In the following century such attacks were mostly concentrated on the mainland. In 878, they led to people in Hampshire taking refuge on the Island. In 897 six fast Viking ships were defeated at the battle of Brading Haven, now known as Bloodstone Copse. This, and later such raids, meant that activities at Fishbourne were moved further up Wootton creek. The Saxon king of Wessex who sent fast galleys to intercept those ships leads us to the name of a woman, Osburga whose appearance in the Island story I have already hinted at. You can get your tongue round her name and, indeed, should take note of the woman herself.

Osburga (Osburh) was the daughter of Isle of Wight-born Oslac, Chief Butler of England (Cup Bearer or Chamberlain) and Thane or Ealdorman of the Island, and of Jute extraction. Her mother is unknown, but her father's parentage, with its firm link to the Island, is. Osburga's paternal grandfather was Wihtgar, born on the Island, and one time king of Wihtwara; (Oslac's mother was Ireland-born **Princess Sabd**, 750–804). Osburga's dates are a total mish-mash: her birth, given in various sources, was somewhere between 794 and 835, possibly 807; her death between 849 and 845, or 855. Phillip Armitage, in *Personae Vectenses* (2022) notes, 'In 1855 Æelwulf [her husband], together with his youngest son, Alfred, went on a pilgrimage to Rome "on the death of his wife".' Because of this, he suggests that her date of death was 854. He also suggests that she was born in *c*.813.

But there is more to Osburga than important Island parentage and confused dates. At a date unknown, she married Æthelwulf, becoming Queen Consort of Wessex. Her importance to history, not just that of the Isle of Wight, was that her youngest son was to become Alfred the Great, and details of her life are only known because of him. Yet, in spite of all that is known about Alfred, his date and place of birth are uncertain; both are squabbled about among historians, so I see no reason not to suggest where he was born. Osburga had inherited Arreton Manor, just to the east of Newport, from her father, and Alfred was to bequeath it to one of his sons. (It was to go on to be owned by King Edward before the Norman Conquest. The rest of the Manor's story will be told in later chapters.) But I suggest that is where Alfred was born, possibly between 847 and 848. There is no reason to suggest that, given the family's long connection with the Island, and Osburga's ownership of the Manor, where she was probably born, she did not spend time there, including when she was pregnant.

If we accept Armitage's dates, Osburga died in 854, when Alfred was young, as did his father (who had, however, married again). Alfred's first and early biographer, the Welsh Bishop Asser, describes her as 'a most religious woman noble by temperament and noble by birth'. But there was more to her than that, as revealed by a story told by Asser about the boy's education. Unsurprisingly, there is more than one version of it, presumably in the translating of Asser; I've chosen the one I prefer. In his childhood, and it must have been before he was seven, his possible age when his mother died, Alfred won a beautifully decorated book of English poetry. It had been offered by Osburga to whichever of her sons was able to memorise it. In order for him to do so, it must have been read to him, most likely by his mother, because he did not learn to read until he was 12. The significance is that Osburga was literate, unusual for a woman of her time. It occurs to me to ask, was it normal for a woman of high rank to be so hands-on with her children? And she seems to have been astute enough to notice something special about her youngest child, suggesting, too, given how Alfred turned out, that she was able to influence her son's early development. It is noteworthy too, that such a woman was from firmly Isle of Wight stock.

The king mentioned earlier, who sent the galleys to defeat the Viking ships in the battle of Brading Haven was, of course, Alfred, an indication that he continued to have an eye on the Isle of Wight, where he still owned Arreton Manor. (It was not, however, the end of Viking raids and, in due course, in 1016, England was united under the Danish king Canute.)

As for Osburga, and her inheritance and ownership of Arreton Manor, which would then have come with considerable landholding, it is fair to see her as the first women by name of those who follow in the next chapter – 'Women of Property'.

3 – Women of Property, 813–1664

Queen Osburga

Queen Osburga ends chapter 2, and she certainly qualifies to begin this one. She inherited Arreton from her Island-born father, and passed it on to her youngest son, Alfred the Great, who, in turn, bequeathed it onwards within the family. Phillip Amitage (2022) writes,

> [Helge] Kokeritz provides another possible link between this royal family and this part of the Island when he traces the derivation of the name 'Alverstone' – the hamlet near Brading – to 'Alfred's Farm'. The close proximity of Arreton and this Alverstone (there are two Alverstnes on the Island) adds weight to the idea that this whole area of the Island was, in Saxon times, one large estate in the ownership of Oslac, then Æthelwulf and Osberga and, later, Oslac's grandson, King Alfred and that this estate probably extended as far as Brading and its haven and possibly encompassed the whole of the early-medieval parish of Brading.

This suggested extension of the family's land would, therefore, have included a port, providing easy access to the mainland, including for trading, for example the export of the produce of its fertile soil. But it also encouraged the Vikings to see it as a useful place from which to invade the Island, resulting, as chapter 2 notes, in their defeat by Alfred at the Battle of Brading Haven.

I see Osberga, a mother of six, as well as seemingly caring for her property on the Island, and carrying out whatever regal duties were required of her, as an Island matriarch. She had only one daughter, Æthelswith (c.838–888); I note sources give only the name of her father, omitting Osburga's name as mother. But I suspect that not only did Osburga see to her upbringing, but she may well have been behind her marriage in 853, aged 15, to King Burgred of Mercia (centred on the River Trent on the mainland). It is not known what power Queen Æthelswith came to wield but, in 868, she witnessed a West Saxon charter and made a grant of fifteen hides (1 hide = 120 acres) of land in her own name in Berkshire, a transaction rare for a queen of the period. One item, presumed to be hers, is a gold ring inscribed with the words *Æthelswith Regina*. Given the large size of the ring, it is more likely that she was the giver of the ring, rather than the wearer. It survives in the British Museum. I don't think it's fanciful to suggest that the Queen of Mercia was educated by her mother to assert herself, if only by example.

While it is not possible to know what Osburga's regal duties might have been, I do clearly see her dealing with her property, even if it was through, say, a bailiff. The fact that it was still intact sufficiently to pass on to the next generation, and to choose who her heir was, is evidence enough. How hands-on she may have been will be given credence by women of property who follow.

Ruth Waller ends her 2006 article with the archaeological purpose behind it:

Although the Anglo-Saxon Chronicle records Viking raids on the Isle of Wight in the late 9th century, late 10th century and early 11th century... there is no direct archaeological evidence for this at all. This neatly leads to the fact that by 1016, and until 1035, all England was ruled by the Danish King Canute. He visited the Island in 1022.

Much of what follows in this chapter owes its life to the Norman Domesday Book covering the whole of England. This was commissioned by William the Conqueror (William I of England) to provide him with details of the least bit of land that, since 1066, he ruled over. The book was dated 1086. It records, for example, that by 1086 there were ten churches and approximately 100 manors on the Isle of Wight, several dating from Anglo-Saxon times, including Arreton. There are no surviving churches from that period, though two are thought to contain Saxon remains: 'the possible sundial and north wall of the chancel at St George's Church, Arreton'.

The Domesday Book harks back to those times when it records of the Isle of Wight that 'The King holds Wroxall. Countess Gytha held it of Earl Godwine in alod [a feudal state with no superior] ... There are 17 slaves.' The term 'held' used in the Domesday Book meant that the land was owned at the pleasure of the King, the real owner. There is no apparent evidence that Gytha ever visited the Isle of Wight or, indeed, the free manor of Wroxall (Warochesselle), but the recording of its 17 slaves implies that there was wealth to be had from there, justifying her inclusion as 'A Woman of Property'. What is more she and her family were powerful within the ruling elite of England, and her position may well have benefitted Wroxall.

Gytha Thorkelsdöttir

Gytha Thorkelsdöttir (Gueda; *c.*997–*c.*1069) was, as her name implies, Danish, the daughter of a Danish chieftain Torgil Sprakling, the sister of Earl Ulf Thorgilsson, who was married to Estrid Svendsdatter, the sister of King Canute. Gytha married the Anglo-Saxon nobleman Godwin, Earl of Wessex, and was the mother of King Harold Godwinson (who was to lose the Battle of Hastings in 1066) and of Edith of Wessex, queen consort of King Edward the Confessor. Gytha was to lose five of her sons in two battles, the last two at the Battle of Hastings, one of them King Harold himself. Shortly after that, she was living in Exeter and it is assumed, and not surprisingly, to have been behind that city's rebellion against King William in 1067; indeed, she was known as 'a symbol of resistance'. The uprising resulted in him laying siege to the city. Gytha pleaded, unsuccessfully, for the return of the body of Harold. According to the *Anglo Saxon Chronicle* she then left England, together with the wives or widows and families of other prominent Anglo-Saxons, all the Godwin family estates having been confiscated by William. She probably then retired to Scandinavia where she had relatives. Only her eldest daughter, Queen Edith (d.1075), still held some power (however nominal) as the widow of King Edward the Confessor.

Queen Edith

Queen Edith (*c.*1025–1075), Gytha's daughter and wife of Edward the Confessor (m 1045), is recorded by the Domesday Book as the richest woman in England, and the fourth richest individual after the King, holding land valued at £1,570 and £2,000. One of her holdings was Wootton (Odeton, later Woditon) which appears in chapter 2 because Fishbourne was part of Wootton Manor. While she was the main holder of Wootton, it is worth noting that at least one member of an Island family held it from her as a freeholder. I mention Galfridus de Insula because he appears to have lived there, and the family is to reappear in due course. Not only was Edith very rich, at least before the Conquest but, having been educated at the Benedictine Wilton Abbey (in what is now Wiltshire), as well as being literate, she spoke several languages. She was an example of increasingly educated women. (The Abbey will continue to have connections with the Isle of Wight.) Again, there is no evidence that Edith visited her Island property, but whatever she gained from it financially, she distributed philanthropically in various ways. I can find no evidence, though, that this included within the Island. Her husband was succeeded as king by her brother Harold Godwinson. She was buried beside her husband in Westminster Abbey.

The Domesday Book notes that Godesa (Godeza) held Nettlestone of King Edward; that is Edward the Confessor and, therefore, before the Conquest. It is impossible to find out anything about Godesa except that it is the feminine of the German name Godezo, so perhaps that gives some intimation of her background. With the Conquest, however, as with all such holdings, Nettlestone (on the east coast of the Island) reverted to the Crown, that is William I.

How did the Island fare when the Norman William invaded England in 1066; defeating the Anglo-Saxons? The king rewarded those knights whom he most esteemed for their part in the conquest with lands in England. He gave the lordship of the Isle of Wight, which was a royal appointment with the rights and privileges that went with it, as well as several other manors on the mainland, and the title Earl of Hereford, to his relative William FitzOsbern. The latter began the construction of Carisbrooke Castle because of constant fear of invasion of the Island; it was to be needed in the years that followed. The Island historian Rupert Willoughby points out in a video clip that it was built by Island labour, and that the local populace was cowed.

Perhaps FitzOsbern did not spend much time on the Island, and his stays at his castle there were brief, because you have to wonder what his wife thought of living or staying there. His first wife, **Adeliza de Tosney** (1028–1066) died aged 38 in the year of the Conquest, having apparently had 14 children. But she lived long enough to be called Countess of Hereford. In 1070 he married, as her third husband, **Richilde, Countess of Hainaut** (*c.*1018, or 1027, or 1031 or 1034–1086). She was an heiress in her own right and used to ruling as co-ruler and regent in Hainault. I suspect that she put her foot down concerning Carisbrooke Castle. I cannot deduce whether or not any of FitzOsbern's 14 children spent time on the Island. Another source gives the names of only four of them, one of whom succeeded him as Earl of Hereford. It is said that he had a son by Richilde, but if her 1018 birthdate (the one most often given) is correct, that seems unlikely: 1034 seems the more probable date in view of the apparent evidence of her fertility. In any case, Richilde may never have had to consider Carisbrooke, as FitzOsbern died the year after their marriage.

FitzOsbern, in his turn, apportioned manors on the Isle of Wight to those he wished to reward, perhaps because they had fought alongside him. Only two names need to be noted here.

Cecil Aspinal-Oglander has already appeared, in chapter 2, in a much later manifestation of the family, and connected with Louisa Oglander who supported and helped finance the excavation of the Brading Roman Villa. At the beginning of his Oglander family history, *Nunwell Symphony* (1945), he writes:

This Seigneur d'Orglandes was present at the Assembly of Lillebonne, where the invasion of England was decided upon. True to family tradition, when the expedition was launched, an adventurous son of his house, Richard d'Orglandes, set out with it; and this Richard, in the train of William Fitz-Osborne, took part in the subjugation of the Isle of Wight. FitzOsborne, in reward for his service, was presented by the Conqueror with the independent Lordship of the Island. Richard d'Orglandes was in turn rewarded by his chief with a grant of land at Nunwell. And here at Nunwell the descendants of Richard have lived and loved and prospered ever since.

The name of Richard's wife eludes me, but the Oglanders, as they became, appear several more times, still at Nunwell, in the chapters that follow.

But there was a name more relevant to Godesa and Nettlestone, though first it should be noted that, in 1101, the lordship of the Island passed to the de Redvers family, taking over from FitzOsbern. This change will be come relevant in due course.

Matilda de Estur

Hugh de Estur also arrived in England with William the Conqueror's Norman army, and was granted lands for distinguished services rendered at the Battle of Hastings. He and his three brothers held lands in the Isle of Wight and Hampshire, as listed in the Domesday Book. One of Hugh's sons was William de Estur, and from him Baldwin de Estur was descended. At last we come to the point: his daughter was **Matilda (Maud) de Estur** (*c.*1224-*c.*1282, or 1288), whose dates, like those for so many others, are uncertain. She was said to have been 'an infant' (mother unknown) when her father, Baldwin de Estur, died in 1224. Sources say that the date of her death is 'unknown', but I've looked at the court cases in which she was involved as plaintiff or defendant; the last one could be either 1282 or 1288. She married Baldwin or Walter de Insula (later changed to de Lisle and then Lisle), in about 1244; he was knighted in 1253, and died in *c*.1265. Matilda kept her own name, and her elder son, William, used de Estur; her other two sons used their father's de Lisle. She was her father's heir and inherited landholdings scattered throughout the Island which, based at Gatcombe House (south of Newport), she seems to have managed herself, adding to them; she is commonly known as Lady Matilda (or Maud) of Gatcombe, or *Domina de* Gatcombe. A lot of her property transactions and, indeed, the court cases that sealed them, seem to be within the family.

'Manor Houses of the Isle of Wight' (posted by the 'Island Eye') notes:

In 1269–70 an agreement was made between Maud de Estur and Walter de Lisle, who was probably her son, by which Maud was to hold for life a messuage and a carucate of land in Nettlestone and Westbrook with reversion to Walter, who was to hold the estate of the heirs of Maud. Walter was in possession in 1293, when he held an eighth of a fee at Nettlestone of William de Estur.

A *messuage* is a dwelling house with outhouses and land assigned to its use; a *carucate* is a medieval unit of land area approximately the land a plough team of eight oxen can till in a single annual unit. Tax was assessed on this.

Another 'Island Eye' posting shows just how complicated property affairs within the de Estur/de Lisle family were:

Westbrook [Manor] appears by name in the 13th century, and was held at the time of the Testa de Neville by the Lord of Whitefield under Maud de Estur of Gatcombe, and was granted to the latter by Walter de Lisle in 1270. Two years later, Ralph de Coleville granted to Walter a messuage and land in Westbrook, Appley and Westhay.

'Testa de Neville' refers to Walter Nevill and his wife Muriel who held several other properties. Another from 'Island Eye':

Appley [Manor], originally a farm of some 200 acres at the north-east extremity of the parish bordering the sea, probably represents the land in Appley which with Westbooks [sic] and Westhey, was granted in 1272 by Ralph de Colville to Walter son of Maud de Estur.

In 'The priory and Manor of Appuldurcombe, Isle of Wight'(?), Dr JL Whitehead writes, again concerning the 'Testa de Nevill', 'The Abbot holds one fee at Wydecoumbe, as a tenant of the Lady Matilda Estour, Lady of Gatcombe.' That was near Whitwell, in the south-east of the Island, which was included in the manor of Gatcombe. It therefore came into the Lisle family by the marriage of Walter de Insula with Maud. She built and endowed the chapel of Saint Rhadegund, now St Mary and St Rhadegund.

It should now be noted that before the time of Matilda, who was a descendant of William de Estur (awarded land by FitzOsbern), the lordship of the Island had passed to the de Redvers family in 1100; this now becomes relevant. A *British History online* posting about Gatcombe suggests that 'In 1263 as Lady Maud de Gatcombe she was holding this manor and other property in the Isle of Wight by the service of guarding the island when necessary and by suit at the court of Carisbrooke Castle.' Carisbrooke comes into its own as the seat of the de Redvers family.

In 'Carisbrooke Castle and the Lords of the Isle of Wight' (1959?), CBR Butchart writes: 'The Battle Abbey Roll records the name of one "Rieurs" as having served at the Battle of Hastings in William the Conqueror's army. This may possibly have been Richard de Redvers'. He was duly rewarded with land in England. In later taking the right side in strife between brothers for the crown of England, 'He was given the town of Tiverton, the Honour of Plympton and created Earl of Devon and Lord of the Isle of Wight. With the Lordship of the Isle of Wight came Carisbroke [sic] Castle.' (In fact, it sees more likely that he was made Baron of Devon; this title was later raised to Earl of Devon – this sequence is rather difficult to untangle). The Lordship had reverted to the Crown when a FitzOsbern had chosen the wrong side. We may skip the other descendants who were also involved in strife, such as that between Matilda and Stephen for the Crown of England, to Baldwin, 6th Earl of Devon, Lord of the Island from 1216 to 1245 (when he died).

Amice de Clare

In 1226 the sixth earl was betrothed to six-year-old **Amice de Clare** (Amicia; 1220–1283/1284), daughter of Gilbert de Clare, Earl of Hertford and Earl of Gloucester, and Isabel Marshal; he was 40, she was 19. (At least one source suggests Amice was married in the year of her betrothal.) She is most known for being the mother of a daughter who was to become unarguably the most famous person in the history of the Isle of Wight – more notable, as far as the Island is concerned, than Queen Victoria. Amice did also have at least a couple of property dealings, both religious. As Countess of Devon, she gave to the nuns of the Abbey of Lacock 'with her heart' her manor of Shorwell. The convent, then recently founded for nuns of the Augustinian Order was in Wiltshire. As usual, what was important was what the manor would earn for the Abbey. Also of importance was the fact that her daughter Margaret was a nun there. Phillip Armitage in his *Personae Vectenses* notes that she owned areas of land around Yarmouth.

Amice and de Redvers had two other children (Margaret, becoming a nun, no longer features in developments on the Island). Their son, Baldwin, 7th Earl of Devon and Lord of the Isle of Wight, was born there in 1236; he inherited the lordship at the age of 10. In 1257 he married the well-connected Avita (Avizia, Marguerita) of Savoy, but he died in 1262 (aged 26), while accompanying Henry III on an expedition to France. (Butchart has it that he was poisoned by his wife's brother.) The couple had one child, a boy, who died in infancy. So it was Baldwin's sister, Amice's daughter, Isabella, who inherited the Lordship.

Isabella de Fortibus

Aged 11 or 12, in *c*.1240, Isabella was married, as his second wife, to William de Fortibus (or Fortz) who owned land in Yorkshire and Cumberland, and was the Count of Aumale (Albermarle; Normandy) and Lord of Holderness (an area of Yorkshire). They had six children, none of whom outlived Isabella. When her husband died, in 1260, part of his estates (her 'dowerlands') were granted to her. When two years later her brother Baldwin died, he left her his lands in Devon, Hampshire, the Isle of Wight and Harewood in Yorkshire. She was in her mid-twenties; thus, **Isabella de Fortibus** (de Forz; 1237–1293), using the titles Countess of Aumale, 8th Countess of Devon, and Lady of the Isle, became one of the richest heiresses in England. As a rich widow she became highly eligible; as a widow of wealth and supreme power on the Island, she was able to run her own, and the Island's, affairs as she saw fit. She determined to keep it that way, fending off all the suitors that swarmed around her; indeed, she was an exceptionally determined woman. From Carisbrooke Castle, which was her main residence from 1262, and which she not only extended and made more comfortable – so that it became known as the New Castle of Carisbrooke – she also administered her personal and Island affairs from there. Many of her accounts have survived; they show that her net income in the 1260s rose from £1,500 to £2,500. (The 'Hidden Heroes' post about her suggests adding three noughts to those figures for some indication of today's values.) In 1266, she held a general audit of her estate accounts at the castle.

As well as being an astute ruler and businesswoman, Isabella was also rather litigious, and that is how I first came across her when I was writing, with my late husband, Derek Roebuck, *Women in Disputes: A History of European Women in Mediation and Arbitration* (2018). I devoted four pages to her, starting, '[She] may not have been a queen, but she tended to act like one, and her power, prestige and property involved her in many disputes, including with the king.' Forgive me if I use here some of what I wrote there.

Isabella was so litigious that she owned her own copy of the statutes of the realm, and with her advisers, she prosecuted dozen of cases, both civil and criminal. One of her earliest disputes was within her own family. It was with her brother's widow, Avita (d.1292), 'in connection with certain of the various estates which she had of Baldwin de Redver'. In addition to that she even had a long-running dispute with her mother. In 1261, the two widows had combined to buy the marriages of the Aumale heir and the remaining two-thirds of Holderness. (It was possible to acquire a marriage or re-marriage; Simon de

Montfort the younger had done so from the king concerning widowed Isabella, though she had made sure he was unsuccessful in carrying it through.)

Tension apparently arose between the two women when Isabella supported the barons in their rebellion against the king, and her mother sided with the king. But their dispute, which lasted from 1265 to 1274, concerned income from the family estates. It was taken first to the king and then to the exchequer court. Because it lasted so long and was so intricate, it is unnecessary to relate it here in detail, as I did in *Women in Disputes*. In 1274, mother and daughter were reconciled, but they never lived together again, which suggests that the reconciliation was merely formal. Isabella did, however, confirm her mother's gift to the nuns of Lacock, granting them the amercements (punishments by fine) of their men of Shorwell. Amice, having outlived her husband, remarried. Just before her death, she founded the Cistercian Abbey of Buckland in Devon, a sister house of Quarr Abbey on the Isle of Wight. Although it is called a 'sister' house, it was for monks, not nuns.

Isabella had other disputes with the burgesses of Newport and the Prior of Carisbrooke. But it was with the Abbot of Quarr Abbey, to the west of Ryde, that her dispute was most protracted and heated, because it was, basically, about who was in charge. Quarr Abbey (perhaps early called Our Lady of the Quarry) had been founded by Baldwin de Redvers, 1st Earl of Devon and 4th Lord of the Island in 1131/2 and, when he died there in 1155, that is where he was buried, together with first wife **Adeliza de Baalum** (Adelise, Alice; *c*.90–*c*.146). (In parenthesis, to give substance to Adeliza, when Baldwin, in rebellion against King Stephen, was besieged in Exeter, Devon, Countess Adeliza, Butchart suggests, 'with dishevelled hair, bare-footed, and in tears implored the king in vain'. Over the years, the de Redvers, and other Islanders donated manors to the Abbey, increasing its wealth and power. Arreton manor was one of the original endowments.)

Though Isabella was a benefactor of this community, there were several tussles over the years between her and the Abbot, so much so that in 1282, the Abbey made application for a writ of protection against her. There are screeds to be found about the increasingly difficult relations between the two sides, and the court hearings that resulted, but I'd like to make it as simple and accessible as possible here. To do so I shall quote from a lively, if quite long, Internet posting under the title 'Isabella de Fortibus' by Therron Welstead, an archaeologist sometimes working on the Island:

> Picture the scene, it is 1283 and you are a proverbial fly on the rafters of the great hall of Winchester Castle (Hampshire) watching the proceedings below. It is a tense court case with hostilities running high. There are many figures making accusations and counter claims; Isabella de Fortibus, Earl of Devon, with 22 of her men, is against the abbot of the Cistercian abbey of Quarr. … The abbot, wearing his white habit, is supported with 18 of his men, a mixture of monks and lay brothers. Overseeing the proceedings are four justices and a jury.

The abbot's accusations include that Isabella was at the centre of 'intolerable oppressions and extortions' at the abbey's expense. Isabella was ignoring that the abbey had been placed under royal protection, and [the] countess's stewards were forcing the abbot and his tenants in defiance of the charter of liberties granted to them to do suit of court (duty of attending court by the lord).

The abbot also brings up a particular incident that occurred following an attempt to collect tithes that he claimed were owed to the abbey (Carisbrooke Priory also claimed them). On 29th July 1282 there was an 'assault with force and arms upon … his fellow monks … lay brothers and men of that abbot, at … Staplehurst … and beat, wounded and ill-treated them, and there stole from the same brethren and led away three horses … of the price of ten marks, and took those brethren and imprisoned them, and took and carried away other goods and chattels … to the value of thirty pounds.'

The response from Isabella's perspective – presented on her behalf by Robert Bardolf, the bailiff of the Isle of Wight – is quite impressively different. The prior of Carisbrooke Priory raised the hue after seeing 50 armed men. Roger, the clerk of Robert Bardolf, went to investigate, but was shot at with arrows by the men of Quarr Abbey. In the confusion, Roger's groom thought his master had been killed and summoned Robert Bardolf. Robert approached with a militia, but their advance was checked by more volleys of arrows. Several of the militia were wounded and one was thought to be fatally wounded. Because of the fatal wounds, the men of Quarr were placed in prison in Carisbrooke Castle … when it was realised that the wounds were not fatal, the imprisoned monks and lay brothers were let free, but they did not collect their belongings when they left.

One of the niggling issues between Isabella and Quarr was the terms under which the abbey existed: a charter of liberties that she had previously granted to it. This meant the monks were exempt from attending her court amongst other privileges. One of her advisors felt that this encroached on Isabella's rights and tore up the charter. The upshot of the case, as J Charles Cox succinctly describes it in *Churches of the Isle of Wight* (1911) was the 'granting by the Countess of a charter of exemption to the abbot and all his tenants from suit and service at her Hundred Courts, and from all manner of tolls and tallage and all other demands both by sea and land, and upon the seashore'.

Many of Isabella's disputes involved her lands in Devon. Although they show that she by no means neglected her responsibilities there, neither do they need to detain us here. Her involvement in disputes were not always on her own account:

[She] frequently appointed attorneys to travel to the royal court whilst she remained on the Island to ensure that it remained secure. As a result of her choice to remain a widow, Isabella was able to bring cases, of which there are numerous examples, to court against people from all levels of society, including the king himself … the record evidence also shows that, through her position as landholder and lord, Isabella's tenants, and sometimes her officials, looked to her to intercede on their behalf when they were involved in a difficult situation.

The one dispute that rumbled on until she was on her deathbed was with the king. On the Island, Isabella was queen in all but name. Edward I not only resented that, but also had his eye on the island for strategic reasons. He repeatedly tried to buy it from her; she constantly refused to sell. In 1281, Edward summoned Isabella to court, asking her to prove her right to rule the island, control its legal system, claim wreck of the sea and taxation. As lord of the Isle, Isabella claimed the 'right of wreck' round the coasts of the Island. At the time, should a shipwreck occurring round the coasts of the mainland have no survivors, any value arising from the sale of what was salvaged and, indeed, the ship itself, belonged to the Crown, seen as an important source of royal revenue. Isabella's defence for her claim was that 'she and all her ancestors from the time of King Richard, and also before that time, had had their wreck of the sea in her fee on the Isle of Wight without any interruption'. Her claim was even firmer: from when Henry I had granted the Lordship of the Island to Richard de Redvers in 1102, the family had enjoyed the privilege of 'right of wreck'. The wording of Henry's grandfather, William the Conqueror, when he awarded the Island to FitzOsbern in 1068, was that it was 'to be held as fully as I myself hold the Realm of England'. The court may well have been biased against Isabella but, not surprisingly, she triumphed.

In 1293, Edward asked Isabella once more to sell him the Island; once again she refused. But, aged 56, she became increasingly ill that summer. When Edward heard that she was dying, he ordered three bishops to travel to where she was resting on her pilgrimage to Canterbury. Admitted to her room, they were the only witnesses to her agreement, which consisted of touching the Bishop of Durham's glove as she died. It hardly mattered to Isabella: her six children were dead and her heir was a 17-year-old second cousin once removed. Her daughter **Aveline de Fortibus** (1259–1274), did live to marry (aged 10) – Edmund Earl of Lancaster, the younger of two surviving sons of Henry III – but she died a year after the marriage was consummated when she was 14.

Following the return of the Island to the Crown for a mere £4,000, it and Carisbrooke Castle ceased to be hereditary, but from then on were granted by the monarch. As Katy Bell puts it in 'Isabella de Fortibus: Queen of the Isle of Wight', Isabella's death marked the end of the Isle of Wight's independence from England; it became an appendage of the Crown.

Isabella, though, had the final laugh from beyond the grave: when Edward I demanded that the knights of the Isle of Wight come to Scotland to fight for him, they all refused, stating that they were not bound to the king's service beyond the Solent. And 50 years after her death, Katy Bell notes, 'there was an investigation by Edward III into why he was failing to receive wreck from the Isle of Wight, due it seems to locals going out in boats and capturing property before it drifted into shore'.

Isabella was buried at Fontevraud Abbey in France. There is no portrait of her; the only possible likeness, but disputed, is a stone sculpted corbel (a type of bracket) jutting out from a wall in Christchurch Priory (Dorset, Diocese of Winchester). Butchart notes that 'She was one of the many women of the feudal age who displayed that capacity for administration which those ignorant of history and psychology deny her sex to be possessed of.'

7. Isabella de Fortibus, stone carved head, from the Internet

A letter that Percy Stone (architect, archaeologist and author) wrote to John Oglander of Nunwell in 1901 can mislead, at least on first reading, in mentioning Matilda d'Estur of Gatcombe: in fact he is concerned about Whitfield (Whytfeld); that is, when it separated from Gatcombe. Having secured the Isle of Wight from Isabella on her deathbed, one of Edward I's actions concerning the Island was to grant the manor of Whitfield, including Brading, to his daughter Mary for her lifetime. Stone wrote,

When Whitfield separated [from ?] Gatcombe is not apparent, as in the list of fees Domina de Whytfeld (I conclude this is the Lady Mary) held of the Lady of Gatcombe, Matilda d'Estur. ... The Sturs of Gatcombe were evidently Chief Lords of the fee, in Brading Parish, of Whitfield, Alverston, Ageston, Brading, Westbrook, North Sandham or Appley, Ninham near Languard – according to the list of Liberties.

Mary of Woodstock

Lady Mary was **Mary of Woodstock** (1278–before 1332), sixth-named daughter of Edward I and Eleanor of Castile. (Although that Eleanor was descended from Eleanor Aquitaine, she is often unhelpfully confused with the latter in the recreation of the Island's history.) From the age of six, when she was veiled, Mary was a nun at Amesbury Priory (Wiltshire), but lived very comfortably thanks to a generous allowance from her parents. Despite a papal prohibition on travel in 1303, she travelled widely round the country, including paying visits to Court. I can find no evidence that she visited the Isle of Wight but, as so often, the purpose of holding a manor was for the wealth it produced.

Mary's mother, Eleanor, had set Mary quite an example. **Eleanor of Castile** (Leonor, Alienor, Alianor; 1241–1290) was notorious for her acquisition of property. Following her death she was to be warmly remembered and, although it was a political marriage, she was much loved by her husband; she was however not universally loved in her own time, and was known primarily as a keen businesswoman, particularly in the land market. The Archbishop of Canterbury warned her servants about these activities:

A rumour is waxing strong throughout the kingdom and has generated much scandal. It is said that the illustrious lady queen, whom you serve, is occupying many manors, lands and other possession of nobles, and has made them her own property.

Walter of Guisborough preserves a contemporary poem:

The king would like to get our gold,
The queen, our manors fair, to hold …

There is evidence, though, that much could be laid at the door of her officials: on her deathbed she asked her husband to look into the matter, and her executors recorded payments of reparations.

By whatever means, she obviously acquired Milton Manor, with land held in Adgestone, of the manor of Appleford on the Isle of Wight. In 1280 she gave it to Christina and Sir John Weston. Christina was one her ladies-in-waiting; she accompanied her to Gascony where the royal couple spent a year following their marriage, and where Eleanor gave birth to her first child who did not survive infancy. As Christina was sent home from there, apparently '*ad pregnandum*', you have to wonder what Eleanor felt in retrospect. Sir John was probably a member of the party during that year.

Following the death of Isabella de Fortibus, and the return of the Isle of Wight to the Crown of England, no woman connected with the Island's manors was ever to reach the heights of ownership of property and involvement that merits detailed inclusion here. Nevertheless, it is worth noting a few with some property connection. In 1355 Edward III granted ownership of Carisbrooke Castle to his eldest daughter, and second child, **Isabella of England, Countess of Bedford** (*c.*1367–1431). Her mother was Philippa of Hainault. Isabella's eventual marriage and how the Castle features in it appears in the following chapter, 'Troubled Times', in connection with an attempted invasion by the French.

Philippa de Mohun

Philippa de Mohun (*c*.1367–1431) was the third daughter and co-heiress of John Mohun, 2nd Baron Mohun, and Joan Burghersh. She married three times, the third time, before 7 October 1398, to Edward of Norwich, 2nd Duke of York, and grandson of Edward III. Following her husband's death at the Battle of Agincourt (1415), she received a grant for life of the Lordship of the Isle of Wight, previously held by him and, on 10 December 1415, was styled Lady of the Isle of Wight. She died at Carisbrooke Castle and her will was drawn up there; though it itemises several bequests of philanthropy, it says nothing about the Island; indeed, I can find no evidence of activity or ownership of property on the Island. She seems only to have had one child, a son, by her first husband, mentioned in her will. She lived for 16 years as a widow and, as she died there, it may have been at Carisbrooke Castle. I can't begin to imagine her life there. Perhaps her activities have simply not been recorded, or I have failed to find mention of them. She was buried in Westminster Abbey.

It is difficult to write accurately about the grant of the Manor of Appuldurcombe to the Abbess of the Nuns Minoresses with Aldgate to settle on the Isle of Wight, firstly because of a confusion of dates, and secondly because I'm not sure that they settled there; it may simply be that they benefitted financially from the grant. Because the history of that manor is interesting enough to appear in other chapters, I feel I should include them. here. Trying to marry various conflicting sources is one of the problems. If it was granted to the Abbess in 1422, that Abbess is said to be Isabella of Gloucester in several lists of abbesses which may well have copied from each other. The Gloucester family were certainly involved in the convent, but the dates of their daughter, who was Abbess there, were 1386–1402.

Johanna Bowerman

Sometimes you have to do a lot of foraging to find enough material about a woman to justify her inclusion; that's what I had to do with **Johanna Bowerman** (Joan; 1451–*c*.1503), and, as usual, not all the sources align. She was Islandborn, and died and was buried at Brook Manor, daughter of John Roucle (or Rockley) of Brook Manor, and **Johanna Gerston** (d.1503). One of the titles by which she was known was Lady of the Brook; her father was known as Lord of Brook. In what follows, I hope to show that this title belonged to Johanna, and not to her husband Thomas Bowerman, as some sources imply.

Brook Manor, just west of Mottistone, only half a mile from the sea, is noted as Brook in the Domesday Book of 1068, probably included Hulverstone and was perhaps in Freshwater Parish. Nineteen families of peasants lived there, working the land. As a Manor it passed through various hands, at one time being held by Carisbrooke Castle. According to *British History online*, Nicholas de Morgan being of unsound mind, it reverted to the King, and at Nicholas's death in 1362–3, it appears to have been divided among his sisters. Geoffrey

Rookley or Roucle seems to have acquired the shares of three at least of the other sisters, and was styled in 1370 as Geoffrey Roucle 'de la Broke' who gave part of the estate to his son John, Johanna Bowerman's father. It then says that he was succeeded by his son-in-law Thomas Bowerman, Johanna's husband. It is fair to assume that it was part of her dowry because Johanna, widowed in 1488, left it to her grandson Nicholas Bowerman; that is, it was hers to give. When Nicholas married in 1503, he was styled Lord of Brook and Austerborne (Osborne).

Brook was not Johanna's only land: an Internet source for Adgestone Manor suggests that 'Joan (Johanna) Bowerman and her grandson Nicholas died seized of land in Adgestone, which they held of the manor of Alverstone'. A dispute Nicholas was to have concerned the chapel at Brook in which Johanna had founded a chantry for one priest to sing for her and her husband and father and mother, John and Joan Roucle, and for all Christian people.

Needless to say, Johanna is remembered by something relatively trivial. In 1499, she entertained Henry VI when he visited the Island. Her hospitality was so appreciated that the king complimented her on his departure with the present of his antique drinking horn, and a warrant for a fat buck of the season, to be annually delivered during her life from his forest at Carisbrooke. Perhaps it is noteworthy that Johanna and her Manor House were considered appropriate to entertain the king. Bowermans were to live at Brook Manor until the late eighteenth century.

Elizabeth Howard, Countess of Peterborough

Johanna Bowerman was very much an Islander; **Elizabeth Howard, Countess of Peterborough** (1603–1671), daughter of William Howard, 3rd Baron of Effingham, was not. But they are both primarily remembered for something trivial. Elizabeth was reputedly a great beauty, so much so that she was painted by Van Dyke in about 1630. The press office for the Ashmolean Museum, Oxford, where it was on display in 2017 (usually in the Mallett Gallery of European Art) described her as dressed 'in lavish silk and lace and wearing pearl and diamond jewellery which is painted with particular delicacy'.

That was not all: a miniature, watercolour on vellum, was painted by the studio of John Hoskins the elder, c.1638–1640, described as 'Head and shoulders portrait, head inclined slightly to the left wearing a gold dress, grey cloak fastened with a pearl rope, pearl necklace and double pearl earrings. Brown eyes, fair hair in ringlets pale face, sidelong glance, dark brown background'. Two years after her death, in 1642, her husband John Mordaunt, 1st Earl of Peterborough, died of consumption. His parents had been Roman Catholics at the wrong time. Taken from his mother by James I and made a ward of the Archbishop, he was educated at Oxford. Later, he was taken to Court by the king (in modern times known to have been homosexual), who was struck, as the Internet source has it, 'by his beauty and intelligence'. This or perhaps in recompense for the treatment of his parents, led, in 1628 to his creation as Earl of Peterborough.

What has all this to do with the Isle of Wight? After twenty years of widowhood, in 1664, Elizabeth, Countess Dowager of Peterborough, together with her second son John, Lord Mordaunt of Reigate, and a James Atham, were granted a 31-year lease of the saltmarsh extending from the port of Newtown, on the north coast, to Shalfleet. As *British History online* also tells us, 'A considerable manufacture of salt was carried on at Newport until the nineteenth century. The salterns were to be seen on the coast.' A saltern is a plot of land laid out in pools for the evaporation of seawater to produce salt. There is no evidence that Elizabeth ever visited the Isle of Wight, let alone the salterns that, no doubt, provided her with some nice pin money.

Newtown was founded in 1256 under the name of Franchville by Isabella de Fortibus, lord of the Isle. As it was said in a text in the Carisbrooke Museum that Newtown was destroyed when French forces invaded the Island and besieged Carisbrooke Castle, that leads neatly into the next chapter, 'Troubled Times'. Four years after Elizabeth's death, when the 31-year lease had yet to come to an end, Newtown Town Hall was built; in its older age, it features in chapter 13.

8. Elizabeth Howard Countess of Peterborough, from the Internet

4 – Troubled Times, 1214–1782

Relations with France 1214–1782

In the Iron Age, the Isle of Wight benefitted from its location because of the ease of trade between it, the mainland across the Solent, and Gaul across the Channel. Thereafter, as has been shown, its position made it particularly prone to invasions, such as those of the Romans, Jutes, Mercians, Vikings and, of course, the Normans. That last invasion caused problems that rumbled on for some time, as the Normans of the Conquest may have become kings of England but they were determined that they should also have all, or parts, of France. This was finally resolved by what is known as the Hundred Years War (more accurately 116 years; 1337–1453). That is why I made the link between the end of the last chapter, and the beginning of this because, in 1377, the French invaded the Isle of Wight and attacked and burnt Newton to the ground. They did rather more than that, as will be shown. What is more, France invaded the Island five times during the Hundred Years War.

But the troubles with the French did not start with that seemingly endless war. King John, determined to regain lands in France, some of them belonging to his wife, others to his mother, Eleanor of Aquitaine. He visited Yarmouth with the same intent in 1201 when (Boucher James suggests) he also wished to meet the Lord of the Isle concerning the garrisoning on the Island of men in the pay of the king. He visited again in 1206 on his way to France to discuss matters concerning Normandy. In 1214, however, his party contained named women and that visit is, naturally, of more interest here. He set sail from Portsmouth for La Rochelle with a large army, but on the way he and his party spent time in Yarmouth. The visits to the Island are confused, depending on the source; as usual I have to decide between them. The most reliable information I have found concerning how the 1212 visit occurred, and the composition of the party, is from the Portsmouth Royal Dockyard Historical Trust:

> King John led an unsuccessful expedition against the French. Ten galleys based at Portsmouth. 1st February. The king, queen, son Richard and niece Eleanor embarked but were delayed a week in the Solent by poor weather.

Isabella of Angoulême (1186 or 1188–1246) was John's second wife; they married in 1200, when she was 12 or 14, after he had annulled the marriage to his first wife. Isabella was heir to her father Aymer Taillefer, Count of Angoulême (she inherited in 1202), and, in addition, came from good French royal stock. John and Isabella had five children, one of whom, the youngest, was called Eleanor, but she was not born until 1215. John's niece, known as **Eleanor Fair Maid of Brittany** (1141–1284), was the eldest daughter of Geoffrey of Brittany, fourth son of Henry II of England and Eleanor of Aquitaine, that is, John's older brother. Following the early death of Geoffrey and her brother, Eleanor not only was heir to vast lands in France, but also would have a claim to the throne of England. A rival, therefore, to be kept close. Richard was John's natural son (the king had five children by more than one mistress).

The phrase 'in the Solent' does not mention Yarmouth, but I am satisfied that the fleet was based there. I had assumed that the royal party stayed on their ship in the harbour. But it appears that, instead, they were based in a large house on shore. The *British History online* account of Yarmouth notes that 'there must have been at that time a mansion of some importance at Yarmouth'. After his visit, either that house, or the land on which it had stood, came to be known as 'The King's House'. There Governor Robert Holmes later built his own mansion (see Chapter 5, 'Irregular Relations'), now The George Hotel.

The king and his army arrived in La Rochelle on 15 February but, by the time they returned to the English mainland in October, John has lost everything he had at first gained. Isabella and Eleanor may have returned to England from Yarmouth. In June 1215, John was forced by the Barons to sign the Magna Carta, and he died a year later.

It could be said of Knighton Manor, to the east of the Island, that fortune did not smile upon it. Although there is some dispute, it is said that Hugh de Morville (*c*.1155–1204), one of the four knights involved in the 1170 assassination of the Archbishop of Canterbury, Thomas Becket, owned it at the time. Having responded to Henry II who, when at the end of his tether with his failed relationship with Becket, and in a temper, conveyed his wish to see the end of the 'tiresome priest', Morville took flight to the Isle of Wight. Sources differ: those not from the Island suggest that afterwards he fled to his castle in Knaresborough, while Island sources, such as an examination by an *Island Echo* posting of 2022, suggest that while he later fled to that castle, in the immediate aftermath, he fled to his Knighton Manor. This story may well be a myth: it is not, for example, mentioned in John L. Whitehead's rather difficult to disentangle, 'Notes on the Manor of Knighton, IoW, and the early Manor Lords, AD1066–1343'. It is, however, taken up by the historical novelist Sarah Sprules in *Knighton Gorges: The Curse of Thomas Becket* (2014).

Hugh de Morville (Odo) (d.1202) certainly married **Helwise de Stuteville** (*c*.1156 to after 1223); he was her second husband. Sarah Sprules has Helwise as very much one of the central characters of her novel, holding the fort at Knighton Manor, while her husband, desperate not to be caught, was holed up for months on end in Carisbrooke Castle, receiving parcels from her and, in due course, visits. As Knighton Manor's later history was to continue tragically, it is, perhaps, worth a read, though like many such novels, there is a young woman, another main character, falling in love, for whom there is no historical record. Helwise was to go on to marry for a third time following Hugh de Morville's death.

As Hugh de Morville (d.1202) was by no means the end of the ill luck falling upon Knighton, inheritance of it needs to be further explored. I cannot vouch for total accuracy concerning the dates of family members who followed because sources differ. John (Ivo, Eudo) de Morville (d.1256) succeeded as Lord of Knighton (his father may have been Hugh). He married the heiress **Isabella de Wrokeshale** and their daughter **Eleanor de Morville** (Helena, Ellen; *c.*280–*c.*341) born at Knighton, was left heiress of Knighton, as well as of lands on the mainland. Aged 14 or under, she married 'under the King's hand' (Henry III), Ralph de Gorges (d.1272), who added his surname to her property, thus Knighton Gorges. It is their daughter, and who she married, who take the story and, indeed, French raids, further.

Eleanore de Gorges (*c.*1307–*c.*1376) heir of Knighton, married Theobold (Tibault; 1303–1340) Russell whose father, William, had been warden of the Island, and constable of Carisbrooke Castle; he had spent much of his life engaged in administering the defence of the Island; more specifically, in 1294, he received royal instructions to put the Island into a proper state to meet the threatened invasion by France of the southern coasts of England. By his second marriage, in about 1280, to **Katherine de Aula**, heiress of the de Aula family of the Isle of Wight, the Manor of Yaverland came to him (this is relevant for later in the story).

As Lord of Knighton, Theobald Russell had wider Island responsibilities: he commanded an Island militia that included the manors of Knighton, St Helens, Kern, Ryde, Quarr, Binstead and Newchurch; his lieutenant was Reynold Oglander of Nunwell. The former diplomat turned medieval historian, Randolph Jones, in his article, 'Sir Hugh Tyrel and the French raid on the isle of Wight, August 1377', sets the scene, propelling a few years back, to 1340, when there was a French raid on St Helens.

We know from taxation records that the population of the Isle of Wight in 1377 was 4,733 souls, excluding paupers and children. In times of emergency, all able-bodied men between the ages of 16 and 60 were expected to assist in the defence of the coast. If we consider one third of the total adult population to be able-bodied males, the militia would have numbered over 1,500 men. However, because of the unexpected appearance of the French fleet, it is unlikely that they would have been gathered together in one place at the time of landing.

So it was that, in 1340, Theobald Russell, commander of the militia responsible for St Helens, gathered together what force he could and set out for the coast. Spare a thought for the feelings of Eleanor, waiting at home for the safe return of her husband. He and his men were successful in driving the raiding party into the sea, and he did arrive home. Unfortunately, he had been mortally wounded. Eleanor retired to the room in which Theobald had lain in state, and remained there grieving. The rest of her story will have to wait, and what followed over the years to come, until the next chapter, 'Outsiders'.

In searching to see what happened to Reynold Oglander, Russell's second in command, without knowing if he took part in repulsing the French then, I failed to find him, but I did find a good enough introduction to what happened when the French invaded again. In *Nunwell Symphony* (1945), Cecil Aspinall-Oglander writes,

> Little is known about Robert [succeeded 1365]… But it was in [his] day that the family achieved the then rare distinction of seeing their house destroyed by an enemy invader. After leaving the Island in peace for a generation, a French force again landed at St Helens in the summer of 1377, the year that saw the accession of Richard II. This time they were not opposed as successfully as in Theobald Russell's day. Advancing inland, they sacked and burnt Nunwell and the forty tenement houses that clustered round its wall. They sacked the town of Newport; and it was only on arrival at Carisbrooke that they at last met their match. The castle garrison, under their Captain Sir Hugh Tyrrell, put up a stiff resistance, and the French losses were heavy. A parley then ensued; and on being offered the rather inglorious bribe of a thousand marks the enemy took the cash and departed out of the island.

Robert's wife was **Alice Hatchett**. They married in 1342, and had one son. That is all I can find out about her. Was she still alive in 1377? If so, it is not difficult to imagine how she felt about seeing Nunwell destroyed, if she was there to watch. Exactly the same is true about the women who lived in the 40 tenement houses.

That description of the destruction of Nunwell is a vignette of the 1377 French invasion. For a full account of it, from beginning to end, the invaluable article by Randolph Jones is the one to turn to; unfortunately there is nothing about women, so one has, as so often, to use one's imagination. To help, you only need a quotation from the Elizabethan historian John Stowe: 'The French therefore having Gotten the island, did much hurt in slaying the inhabitants, burning certain towns, and taking the substance from the people.' And Jones helpfully reports the 'inquisitions' held in 1380 and 1387:

> These reported that the towns of Whippingham, Pan, Fairlee, Wootten, Barnsley, Shide, Park, Carisbrooke, Thorley, Newport, Yarmouth, Afton, Northwood, Watchingwell, Freshwater and Ashey had been burnt by the King's enemies in the first year of his reign (ie 1377).

Aspinall-Oglander goes on to remark that 'The next forty years were lean indeed'. And he quotes from Sir John Oglander's manuscripts: 'In those wars between France and England, the Island was more subject to incursion than any other parts, as having then no castles. Whereupon many forsook the Island, and placed themselves in the mainland.'

In spite of that, he goes on to recount how Robert Oglander 'Rode out the storm. Rebuilt his house, making the new one, we will hope, a little more comfortable than its predecessor.' He adds that not a trace of either house remains. He does, however, suggest what they would have been like. Suffice it to say that, regarding this new one, it is likely that it contained a '"lady's bower" or parlour'.

And there would have been a '"dortor" or dormitory for female dependents'. **Alice Hatchett Oglander**, if still alive, would doubtless have been involved.

Meanwhile at Carisbrooke Castle, Sir Hugh Tyrrel (1341–1378) was holding out against the French. Jones goes into the details of his life in the service of his country before and after 1377; by May that year he was keeper of the castle. Following the death of his first wife, he had married **Katherine de la Plaunche** (Plaunk; 1340–1398). Was she with him in the besieged castle? I can find no record; even the date of her marriage to Tyrell is given as 1330 when she was not yet born, and he only 11.

One other woman may have been involved. Most simple Internet sources give the name of the hero of the hour as Peter de Heynoe (or various spellings). Jones uses a quotation from Sir John Oglander to give the liveliest, and probably most romantic, account of his involvement:

> The de Heynoes were Lords of Stenbury … when the Franch had taken the Island and besieged Carisbrooke castle. One Peter de Heynoe came to Sir Hugh Tyrell, then Captain of the Island, and told him he would undertake with his silver bow to kill the commander of the French taking his time, for he had observed … how nights and mornings he came near the castle; which on leave he killed out of a loophole on the west side of the castle, and by that means brought the French to a composition to take 1,000 marks to be begone, and to do no further harm; on which embassage one of the Oglanders was employed and effected it.

But, as Jones points out, a Peter de Heynoe is named as the Lord of Stenbury in the militia list of circa 1340, with under his command, Stenbury, Whitwell, Wroxall, Bonchurch, Cliffe, Apse, Nyweton [Newton], and Sandham. 'However, in 1377 the Lord of Stenbury was one Guy de Heynoe, a minor then fourteen years of age. His father, William, had died in 1375. Perhaps Peter was Guy's guardian.' I can find no wife or mother concerned to be proud. Jones then goes on to explore who might have been the commander concerned. This search would seem to have been impossible, as the French force was Franco-Castilian, and several men might have been the commander concerned. So I am left to suggest that there would have been women across the Channel mourning their dead men, just as those on the Island would have been doing the same, as well as losing their homes. And girls growing up without their fathers.

Jones sums up that the French (who had been blown to the Island by a storm),

> having achieved as much as they could, in the short time available, they decided to leave. It is clear that the English did not defeat them: in the end they brought off the raiders with a ransom … The Wightmen also promised not to oppose any future land within the space of a year. Therefore, Sir Hugh's defence of Carisbrooke castle and the Isle of Wight was probably not as glorious as it first seems.

Wherever Katherine de la Plaunk Tyrell was at this time, her husband died the following year, and she re-married. As for so-called Peter de Heynoe's clever shot with his bow and arrow through a castle wall loophole, it is still there, and called Heynoe's Loop. Put that into an Internet browser and a photograph comes up – it is an interesting shape, reminiscent of the club on a playing card. Getting to the bottom, via the Internet, of which Heynoe was involved, let alone whether any wife, mother or daughter was present, is less rewarding. The *History of Manor Houses of the Isle of Wight* entry for Stenbury Manor whizzes you through the men. There is a Peter de Heyno in the reign of Edward III (which ended with his death in 1377), with no dates for Peter; and it tends to follow what Jones discovered. But I can't resist noting that a Thomas Heyno in possession died in 1505 leaving five daughters, one of whom, Grace, the posting calls 'an idiot'. The Manor was, therefore, divided between the other four sisters, and you can follow their trajectory thereafter, but I mustn't get carried away here!

In chapter 3, I mentioned that in 1355 Edward III granted ownership of Carisbrooke Castle to Isabella, his eldest and favourite daughter. I wrote that more about her would appear in this chapter. She may have been difficult, as Rebecca Starr Brown suggests in 'The Willful Isabella of England, Countess of Bedford' (2017), but she was the king's daughter so it is worth noting that marriage arrangements for her fell through several times, for one reason or another. Eventually, in 1360, aged 28, she met Enguerrand VII, Lord of Coucy, a Frenchman who had been brought to the English court as a hostage in exchange for the freedom of King Jean II of France. They married in 1365, and de Coucy was so much accepted in the family that he was made Earl of Bedford, his lands in England were restored to him, and the couple was allowed to journey to France. Although they had two children, Isabella, as Rebecca Starr Brown suggests, 'seemed to have[had] little interest in taking up the mantle of "wife" or mistress of his household lands'. She spent much time in England in the 'role of Edward's favourite daughter'. The couple drifted apart, de Coucy increasingly conscious of his split loyalties, though he was careful to remain as politically neutral as possible during the Hundred Years War. Then came 1377, the death of Edward III, and the accession of Richard II. De Coucy, without owing anything to the new king, 'acted quickly and decisively to sever all his ties with England'. He also severed ties with Isabella; they never saw each other again. Meanwhile, Isabella owned Carisbrooke Castle, which the French attacked that year. There is no evidence that de Coucy took part, but it is worth noting where, under the circumstances, his loyalties would lie, and he was forced to surrender his English lands to King Richard.

Over more than a hundred years later, the 1488 encounter with the French and the Isle of Wight was a one-off. It was a venture, or adventure, cobbled together by Edward Woodville, Lord Scales, Lord of the Isle of Wight, the last to hold that title. He was part of the eminent Woodville family – his sister Elizabeth Woodville had married King Edward IV – and he had gained recognition for his help in securing the throne for the man who became Henry

VII. Edward was known as 'the last knight errant', which just about sums up his undertaking of a personal expedition – probably unsanctioned by King Henry – to help the Duke of Brittany against France. To achieve this, he recruited from among the Islanders, from a population of only 5,000, a force of 440; it included 40 knights and squires – from such families as the Roucley, Lisle, Knight, Mewys, Popham, Bremshet, Brutenell, Hacket and Oglander (names I've garnered from a poem about the event) and 400 yeomen (no names). Aspinall-Oglander describes how Woodville dressed his force in white coats, embroidered with a red rose, and when it set sail from St Helens and arrived in Britanny, they were reinforced by 1,600 Bretons dressed the same, so as to suggest a stronger English force. At the ensuing battle of St Aubyn, on 28 July, they were completely routed:

> Woodville himself was killed; and of the 440 English who had set out so full of enthusiasm – the flower of the Isle of Wight – tradition asserts that only one boy returned to tell the tale. 'There was not any family of any account in the Island,' writes Sir John [Oglander], 'but lost a father, brother or uncle. We lost two young gentlemen of our house at the battle, George and Richard Oglander'.

> The effect of these heavy losses upon the already sparsely populated Isle of Wight can be judged from an Act of Parliament that was passed the following year. In that Act the Island was described as 'desolate and not inhabited, but occupied with beasts and cattle, so that if hasty remedy be not provided, the Isle cannot long be kept and defended but open and ready to the hands of the King's enemies, which God forbid'.

The sole survivor of that Island force who managed to return home was Diccon Cheke, surely of the Cheke family of the Manor of Mottistone; they had owned the property from 1300 and were to do so until 1600. From Randolph Jones's list of commanders of militias (1340) is 'The Ld of Modeston [Mottistone] (Tho.Chyke) had the command of Modeston, Newtown, Caulborn and Brixton.' The family built the present house in the fifteenth and sixteenth centuries, so presumably it was started in the lifetime of Diccon. The owner of Mottistone Manor in 1488 seems to be Robert Cheke (*c.*1448–*c.*1500), who was born there; his wife was **Lady Margaret Elizabeth Bramshott** (1450–1498), but among their named children there is no Diccon; he seems to have disappeared from history after 1488. The same applies to the two Oglanders, George and Richard, and nothing about either being married. But their mother, **Joan Oglander** (née Molendarius; 1400–1500), was alive at Nunwell, aged 48, to mourn them, and she apparently lived to 100. There was also a sister, **Dorothy Oglander**, who married a T. Cheke, surely of Diccon's family. There must be a story there.

Of the 400 yeoman, who must also have died, not a word. But most will have had wives who would now have to add their husband's farm work to their own, as well as mourn their husbands, and bring up their children. And I cannot help asking, who embroidered all those red roses?

The plaque that Dorothy Davies, author of *Captain of the Wight*, campaigned to have erected in the Carisbrooke Castle Museum reads:

In Memoriam
Sir Edward Woodville
And the 440 gallant men of the Island
Who died at the battle of St Aubin, July 28th 1488
And to Diccon Cheke, sole survivor of the massacre,
Who returned with the story.
Requiescat in Pace.

The next notable French invasion was in 1545, and is best known for the battle of the Solent and, in particular, the sinking of the *Mary Rose*, watched from the Portsmouth naval base by Henry VIII, and no doubt by Islanders on their north coast. It was caused by a variation of political problems between England and France; at root this time was Henry's leaving the Roman Catholic Church, and taking his country with him. A good source for what follows is Ben Jones's 'The Great French Armada 1545 & The Battle of The Solent'; he writes,

Late in the afternoon [of 19th July] the wind picked up again and the English were able to beat off the French Galleys. Unable to get an advantage at sea, the French invaded the Isle of Wight. [Owing to] frequent raids and invasions by the French during the Hundred Years War, the islanders were well prepared. All the men underwent compulsory military training and some women were even trained as archers.

The French admiral ordered three attacks on the island, at St Helens, Bonchurch and Sandown. The troops then spread out and laid waste to the villages of Bembridge, Seaview, St Helens and Nettlestone. Once again, how this would have affected families, particularly women and terrified children does not leave much to the imagination.

The largest force landed at Bonchurch; it is there that the women archers are said to have been used. This was the only place where the Islanders were forced to retreat, their rather portly captain, Robert Fischer (Fyssher), unable to run, reportedly crying out '£100 for a horse.' I can find out nothing more about him, particularly a wife who might have been at first frightened, then a bit shamed. And, in fact, the terrain at Bonchurch – steep, thickly wooded slopes – would not have lent itself well to a horse, even with a trim rider. More than one source, including Ben Jones, wonders if Shakespeare might not have developed that cry for help for *Richard III* ('A horse, my Kingdom for a horse'). Although the French were able to move inland from Bonchurch, their Admiral called everyone back to the fleet and returned to France. Different sources suggest that the French force of 500 'won' the battle for Bonchurch, others that the 300 Islander militia did. An edited version of the 'Battle of Bonchurch' (2014) by CT Witherby reads,

> The English on top of the downs must have seen the galleys moving towards Bonchurch, then men landing and finally must have seen the French party slowly climbing towards the summit of the hill. To the defenders this must have seemed a clear indication of another French attack, but from a new direction. At once, all available men were collected to drive the French off the summit.

> As soon as the French neared the summit, they were greeted by a shower of arrows and suddenly saw Englishmen running down towards them. The French commander was slain but the chase continued down the hill towards Bonchurch and the French soldiers were swept away.

I am, of course, interested in the women archers. Were they among those described above? History does not appear to record any more than their existence. I even hoped that there might have been a plaque in their honour, but looked in vain. There is a general one at the front in Seaview, easily visible: I came upon it by accident. It reads:

> During the last invasion of this country hundreds of French troops landed on the foreshore nearby. This armed invasion was bloodily defeated and repulsed by local militia 21st July 1545.

The Seven Years War (1756–1763) became a global conflict but was essentially a tussle for dominance between Britain and France, the details of which are not relevant here except in one respect. Britain's shipyards were kept busy bolstering the navy, and one of the warships that came off the slipway in 1756 was first called the *Royal Anne*, but was renamed for George II before the launch. In 1782, the ships assembled at Spithead, the sea lane between Portsmouth and the Isle of Wight, including the *Royal George*. It was ready to set sail with the rest of the fleet for Gibraltar, which was under a Franco-Spanish siege, when it was discovered that some repair work needed to be done below sea level; this required the ship to be turned slightly on its side. When it was found that the problem required a replacement part, it began to take a little longer than expected. That didn't worry the 300 or so women and children below deck, on board to say goodbye to their husbands and fathers, as well as some traders and a few prostitutes. But a complication caused the ship to list more and, when a workman clambered aboard to warn that it was listing too much, and steps needed to be taken to right it, the lieutenant to whom this information was vouchsafed refused to listen to a mere workman. The upshot was that water began to enter the ship, more and more of it, until finally and very quickly, it sank. There were 1,200 on board at the time; of these about

200 saved themselves by going out on the topsail yards which remained above water after the ship reached the bottom. About 70 more were picked up by the boats from other ships at Spithead, among them 11 women. At least 900 drowned, including women and children.

What has this got to do with the Isle of Wight the other side of the Solent? Quite soon, many bodies, including those of women and children, began to be washed up on the beach at Ryde. The townspeople did their best to honour the dead, and they were buried where Dover Street meets the Strand, on land that is now the Esplanade. Unfortunately, in 1835, when there were some heavy gales, some of the skeletons were unearthed, drifting south until they were exposed to view at Bembridge.

When I came to the end of that wretched story, first prompted by Rosa Raine's *The Queen's Isle* (1861) and then helped to reconstitute it by the postings such as the National Maritime Museum's 'An Account of the Loss of the "Royal George" at Spithead, August 1782' (2010), I thought that surely some women must have survived. Nothing daunted, I came across Hilary L. Rubenstein's 2020 article 'The Only Female Survivor of the Sinking of the Royal George', published to accompany the publication of her book *Catastrophe at Spithead: The Sinking of the Royal George* (2020).

Elizabeth (Betty) Horn (née Badcock; 1758–1837), was the daughter of a Plymouth shipwright, and the wife of Jack Horn, an experienced seaman, by then a petty officer, serving as one of the ship's quartermasters, probably supervising last minute loading of provisions. While most of those on deck found ways to save themselves, those below, including Betty, made for the portholes. A seaman dragged the struggling Betty, surrounded as she was by others, through one of them, and threw her clear. He, a good swimmer, then saw the barely conscious Betty float past. It wasn't easy, even with the help of one of his shipmates, but her original saviour kept an eye on her and pointed her out to one of the rescue vessels. A few days later, recovered, she was reunited with her husband. Some other women were saved from the ship, but unable to swim, and hampered by their long and bulky clothes, drowned immediately; another casualty was, apparently, a woman disguised as a sailor. Among the 60 children who perished, were babies swept from their mother's arms. The terrible screaming described can be imagined.

Following her husband's death in 1827, Betty sank into poverty. Some months before her death in 1837, aged 77, someone alerted William IV, who authorised a payment to her of £50. Found in her possession, it was said, was a list of everyone who had been saved from the *Royal George*.

The Plague, 1349–1743

Newtown or, as it was originally called, Francheville, on the north-east coast of the Island, provides a useful link between French invasions and the plague. It was re-named, as an oceanic posting about the town put it, 'to inspire hoped-for resurrection of its fortunes after being sacked by the French in 1377'. What made 1377 even worse is that 'In 1349 the Black Death came to Hampshire and the Isle of Wight, with [the] coastal area taking the brunt of the suffering. Losses of over 50% of [the] coastal populations were experienced in a number of cases.'

Carenza Lewis notes in 'Settlement in Hampshire and the Isle of Wight' that 'at Wooton [Hampshire] specific reference is made in 1354 to the pestilence in records of tenants' arrears. On the Isle of Wight the toll seems to have been even higher: nearly every benefice fell vacant during the period of the Black Death and by 1350 the king was forced to remit all tax due from his tenants.' The posting on the Wilcuma website of 'Hampshire During the Black Death and the 100 Years War (1337–1444)' notes that 'The Isle of Wight is said to have been virtually depopulated; Brading sea mill was vacant in 1349 for "no Miller would come because of the mortality; the average number of Inquisitions post mortem, in the Island (inquiries after death concerning the property of notable persons) was one a year, but in 1340 there were seven deaths thus recorded, all people of considerable local importance."'

I have not found any 'people of local importance' for the Black Death then but, as Boucher James puts it in volume 1 concerning the next onslaught of plague – and it is easy to confuse Newport with Newton,

As early as 1582 the pestilence raged to a considerable extent in Newport and its neighbourhood. Edward Horsey, who had been Captain of the Island from 1565, a man of dissolute life, died of the plague in the same year, 1582 at Hasely.

Horsey, a soldier, ambassador and courtier under Queen Elizabeth I, had led a full and colourful life before being appointed a justice of the peace for Hampshire and the Isle of Wight in 1569. By1580, he was living at Great Haseley Manor near Arreton. In fact, it appears that having caught the plague in 1582, probably because members of a visitor's household had it, he seemed to have recovered, but died the following February. There was a woman in his life, one of some substance and ingenuity, but that story is best kept for chapter 5, 'Irregular Relations'.

Newport seems to have been particularly prone to episodes of plague, probably because it was a port at the end of the navigable section of the Medina river. Boucher James, continuing his account of the plague there in 1582, writes,

Some of the townspeople may have tried to escape from the plague, but there is no evidence of … desertion from their duties. The registers of the dead were … carefully kept. At such seasons the disposal of the dead bodies becomes a ghastly and terrible office. Ever since that early date when a few huts or hovels had gathered round the estuary of the Medina river the people of Newport had been accustomed to bury their dead under the shadow of the mother church of Carisbrooke; with the arrival of the plague that church-yard became either insufficient or more probably was at too great a distance to carry the bodies which had to be buried almost instantaneously. A new burial-ground had in consequence to be formed at Newport, where the gaping, ever-opened graves received … nearly one sixth of the population, or reckoning five persons for each household not very short of one person in each family.

Interpreting that last sentence, it seems that more than one family lived in each house; surely in the poorer houses there would not have been servants – who might well be counted as a different family. Sir Edward Horsey was buried in Carisbrooke church. His alabaster and marble monument with effigy survives in St Thomas's Church, Newport. A modern online travel snippet brings the Newport graveyard of 1582 up to date.

In Newport's town centre there's a small public park with some fine trees, a formal rose garden and a new brightly coloured children's playground. Yet propped against a wall near the public library are some old tombstones and beside the busy road there's a solid-looking stone archway. This was the gateway to 'Church Litten', Saxon for a burial ground, created especially for victims of the Plague. In Newport two hundred people died of the disease, even the Governor of the Isle of Wight.

Newport features in the next plague, once again it seems because of its port allowing arrivals from the mainland, including London. It always raises the spirits to find, just by a hint, a new woman of interest – even when there seem to be more than enough women to write about! So it was, when I read this in an online posting 'History of the Isle' about Bembridge:

Even in 1665, there were still only three routes into Bembridge Isle, so poign-antly emphasized in a petition from the inhabitants of Yaverland, requesting that Lady Richards not be allowed home to Yaverland Manor, since they feared she had become contaminated with the plague in Newport.

That is all, but it started me digging until, indeed, I discovered that the plague seems to have arrived in Newport from London. But my first task was to identify who Lady Richards of Yaverland was, then to discover the location of Yaverland, and finally to locate the petition. I discovered that the Manor of Yaverland was held in trust for German [Jermyn] Richards, but then I realised that this reference was too early as he died in 1563. Still it was clearly the family into which Lady Richards had eventually married.

An unlikely blog, 'Covent Garden and Sir John Baber physician to Charles II', contains the petition itself, sent to Sir William Oglander, 1st Baronet, MP for Newport and deputy governor of the Island since 1664:

The Humble desire of ye Inhabitants of yaverland August the 30th.
Sir,
These few lines are to entreate yor Worpp for to send to Brading yt they might sett a watch & ward to keepe out all Newport people out of the town

wee are resolved to keepe a gard day & night att yarbridge & wee have beene with Major Holmes att the fort & he hath promise that none shall come that way & we doe understand that the Lady Richards is minded to come to Yaverland too morrow but we are resolved for to stop her & not to lett her come & wee are fearfull if she might come in thorough Brading & soe to come over the wall by ye sluice therefore we thought fitt to acquainte your worship- with it hopeinge that yor worship will send to Bradinge that they might secure that way.

That same blog notes that Sir John Baber had married Elizabeth Richards, daughter of Sir John Richards of Yaverland on the Isle of Wight. They had four children, the last born in 1658, but Elizabeth died the following year, leaving John Baber a widower with full responsibility for his children. 'With plague breaking out so close to his home, he must have decided to send his children out to the countryside. Lady Richards who may have been the children's grand-mother, took the children to their home in Yaverland on the Isle of Wight.' By late August, the people of Yaverland would have been aware of the plague in London, and of the coming arrival home of the Lady of the Manor. Lady **Richards**, mother of Elizabeth Baber, may have been born **Elizabeth** Hunger-ford, daughter of Sir John Hungerford of Down Ampney (Gloucestershire). She was Sir John's second wife and had been widowed for some years by 1665.

John Baber was wise to send his children away from London and the plague of 1665–1666. A National Archives online database describes it as 'the worst outbreak of plague in England since the black death of 1348[.] London lost roughly 15% of its population.' In total 68,596 deaths were recorded in the city, but the figure may well have been higher; and it was followed by the Great Fire of London of 1666. Baber married again, twice, after Elizabeth's death, so their children may not have stayed long in Yaverland.

It is worth explaining why the location of Yaverland enabled its inhabitants to cut themselves off. An online posting about the history of Bembridge Island states:

The area containing Yaverland and Bembridge was for much of its history an island, cut off from the Wight mainland by an encircling arm of sea at high tide and a muddy gulf at low tide. Hence its former name, 'Bembridge Island'. A wide area of sea flowed up between Bembridge and St Helens, past Brading and Yaverland and then joined up with another branch of sea that emerged through a gap between Yaverland and Sandown, where the boating lake is situated today. ... Even in 1665, there were still only three routes into Bembridge Isle.

The Yaverland petitioners who tried to prevent Elizabeth Richards arriving home from Newport may not have been aware that she was returning from plague-ridden London with four children. History does not relate what happened, but my guess is that she arrived home safely at her fine Elizabethan or Jacobean manor house, so nicely described and illustrated by Johanna Jones in a *Wight Life* posting about Yaverland Manor.

The Isle of Wight narrowly avoided the plague again in 1743, when a vessel carrying it anchored off the south coast while seeking provisions. The danger was quickly dealt with, as detailed in an *Island Echo* posting: 'On this day: the Isle of Wight had a narrow brush with the plague in 1743.'

Carisbrooke Castle, the Civil War and Charles I, 1641–1651

There is no need to tell here the story of the English Civil War between the Royalists supporting Charles I and the Parliamentarians (Roundheads, Ironsides). The importance is how it tore families apart, and how it affected the Isle of Wight and, in particular, Carisbrooke Castle.

Sir John Oglander was to play a part in the events of that time; his was a family typical of those that were long established land-owning gentry. Memories would linger of two sons of an earlier generation killed during the ill-starred misadventure of Edward Woodward to Brittany in 1448. The Island had officially fallen to the Parliamentarians in 1642, but there were pockets of support for the king. A known Royalist, Sir John was detained several times, starting in 1643, when there were the increasing problems between Charles I and Parliament that were to lead to the fighting of the Civil War. The importance of Sir John is also that he kept a diary which was used by Richard Worsley for his *History of the Isle of Wight* (1781), and was published in 1888 as *The Oglander Memoirs*. The family historian Cecil Aspinall-Oglander provides extracts and stories from the papers, including personal letters, held at Nunwell, setting the scene of what was to follow, particularly from a Royalist point of view:

> Thou wouldest think it strange if I should tell thee there was a time in England when brothers killed brothers, cousins, and friends their friends. Nay, when they considered it no offence to commit murder. I believe such times were never before seen in England, when the gentry were made slaves to the commonalty and in their power, not only to abuse but to plunder …

My thoughts turned naturally to Oglander's family. In 1606, he had married **Frances Franck More Oglander** (1590–1644) daughter of Sir George More and Anne Poynings. By the start of the Civil War in 1644, they had nine children, four of them girls. They had to live through the times when Oglander was detained, though not charged, and the events in which he took part. But Frances died that year (cause unrevealed, though a letter of 1631 mentions her improved health), and before the strife reached the Island in full measure. Her oldest son, George, had died in 1632 – of smallpox in Normandy – causing both parents grief; Sir John's at the death of his eldest son, carefully educated to be his heir, is described in his Parliamentary records biography. By 1644 the children still living were grown up; a boy and a daughter, Elizabeth, born *c.*1621, had died of smallpox in 1629. Of the two daughters called Anne the first had died young, the second, born 1612 or 1614, presumably named after her, and known as *Trés Belle Anna*, married, aged 21, Sir Stephan Lennard as his third wife, though he was only 31. Frances, born *c.*1611, was said to be 'plain', though she still managed to marry Captain Francis Clerke, and Bridget, born *c.*1619, married Sir Robert Eyton. The dates vary, but what is certain, from remarks sprinkled throughout *Nunwell Symphony*, is the importance of good looks (preferably beauty), the need to find a husband of appropriate status, and problems of dowry; brains, character and education, for the girls, were inconsequential. I have found nothing, either, to indicate whether or not the girls were still living at Nunwell, nor to ascertain what they went through during the events that were to unfold, starting in 1647.

During a court case which detained Oglander in London in 1643, he wrote to his wife, whom he called Franck. His letter, of 11 July, says much about their relationship, his political leanings, and the effects of them, how she needed to take on some of his work of making sure Nunwell farm ran smoothly during his enforced absence, and the securing of the income derived from it. Here are the more relevant paragraphs:

All that I desire of you is that you bear it with a good courage, and not by your grief to let our enemies see you grieve and be not cast down although our case is bad enough, yet there are many worse …

You and my son must take care of the business I cannot do. I am glad the baili proves so well. Pray encourage him, and let him follow the haying when fair weather comes, and to let the wheat out by the acre for cutting, and the barley for raking. If you want money, take the Baili's account of his corn, and if he doth not sell it fast enough, let a load be carried to Newport if it will yield 5s a bushel.

Commend me to Bridget, and tell her that her jewell will yield £40. My son [in-law] Lennard and my daughter [Anne] are well. They are not without their troubles.

I have bought your gown, which cost twenty shillings, more than your money. I hope you shall have it by this. Your stockings you shall receive of this bearer.

My black suit begins to be torn. Wherefore, pray, in the trunk in cellar, where the tobacco is, send up my satin doublet and cloth hose, and cloak lined with plush, and some tobacco; and put the other tobacco in the bin.

Good Franck, be merry, and let him have your prayers who loves you dearer than his own life.

Your loving husband,
John Oglander.

John Lisle, now in the Island, I fear is my greatest enemy and most incenseth my Lord against me.

John Lisle of Wootton Manor was a Member of Parliament sitting as an anti-royalist. Later he was accused of regicide and, as a result, was assassinated in Switzerland in 1664. Probably affected by his politics, his second wife, **Alice Beconshaw Lisle** (*c.*1614–1685), having borne seven children, was tried by the notorious Judge Jeffreys and executed, aged 71, in 1685 at Winchester on a charge of harbouring fugitives after the Battle of Sedgemoor. The new King James refused to pardon her. (She is the last woman in England executed by a judicial sentence of beheading.)

In his next letter Oglander tells his wife that he still can't get a hearing and fears that money may have to change hands. Franck is exhorted to bear the situation with 'masculine courage'! Thereafter connection between them is made more difficult, the letter from him of 3 August seems to be the last. There is also one from her to him of 30 July which ends, 'I give God thanks we are all well here. Only we want your company, for which I, your most faithful wife, will never cease to pray to obtain while I have life.' The last letter quoted, of 13 September, is one from his daughter Frances, by then Mrs Clerke and obviously not living at Nunwell because she has only just heard of his arrest. Her PS reads, 'You shall a cheese by Gardner by next return from your poor daughter.'

Oglander's wife Frances was to die the following year, 1664, aged 54; perhaps it had all been too much for her.

Her husband's misfortunes may have dated from the time in 1637 when Jerome Weston, 2nd Earl of Portland, 'that rather gay and dissolute Royalist' governor of the Island, had put pressure on him to become a sheriff of Hampshire responsible for collecting ship money. As Aspinall-Oglander explains, 'This unwelcome appointment was the beginning of John's undoing for it was during its tenure that his popularity in the Island began to wane. A royalist to his backbone, he threw himself at once, as the King had gauged he would, into the very unpopular task of collecting Ship money.' As its name suggests money was raised to fund the building of new ships for the navy.

But it is Portland or, rather, his wife, following his arrest, who now moves briefly to centre stage. **Lady Francis Stewart, Countess of Portland** (1617–1693/4) was the daughter of the 3rd Duke of Lennox and Katherine Clifton, Baroness Clifton, and a cousin of Charles I. She married Portland in 1632. And we know she lived with him at Carisbrooke Castle because of the story about her that is so good that not only is it told in detail in *Nunwell Symphony*, but there is also a text on a wall of the Castle Museum which takes it from Worsley, who took it from Oglander. By 1642, Portland had been removed from office by Parliament and imprisoned. Lady Frances was allowed to stay in the castle with her five young children, her brother and sister-in-law, and a force of 20 Royalist gunners led by a Colonel Brett. They had fewer than three days' provisions. Aspinall-Oglander writes:

Following the arrest of Lord Portland and the coercive persuasions of Richard Swanley's marines, the majority of the Isle of Wight gentry began to trim their sail to the Parliament wind. Not so, however, the gallant Lady Portland. …This spirited lady … as obviously much more to John's fancy than her very rollicking husband …[When] an order arrived from Parliament the local militia and the crews of the men-of-war were to take possession of the castle, 'the intrepid Countess behaved like a Roman matron'. [And] when the attacking force of at least five hundred men approached the castle walls, Lady Portland 'mounted the platform and, match in hand, declared that she herself would fire the first cannon, and defend the castle to the last extremity, unless honourable terms of capitulation were granted. Once again, as on an earlier occasion in 1377, a parley then ensued at the entrance, and it was agreed that, on surrender of the castle, the inmates should be allowed the freedom of the Island. This concession, however, was soon revoked; and the 'Lords in Parliament' issued a decree that the Countess of Portland was to be given two days' notice to quit the Isle of Wight.

Lady Portland was helped to travel to France, while the children went to their father, by then released; it was John Oglander who arranged their successful journey. What happened to Lady Portland thereafter does not seem to have been recorded.

9. The Countess of Portland, © National Portrait Gallery, London

Meanwhile, the Battle of Edgehill, the first pitched battle of the Civil War, had taken place (23 October 1642) and, although the king's forces had been routed, war continued to be waged. I have commented before that how it affected families had to be imagined. But now I suggest that historical novels can be helpful in aiding that. I recommended a novel when it came to the escape of Sir High Morville from the scene of the assassination of Archbishop Thomas Becket. The novels are not necessarily well written, and sometimes imaginary love affairs are dreamed up which may be a bit annoying, but I shall continue to include them. Usually the writer lives or has lived on the Island, and has done their research. These recommendations are quite apart from the information in chapter 10, 'Women Writers', which concerns women writing about the times in which they lived.

For what it was like during the Civil War on the mainland, as well as illustrating family rifts over which side to support, the first few chapters of Vanessa Hannam's historical novel, *The Hostage Prince* (2006), are effective, though most of the book concentrates on the part the heroine later played on the Island. At the family's estate, Hatherton Manor, her father, Sir Edwin Jones, suffered:

There was little to believe in now. Parliament had destroyed the old order, and had nothing with which to replace it. He could no longer look after the land: so many young men had left to fight for the King that the fields were left untended. His bounteous Kentish apples, which stored the winter like no other, remained unpicked on the trees, … He didn't blame the men for leaving. How could they refuse when they were offered four shillings a week – far beyond anything he could pay them? Somehow, though, the Judas money did not find its way to the families, and the tenants couldn't pay the rents. There was little he could do to help. Ironically, it was the King's taxes that had all but finished him, the most ruinous of all being the 'Ship money', squandered on a useless navy, most of which lay rotting on the sea bed. The last lot of soldiers who'd been billeted at the manor had emptied the store room and granaries of all that was not hidden, and he knew the debt would never be paid.

After battles and sieges in the years that followed that first battle, the king, following the Battle of Naseby, was finally corralled at Hampton Court from where, in November 1647, he escaped and fled across the Solent to the Isle of Wight, to Carisbrooke Castle, where he had happy memories of visiting as a young prince. It was yet another mismanagement, or lack of knowledge, on the part of his advisers and entourage of what was going on there; it was not the place of refuge that he had expected. The governor of the castle was a Parliamentarian, Colonel Robert Hammond, who had no choice but to advise those now in charge in London of the royal arrival; in reply, he was instructed to confine the king, though in those early days, on a loose rein: he was able, for example, to visit loyal Royalist John Oglander at Nunwell.

By chance a year later, a young cousin of Hammond – 20-year-old William Temple – was on the Island to visit his uncle, Sir John Dingley and his wife **Jane Dingley** (née Hammond; 1589–*c*.1691) at Wolverton Manor, in the parish of Shorwell. What the Dingleys' politics were is not of particular issue here, but William Temple had definite Parliamentarian leanings. He was on his way to visit his father in exile at St Malo. He is likely to have visited his cousin Colonel Hammond at Carisbrooke and, from a later disparaging remark about Charles I's appearance, to have seen him.

At the same time, 21-year-old **Dorothy Osborne** (1627–1695), the youngest daughter of 12 children of Sir Peter Osborne, in the service of the king, governor of the island of Guernsey, was part of a family visit to the Island on their way to France. Dorothy's kinsman, Richard Osborne, was Gentleman-of-the-Bedchamber to the king. Two of her brothers had died in battle, and her parents had lost most of their lands and fortune in support of the king.

The time and circumstances of the meeting of the couple are not clear, but what is clear is an incident in the inn where the Osbornes had been staying.

10. Dorothy Osborne Temple, © National Portrait Gallery, London

They had already left, when young Robin Osborne ran back, and with his diamond ring scratched on the window, 'And Haman was hanged upon the gallows he had prepared for Mordecai. Then was the King's heart pacified.' Jane Dunn in her large joint biography, *Read My Heart: Dorothy Osborne & Sir William Temple A Love Story in the Age of Revolution* (2008) explains the biblical and political reference. Under the circumstances, it was an incendiary act, and of the party, at least Robin and Dorothy were detained, and Robin was to be charged and brought before Governor Hammond. Quick-witted Dorothy, deducing that a young woman would fare better, claimed it was she who had done it. William was apparently there to see what happened, and it was then that he fell in love with her. They were released, and were on the boat together to St Malo where William spent a month able to visit Dorothy. The upshot was the confirmation of the love affair between them, but it could not lead to marriage, because of family resistance for financial reasons on both sides, until 1654. During that time, with only a few short clandestine meetings, Dorothy wrote 79 letters to William which he kept and which survived. They were found and published in 1886, when they proved a sensation, well received, for example, by Virginia Woolf who wrote admiringly about them (her full quotation is in a useful Internet article, 'Dispatches From the Former New World' (2021). The originals of Dorothy's letters are to be found in the British Library (Add.MSS: 33975); none of his replies have survived. It appeared that Dorothy, because of the constraints she was under, had to destroy them as soon as she'd read them. The marriage, not only of two hearts but also of two compatible intellectual and political lives, lasted until Dorothy's death.

Not surprisingly, notice of Charles I's imminent arrival threw those on the Island and, in particular, staff at Carisbrooke Castle, into turmoil. And once again I am going to turn to a historical novel, this time *Mary of Carisbrooke* (1956) by **Margaret Campbell Barnes** (1891–1963), already an established writer in the genre, who lived on the Island from 1945 until her death. It is clear that she did some serious research on the subject, and her scene setting of the events of the king's incarceration is valuable, but she was also a novelist. That means that she did not so much invent characters as sometimes give them different family relations. Hence 17-year-old heroine, Mary Lee, is given a father, Sergeant Floyd and, therefore, becomes instead Mary Floyd. (I can find no one of that name, sergeant or otherwise, at Carisbrooke.) When the conditions of the king became increasingly restricted, not only is she known to have been responsible for his laundry but also, because of her position, she was able to secrete his letters out of the castle, as well as those coming in. And Mrs Jane Wheeler, who had overall housekeeping duties, is made her aunt with the first name Druscilla.

Last, but not least, the author has not avoided the love affair bug affecting such novels, so that Mary, as the title suggests, is given a major role and has romances with two of the king's Gentlemen. They were both true characters involved in the king's failed attempts to escape – Harry Firebrace and the already mentioned Richard Osborne. The attempts are described in detail, Mary and Druscilla being integral to their planning – of course.

There is no doubt that Mary was important to the king, even if one goes only by the text on the wall in the Carisbrooke Castle Museum with the title 'Mary – Assistant Laundress and King's Messenger'. The king wrote to her, 'I know that nothing will do amiss that comes in thy hand'. But the Parliamentarians, many of whom had come over to guard the king, became suspicious of her; Colonel Hammond was warned: 'The King hath constant Intelligence given him of all things which he receives by the hands of a Woman that bringeth it to him when she bringeth his clean linen.' Hammond put Mary under surveillance and in February, after a messenger asked for her by name, he had evidence of her activities. Mary pleaded innocence, but was dismissed. The novel includes that last incident, but says that another maid took the blame upon herself; Mary survived, and when the king had cause to be particularly low, even became his confidante. Another real woman, a 'gentlewoman', Jane Whorwood, with her connections, was mainly involved in the escape plans on the outside. But I am going to leave her hanging here, to be retrieved in the following chapter, 'Irregular Relations'.

Mary had a friend in Newport, Frances Trattle whose parents ran a pub. The author describes an incident as the king, on his arrival on the Island, rides through the town: Frances steps forward and throws a red rose in his path –

11. King Charles receiving the rose. Photograph from the Internet

pure fiction, surely. But it turns out to be absolutely true; indeed, as is shown here, there is even a painting of the event by the French painter Eugene Lami in 1829. ('Charles Receiving a Rose' is currently in the Louvre.) The pub was renamed The Rose and Crown but no longer exists.

The sort of colour that pleasingly pervades the novel is also illustrated by Mary's memory and opinion of Lady Portland. She and her aunt are preparing the bedroom that must be fit for a king:

Somehow the four-poster did not look as good now, only rather shabby and faded. 'There are three red velvet hangings milady Portland was wont to use in the winter' Mary remembered suddenly.

'Red Velvet?' In the ferment of the afternoon's work aunt and niece had each come to respect the other's ability, so that much of the authoritative manner and meekness had gone.

Yes, Aunt Druscilla, do you remember? They had little silver stags embroidered on them, which I adored. They may be in one of the attics. I know they were all packed up ready to take to France but milady had to leave so much behind when the Parliamentarians turned her out of the castle.

The material had been as brave and beautiful as the Governor's wife who had owned them.

As well as the story of Charles I's incarceration in Carisbrooke Castle, his departure and, indeed, his end, are described in the novel. For, as we know only too well, nothing that took place there was to save his life. The castle was not, however, done with the Royal Family.

Charles I and his French Catholic wife, Henrietta Maria, had nine children, five of whom were alive at the outbreak of the Civil War in 1642. A final child, Princess Henrietta, was born in 1644, while her mother, fleeing Oxford where the Court had been forced to move, sought sanctuary in Exeter, surrounded by Parliamentarian forces. The other children included Charles, Prince of Wales, who became Charles II after the years of Oliver Cromwell and the Protectorate of his son Richard. He had escaped abroad but returned to attempt an invasion. Another daughter was Mary, Princess Royal who, before the Civil War, had been sent to the Netherlands as the child bride of William Prince of Orange. Her siblings were later able to find refuge there. The second son, James, Duke of York, remained in Oxford until the City surrendered in 1646. He was then removed by order of Parliament to St James's Palace in Central London where he was held with his young sister, Elizabeth. She had been born and baptised there, and was taken back there when she was six, together with her even younger brother, Henry. With his father imprisoned and his older brother on the run, James was seen as a serious contender for the Crown. But in April 1648, pressed by Elizabeth to escape, dressed as a woman in her clothes, he joined the family in the Netherlands. Two years earlier, the children's mother returned home to France to solicit aid for her husband's cause from her nephew Louis XIV, leaving infant Henrietta in the care of Anne Villiers, Lady Dalkeith. When the order came from Parliament for the infant to join her siblings in St James's Palace, her governess, determined to resist this, set out from there on foot for Dover on 25 July 1646, carrying the toddler dressed as a boy, and took her safely to her mother. She was later to become well known to modern readers as Charles II's beloved sister Minette, locked in an unhappy marriage to the Dauphin of France until her death in 1670. Her father did manage to see her before events overtook him.

But it is **Princess Elizabeth** (1635–1650) who is now the main subject of interest here. On the last morning of their father's life – having not seen him for 15 months – she and her brother Henry were able to talk to their father. Elizabeth clung to him, sobbing. The meeting was to scar and sustain her, particularly as he gave her special messages for the family which it became her mission to pass on. From early on she had been tutored and this experience, given her quick intelligence, enabled her, by 1644, to read and write in Hebrew, Greek, Italian, French, and Latin; scholars dedicated their religious works to her, so conversant was she with the Bible. She seems to have been too good to be true. She was called Temperance by her family because of her calm, patient and kind nature, and the French ambassador described her as 'a budding beauty' who had 'grace, dignity, intelligence and sensibility'. No doubt that was part of an ambassador's tools of the trade. But to counter all that learnedness and goodness, she had poor health; examination of her remains diagnosed rickets, which would have accounted for her misshapen body and difficulty in walking, as well as a weak chest. In spite of the persuasive letters she wrote to the authorities asking that she and 10-year-old Henry be allowed to join their family abroad, on 13 August 1650, they were brought to Carisbrooke Castle while their future was considered.

A frail and fragile 14-year-old girl, old and wise for her age, arrived there with her brother on 9 August 1650. The party had been delayed a few days because of Elizabeth's short illness. But who greeted her? Who was to look after her? Both Margaret Campbell Barnes and Vanessa Hannam are clear: for the first of them, it is 18-year-old Royalist Mary of Carisbrooke, so caring of Elizabeth's father; for the other it is 17-year-old Lizzie, the daughter of Hatherford Manor in Kent whose father, squire Sir Edwin Jones, introduced us to the ravages caused by the war. By this time, Lizzie was firmly on the side of Parliament.

I'm going to go with Boucher James's account; much of the writing of his two volumes (edited, remember, by his wife Rachel) depended on letters he wrote to people who would know. He tells us that Colonel Hammond had been replaced as governor of the castle by another Parliamentarian, Colonel William Sydenham. He had a wife, but there is no evidence that she was there with him. The royal children left the kindly care they received at Penshurst Castle on 9 August 1650, arriving at Cowes on the 13th, and at the castle on the 15th – there was a short delay for the Princess to recover from a bout of fever. They were accompanied by Anthony Mildmay, a Parliament supporter, part of the king's suite during his imprisonment, but as Mary Floyd (Lee), found, not hidebound.

Lizzie's experience of him in Vanessa Hannam's novel was more extensive, for a Captain Mildmay arrived during the night with his troop of Cromwell's men to arrest her father, which was only the beginning. During that visit, Lizzie, to save her father secreted in the Manor's priest hole, had laid before Mildmay her Parliamentary credentials, which were, indeed, increasingly true. But her governess, Ruth, nearly scuppered the subterfuge when she ranted at Mildmay:

> 'I've read about that man,' Ruth sneered … 'In your father's news sheet, the *Murcurias Politicas* … he must be the Mildmay who betrayed the King. He was part of his Majesty's retinue … No less than the Royal Carver, and then he turned to the other side. We are in the presence of a traitor. I would no more pander to him and his like than trade with the devil.' Ruth crossed herself vigorously.

> 'Listen to me, Ruth,' hissed Lizzie 'we have to dissemble. I'll do anything to spare us all the terrible things we know are going on in the name of Parliament.'

(Ruth was talking about the right Mildmay, but Anthony can be easily confused with his brother, Henry who, as a Member of Parliament, switched from being a Royalist. The latter has a long entry in *The Oxford Dictionary of National Biography*, in which Anthony is only mentioned as governor of the castle when the royal children arrived. This statement is an error taken from Mary Anne Everett Green's *Princesses of England*. She was, though, a well-regarded nineteenth-century historian.)

The order received at the castle was that the children were not to be treated as royalty – no person was to kiss hands – but with respect. Boucher James records that,

> Their household included Mr Lovel, tutor to the young Duke; Mr Anthony Mildmay, an 'honest and faithful gentleman,' who had special charge of them; John Barmeston, gentleman usher; Judith Briot, gentlewoman; Elizabeth Jones, laundry-maid; John Clarke, groom of the chamber. A yearly allowance of £1,000 was granted for the maintenance of the household.

Apart from the mention of **Judith Briot** in *Mary of Carisbrooke*, in which she certainly plays a part during the short time the Princess was imprisoned in the castle, I could initially find no other details of her. She could have been related to the English coin engraver, Nicholas Briot, whom the king appointed chief engraver to the Royal Mint. As for Lizzie Jones, did Vanessa Hannam pluck her out and make her a spirited gentlewoman, heroine of her novel, rather than a laundry-maid? (So spirited was she that her father rejoiced in 'a daughter with a man's courage', a remark reminiscent of that in one of Sir John Oglander's letters to his wife. I need make no comment!)

The differences between accounts develops. Because of Lizzie's pro-Parliament discussion with Mildmay during his first visit, she was to find herself invited – no, instructed – to travel to Syon House outside London where the children were being cared for, to become a companion to them. There she meets Mrs Briott, a middle-aged servant of the children, who tells Lizzie that she is married to the son of 'the King's silversmith', and Sir Richard Lovell, the children's teacher, with whom there is an immediate spark. She also hears young Henry's negative opinion of Anthony Mildmay, and meets his dog, Rogue. In *Mary of Carisbrooke*, Rogue belongs to Mary and is given to the king when he is at his lowest. The scene, on different historical novel and reality levels, is set, leaving the reader who comes to both novels, and what is known of reality, to do their own disentangling, as I have tried to do. One cannot completely ignore fictional reconstructions, given the gaps in historical knowledge, even the facts of which are open to their own interpretation.

A few days after the Princess's arrival, she got caught in the rain while playing bowls on the green laid out for her father, and developed a chill which turned into pneumonia; she may well have had tuberculosis. Boucher James maintains that 'Notwithstanding the care of that "honest and faithful gentleman" Anthony Mildmay, Esq. and all the art of her physicians, her disease grew upon her ...'. While, for Margaret Campbell Barnes, Judith Briot of the novel proving a bit flighty, Mary nursed her devotedly, but in vain. Within a few days she was dead, though first passing on to Mary the messages her father had entrusted to her. It is known that the Princess spent much of her short time at the castle writing down what she remembered, in spite of being in a paroxysm of weeping as he spoke. The document has been preserved; the part of the text here is taken from an *Island Echo* web posting:

He bid us tell my mother that his thoughts had never strayed from her and that his love would be the same to the last. Withall, he commanded me and my brother to be obedient to her; and bid me send his blessing to the rest of my brothers and sisters, with communications to all his friends. Then, taking my brother Gloucester on his knee, he said 'Sweetheart, now they will cut off thy father's head.

And he desired [me] not to grieve for him, for he should die a martyr, and that he doubted not the Lord would settle his throne upon his son, and that we shall all be happier than we could have expected to have been if he had lived.

Boucher James writes that at Carisbrooke Castle Elizabeth's body was embalmed and, after lying in state for 16 days, was carried to Newport in a hired coach, accompanied by her household. There her body was received by the mayor and aldermen, and finally buried in St Thomas's Chapel, 'about the middle of the east part of the chapel'. The plaque on her coffin read: 'Elizabeth, and daughter of the late King Charles, deceased September 8, MDCI.' A few days after her death, permission arrived from London for her to join her family in the Netherlands.

Henry remained detained in the castle for two years before he was allowed to join the Royal Family abroad; he died in 1660. The monarchy was restored under his brother Charles II the following year. Charles visited the Isle of Wight in 1665 in order to knight Edward Worsley who was 'Z' in his father's code in the letters secreted out concerning escape plans; a copy of one of the letters can be seen online. Charles I probably visited Worsley and his wife **Jane Barker Worsley** at Gatcombe Manor before restrictions forbade movement outside Carisbrooke Castle. Lord Portland was governor of the Isle of Wight in 1660–1661. I can find no evidence that the Countess returned.

During Queen Victoria's time at Osborne, when the church was being rebuilt in the years 1854–1856, she learned of Princess Elizabeth's fate and commissioned an effigy of white marble by the sculptor Baron Marochetti. He used as a model for his sculpture a girl the same age as the princess; she was Julia Jackson, Julia Margaret Cameron's niece, and Virginia Woolf's mother – all of whom will appear in detail in chapter 8 – 'Freshwater: Dimbola and Farringford'. Elizabeth is depicted as a long figure asleep with her head resting on a Bible – remembering that her father had given her his Bible at their last meeting. Added to the plaque is the inscription: 'erected as a token of respect for her virtues and sympathy for her misfortunes by Victoria R'. The effigy, which lies over the Princess's tomb, and dating from 1856, is easily seen in the church; a model of it, as well as some of her possessions, are in the Carisbrooke Castle Museum.

The last stanza of a poem of 1866, to be found at the end of the Internet details about the Princess reads:

And long unknown, unhonoured, her sacred dust had slept
When to the Stuart maiden's grave a mourner came and wept.
Go, read the Royal Martyr's woe in lines the world reveres
And see the tomb of Charles's child wet with Victoria's tears.

12. Princess Elizabeth marble effigy, from Carisbrooke Castle Museum,
photograph by the author

5 – Irregular Relations, 1502–1830

Princess Cecily Plantagenet

Princess Cecily Plantagenet (Cecilia; 1477–1507) third daughter of Edward IV and his wife Elizabeth Woodville, may not seem to have been in the most eye-catching example of an irregular relationship, but she is first in this chapter because her third marriage enters the scene chronologically with those that follow. Not only that, but the marriage is known to have immediately upset and angered the new king, Henry VII. The date is unconfirmed (probably 1502), but it was done in secret, and the princess did not, as required by royal protocol, request permission from the king. What is more, her new husband was a mere esquire – Sir Thomas Kyme of Frisney, a Lincolnshire squire. Mary Anne Green suggests that 'the English royal family had never known such an unequal union'.

To detail Cecily's life before this marriage is beyond the scope of this chapter, or this book. As is the War of the Roses, in which Cecily's Yorkist father fled to Flanders, while his predecessor, Lancastrian Henry VI returned to the throne (and then her father did the same, dying in 1470). Suffice it to say that in all her younger life she was used as a pawn, with her siblings declared 'bastards' when her uncle Richard III, who was supposed to be Lord Protector to her under-age brother (her father's heir), took the throne. And she was in serious danger when Richard confined her two little brothers in the Tower of London, never, as history hitherto has suggested, to be seen again. When she was allowed back at Court, there was the possibility that Richard would marry her or her sister Elizabeth (the second of the sisters, Mary, had died in 1483); instead, Cecily was, at 17, married off, *c.*1484, to Ralph Scrope, the younger brother of the 6th Baron Scrope of Masham. Richard having been defeated and killed at the Battle of Bosworth Field in 1485, the victor, who became Henry VII, married Elizabeth, the eldest sister, and repealed the Act that had not only delegitimised but deprived her and her siblings of their lands and, in 1486, Cecily's marriage to Scrope was annulled. Are you still with me?!

It is likely that the King's mother, Lady Margaret Beaufort, a long-standing friend of Cecily's, arranged her next marriage, to John Welles, 1st Viscount Welles, heir to the ancient Welles family and younger half-brother of the king; Cecily herself may have had a hand in it. Henry VII might well have preferred her to remain unmarried as, being his wife's sister, she could be seen as heir presumptive until he had sons. The marriage probably took place on New Year's Day 1488. Cecily's new husband was 20 years her senior, but it does not seem to have been an unhappy marriage and they had two daughters. Unfortunately, in February 1498, her husband died of pleurisy (their daughters did not survive childhood, dying in 1498 and 1499). On his deathbed Welles signed his will, leaving all his property for life to his 'dere beloved lady and wife Cecille'. It was Margaret Beaufort who helped Cecily protect her rights to her late husband's property. By the time of her sister Queen Elizabeth's early death, Cecily had married Thomas Kyme. She had to do a financial deal with the king in order to protect her rights, knowing that he had his eye on her lands. Once again Lady Margaret was to step in to help her financially.

I'm afraid the Isle of Wight has been a long time emerging from this unruly saga of Princess Cecily. Why the couple chose to move to the Island is uncertain – so many historians have written about her life and, indeed, muddied the waters. But I have found an Ancestry Family Search source for Sir Thomas Kyme that quite clearly gives his parents as of Friskney, but Thomas himself was born, died and was buried on the Island. The date of marriage is firmly given as 13 May 1502. Another, or supporting, reason could be that Lady Margaret suggested it as a suitable place because she trusted Sir Reginald Bray who was not only an executor of Welles's will (along with Cecily), but had also been a senior member of her late husband's household, and was Lord of the Manor of Niton there. (The manor 'followed the same descent as the honour of Carisbrooke … Until the death of the last lord, Sir Reginald Bray'.) Whatever the reason for choosing the Island, soon after Elizabeth's death, Cecily sought permission to retire from Court and, some time after February 1503, she and her husband arrived at East Standen Manor near Arreton, which they rented rather than bought, and they did not live in luxury. It has to be said that the claim of Kyme's Island connection is knocked on the head by Susan Higginbotham in her article, 'The Queen's Sister: Cecily, Viscountess Welles', as is the claim that the couple lived there following their marriage. I am unhappy to accept that: too many suggestions connect her with the Isle of Wight; I have, for example, found the Internet article by Sharon Champion, '"Not so Fortunate as Fair": The Life of Princess Cecily Plantagenet' useful. There is also an interesting disagreement about her burial that is worth raising.

Very little is known about Cecily's short life at East Standen, except the birth of two children, Richard Kyme (1504–1573), and **Margaret Kyme** (1505–1563; m John Wetherby). Cecily had no financial help from the king; indeed, if mentioned at all in Court circles, she was called Viscountess Welles, and her children by Kyme were unrecognised. In 1506, Margaret Beaufort arranged funds for her to visit the mainland. By the following year, Cecily was dead. As I have intimated, the place of her death and burial is disputed. Susan Higginbotham, drawing on Rosemary Horrox's entry for *The Oxford Dictionary of National Biography* (2004), who, in turn, drew on Lady Margaret Beaufort's account books, has her spending the last three weeks of her life at Hatfield House, Hertfordshire. But she gives no identifiable burial place, simply that it was at 'the Friars', paid for by Margaret Beaufort. No tombstone has apparently been found in any of the suggestions for that incomplete location. Other sources are quite clear that she died on the Island and was buried in Quarr Abbey. It is reasonable to take at face value what J Charles Cox – well regarded clergyman and historian – writes in *Isle of Wight its Churches and Religious Houses* (1911):

In 1507 there was a royal funeral and burial within the abbey church, attended by great solemnity and ceremony. Cecily, the third daughter of Edward IV, and sister of Elizabeth the Queen of Henry VII, married in 1504, for her second husband, John Kynd, a gentleman of Lincolnshire extraction, who occupied the retired manor-house of East Standen amid the Arreton Downs. Here the royal Cecily died, and the Island gentry attended the bier from Standen to Quarr.

'The Friars' presumably could be shorthand for Quarr Abbey. There would be no concrete evidence of that burial because Henry VIII's Dissolution of the Monasteries took place between 1536 and 1541; that included all monasteries, priories, convents and friaries in England, Wales and Ireland. They were also destroyed and ghostly remains of them can be seen all over the country. Quarr Abbey was, of course, dissolved, so it is not surprising that there is no burial site for Cecily to be found there.

To visit the remains of the old Abbey, you go up the drive towards today's Benedictine Quarr Abbey but, before you get there, turn right along a narrow road until, on your left, past a couple of houses, and, again on your left, you come to a gap in the hedge. There you find a map of the old Abbey and a bench for the weary. Leaning over the barrier, in the far distance you can discern the ruins; you regret that you cannot get closer. The destruction of the buildings of the original abbey does lead rather neatly into the next irregular relationship.

John Mills (Mill, Milles) was a Southampton merchant doing well financially, which had, as Sir John Oglander says in his memoirs, 'Made [him] a gentleman'. He had not become rich by missing the main chance, in this case, how Quarr Abbey, dating back to 1132, had been left by the Dissolution of the Monasteries. Some sources suggest that he bought the abbey outright, others that at first he rented the rights (1536), and later purchased them (1544). His purpose was to dismantle the buildings and sell the stone and monuments, building materials being at a premium; every stone and slate had a value. He was very successful in this endeavour, leaving the family even better off than before. Sir John Oglander also says that, at the same time, Mills bought the manors of Nunham, Heasley (Hasley) and Combley 'of Henry VIII'. That meant that on his death he left his son George and his daughter-in-law well provided for and living in Hasley Manor. The manor dated back to at least the Domesday Book, where it was called Haslie. It was later bequeathed by its owner to Quarr Abbey, the monks of which improved its farming potential and built a chapel.

Dowsabel Mills

It is George's wife who is of concern in this chapter of irregular relationships, though that with her husband is not at issue. But Sir John's introduction of **Dowsabel Mills** (Dowsabel, née Burton; 1567–1603) as John's 'fast-living daughter-in-law' provides a clue to revelations later in this chapter. I am relying to a large extent on Sir John Oglander's memoirs because their lives did overlap, at least at the end of her life. In chapter 4 he emerged as a loving husband and father, a responsible landowner, and a committed Royalist; his memoirs show him to have been a delightful gossip as well.

Getting to understand Dowsabel, whom I took to immediately, partly because of her unusual name (though it was not particularly rare in her times), but also because of her spirit, was not initially easy: it took a lot of determination to uncover her background. Because no other source has come to hand, I am having to depend on an article posted by Henry Thomas Burton with the rather highfalutin title, 'Descent from Edward III for Dowsabel Burton, heiress of Kins[ley House]' (2007). He writes, so that I can be sure it is the right Dowsabel:

> When the IPM [inquisition post mortem] of Sir John Burton was taken in 1583, it returned his 16-year-old granddaughter Dowsabel Burton, wife of George Mill, gentleman, as his heir. The 19th-century editors of the Visitation pedigrees [record of pedigrees] could not uncover what became of George Mill and Dowsabel Burton …

I hope what I write here is helpful! Picking up on Dowsabel and George's lifestyle at Hasley, Oglander recorded that George 'kept a brave howse and lived worshipfully'. I suspect that Dowsabel, as the future will tell, was largely responsible for the brave house. John D Whitehead, posting in 1974 about the people of Haseley on a Woottonbridge website, moves the story along:

> So, with Quarr and other similar projects, both on the Island and on the mainland, successfully completed, George was, at his death, able to leave his widow very comfortably provided for, as well as being undisputed mistress of Haseley. She, apparently, heaved a sigh of relief and made haste to find other amusements.

Whitehead seems unaware that Dowsabel was an heiress in her own right, and she continued to keep a brave house. Enter now Sir Edward Horsley who appeared in chapter 4 concerning the plague of 1582. But Oglander tells the whole story best:

> In this time, Mr Worsley dying, Sir Edward Horsey, a brave soldier, obtained to be Captain of our Island [1565] and, hearing of Mistress Milles' noble housekeeping, did desire to sojourn there. So they lived together and, had he not had a wife then living in France, a Frenchwoman, there is no doubt but they would have been man and wife, for a goodlier pair, both man and woman, you could hardly find. In those days there was more innocent mirth than now, for Mistress Worsley … and Mistress Milles, two handsome, tall, proper women, would dance a poor tabor and pipe from Heasley House to the foot of the hill.

Though their love was answerable, Sir Edward and Mistress Milles kept a worthy house, spent a beef or two every week, 8 sheep, 2 quarters of wheat and malt, with all things proportionable. But Fortune that desires mutability took him away with the infection of the plague, as it was generally thought. Yet this is strange: that all men giving him visits in his sickness, none were affected. He was first buried in Carisbrooke Castle, afterwards removed to Newport. She lived long after, maintained the same house and brought up most of the young gentlewoman in the Island and had the sway of the Island for many years till, blind with age and weak in body, she departed this life Anno Domino 1603, and was buried at Arreton. She never had a child, although very handsome, and spent her estate in housekeeping.

Not only was Dowsabel buried at Arreton, but she joined her late husband George inside St George's Church, Arreton. A Wootton Bridge historical posting on the church notes that 'Under a blue marble stone, (now disappeared) as you go up to the communion table in the chancel is buried Dowsabell Mill, wife of George Mill who owned Quarr and Heasley Manor.' I prefer to think of Dowsabel dancing down the hill and teaching the young gentlewomen of the Island; it would be good to know what she taught them – dancing, certainly. Whitehead, about whom I can find nothing, has a suggestion that takes into account not so much later morality as twentieth-century tabloid writing, making the enterprise sound sleazy. He claims that Dowsabel started the school while Horsey, 'a rough, hard-drinking sea captain whose credit had been swollen by numerous victories against French pirates', was still alive and continues,

She turned Haseley into a 'finishing school' for the young ladies of the Island. Even in these days of easy morals the mind boggles at the picture of such a menage. There can be little doubt that those young ladies had no need to ask their mothers any questions by the time they 'finished'.

It is fair enough to suggest, though, that while Horsey was alive and living with Dowsabel, that was an irregular relationship, but by no means as irregular as some of those that follow.

In chapter 4, where the part played by the women, such as Jane Wheeler and Mary Lee, involved in the incarceration of Charles I in Carisbrooke Castle is discussed, I mentioned Jane Whorwood. But she and the part she played were deliberately left hanging, to be picked up in this chapter because of her supposed irregular relationship with, rather surprisingly, the king himself. Surprising because he is more generally depicted as a loving and faithful husband of Queen Henrietta Maria of France, spending much of his time during his incarceration reading the Bible and praying.

Jane Whorwood

Jane Whorwood (née Ryder; 1612–1684) was the daughter of Scots courtier (surveyor of the royal stables) William Ryder, and Elizabeth de Bousy, laundress to Anne of Denmark, wife of James I. When her father died in 1617, her mother married a more influential courtier. In 1634 Jane's marriage to Brome Whorwood, four years her junior, was arranged. In 1642, at the outbreak of the Civil War, he fled abroad, and did not return until 1645. Meanwhile Jane and their two children, a boy and a girl, lived in the family property, Holton House, on the outskirts of Oxford, to which the Royal Court had retreated. It was this propinquity, as well as her stepfather's established access to the Royal Family, that laid the groundwork of Jane's career as a royal agent. Her stepfather had assumed the office of Black Rod in 1622, giving him parliamentary connections and, upon the dissolution of Parliament by Charles I in 1629, her stepfather became a pawnbroker and private financial adviser to the king.

Jane was a successful agent, for example arranging, in 1644, and with the help of a laundress, the smuggling of 1,705 lbs (775kg) of gold, concealed in barrels of soap, from a London Royalist merchant to Oxford. This enabled the Prince of Wales (later Charles II) and Queen Henrietta Maria, to be spirited abroad. On another occasion it was the king's stockings. Jane's work as an active agent, supporter and, indeed, friend, of the king continued throughout the 1640s. She was particularly adept at setting up a countrywide network of Royalist contacts and was involved in attempts to coordinate assistance to the king's attempts to flee, before his final arrival on the Isle of Wight to seek refuge in Carisbrooke Castle, as he thought, in 1647. (You would have thought that the Parliamentary presence on the island, and the recent appointment by Parliament of a new governor of the castle would have been known.)

The king's presence at Carisbrooke Castle and the failed attempts to facilitate his escape were discussed in chapter 4. All the time, Jane was involved, on two occasions in procuring acid from London to melt the bars on his window to enable his escape from his room in the castle, and in arranging a ship to take him from the Island to safety abroad. Their exchange of letters and, indeed, all his correspondence, some in cipher, and other writings, are being collected and edited by the Keele University historian specialising in the period, Sarah Poynting, to be published in three volumes as *The Writings of Charles I*. The need to decode whole, or parts of, letters during his confinement presents no easy task. It has been attempted before but Sarah Poynting has redone it. In one of the two letters sent from the king to Jane Whorwood, holed up in Newport ready to spring into action, was a sentence that particularly caught her eye and, in that sentence, one word.

At one stage when access to Charles was relaxed, he wrote that Jane could easily visit him, but warned that they would not be able to speak privately without special permission. His letter then switched to cipher. According to an earlier decoding, the next sentence read, 'Yet I imagine that there is one way possible that you may get answering from me.' Then not in cipher 'You must excuse my plain expressions.' Donald MacLeod explains in a *Guardian* article entitled 'Historian exposes secret sex life of Charles I' (2007) written when Sarah Poynting's revelation widely hit the headlines:

> Dr Pointing realised that 'answering' could only be correct if the king had made three separate mistakes in the cipher for one word. When she worked through the passage, a rather different meaning emerged: 'I imagine that there is one way possible that you may get a swiving from me'. He then describes how she could have secret access to his rooms.

In the seventeenth century, 'swiving' was a wholly obscene word for sex, found most commonly in the pornographic verses of the Earl of Rochester, who used it to describe the notorious sexual activity of Charles's son after the restoration.

Sarah Poynting published her own article, 'Deciphering the King: Charles I's Letters to Jane Whorwood' (2006) which, unfortunately, as it appeared in the learned history journal, *Seventeenth Century*, is not so easy to access. In it she notes, 'There has been a marked reluctance to examine how the public image relates to the private man'. She does not display that reluctance:

> The king is known to have been devoted to his wife, Henrietta Maria, and remembered for refusing to tolerate the drunkenness and immorality that marked the court of his father, James VI and I. Charles's sexual probity has been so taken for granted that when I first told colleagues about my discovery, they didn't believe I could be right until I went step-by-step through the cipher. There is no reason, though to find such apparent con-tradictions incredible; it simply means that we have begun to understand a little more about a complex man at one critical time. Charles may have been a unique captive, but there were moments when he shared the concerns of other prisoners: Self-justification, escape, and sex.

As a result of her work, John Fox, in the second edition of *The King's Smuggler: Jane Whorwood, Secret Agent to Charles I* (2022) brings up to date his 2010 less revelatory edition.

What I really like is how Margaret Campbell Barnes's much earlier historical novel *Mary of Carisbrooke* (1956) (introduced in chapter 4) was rather ahead of the play. The other women, part of the Carisbrooke Castle household staff who were also helping the king, were impressed by Jane Whorwood. Not only did she exude competence, enthusiasm and unflappability, but she was also friendly, charming and inclusive. In appearance, as contemporary descriptions suggest, she was tall, red-haired, and although her face was pockmarked, she was striking (no portrait of her exists). The women who, during the previous months had discovered parts of the living quarters that made it easier to help the king, suggested how Jane could get up to his room:

It seemed that nothing ever deterred Jane Whorwood from her objectives. 'What a surprise it will be for Charles!' she exclaimed delightedly. 'He was furious because Hammond would not let me in yesterday. But how shall I get out?'

'I will wait for you at the foot of the stairs. Major Rolph usually sits there in the doorway of his room, but now he is away the guards are getting lax' ...

After the King had supped and locked himself into his bedroom as usual, Mary waited a long time. Much longer even than it should take for so concise a woman as Jane Whorwood to convince the King of his danger and to give him a clear idea of the proposed plot. So long that the shortening summer evening had grown dark and Mary was beginning to worry lest the friendly sentries at the gatehouse would be changed before she came. But at last there were cautious footsteps on the stairs and the King's visitor joined her with just that nice margin of safety which suggested that the whole business would indeed have been better left in her hands. She had the air of one whose visit had been successful, and seemed as humorous and unruffled as before. 'They will think you are letting out a lover!' she said with her deep gurgling laugh as Mary flung a cloak about her. 'Do you not mind?'

'I have been called upon to do so many unlikely things since the King came here that I think I have come past minding' said Mary, half-rueful and half-laughing too.

On 15 September 1648 the king and Parliamentary commissioners began another round of their negotiations, but both sides knew that they were insincere and pointless, as the army hardliners in London would never agree to a moderate settlement. On 13 November, Jane wrote warning the king that she knew Parliament would insist on absolute compliance with their terms and advising escape. On the 25th Jane was in Newport and the means were in place for an escape, but the weary king dismissed yet another attempt. From that missed opportunity, the end became inexorable.

You have to wonder about Jane Whorwood's feelings and her state of mind following Charles I's trial for treason and execution in 1649. Over and above whatever she felt for him as a man, as her lover, as the king she had devoted her life to as a secret agent and, once he was detained and she became deeply involved at the top of several plots to help him escape abroad, the adrenalin rush would have been all-consuming. We know that she was forced to return to her husband who was by then in England, together with a mistress. He had not only betrayed his king by scurrying abroad, but now became a violently abusive husband. His mother blamed Jane for his violence, for not having been a better wife. In 1651, she was imprisoned for having aided the king, and, when she returned to her husband he, too, confined her. John Fox describes all she went through thereafter. She was not free until Brome's death in April 1684. But she died that December.

Thomas Colpeper, 2nd Baron Colpeper (Culpeper), known generally as a colonial administrator, particularly of the State of Virginia, served as captain, then governor, of the Isle of Wight from 1661 to 1667. Following Charles I's execution, his father, a Royalist, had been forced to flee abroad, and that was where Thomas was brought up. It was natural, therefore, that he should marry there, and in 1659, he married the Dutch heiress Margaret van Hesse. With the Restoration of Charles II, Colpeper returned to England with his wife; there she was naturalised as English by an Act of Parliament, and he retrieved the family lands by the same means. The couple may well have become estranged by the time he arrived on the Isle of Wight, living in Carisbrooke Castle while his wife stayed in Leeds Castle, Kent. That property had come into the Colpeper family when an ancestor was on Parliament's side in the Civil War.

Susanna Willis

At what stage Colpeper's mistress, **Susanna Willis** (b. *c.*1645), joined him in the castle is unclear, as is her background. Whenever it was, it created a stink on the Island. The most useful source for what happened next is 'The Proprietors of the Northern Neck' (1926*)* by Fairfax Harrison, an industrialist and later historian with a particular interest in the State of Virginia. The Northern Neck property is in Virginia where Colpeper was later governor (1677–1683). Susanna seems to have accompanied him there. The chapter on which I have drawn is '3c Hollingbourne' (the village nearest to Leeds Castle) which can be accessed online. Harrison does not have a high opinion of Colpeper, nor indeed of colonialism:

> His vices were those bred of extravagant living in a society which was reacting from puritanism. Aggrieved by what he deemed the injustice which kept him pinched for money all his life, he grew hard and, indeed, unscrupulous. He belonged to a generation and to a class which ... believed the world owed it a living and which, coming to particulars, regarded the colonies chiefly as a field to be exploited.

> More than that, he flagrantly offended public opinion, and embarrassed even his friend Charles II by a cynical disregard of appearances in domestic relations.

Colpeper so scandalised Isle of Wight society by living openly with his mistress that, although he was an able enough administrator, in 1666 they petitioned the king to have him removed. The reason they gave was that, 'being purely a military officer, he meddled in civil affairs and did not keep up the fortifications'. Clarendon sent an 'illuminating' reply 'in which the petitioners were "politely rebuked for their temerity and assured that Culpeper had the King's confidence". The minister added:

> My lord Culpeper, had not this petition been presented, would, before this time, have been removed and another put in his place, for as much as the King, being in the island, took notice that he was not respected by the gentry, as became his government … But I believe though you may possibly have one that shall live more socially among you, you may never have one that will use his power less than my lord Culpeper.

Charles II visited the Island more than once, and it is known that he did so in 1665, as chapter 4 notes, in order to knight Edward Worsley for his service to his late father. He may well have seen the situation for himself before the petition of a year later. Colpeper did not leave immediately, but in 1667. For the sake of appearances, he even tried to persuade his wife to join him in Carisbrooke Castle; not surprisingly, given that he was living with another women, she refused. For the next few years he lived in England, and was given appointments which prepared him for his eventual posting to Virginia. More important for this story, during that time his wife gave birth to **Catherine Colpeper** (1670–1710), and his mistress to two daughters, **Susanna Colpeper** (1672–1720), and **Charlotte Colpeper** (1677–1756). I have seen no comment on the fact that while living in a long-term relationship with Mrs Willis, offensive to his estranged wife, she is said to have had a daughter by him, important in the later context.

During his Virginia tenure, Colpeper did not spend much time there, and when he was superseded he lived in London with, as Harrison calls her, his *maitresse en titre* and their daughters. That brings us to the involvement of the women in his life in his death in 1689 and its aftermath. And we owe the details of that to his lawful wife, Margaret Van Hesse, at that time living at the Colpeper property in Kent. She didn't initially know about her husband's death, or even that he was ill; Susanna Willis, as Harrison explains, 'seems to have buried him privately, for there is no record extant of where or when he was buried'. Susanna then apparently took 'the key to his [as]sets and possessed herself of everything'. When the news did eventually reach Leeds Castle, Margaret hastened to London, and

> sued out letters of administration upon her husband's estate. Armed with this weapon, she demanded possession of his effects, only to learn that he had in the preceding October settled his estate upon trustees largely for the benefit of his two daughters by Mrs Willis, and that by a will dated 17 January 1689, he confirmed this bounty, leaving the lands which he had acquired with his wife's fortune, charged with his debts.

It is not difficult to imagine the reaction to this betrayal by Margaret, whose daughter Catherine was Colpeper's only legitimate child. But, without the documents ferreted out, presumably by Harrison, we would be left hanging.

Lady Culpeper rose to the defence of her own daughter. She filed a bill in chancery against Mrs Willis, alleging fraud and undue influence, and praying that the settlement and will be set aside. Mrs Willis countered effectively: being in possession, she was content to settle down to a long drawn out chancery suit.

Such a delay was patently unacceptable to Margaret: she turned to the high court of Parliament and had introduced into the House of Lords this fury-infused bill which is worth quoting in full:

Whereas Thomas, Lord Culpeper, being seized in fee of divers manors etc., in the counties of Southampton, Kent, Sussex, Warwick and Lincoln, and being also possessed of divers messuages, etc., during some certain terms of years, unhappily fell into the acquaintance and conversation of Susanna Willis, otherwise Welden, otherwise Laycock, who by her artifices so far seduced him that he, for many years before his death, lived apart from his Lady, who never gave him the least occasion of offence, and with whom he had a very great fortune, with which he purchased a very considerable estate of inheritance in fee simple, and the said Lord Culpeper was to that degree ensnared by the said Susanna, that he spent most of the revenue of his estate upon her, which expense amounted to at least £60,000, and by that means had but little left to allow his said Lady, and his only child, Mrs Katherine Culpeper, for their support and maintenance; and although he was sensible of his miscarriages and often declared to his chief confidents that he would not do anything in reference to his estate to the prejudice of his wife and child, yet the said Susanna by fraud, circumvention and evil practices prevailed on him to make several settlements, which she conceals or has in her custody, for the benefit of her and her two children, which she caused him to own as his; and at length when Lord Culpeper approached his death and had not the exercise of his reason, caused him to declare a writing, prepared by her and her accomplices, to be his will, whereby a great part of his estate is by pretence disposed of to her and her children, and no provision is made for the payment of his debts, which are great, and contracted for the buying of rich household stuff, plate, jewels etc., for the said Susanna, which she possesses to great value, pretending them to be the said Lord Culpeper's gift.

There was then a similar, but short proposal. The result was not very helpful to Lady Culpeper: their Lordships were sympathetic towards the 'insulted wife' but, and here, I suggest, her advisers had let her down, 'the recitals of her bill smacked too much of pleading to make it possible of enactment'. When it came to a vote before the House of Lords it failed to pass by a vote of 36 to 35, 'the determination being that Lady Culpeper should pursue her remedy in chancery'.

At this stage, Lady Culpeper managed to get her own daughter married well – to Thomas, 5th Baron Fairfax of Cameron, in Scotland. Interestingly, through the marriage of Catherine's own daughter, her husband conveyed the estate of Leeds Castle to his family. In the meantime, Margaret's son-in-law, Lord Fairfax, took the burden of further attempts at securing justice off her shoulders. He negotiated a compromise with Mrs Willis. Susanna, her elder daughter, had, in 1685/6 married Sir Charles Englefield; Charlotte, the younger, had in 1690, in the middle of all this rumpus, safely married John Peshell (whose father was a baronet). The girls' parentage was obviously no bar to a good marriage.

The intricate details of the outcome of this compromise need not be detailed here, but everyone was provided for, including husbands, and it was agreed that 'both Lord Culpeper's settlement and will should be suppressed, so that his legitimate daughter might be vested with the remainder of his estate at law.' To ratify this arrangement a new bill was introduced into Parliament in March, 1696/7'.

All but one of Colpeper's various manors and messuages were on the mainland. What is of more interest is that the youngest of the three daughters, Charlotte, as well as receiving £3,000, was also to receive Redway Manor, with its farm, in the parish of Arreton, Isle of Wight. Unfortunately, the fate of this outcome is not clear. Colpeper's brother John, heir to the title, was unhappy with the whole arrangement. He tried, but failed, to have it set aside in the House of Commons, but took it to the House of Lords where he was able to get it blocked by one vote. Harrison ends the saga:

> While gratifying revenge, this success did not, however, accomplish John's larger purpose of securing a vested interest in his brother's estate, but he pursued his particular claim in the Court of Chancery and there, in 1700, at last had a decree establishing in his favour an annuity charged upon a manor in the Isle of Wight.

A short Internet entry for Redway Manor, perhaps unaware of Harrison's finding, states that 'It was devised by Thomas Lord Colpeper to his natural daughter Charlotte, who married Robert Pushall towards the close of the 17th century.' Annoyingly, I cannot ignore what Harrison says, how he left things hanging in the air. He was not to know in 1926 that my main interest would be Charlotte and Redway Manor; but does John Colpeper's intervention mean that Charlotte was left with no interest in the Manor?

Grace Hooke

Colpeper was followed as governor of the Island by Sir Robert Holmes (1668–1692) who was part of a saga that even outdoes his predecessor as a participant in an irregular relationship. At its centre is **Grace Hooke** (1660–1687). At first glance, Grace came from a respectable Freshwater family. Her grandfather, University-educated John Hooke, was curate at the Freshwater Parish Church.

Her parents, John Hooke and **Elizabeth Maynard Hooke** (*c.*1638–1684) were respectably married (1658); her father ran a greengrocer's in Newport, which prospered and expanded, and in due course he became an alderman and then twice mayor. Her uncle, Robert Hooke, is still so well known that I have found on my late husband's legal history bookshelves two books about him, Michael Cooper's '*A More Beautiful City': Robert Hooke and the Rebuilding of London after the Great Fire* (2003), and Lisa Jardine's *The Curious Life of Robert Hooke: The Man Who Measured London* (2003). As well as being Surveyor to the City of London, he was Professor of Geometry at Gresham College, founded in London in 1597, and Curator of Experiments to the Royal Society. Yet, even while detailing what appears to be a brilliant career in London, neither author omits the details of a most irregular relationship. That is why I'm devoting so much detail to him.

To that end, it is worth turning to Boucher James (and his editor wife, Rachel) for a nineteenth-century perspective on Hooke. He writes first in praise of him:

> Two hundred and fifty years ago Freshwater was the birthplace of one of the most devoted cultivators of natural philosophy of his age, and certainly the most scientific inquirer that the Isle of Wight has ever produced – Robert Hooke.

But then he delves deeper, in a quick word sketch bringing Hooke to life and possibly explaining some his behaviour:

> His jealous and rapacious temper and sordid personal habits, which made him an object of dislike in his own day, have probably somewhat affected the judgement of posterity. In all fairness the constitution of his bodily frame, which was small of stature, thin, and crooked, must be taken as an excuse for what in his day would have been called Hooke's splenetic temperament. Yet spleen is no apology for his practice of laying claim to the inventions and discoveries of other men, which involved him in much personal controversy.

If you expect the sordid details to involve his behaviour at home, this is all you are vouchsafed at the end of several pages about his work and quarrels with his peers:

> The indefatigable student of science had his share of the 'cares of life', like the rest of us, and in this touching expression of devout feeling we may look with more indulgence upon the outbursts of acrimony to which he gave way. He had his sorrows also, one of which was the death of his niece, Mrs Grace Hooke, who had kept his house for him for many years.

Poor Robert Hooke, as a professor of Gresham College he had to remain celibate. And so he was to the outside world of his day, remaining unmarried, and not living openly, or even covertly, with a woman. But he harboured a nasty little secret: over the years, he had sexual relations with several of the maids who passed through his household, his favourite being Nell who had Isle of Wight connections. And when his 10-year-old niece came to London to be cared for by him and, indeed, to receive the sort of education not available on the Island, in due course he had sexual relations with her too – perhaps not the sort of education envisaged by his brother and sister-in-law. What is more, he kept a diary of the encounters, with maids and with Grace, so that we can see exactly when he started having sex with her, and the further times over several years, and even how he berated himself for doing so. His short diary entries are drawn on by Michael Cooper and, particularly, by Lisa Jardine; they are also available online.

Hooke notes on 4 June 1676, 'Slept with Grace'. That is all. She was 16. Today we would call it not only incest but also child sexual abuse. Sometimes he did spell out when he had sex with Grace, but from 11 February 1677 he often just used a symbol he devised, so the entry might simply read, 'Grace γ'. The symbol meant either sex or orgasm. On 15 March he wrote, 'Grace perfect intime omene γ.' Presumably that meant full penetrative sex. While it seems that Grace was so attractive that she was to be much sought after in the years that followed (also noted in Hooke's diary with some dismay), and that he was forced to be celibate, she was his niece, confined to his care for raising, educating and safekeeping. Of those, he did fulfil educating, sending her to Mrs Whistler's school, later himself teaching her algebra and French, as well as lending her books, and throughout the years producing a cultured young woman ready to go out and up in the world, if his true relations with her were kept secret. Perhaps they were, though an engagement to the son of a wealthy London merchant who had been both a Sherriff and Lord Mayor at the time of the Great Fire, that had gone as far as contacts signed, was called off, requiring a legal release.

Hooke did try and stop himself from having sex with Grace and, incidentally, we have no idea what she felt about such matters but, as he intimates that she was a bit free and easy with other men, it does not mean that she was happy with the situation, more likely that he had corrupted her (my word). On 13 December 1676 he wrote 'Grace out. I resolvd to rid myself of her.' But by 16 January 1677 he was writing 'Grace γ, paid me 1s' (which presumably she had borrowed), and on 25 January he noted, 'I wrote to Brother about removing Grace'. But in February and March, there were the usual entries and in June a variation, 'Playd with Grace γ'.

Grace did write home, and the year before sexual relations with her brother started, her aunt, Katherine Hooke visited London, perhaps to see that all was well, perhaps also to have a jolly in the big city. Grace was then 15. Her mother may once have visited, and Grace did go home, sometimes staying there for a while. Hooke noted on 3 October, 'heard of Sir R Holmes courting Grace', and on 3 November, 'I wrote to Brother J Hooke about Grace and Sir R. Holmes'. Grace was by then 17, Holmes was 55.

As governor of the Island, Holmes chose to live in Yarmouth on the north-west coast, and carry out his duties and operations from there; indeed, he built a mansion close to the waterfront, on the land where King John and his party had stayed in 1214. Holmes's mansion still exists, hard by Yarmouth Castle, and is now the George Hotel. Holmes was a different character to Robert Hooke. His career had started well enough, leading to his eventually being appointed governor of the Isle of Wight. During the Civil War he fought in the army on the king's side, and in 1646 he left England for the Continent to join Prince Rupert of the Rhine, Duke of Cumberland, the Royalist cavalier commander, dubbed the archetypal 'Cavalier'. This led to Holmes joining the prince's piratical fleet. In 1660, as well as commanding a squadron off the west coast of Africa, Holmes was appointed Captain and Commander of Sandown Castle (built by Henry VIII to protect the Island and the south coast of the mainland against French attack). In 1665, he was not only knighted by Charles II, but also promoted to acting Rear-Admiral. Two years later he was appointed Commander-in-Chief of a squadron to operate from Portsmouth and the Isle of Wight. In 1668 he 'purchased' the governorship of the Island from Lord Colpeper. It is not surprising that he chose to make his base in Yarmouth, rather than Carisbrooke Castle, and he devoted much of his time as governor to rebuilding the Island's castles against French invasion. In 1670 King Charles II visited him, staying at his new mansion, and the story is still told of the king riding his horse up the staircase to his rooms. Presumably he also came to see how defences, such as Yarmouth Castle next door, were being reinforced.

This is the man with whom Grace Hooke now became involved during a visit home to the Island. History does not seem to record exactly how and where she and Holmes met but, in spite of the age difference, he will have been surrounded by a rather dashing aura, and he will have found her, at the age of 17, most attractive, charming, and cultured. Hooke's diary indicates how attractive men found her in London. At the beginning of 1678, Grace was confined to Yarmouth suffering from measles, unable to travel back to London. It seems clear that measles was an excuse; it was, in fact, when she gave birth to Mary, a baby who was to grow up known as Mary Holmes. The Newport Corporation Books in the court held on 8 May 1678 record that the Council ordered that Dr Edward Harrison be paid for the 'diet and board' of Mrs Hooke, Grace and Jane Young, possibly a servant. It is presumed that the baby was then placed with a nurse, for on 7 June Grace returned to London.

Meanwhile Fate had dealt the family a sharp blow: on the morning of 17 March 1678, Grace's father, John Hooke, was found hanging in his house in Newport. There is more than one possible reason for his suicide. Hearing from his brother of Mary's entanglement with Holmes – it would seem that he didn't know about Robert's own involvement with her – was perhaps just one blow too many. But there were other factors. Being mayor of Newport twice, the second time 1676–1677, meant that, while he was at the pinnacle of his career and, although there were privileges and economic advantages, there were a lot of outgoings. As there was also a hiatus in providing the mayor with a stipend, it was ultimately a great financial drain. In fact, Robert's diary records that John had stopped paying for Grace's upkeep in London – sending produce instead – and was constantly asking his brother for money. There is also evidence that in his business he started using light-weight and false measures. Margaret Espinasse, author of *Robert Hooke* (1956), proposes an exacerbating factor: 'The melancholy which also oppressed his brother Robert grew upon him with his financial troubles and at last overwhelmed him.'

John was buried discreetly. Robert Hooke contacted the king about financial help for his brother's widow, Elizabeth, only to find that Robert Holmes had already done so.

Grace continued living with her uncle as his housekeeper. She was now his close companion. He taught her bookbinding, and she rebound some of his books; they went for long walks together, and trips down the Thames. It is not known what she died of, but she was only 28, and was probably buried in London. It is hardly surprising that Robert so mourned her. His friend and biographer wrote:

In the beginning of the year 1687 [?], his Brother's Daughter, Mrs Grace Hooke dy'd, who had liv'd with him several Years, the concern for whose Death he hardly ever wore off, being observed from that time to grow less active, more Melancholy and Cynical.

It is not clear if Grace ever saw her daughter again, or how Mary was brought up. It might have been by a woman hired to do so living in Holmes' mansion. I like to think so, and I stayed a night at the George Hotel in the hopes of feeling the presence of both mother and daughter, as Grace and Holmes must have had their trysts there. Why he did not marry Grace is of course unknown but it is sometimes assumed that it was because of a difference in social class, in spite of the education she had received in order to marry well. Perhaps he had heard gossip via the bush telegraph about her chequered past. I surmise that her father's suicide may have been a factor. But this paragraph is based on supposition. That there has been some scepticism that Grace was Mary's mother, is intimated by an Isle of Wight History Centre article posted online, 'The Scientist The Grocer, the Governor and Grace' (2000) by Robert Martin. But if she was not her mother, why would Holmes have used up a favour from the king by approaching him about John Hooke's estate and the financial situation of his 'wife and child'. The Newport Corporation, raising John's debts, claimed his estate, but did agree an annual maintenance to Elizabeth of £10.

Whatever the truth of why Holmes did not marry Grace, Mary Holmes does not disappear from history. He certainly acknowledged her as his daughter: when he died in 1692 his will was made in favour of his nephew Henry Holmes, but only on the understanding that he marry his uncle's daughter, Mary Holmes, which, unsurprisingly, he did. Mary went on to give birth to eight daughters, one of whom died as a young child, and eight sons, four of whom died in infancy, which must have kept her busy, though she would have had help once they were born. You also have to imagine her grief at each loss. In spite of what must have been a strain on her body, she seems to have lived until 1760 when she was 82. Meanwhile, her husband had a distinguished career, as an Anglo-Irish officer, lieutenant-governor of the Isle of Wight (1710–1714), and a Tory member of Parliament from 1695 to 1717. He left Mary a widow in 1738, presumably as a comfortably-off, happy grandmother. She died and was buried in Yarmouth, though I could not find her grave; it was raining very heavily and the inscriptions had all worn off the gravestones.

Robert Holmes's reputation suffered not a jot from Mary's birth and his acknowledgement of her as his daughter. A statue of him, for which he was responsible, dominates nearby St Mary's Church where he was buried.

Celia Fiennes (1662–1741) was one of the first of a number of English women travellers, particularly noted for riding side-saddle on horseback throughout England, including a few days on the Island, between 1685 and 1741. Her account of her travels was written primarily for her family in 1702, and only later went through several editions, starting in 1812, under different titles and in different forms. I have two versions, one a portable paperback (1983), the other a large format, nicely illustrated, one (1995). Useful maps leave out her side trip to the Island! Passing briefly through Yarmouth, she wrote in *The Journeys of Celia Fiennes*, presumably following local gossip:

> Sir Robert Holmes has a good estate there he was Governor of the Island and of Yarmouth Castle, and there he is buried where is his Statue cutt in length in white marble in the Church and railed in with Iron-Gates, he was raised from nothing and an imperious Governor and what he scrap'd together was forced to leave to his Nephew and base Daughter, having no other, and they have set up this stately Monument which cost a great deal.

Seymour Fleming (Lady Worsley)

The name of **Lady Worsley** (née **Seymour Dorothy Fleming**; 1758–1818) is mired in scandal, dating from her involvement in a high-profile 'criminal conversion' trial. She was the daughter and co-heir of Irish-born Sir John Fleming Bt and his wife Jane Coleman. Her father and two of her sisters died when she was five, and. seven years later her mother married the elderly Edwin Lascelles, 1st Baron Harewood, whose wealth came from slavery plantations in the West Indies. In 1775, aged 17, Seymour Fleming married 24-year-old Sir Richard Worsley, 7th Baronet of Appuldurcombe Manor, Isle of Wight, bringing with her a jointure (dowry) of £52,000 (today's £6,682,900). Her husband's English baroque manor house was by then filling up with antiques, following the Grand Tour that Richard Worsley went on after his Oxford degree (Corpus Christi College). As for the man she married, LOJ Boynton, in his slender booklet *Appuldurcombe House* (nd) uses a quotation from the historian Edward Gibbon who confided to his journal:

From an honest wild English buck, he is grown a Philosopher ... He speaks in short sentences, quotes Montaigne, seldom smiles, never laughs, drinks only Water, professes to command his passions and intends to marry in five months.

Appuldurcombe, near Wroxall to the south-east, was quite a place in those days – indeed, it was known as the grandest building on the Island, 'without a doubt' – and Seymour had the looks, charm, elegance and fortune to grace it. Her looks and place in society were such that she was painted in 1775/6 by Joshua Reynolds in a red riding habit adapted from her husband's regimental uniform, with a long-plumed hat – a painting now in Harewood House, her stepfather's property. At the same time, Reynolds painted the matching portrait, Worsley in his uniform (in a private collection); he was already Member of Parliament for Newport. What could go wrong?

The marriage seems to have been unhappy from the start. Seymour was the sort of woman who needed attention; her husband spent a lot of time away from home, either in London fulfilling various duties or involved, as governor (1780–1782) in further strengthening the defences of the Island. Christine Fleming in her article 'The Lady in Red' says that the sight of the Reynolds portrait made her decide to use it as the basis for her Master's dissertation topic. To her, an unequal relationship and its consequences were revealed, and she wrote:

Even when the couple's portraits are viewed together Lady Worsley stands apart, separate. Lady Worsley's military inspired riding habit challenged the role of gender and female power during her lifetime, and I'd argue continue to do so today. Her pose is one of supreme confidence, her body less angled than her husband's she stands with bristling posture, her hand on her hip as if challenging the viewer. The vibrant red of her riding habit sharply contrasts [with] the muted earthen tone of the landscape around her. Seymour's pensive gaze is determined and hard to read. I find it full of unanswered questions I have about her life, her perspective as a female and the hardships of her bizarre marriage. Although her and Lord [sic] Worsley's portraits were commissioned to hang together they reflect the stark indifference they felt for one another. In reality we know the two portraits, much like the couple, weren't meant to hang together.

Seeing the portrait, with Seymour confidently holding her riding crop, had much the same effect on Hallie Rubenhold: 'I remember thinking there has to be an extraordinary story behind this woman,' she said. And as a result she wrote the biography *Lady Worsley's Whim: An Eighteenth-Century Tale of Sex, Scandal and Divorce* (2011). That led to the BBC film *The Scandalous Lady W* (2015) which is available on DVD. This is very much a Georgian romp, with Keira Knightley giving it her all as Georgiana of Devonshire.

This is all because Seymour, as a result of her unhappiness, or dissatisfaction, began to take lovers. She had begun trying to do her duty and produce a son to inherit the title and Appuldurcombe, but one source says that the marriage was not consummated for three months. But in 1776, a year after the marriage, a son, Richard, was born. How her husband responded to her subsequent adultery will have to wait for the trial.

Into the picture now steps Maurice George Bisset of the already introduced Knighton Gorges Manor which he, at the age of eight, had inherited from his grandfather. In due course, he became a captain in the South Hampton Militia, which covered the Isle of Wight and, not surprisingly, became a close friend of his neighbour Richard Worsley. That friendship meant constant visits between Knighton and Appuldurcombe, and Bisset and Seymour became lovers. In August 1781, she gave birth to his daughter. To avoid scandal, paternity was accepted by her husband, and the baby was christened Jane Seymour Worsley. But in November that year, Seymour ran away with Bisset. For Worsley this was going too far and, in spite of the scandal which must, and did, ensue, in 1782 he sued Bisset for damages of £20,000 (over two million pounds today) for having 'criminal conversation' with his wife – for adultery with his wife which entitled him to sue for compensation. (He had failed to win a seat in 1779, and lost all his offices when the North administration fell in 1782, which may have been a factor: he had lost status, and his wife's behaviour was the last straw.) The case was held in the Court of King's Bench in London before Chief Justice Lord Mansfield and it was opened by the Attorney General.

It is already clear from discussion of her portrait, and her behaviour in her marriage, that Seymour was a woman of some spirit; she was by then 24 years old, in her prime, and she made the most of it, testifying in court herself on Bisset's behalf. The rumour was allowed to float that she had already had 27 lovers since her marriage; indeed, her lawyers called several of them to give evidence. Her doctor was also called to state that she had contracted venereal disease from the Marquess of Grantham, meaning that Bisset was not unique. None of this really helped Bisset, however much the salacious details appearing in the newspapers appealed to the public, and showed Worsley to be a cuckold. But there was a clincher. The couple did not only move in Society on the Isle of Wight, they did the same in London and other places where Society moved during the season, and evidence was brought that on at least one occasion Worsley had made it possible for Bisset to spy on his naked wife washing herself in a bathhouse in Maidstone. This proved that he had encouraged Bisset to have an affair with his wife; indeed, he had connived at the adultery. Not only was Worsley awarded just 1s in damages by the jury, but he was also subjected to much mockery, given traction by the cartoon showing Bisset sitting on Worsley's shoulders as he spied on naked Seymour through a window, captioned by Gillray, famous for his political and social satires,

'Sir Richard Worse-than-sly,
exposing his wife's bottom; – o fye.'

A reproduction of the cartoon vies with the portrait of Seymour that emerges from material written about the scandal. Even worse, it is said that this poem, which was also well circulated, and which apparently raised outrage among the public, was penned by Seymour herself:

> ... with B ----t stopt, for he could give
> What from thine arms I never could receive.
> From him no tiezing titillations came,
> He rais'd those passions which he could well tame.
> Dissolv'd in thrilling extacy we lay,
> Kiss'd till the morn, then curs'd the coming day.
> Oh, had you seen me on his breast reclin'd
> Lips glu'd to lips, and limbs with limbs entwin'd.
> With oft repeated acts of dalliance spent,
> My lust quite sates and my heart content.

However much all this damaged Worsley, he did manage to turn the tables on Seymour: he separated from her, rather than suing for divorce, not only thus keeping her jointure, but it also meant that she could not marry Bisset. He quite soon left her, but not before she became pregnant by him, or perhaps because of that, more likely because she did not have access to her fortune. As she was left penniless, Seymour entered the London demi-monde, becoming an upper-class mistress, as well as joining the club for aristocratic women shamed for promiscuity or adultery, the New Female Coterie. In due course, she went to Paris to escape her debtors. When she returned to England with a new lover in 1788, Worsley entered into formal articles of separation, on the understanding that she spend four years in exile in France. There she got caught up in the French Revolution and, during the Reign of Terror, may have been imprisoned. During that time, her son, Worsley's heir, Richard, died. She did manage to return to England and went to live with her mother until her brother-in-law arranged for her to live in her former home in London, Brompton Park, though without owning it. When she was 47, in 1805, Worsley died, enabling her to retrieve her jointure and marry her current lover, John Lewis Cuchet, twenty years her junior. At the same time, by royal licence she resumed her maiden name of Fleming, which Cuchet adopted. At the end of the Napoleonic Wars, the couple settled in France, and there, in 1818, aged 60, Seymour died. She is buried in the Père Lachaise Cemetery in Paris. Details of Worsley's life after the trial, including mention of his 'housekeeper', Mrs Smith, and his further accumulation of treasures during his travels, are neatly summarised by Boynton.

It is worth just sketching what became of Seymour's erstwhile Island home. On Worsley's death, the title passed to a fourth cousin, while Appuldurcombe itself, which was left deeply in debt, passed to his niece Anna Maria Charlotte Bridgeman Simpson. A year later she married the Hon Charles Anderson-Pelham, but died in 1813. In 1837, he was created 1st Baron Worsley of Appuldurcombe and 1st Earl of Yarborough. His main home remained Brocklesby Park in Lincolnshire, much grander than Appuldurcombe, but his Island manor house was useful when, as effective founder of the Royal Yacht Squadron, he came over to Cowes to sail. Appuldurcombe was never the same again. There is no evidence that Seymour Fleming came back to haunt the place, bombed during the Second World War, and left partly in ruins and empty. There are however ghosts seen there, but not, apparently, of a woman. Appuldurcombe is by no means the only Island house with its ghosts: Bisset's Knighton Gorges certainly has its share, as the next chapter will show.

In 1788, the year in which Seymour returned from France for the first time with a new lover, and when her husband agreed to a formal separation on the understanding that she go abroad for four years, John Wilkes arrived on the Island. He was not only a radical and trouble-maker as a Member of Parliament and as a journalist, with a rapier wit, but he was also a well-known rake, including being a member of the Hell-Fire Club which held 'tasteful' orgies in the 'romantic' in the ruins of St Mary's Abbey. That did not change, in spite of his appearance being particularly unprepossessing, which he countered with charm, when he arrived on the Isle of Wight, aged 63. He took a lease on Sandham Cottage, which he called Villakin – it was not so much a cosy thatched cottage in the then village of Sandown, more a three-storeyed villa on a cliff overlooking the Sandown Bay, with four acres of land. He was to live in it for long periods between 1788 and 1797 (the year he died) and make it a book and treasure-filled home, with a much-loved and cared-for garden, where he welcomed ornamental chickens, Chinese pigs and numerous guests with well-known names. Going to church in Shanklin, he met, for example, the actor Richard Garrick and 'his charming wife'.

Catherine Smith

Wilkes had married Mary Meade, 10 years his senior, in 1747 and came into possession of an estate in Buckinghamshire and a comfortable fortune, which gave him status among the local gentry. It had been an arranged marriage, during which Wilkes had several affairs. Jan Toms, in the posting 'John Wilkes on the Isle of Wight' (2018) in her series 'Brief Biographies', notes that 'he boasted that he loved all women except his wife'. The couple separated in 1756, a separation which became permanent. But they had a daughter, also called Mary, whom Wilkes called Polly, and he remained totally devoted to her for the rest of his life. By **Catherine Smith**, his housekeeper, whom he called 'a low, illiterate woman', and who accompanied him to the Island, he had a son, John Henry Smith, born in 1762. He was not close to this son but did later obtain a post for him in the East India Company. His other mistress, **Amelia Arnold** (d.1795), lived separately nearby in Sandown. By her he had a daughter, **Harriet Wilkes** (b.1778). He passed the two children off as a nephew and niece. **Polly Wilkes** (1750 –1802) was to visit him at the Villakin at least twice and between times he kept up a regular correspondence with her, which is how his life on the Island can often be viewed. What is, perhaps, less known about Polly, apart from her being intellectually bright, is that she was a good enough pastelist to be included in Neil Jeffares' online *Dictionary of Pastelists before 1800*.

Sandham was equidistant between Knighton Gorges, where Bisset lived, and Appuldurcombe, the property of Worsley. Wilkes wrote to Polly in July 1791, 'Captain Bissett dined here yesterday, but I have neither seen nor heard of Sir Richard Worsley'. Bisset also kept Wilkes supplied with melons and other fruit. Following Bisset's affair with Seymour Fleming he had, in 1787, married **Harriat Mordaunt** (b.1753), an illegitimate daughter of Charles Mordaunt, 4th Earl of Peterborough. Wilkes had obviously known Harriat before both came to the Island, because he wrote to Polly in 1775, 'Lady Peterborough, Miss M------t more gloomy and dejected than ever'. Although in one letter Wilkes told Polly that he had not had contact with Richard Worsley, Jan Toms notes that the Garricks took him with them to Bisset's Knighton Gorges and:

Here he found Sir Richard Worsley and some of the 'Neapolitan acquaintance'. Sir Richard promptly invited him to his seat at Appuldurcombe the following day where he entertained the whole Knighton set at a grand breakfast.

Wilkes reported that Mrs Garrick was, as usual, the most captivating of the whole circle. Worsley had returned from a long sojourn abroad including Italy in 1788, and had obviously let bygones be bygones with Bisset. In a letter written in May 1789, Wilkes reported that 'On Wednesday we make war on the rooks at Sir W Oglander's (Nunwell House), and on Friday we make war on the foreigners who keep up such an uproar at Freshwater Rocks.' Once when Polly was coming to stay, her father asked her to bring half a dozen tablespoons and a dozen silver-handled knives and forks, plus a marrow spoon and 6 desert spoons. There was always something he needed.

By 1797, Wilkes was growing tired; he shut up the Villakin and returned to live with Polly in London. On Boxing Day he died. The main beneficiary of his will was Polly, but he made provision for Amelia, leaving her £1,000 and the lease and all the contents of the Kensington house where she lived. Harriet inherited Sandham Cottage, its treasures and £2,000 to be held in trust for her until she reached 21 (she was then 17). His other natural child, John Henry Wilkes, was left only £100. Jan Toms notes:

Ironically in the end, it was John Henry who perhaps came off least badly as far as the will was concerned, because when John Senior's affairs were examined, he turned out to be insolvent. The windfalls turned to dust.

Young Harriet was in the end all right: she married a barrister and produced five children. Polly was all right, as she inherited her mother's fortune. As for Sandham Cottage, it no longer exists, but the site is on Sandown High Street.

There is an interesting portrait of John Wilkes and his daughter Polly, painted *c*.1779, by Johann Zoffany in the National Portrait Gallery. Instead of the usual pose of the woman sitting, the man standing behind her, it is Wilkes sitting, and looking half tenderly, half questioningly up at his daughter; while Polly, dressed – or perhaps over-dressed – as a very elegant and rich lady, sporting a tall, powdered wig, looks unreadably into the middle distance. She remained unmarried; perhaps she'd seen enough of marriage. The dog at the couple's feet belonged to Zoffany.

It would be a mistake to suggest that irregular relationships only took place on the Island: they were commonplace elsewhere, particularly among the upper classes when the Hanoverian Georges were on the throne, and it was not only Georgian women who were drawn into them.

Sophie Dawes, Baronne de Feuchères

Seymour Fleming, in her New Female Coterie days, after Appuldurcombe, and after trial, may well have been known as a 'demi-rep', a term coined by Henry Fielding in his 1749 novel *Tom Jones*. This meant a woman 'who intrigues with every Man she likes, under the Name and Appearance of Virtue'. Or, put more simply, a woman of doubtful reputation. **Sophie Dawes, Baronne de Feuchères** (*c.*1790–1840) is said to have inspired the character of Becky Sharpe in William Makepeace Thackeray's *Vanity Fair* (1847–1848). Sophie was the supreme social climber. She had a long way to climb.

Sophie Dawes' date of birth is uncertain, as she liked to change it, and those who write about her can't agree, but it was somewhere between 1790 and 1792. Her mother was **Jane Calloway** (1754–1838) of St Helen's, her father, Richard Daw or Dawes, was a fisherman by day, but by night the 'celebrated' smuggler Dickie Dawes, on a coastline where that activity was rife. As the National Trust Internet posting, 'St Helen's Duver History', tells it, he would run the gauntlet of the customs men through a narrow channel known as 'Dickie Dawes Gut' to store his contraband of brandy, silk and tobacco. The booty would often be hidden beneath the tombstones of St Helen's Old Church before being brought inland along secret passages. Another common practice was to lash and weight down barrels of brandy before 'rafting' them in when the coast was clear. No doubt his drinking, becoming heavier over time, came from some of the goods he handled. These details of Sophie's father suggest that she was taught by example from a young age to dissemble and beat the system. And it is hard to believe that Jane Calloway did not help him in his smuggling endeavours, as wives often did; if that was the case the couple could have been included in the next chapter, 'Outsiders'.

Some accounts suggest that Sophie's parents were not married, but Warwick Kellaway, for example, in his Internet posting, 'Sophie's Story: From Winkles to Wealth on the Isle of Wight' dates their marriage to 1775. They had 10 children, only four of whom grew up. They lived in Freefolk Cottage, overlooking St Helen's Green, and all was well enough until 1796, when most sources suggest Dickie Dawes died. The family tried to survive on winkle picking on St Helen's and Bembridge beaches – Sophie apparently barefoot – hence Kellaway's title and, indeed, one of the several books about Sophie – Violet Stuart Wortley's *Sophy, the Winkle Picker* (1941). But Sophie was six years old at most, William was four and sister Charlotte was a babe in arms. Soon the older children were in Newport House of Industry (Workhouse), and baby Charlotte joined them two years later. Their elder brother, James, born in 1777, seems to have already left home. Sophie was to remain in the workhouse for anything from two to nine years, and, usefully, she learned to read and write, as well as gaining some basic domestic skills. Not all sources agree that she was there for nine years; one source say two. As so often when using many sources, I have to go with my instinct or common sense. But I think I will accept that she was 15 years when she left, as Robert Stephen Parry suggests in his article 'Sophie Dawes (*c*.1792– 1840) Her History' (2020).

There are advantages to relying on several articles and postings: it allows you to be concise in a book that covers several centuries, and a plethora of women, books and places. But there are disadvantages, too: concision may mean leaving out important details and colour, as came home to me strongly on reading the late Adrian Searle's most up-to-date biography of Sophie, *The Infamous Sophie Dawes: New Light on the Queen of Chantilly* (2020). Two examples hit me almost immediately as I read: one was his careful research into the Newport Workhouse which showed, with full details, that it was not a very nice place. The second fact that he unearthed is that Dickie Dawes did not die in 1796 but, instead, sank into the depths of alcoholism, unable to deal with family nor, indeed, life. He, too, was in and out of the workhouse. But, as far as his family was concerned, he was no longer there.

It was not surprising that Sophie left the workhouse as soon as possible. She was found menial work on Cliff Farm, Victoria Road, Shanklin, but soon, knowing that there must be more to life than that, she ran away to Portsmouth and worked as a chamber maid in a hotel. That was not enough either, and she set her sights on London where she was first an assistant in a milliner's shop. But she was becoming conscious of her attractions and was dismissed for an affair with a young water-carrier. She then sold oranges in Covent Garden, and probably dabbled as a mediocre actress in nearby Drury Lane. Soon she was the mistress of a wealthy gentleman, also called a rich army officer, who installed her in a house on Turnham Green. When they split up, he settled on her an annuity of £50 a year. She sold that and in 1800 placed herself in a school in Chelsea.

Her next step may have seemed a step down: she worked in some capacity in a high-class house of ill repute frequented by émigrés from the French Revolution who were forced to remain there during the Napoleonic Wars. But the valet of the Duc de Bourbon of the Condé Royal House spotted her and drew her to his master's attention. As I have confessed unashamedly to cherry picking from a myriad articles about Sophie, I can't resist this from Warren Whitmore's 'Isle of Wight Villains: Sophie Dawes: from Fisherman's Daughter to Infamous Femme Fatale' (2022): 'One story of her life recounts the tale of the

Duke of Condé playing cards with the Duke of Kent – father of Queen Victoria – with the radiant Sophie as the prize.'

A small correction here: the Duc with whom Sophie now entered a relationship was Louis Henri, Duc de Bourbon; his father was Louis Joseph Prince of Condé, and was also in London. Louis Henri would not become Prince of Condé until the death of his father. Adrian Searle, author of the most recent of the biographies about Sophie, found, as so many had before him, that the known facts of her life, at least until she met the Duc, were limited, much had to be deduced. When, therefore, it was possible to do serious research he tended to do so, as he did with the workhouse. That means there is a long chapter on the back story of Sophie's Duc which, I have to say, rather slows down the narrative.

His valet obviously knew the 52-year-old Duc's taste well: he had, after all, been around the block a few times. He had one son by his royal wife whom he married in 1770, and separated from in 1780; with the Paris Opera singer Marguerite 'Mimi' Michelot he had two daughters, and he hardly frequented the house of ill repute only to play cards. He was, therefore, not slow to take to Sophie, and it wasn't just a short tryst: she became his mistress, sensing how to obtain and then retain his affection. He not only lavished a residence – off Queen's Square in Bloomsbury – and servants, money, and gifts, often jewellery, upon her, but he also had her educated by the best, money no object: she was taught French, Greek, Latin, Music, dancing, deportment and comportment. Her mother also lived in the house and her presence gave it a layer of respectability.

In 1814, Napoleon was defeated, though not for the last time, the monarchy was restored and the Duc returned to Paris to live in the Palais de Bourbon. Many sources suggest that Sophie followed him, but she could not live with him there or on any of the several family estates – Montmorency, Guise, Enghein and Chantilly – because the Duc's father was still alive. For four years, she lived in lodgings apart from her lover, retaining his affection by occasional visits from him and, between times, loving letters from her. But Searle suggests it was some time before she arrived in Paris. That may well be so as a Sophie Harris is said to have borne him two children, one in 1817, the other in 1819, neither of which survived. Whatever the chronology, in 1818 the prince died and her Duc inherited the title Prince de Condé, the family estates and fortune. He was to be the last in his line as Napoleon, or those under his command, had his only son, the Duc d'Enghien, tried and shot for treason.

At some stage then, Sophie arrived in Paris and could now live with her lover, but not as his official mistress. She had become an elegant French-speaking lady, the Prince felt able to contrive a suitable marriage for her, and provided her dowry, with Adrien-Victor de Feuchères, a major in the Royal Guards. On the 1818 marriage licence Sophie described herself as a widow, and in the marriage contract she said she was the daughter of Richard Clark, and the widow of William Dawes. With her husband, now her lover's aide-de-camp, as well as a baron, the three of them lived together, apparently contentedly.

Sophie became not just the Baronne de Feuchères but conducted herself in aristocratic French Society attached to the Court in such a way that she was known as the Queen of Chantilly – hence the title of Violet Montagu's *Sophie Dawes: Queen of Chantilly* (1912), Shane Lloyd Price's *Sophie Dawes: Queen of Chantilly* (2018), and that of Adrian Searle. No one was quite sure where she came from, hence the French lawyer André Louis' *The Mysterious Baronne de Feuchères* (1929). In due course Sophie was to bring over her mother, her niece Matilda, and nephew James, both children of her brother James. So strong was Sophie's hold over her ageing and increasingly infirm lover that through him she arranged for Matilda to marry a marquis, and young James, who had been a butcher's boy in London, became Baron de Flassons and equerry to the Prince (who actually preferred still to be called the Duc de Bourbon).

A view of Sophie after she left the Isle of Wight, and started her new life of social climbing can be gleaned from portraits of her. The historical novelist Robert Stephen Parry provides images of her over time, and details of them, in several blogs entitled 'Sophie Dawes "Extra Pages"'. In 1812, François Huet Villiers painted a miniature of her (now in the Musée Condé, outside the Chateau de Chantilly, 40km north of Paris). I suspect the portrait was commissioned by the Duc, and that the artist was another French émigré. When Sophie had become the Baronne de Feuchères, a French landscape by Adolphe Ladurner 'The Hunt at the Ponds' shows her in the distance, mounted side-saddle, and there is a watercolour sketch of her painted in preparation for that. The 1829 three-quarter-length portrait of her in riding habit was by Alexis Leon Louis Lalbrun. It is that most often reproduced. Her pose is reminiscent of that of Lady Worsley in her telling portrait. Sophie's black habit, with leg-o'-mutton sleeves, has frogging down the front that conveys a military effect, and the chain belt, probably gold, cinching her waist has an almost threatening outsize buckle. Her hair is piled up, ending in a topknot, with large frizzes on each side. She stands straight, looking sideways into the distance in a non-engaging way, and holds her riding crop upwards as if she is about to bring it down on something or someone. The crop in both cases may well represent the sword carried by Richard Worsley and other male military portrait subjects. Sophie is in charge of her life.

Things changed, however, when Sophie's husband, who had thought the Prince was Sophie's father, discovered that he was, in fact, her lover. He left her in a rage which included a beating, obtained a legal separation from her in 1827, and told the king who thereupon forbade her to continue appearing at Court. It became a scandal: the Prince was the last of the royal Bourbon line and Sophie was banned from Court, hence Marjorie Bowen's *The Scandal of Sophie Dawes* (1948). She had not, however, lost her influence with the Prince, which Seale suggests was malign, rather than that of a lover. He was induced, against his will, in 1829, to sign a document put in front of him, in which she was to be bequeathed about 10,000,000 francs, and the rest of his fortune. Many properties were to go to the Duc d'Aumale, scion of the Orléans family, a

13. Sophie Dawes, Baronne de
Feuchères, from the Internet

transaction which Sophie arranged through secret negotiations with his father, who was to become Charles X.

By 1830 her lover was beginning to tire of Sophie's importunings, and planned to leave France secretly and flee to England. But he was found slumped against the wall, hanged by handkerchiefs tied together and attached to his bedroom window. It was at first assumed to be suicide, but soon rumour suggested that Sophie was responsible for arranging his murder. Drawings show his feet on the floor. An enquiry was held but, with the connivance of Orléans, the evidence of the death being the result of criminal means was insufficient, and she was not charged. Most biographical details assume that she was in some way involved, and she became hated by the French and ostracised by Paris society. Not surprisingly, she decided to return to London, and set about selling the French properties she had acquired.

Somehow, in the midst of all the fuss in 1830, she found time and inclination to sit for a portrait by Aimée Brune-Pagès (1803–1866), a respected woman painter during the Restoration, the July Monarchy, the Second Republic and the Second Empire, and who exhibited often in the Salon. Sophie wears a low-cut dress in mourning black. Although her shoulders are bare, a white lace fichou makes sure that the v-shaped neckline is not décolleté; her only ornament is a very long gold chain; there is a touch of rouge on her cheeks. She sits against a dark background in a feminine pose, one arm resting lightly on the arm of the chair, but with a hard-to-read expression. It is quite unlike the earlier taking-the-world-on portrait.

Not surprisingly, Sophie did not choose to settle at St Helens on the Island, but she did return there at least once. Her nephew did not live long to enjoy his title, dying in Calais on the way back to England. In 1831 Sophie paid a brief visit to her home place to bury him, and commission a memorial to him in the churchyard. Some accounts even suggest that she poisoned him. While we're in St Helens, I should draw your attention to AW Ellwishr's *The Sophie Dawes Trail: A Leisurely Stroll through the Historic Village of St Helens and the Duver* (2020). (A duver, pronounced to rhyme with cover, is Isle of Wight dialect for an area of sand dunes.) You would be disappointed if that were all you read about Sophie, but it is an indicator of how much her stratospheric rise, even her notoriety, is known about locally. Freefolk Cottage, Upper Green Road, even has a blue plaque, partly obscured by wisteria when I went to look for it. It reads:

> Sophie Dawes
> Madame de Feuchères
> Daughter of Richard Dawes
> Fisherman and Smuggler
> known as
> The Queen of Chantilly
> was born here
> about 1792

Crime historian Angela Buckley, much taken by Sophie's possible crimes, and enjoying research into stories about smuggling, contributes the posting with photographs, 'The Secrets of Sophie Dawes' (2019). It's useful for including not only the usual portrait of Sophie in her riding habit, but also a photograph of Freefolk cottage, rather attractive in its modern setting, with its blue plaque, then the blue plaque itself, and James's handsome, if lichen-spattered, elaborate tombstone, with its added inscription 'Erected by his aunt, Madame la Baronne de Feuchères'. Of added interest are portraits of Sophie's lover, the Duc, and her husband, de Feuchères, not an unpleasing young man to look at. All of these are full page.

Once back in England, Sophie, rich and titled, bought a house in Hyde Park Square, London, and an estate near Christchurch, Dorset. Her mother, who had been with her in Paris, retired to a convent in Hammersmith where she died aged nearly 90. Sophie became a pious Roman Catholic and began to give much of her fortune to charity, to the poor – it would be easy to dissect her motives. She became known as a benefactor on the Isle of Wight. She apparently grew grossly overweight, possibly from dropsy and, in 1840, died in London of a heart attack aged about 50. She was buried in Kensal Green Cemetery.

But that is not quite the end of Sophie, and not only because the saga of her rise from rags to riches lingers on, and on, re-constituted in print and on the Internet. She even merits an entry in *The Oxford Dictionary of National Biography*. Robert Stephen Parry's *The Testament of Sophie Dawes: The Queen of Chantilly and a Scandal at the Heart of Victorian Society* (2016) is not yet another biography but, as is his usual treatment of historical events and characters, a novel, and a rather engaging take on Sophie's life. It starts in 1862, in Osborne House, Queen Victoria and Prince Albert's retreat on the Isle of Wight; Albert has recently died. In the months that follow, in the stifling atmosphere that surrounds him, an archivist is working there sorting out Albert's papers and, because of what he finds, an unexpected letter from Sophie to Albert, detailing her life, his own life changes.

The archivist, the book's narrator, adds the details to the journal he has been keeping since his arrival to live in St Helens and commute by carriage to Osborne (he also walks all over the Island). It builds up to a crescendo while all the time recounting in detail his pleasure as an ornithologist, as well as life at Osborne with and without Queen Victoria. Parry calls his book an 'epistolary novel', with its combination of the letter and journal, as not only Sophie's life and the characters and places in it unfold, but also that of the archivist. It is not without twists of Parry's devising.

If you are inclined to read books that elaborate on what is sketched here, I'd suggest you stick to Searle and Parry, partly as they are the easiest to get hold of. To be honest, I preferred Parry, particularly because he tells the story from Sophie's rather partial point of view. Searle's formal biography very much shows her, warts and all, with emphasis on the warts. Doubtless, once she was in Paris, with a title, living in one of the Bourbon palaces, ruling over its staff and the Duc's family, and conniving to maintain her hold over her ageing lover, there is evidence that she was manipulative, scheming, narcissistic, not to mention despotic and vindictive, but there are no redeeming features to make her seem made of flesh and blood.

6 – Outsiders: Witches and Witchcraft, Ghosts, Smugglers and Wreckers, Prostitutes, 1528–1964

Introduction

This may at first sight seem a rather disparate chapter but look at Molly Downer: she was a smuggler, and her community was quite sure that she was a practising witch. Smugglers were also sometimes allied with ghosts. Gay Baldwin, doyenne of writing about ghosts, notes in one of her many ghost books, *Ghosts of the Isle of Wight* (1977) that, in the great days of smuggling, from the mid-eighteenth to the mid-nineteenth century, ghosts were used 'to keep honest folk abed' and, therefore, unlikely to see what was going on and, perhaps, even report it. Those smugglers who plied their trade on the east coast, between Ryde and Bembridge, exploited the ghost known as the 'Blue Lady' of Nettlestone Priory, forcing her to wander further and further away from her ancestral home. Her story, and Molly's, will be told later in this chapter.

Ethel Hargrove (1866–1932) of Sandown makes a link between witches and ghosts in her short story 'Cats and Dogs', drawn from her *Wanderings in the Isle of Wight* (1913) and adapted by Alan R Phillips in *Cock and Bull Stories* (2008):

At Wackland near Hale Common in the early nineteenth century Squire Thatcher's cook received a visit from a witch in the appearance of a black cat. The cook was frying pancakes at the time and threw a spoonful of lard on the cat, whereupon the creature ran off mewing with pain, and the witch-woman suffered from a painful back from then on. This is a fairly standard version of the widely held belief that witches possessed familiar spirits in the form of a cat or dog, and their lives were so closely entwined that if a familiar suffered a physical injury, so did the witch.

Haseley Manor at Arreton has long displayed a mummified cat with two attendant rats in a wall cavity, where all three were found. Between the fifteenth and eighteenth centuries it was a common practice to bury mummified cats in the walls and roof cavities of houses to repel the plague of rats and mice. But because cats were so readily associated with witches, they could also act to ward them off, so a dead cat would be placed in a location that was vulnerable to witches and evil spirits entering the house. Cats were also known to sense ghosts and other supernatural beings, and therefore it was believed that their presence in the walls of the house helped guard against such malign forces.

Haseley Manor, you may remember from the last chapter, 'Irregular Relations', is where Dowsabel Mills lived, and where she set up her 'school for young ladies'.

A twentieth century medium was charged under the Witchcraft Act of 1775.

Witches and Witchcraft, 1528–1962

The earliest named woman on the Isle of Wight regarded as a witch that I can find lived in the reign of Elizabeth I (reigned 1558–1603). The story is told by J Albin in *A New, Correct, and Much Improved History of the Isle of Wight …* (1795). He writes,

> As a manor (Athey) it is both ancient and extensive having free warren and the government of the passage of Ride. Its courts were held twice a year and two clerks were presented at it in the twenty-eighth [year] of Henry the sixth for taking pheasants within the boundary. So late as the reign of queen Elizabeth, a widow named Agnes Porter was attained of witchcraft and all her lands, goods and chattels, forfeited to the Lord of this manor, the boundaries of which were as follows from the boundary stone at New Mooth, near Ride so far into the sea beyond the low water mark as a man could reach the ground with an oar of eighteen feet long. On the north it extended from thence into the boat lake by the same rule as far as Binstead lake. All wrecks of the sea within these limits were the property of the Lords of Athey.

It was worse for Agnes than that: Athey enjoyed the privileges of a Court Leet, so that not only did its Lord find her guilty but also she was sentenced to death by burning on Ashey Down, and the sentence was carried out.

'Leet' denotes a territorial and jurisdictional area spread throughout England in the fourteenth century, and the term 'court leet 'came to mean a court in which a private lord assumed, for his own profit, jurisdiction that had previously been exercised by the sheriff.

I have tried to deduce who would have been the Lord of the Manor of Athey (Ashey) at that time. From the time of Edward I, until the dissolution of the monasteries by Henry VIII, it had been a religious house connected to the Abbey of Wherewell (Hampshire), founded by Queen Elfrida. But by the time of Henry's daughter, Elizabeth, I suggest the lord may have been Anthony Dillington to whom it was sold in 1565. By the time of his son, Sir Robert, in 1604, it was called, as the 'History of Manor Houses of the Isle of Wight' relates, 'the Manors of Ashley and Ryde'. It is still a wonderful looking house and property, including a farm, in the Ashey area.

At least Agnes Porter has a name, and some details, though limited, regarding her background and death. An 'Isle of Wight Timeline of History' suggests only that in 1528 – in Henry VIII's reign – there was an 'Accusation of witchcraft against two Newport residents'. There is not much one can do with that except to hope that further particulars will emerge. The date does not fit with the description in Joanne Thornton's 2022 *County Press* article, 'Exploring Elizabethan Newport and historical events beyond':

> The area of the beast market was also used as an area for punishment. A witch was burnt at the stake here in the Elizabethan period. The father of Edward

Denys had accused her of bewitching his sister. The Newport accounts also detail payment for a stake on which to put the traitor's head.

Together with a map, the article helps the imagination by describing the Newport market designated areas. They consisted mainly of trading spaces, of which there were three. St Thomas's church was in the middle of the square, with the corn market around it. To the north was the fish and meat shambles (or slaughterhouses) and to the south were the retail shops. Each of the entities had its own strict rules and regulations, and a licence was required.

In the centre was the Town Hall, which contained the audit house and nearby was a building where the Knighten [sic] Court was held. In Norman times the Governor of the Island had considerable power within the court. By the seventeenth century 'this power had been considerably reduced'.

As for the 'beast market', that was held in St James's Square which had a bull ring and a stake. This was 'a necessity for butchers in the Tudor period, as they were forbidden to kill a bull that had not been first baited'. To make that area appear even more gruesome it 'was also used as an area for punishment'. And that is where the woman who allegedly practised witchcraft on Edward Denys's aunt was burnt at the stake.

It is fair to assume that Edward Denys was well enough known for him to be mentioned, but that his father, let alone his aunt, were not. But who was Edward Denys? The only possible answer apparently available is that it was Sir Edward Dennis, deputy governor of the Island. But there are only scraps of information about Dennis. An Internet entry about Holloway Manor in the Newchurch parish ends 'Sir Edward Dennis' ancestors kept court and law day at Holloway, where his tenants did suit royal.' In a posting, 'Lordship title of Holloway or Ventnor', at the end of a long list is '12th Lord – Sir Edward Dennys is elected Member of Parliament for Yarmouth.' On a posting about Westcourt Farm (Shorwell) is the following information:

The Dennis family held West Court from 1539 to 1717, but they lost it through failing to produce a son. The most notable of the Dennis family was Sir Edward who was Deputy Governor of the island and a colleague of Sir John Oglander. It was possibly Sir Edward's father, Sir Thomas Dennis, who built the main part of the present manor house towards the end of the Elizabethan reign.

If Sir Edward Dennis (or Dennys) is the Edward Denys involved in the witch trial in Newport, then the father concerned would be Sir Thomas. But that is as far as I have been able to go. I emailed Joanne Thornton, in case she knew more; but she had got only as far as I have. So it is probably best if we just think of a wretched woman, regarded as a witch, and burned at the stake for that.

A bit more is known about Molly Downer (fl 1847), but not her dates; even 1847 concerns her behaviour towards another woman. I suggest that your best bet, as it was mine, is to read Sarah Sprules's historical novel, *The Last Wight*

Witch (2015). She has succeeded in taking the bare bones of what is known about Molly and building a convincing life. The novel starts with the setting of Molly's conception, at a village celebration of the harvest, the day most anticipated in the year. The villagers have had a lot to drink, particularly the young, who are not so familiar with its effects. Molly's mother has noticed a rather attractive young man and allows herself to follow him to a secluded place where they have sex without the young woman having much clue as to what is happening to her. Needless to say, when her resulting pregnancy shows, she is kicked out by her family and becomes a village pariah.

Several years pass, Molly's mother has moved to Bembridge where she has made a new life for herself as a herbalist and renowned healer of village ailments. Molly is now a young woman and already initiated into her ailing mother's healing secrets; indeed, as her mother becomes less able to cope, she finds herself filling the herbal requests. Meanwhile, you couldn't make it up, but it is one of the only known facts, her father has become a vicar and, what is more, is sent to the Bembridge local church. As a man of the cloth, he is filled with shame, and remorse when Molly finds out that he is her father. They strike up a sort of relationship when Molly visits the church, one that sustains her: he is someone she can talk to.

Molly is already a bit of a loner, an outsider, so much so that a girl called Harriet bullies her. What is more, the boy that Molly was sweet on, and who appears to reciprocate, leaves her and takes up with Harriet, allowing her to taunt Molly all the more. So when Harriet has an accident, and develops an illness that only gets worse, Molly is heard to rejoice and wish her harm. The die is cast. Meanwhile, not only has Molly's best friend married, leaving her without a girl her age she can talk to and enjoy outings with, but also her mother has died and, in due course, her father dies too. Molly becomes more and more isolated. She discovers that her mother had been allowing the local smugglers to use the cottage as a resting place for their goods. Not only does Molly let herself be persuaded to continue doing this but she also starts to avail herself of the brandy that is an integral part of Isle of Wight smuggling. Then the lonely young woman becomes attracted to the leader of the gang and little by little finds herself a useful member of the gang, loving the excitement of smuggling. Then her lover is killed. Molly becomes more of a hermit, and finds solace in putting witchlike symbols in the cottage window. Her reputation as a witch has become self-fulfilling and she is ostracised by the villagers; she stops opening her door to those with ailments, or needing help with the birth of a baby. Her needs for food are discreetly met by religious strangers who leave parcels of provisions and books outside the cottage. It is they who discover that Molly is dead.

I hope I have only provided you with Molly's possible life story, and not spoilt Sarah Sprules's sales! Molly's story, at least the backbones of it, are so well known that a recent musical has been produced, which I regret I have not seen, though it is possible to hear a snatch on YouTube. More esoteric is the introduction by The Ventnor Brewery, founded in 1840, of a Molly Downer ale. I cannot say I like the label which has Molly drawn as a typical old crone. It's 4.2% – 'amber brown in colour, not as heavy as expected, in depth hoppy bitterness, followed by an overwhelming aroma to [complement] the bitterness …'.

The more I look into Molly's story, the more I wonder. She is apparently first mentioned by Ebenezer Hartnall who, according to 'Beyond the Graves' (2019) posted by the Ryde Social Heritage Group, was orphaned in Ipswich aged 12, and became apprenticed to a bookseller and printer. He arrived in Ryde 'just coming of age' and set up in business. For a few months early in 1840 he published a mixture of true and fictional stories in the 'IW Miscellany' (1844), 'including one about the last of the witches, Molly Downer of Bembridge'. In 1870 he started a small paper, *The Ventilator*, 'which did not hold back on local comment'. One piece resulted in him being sued for libel by VA Webber, a case which he lost. It much affected his health and he died aged 39. I have tried without success to locate the 'IW Miscellany'. The same applies to J Brammell's 'The Ballad of the Wight' (1979), a poem which, it is said, 'paints a different picture to that of 1844'. JE Meadows' 'Genealogist's View of Bembridge' (1996) also eludes me. Far be it from me to prompt any questions, but where is an impeccable and accessible source? And that is not a rhetorical question. Molly is said to have lived in Witches Hatch, Hillway, Bembridge. I went looking for it and found the spot where it should be, but it wasn't there. One person told me it had been burnt down, another that it had been rebuilt. I didn't know when I looked for Witches Hatch that, according to folklorist Paul Wilson, there is an 'unambiguous stone … that marks the site of Molly Downer'. Although there is a photograph of the quite large round stone, I cannot see an inscription.

Paul Wilson in that same posting says that Freshwater Bay has a cave in which Gretchen Eve lived. He provides a photograph of the location. 'She used to help sick villagers until they turned on her and burned her alive in her cave. She is said still to haunt the land.' A woman both witch and ghost. I can find nothing more about Gretchen. Those meagre details of her, mythical or otherwise, suggest that she was typical of the sort of woman who might be called a witch. A 'patient' to whom she had given herbal treatment only needed to die for a hostile family member to know who to blame, and why – she was a witch, one who practised the dark arts.

You come across some jokey postings when you're trying to do serious research. Thus it was with the anonymous posting on 'The Spooky Things' website – 'Godshill Village', part of the Appuldurcombe estate. This 'myth' allows one to blame either a witch or, given the word 'spooky', a ghost, though as she (I'm assuming it's a woman, and a visitor to the Island) maintains that 'the place seems to be teeming with witchcraft – in fact it seems that at one time [G]odshill was the witch capital of the UK … one of the cottages is 'actually called "The Bats Wing"'. The author writes of the birth-pangs of All Saints Church, with the sort of typos that fill my first drafts,

Originally the church was to be built within the village, footings [the bottom part of a foundation] where [sic] dug ready for construction – and that's where the trouble started. Every morning the workmen would report onsite, ready to being [sic] the day's work.

One problem – their tools would not be where they place [sic] them the night before.

Someone must be playing a joke on them, night watchmen where [sic] employed to keep any stays [sic] away from the site – but by morning the tools would still have disappeared, or moved locations. By now the construction workers where [sic] becoming more than a little frightened, it was rumoured that bad magic was involved.

One bright morning the workmen turned up for work expecting the worse [sic] for their tools, only to find that EVERYTHING was missing. All the tools, materials, huge stonework, everything had gone. The whole village was searched from top to toe, eventually they found the missing items …

ON TOP OF THE HILL! Yes, where the church is now positioned – is where the items were found. As incredible as it sounds, something wanted the church built on top of the hill – so that's where they finally built it.

Molly is said to have been the last witch of the Isle of Wight, but it is so easy, both historically, and more recently, to bandy the term about when there are possible explanations for a woman so designated; Molly could, it is suggested, have suffered from Diogenes syndrome. There have been other witchcraft cases connected with the Island, though not so straightforward: it has been possible to try at least one woman under a centuries old witchcraft act.

The Scottish medium known as **Helen Duncan** (née Victoria Helen McCrae MacFarlane; 1897–1956) developed in 1926 from clairvoyant to physical medium by offering séances in which she claimed to be able to permit the spirits of recently deceased persons to materialise, by emitting ectoplasm from her mouth which a photographer showed, in 1928, to be fraudulent. Nothing daunted, on 11 and 12 July 1940, she visited and held séances in the Ventnor Spiritualists' Church (which opened in 1938).When the church was renovated in 2015, her visit was commemorated by a plaque that had been left to the adherents by the previous committee. This read: 'The Helen Duncan Room; showing their intentions to honour the famous Spiritualist who once held a séance in this room. We have now dedicated this special room to her and have put up the plaque in pride of place.'

It seems that Helen was not just on the Island to hold the séances in Ventnor but that she spent some time during the Second World War in Ryde. As the *County Press* posting, 'Infamous Women of the Isle of Wight', records, during one of her séances on the Island she told of the sinking of the warship *HMS Barham*. As news of this tragedy had not yet been released (indeed, it had been kept secret from the public), the authorities expected her knowledge to have come via enemy sources. Upon investigation, no evidence for this supposition could be found; therefore she was arrested in 1944 and imprisoned for nine months, sentenced under the Witchcraft Act of 1735. Winston Churchill called her trial, conviction and the whole affair 'utter tomfoolery'. Helen's was one of the last witchcraft trials ever held in the United Kingdom.

The date of Helen's trial under the Witchcraft Act of 1735 is a bit of an eye-opener, so it is worth looking at the dates of the several such Acts. The first was under Henry VIII in 1541; it was repealed by Henry's son Edward VI in 1547. A new one was passed in 1562 under Elizabeth I – *Act Against Conjurations, Enchantments and Witchcrafts*. It was said to be in some respects more merciful towards those found guilty of witchcraft than its predecessor, demanding the death penalty only when harm had been caused; lesser offences were punishable by a term of imprisonment. Nevertheless Agnes Porter must have been tried under that Act, although there was no evidence of any harm caused in the only source for it. Perhaps Lords of the Manor simply went their own way; perhaps they didn't know that the law had changed. That same lack of knowledge must have applied to the sentence given to the woman burned at the stake in Newport for some offence against the Denys family. The verdicts handed down in Newport in Henry VIII's reign to the nameless women would have been harsh under the law. There were separate Acts passed for Scotland (1563) and Ireland (1586).

The Witchcraft Act under which Helen Duncan was tried, dated 1735, luckily for her, marked a complete reversal in attitudes. Penalties for the practice of witchcraft as traditionally constituted, which by that time was considered by many influential figures to be an impossible crime, were replaced by penalties for the pretence of witchcraft. A person who claimed to have the power to call up spirits, or foretell the future, or cast spells, or discover the whereabouts of stolen goods, was to be punished as a vagrant and a con artist, subject to fines and imprisonment. This act remained in force well into the twentieth century, until its eventual repeal with the enactment of the Fraudulent Mediums Act of 1951. That is how, in 1944, Helen came to be tried under the 1735 Act. But she was the last person to be tried under that act and, indeed, her conviction led to its repeal and the introduction of the 1951 Act.

Although there are modern, self-proclaimed and practising 'witches' on the Isle of Wight and elsewhere in the United Kingdom, they are beyond the scope of this chapter and history. But what does fit into the title of this chapter – 'Outsiders' – continues beyond Molly Downer and other witches who were often simply outsiders. A prime twentieth century example of an outsider who in some ways was treated in the same way as earlier so-called witches, was **Olivia Parkes** (1881–1962), also known in Ventnor as 'Britannia' or 'The Old Lady of the Sea'. The difference between earlier such women and Olivia is that her state is a subject of great sympathy by local people, and wider society, and particularly by Teresa Grimaldi and Sarah Vardy. They have conducted research into her life and are, by several means, calling attention to it and celebrating her as a woman who lived as she chose. Olivia's later life also throws light on the problems of alienation and loneliness, and provides opportunities for doing something about them. Such problems may have something to do with the reason for Olivia's choice; otherwise her motivation can only be surmised.

The earliest sighting of Olivia Parkes seems to be of a youngish woman living in London in the 1920s where she led an ordinary enough life, enjoying ballet dancing and swimming. This precious hint is captured by the records of life drawing classes held in The Better Days Café project for adults and young people of St Catherine's school. These are kept in the Longshoreman's Museum on Ventnor's seafront. Sophie Blake from the Longshoreman's Museum had provided the artists with material that shows Olivia in her pre-Ventnor days. The connection between Olivia and the Blake family of longshoremen will be revealed.

Why Olivia chose to move to the Isle of Wight, and to Ventnor in the late 1920s, does not seem to be known, but she set up a sweet shop in Pier Street. Her later disregard for convention, and for the law, led to her being charged for selling sweets out of hours, found guilty and imprisoned for a month. Such a sentence seems harsh, and I, at least, wonder whether her behaviour in court may have led to it, and whether a month in prison influenced the behaviour that followed. (The shop still remains, one of the longest-running shops in town.) Again my question is: was she perhaps going through the menopause? It was soon after that experience that she moved into the shack on stilts in Myrtle Bay, just west of Ventnor Beach.

The shack had been built in the 1880s for the Swimming Club; perhaps Olivia knew that and it prompted happy memories of her different life in London. It was then bought by the Blake family to store some of their boats. It had become dilapidated following a disastrous storm in 1881. Olivia was to live there for the next 30 or more years, without running water, sanitation or electricity, isolated from society. There were steps leading up to it, with a drop to rocks 15 feet below. She would walk west along the beach to Flowers Brook to collect fresh water and do her washing. Flowers Brook was, and is still, west of the Botanic Gardens where streams from two springs from the Downs above join and flow into a small pond.

But Olivia's eccentricity drew attention, sometimes hostile; she was seen as an outcast. Children threw stones on to the roof of the hut from the cliff, further damaging the roof. She must still have been venturing out to shop, perhaps to secure provisions, because she bought, or somehow obtained, a tent which she put up in the hut to sleep in, protecting her from the elements. In November 1931, during a severe gale, she became marooned; during the night the sea washed away her steps. A passing errand boy, hearing her cries for help the following day, brought the police and fire-fighters to rescue her. But she seems to have returned, becoming increasingly isolated, venturing out only in the evening when there were few local people about, and the visitors had left the town.

In 1958, when she was nearly 80, the Council stepped in. When Olivia refused to leave her 'home', she was forcibly removed and housed in a flat on the High Street. There she died in January 1962, and was buried in Ventnor Cemetery. The shack was dismantled by the Blakes. I've read no evidence that Olivia was known as, or called, a witch, but she lived the sort of life that would probably have been seen as such in earlier times; she was certainly an outsider.

Ghosts, 1340–1964

Just as the witches described were unhappy in life, or in how they met their end, the same tends to apply to ghosts. I need to say here that I am not a believer; that is, I have never seen a ghost nor even felt the presence of one, nor had a strange sensation. During the course of my research on the Island, I was shown round Northwood House by Tim Wander (historic consultant with a special care of Northwood), not primarily for ghosts, but for its interesting history. But as we went along a particular corridor, Tim pointed out the door through which, during the First World War when the house was a hospital, the matron, long after her death, was seen to pass. I was able then at least to use my imagination; indeed, I can still see the door in my mind, though not the matron. She may not have had an unhappy life nor wretched death, but she would have seen enough horrors to give her the impetus to return to the scene – she is known as either just 'Matron' or 'The Matron Who Walks'. But then I read Tim's exhaustively documented *The Ghosts of Northwood House* (2018), and came across the 'ghost hunters', organised groups who spend much of their time visiting places such as Northwood House, often armed with technological paraphernalia, and a technical language, intent upon seeing paranormal apparitions or simply feeling, or recording on their devices, intimations of some presence, sometimes for hours on end. My imagination closed down; a mental barrier came up. I should perhaps add that at the start of the Preface to his book, he writes 'I do not know if ghosts exist. If they do, I do not know what they are.'

I will come back to Northwood House after an attempt to draw up a chronological list of the Island's ghostly people. Frustratingly, the date is not always revealed, and some places, such as Knighton Gorges, have ghosts of different people living at different times. What interests me is not so much the ghostliness of a person who once lived, as the lives they led, the manner of, and the reason behind, their death, as well as the people who describe having seen or felt them. Some of the people or places will have cropped up in an earlier chapter, or will do so in a later one.

Knighton Manor appeared in chapter 4, 'Troubled Times', when, in 1170, Hugh de Morville, one of the assassins of Thomas Beckett and owner of the Manor, fled to the Island. And again, in 1340, when Theobold Russell, commander of the Militia deployed to repel the French landing at St Helens, was mortally wounded and taken home to die at Knighton Gorges, as it had become. After his funeral his inconsolable widow, **Eleanor Gorges** (*c*.1303–after 1357), returned to the room in which he had lain in state and died there not long after of a broken heart. Thereafter, it was called 'The Room of Tears', with the title engraved over the doorway, and tradition has it that the room is haunted, and that sweet music can be heard emanating from it. Their son took his mother's maiden name, thus Ralph Gorges.

Another out-of-the-ordinary death attached to Knighton Gorges occurred in 1721, this time producing the ghost of a man on horseback. Tristram Dillington, MP for Newport and a reckless man whose horse was called Thunderbolt, shot himself, aged 41, it is said over grief at the death of his wife and all his children, save a daughter, Judith, possibly from smallpox. Others say his death may have been caused by his gambling: he lost his townhouse in Newport in a game of cards. This haunting began to earn the house the reputation of being among the most haunted of the many haunted places on the Island; but there was more to come.

Knighton Gorges, as chapter 5, 'Irregular Relations', relates, was inherited in 1765 by Maurice George Bisset, later lover of Lady Worsley. Settled back there following the trial at which her husband, Sir Richard, sued her lover for adultery, Bisset married Harriat Mordaunt (introduced in the last chapter), with whom he had two daughters, the elder of whom was **Jane Harriet Bisset** (d.1866). One version of the story has it that when in due course Jane chose to marry, the man, a cousin and clergyman, did not meet with Bisset's approval. So enraged was he, indeed, that, rather than have his heir and her husband inherit Knighton Gorges, he had it burned to the ground. All that was left were two decaying stone gate posts topped with weeds, now joined by a modern wooden gate, at the end of an overgrown drive. However, in Bisset's will of 1818, he left provision for both daughters, with no mention of disinheriting either.

Another version is that Bisset, following the court case, was shunned by society and lost his mind due to venereal disease. He destroyed the house believing it to be cursed. That doesn't really fit with his marriage, two daughters and being a genial host to his neighbours such as John Wilkes MP (also featured in chapter 5), and Sir Richard Worsley.

However and for whatever reason the house was destroyed, it was to breed its own ghosts, to be seen on New Year's Eve and best described by Ethel Hargrove who claimed that on New Year's Eve 1915 she saw the non-existent house, and continues:

A few minutes before midnight a flood of melody arose from the site of the former mansion. It was varied in character; dance music played on a harpsichord, Georgian airs, slow and stately, then a duet between tenor and soprano voices. At 12.00, the party seemed to break up, a pistol or gun was fired, dogs bayed and the sound of carriage wheels was heard.

As if that weren't enough, a woman, presumed to be Jane Bisset, is said to have been seen running towards the gate posts dressed in blue and purple. The Ethel Hargrove quotation is from Warren Whitmore's 'Halloween: The

History and Hauntings of Knighton Gorges …' (2022), posted on the *Island Echo* website.

For a straight history of Knighton Gorges, without ghosts, it is best to stick with 'Historical Notes on the Manor of Knighton, in the Isle of Wight' by the Revd RG Davis.

Because stories of ghosts attached to Knighton Gorges Manor extend over several centuries, attempts at a chronology have become somewhat skewed, extending from Eleanor Russell in her Room of Tears in 1340 to what Ethel Hargrove experienced on New Year's Eve in about 1915. But the chronology now travels back to 1507 and the death of Princess Cecily of York, who started chapter 5) and who spent five short years at Great East Standen Manor near Arreton. She may have died there, but there is also evidence that she died in England. Where she is buried is also questioned, but I have gone with the Island's Quarr Abbey. Why would she haunt East Standen, that is the question to which I have no answer. But according to a former member of the household, Mrs Rene Cooper, she does, or still did in 1911, her ghost appearing in one of the attic rooms. J. Charles Cox continues:

It's the sudden pressure in the middle of the night, of an invisible someone sitting on the end of the bed. It's not frightening, though a little disconcerting. 'Just as if a girl, someone who doesn't weigh very much, has sat there', said Mrs Cooper cheerfully. 'There's nothing to see and it didn't worry me. I'd have to see a ghost to believe in it'. But she felt the weight just the same.

Mrs Deborah Sutherland, who until recently lived at the manor with her husband and farmed the estate, told us that there's also a tradition that an 18th century maid haunts the house. Mrs Sutherland isn't susceptible to ghosts, but in one room had a vivid nightmare that something inimical was present. She was very frightened. Others have refused to sleep in that room.

Back now to 1560 and to nearby Arreton Manor – which before the Norman Conquest was owned by Queen Osburga (who was introduced at the end of chapter 2), and her son King Alfred the Great. By the time of the Domesday Book of 1086 it was owned by William the Conqueror. In 1132, under Richard de Redvers, to whom he rewarded the Isle of Wight, it came to be farmed by the monks of Quarr Abbey. In 1523, John Leigh took out a lease from the Abbot for 70 years. Following the dissolution of the monasteries by Henry VIII, ownership of the Manor reverted to the Crown, but the lease to the Leigh family continued.

Sons in the Leigh family seem to have been particularly keen to fight each other over the inheritance of Arreton, until eventually, by 1560, it was held by a third son, Barnaby Leigh. But still inheritance was an issue so that one night, when he was asleep, possibly already on his deathbed, his 13-year-old-son John placed a pillow over his father's face and smothered him. Having accomplished his horrible deed, he looked up and saw his younger sister Annabelle watching. Scooping her up, he dragged her upstairs and threw her from the highest window. The origin of the story is to be found in Sir John Oglander's *Chronicles of the Isle of Wight.*

Of course, the story does not end there because the part of the room from which **Annabelle Leigh** (d.1560) was thrown became permanently cold, and the ghost of fair-haired young Annabelle can be seen running through the house and gardens, wearing a blue dress and white slippers and often crying 'Mamma, Mamma'. It is in the solar room that the child was said to have been defenestrated, and there cupboard doors swing open by themselves, and towels that have fallen out are neatly arranged on the floor by unseen hands. One girl visitor to the house told her mother that she had tried to make friends with the little girl in blue.

Annabelle is by no means the only ghost infesting the manor house and grounds. There is a mysterious woman in a purple dress; a silver-grey figure followed by an overpowering sweet smell; and a woman in a red, tight-waisted, puff-sleeved dress. She is also said to have long curly black hair and to be accompanied by a sweet floral smell. Sounds include the rustle of skirts, and footsteps, as well as monks singing. Half a dozen other manifestations could be listed. What I do not understand is that no children of Barnaby Leigh are mentioned other than John and Annabelle, John's brothers having already dispatched each other. If that is so, John did not need to smother his father.

The Black Death that affected Newport in 1582 has been described in chapter 4 but, while that episode of plague led to deaths, those sheltering in the bakery, what came to be called God's Providence House, proved to be immune, its name given because of that. Its modern business is a tearoom run by a wife and husband who are proud, it would seem, of the building's 'resident spirits'. They include a little girl who resides in the first-floor corridors, and an older woman who occupies the Ghost Room, sometimes in the company of a young Brazilian slave boy.

John Ruffin was mayor of Newport in 1632 when his youngest daughter **Elizabeth Ruffin** threw herself into the well in the courtyard of Carisbrooke Castle. The bare bones of the story come from John Oglander's papers; it is suggested that her lover, an officer stationed at the Castle, had left her. Now, it is said, some visitors peering into the well see the face of a pale young woman floating there, entangled in a billowing dress. There is also a 'Grey Lady' wearing a long, dark cloak and accompanied by four dogs. The cloak covering what she is wearing underneath it, prevents dating and therefore when she may have lived and who, therefore, she might have been.

There were two reasons I stayed at The Union Inn, Watchouse Lane, in West Cowes during my fourth and last research trip to the Isle of Wight: first, it was round the corner from where Berthe Morisot stayed on her honeymoon in 1875, and from where she painted the scene on my front cover (Berthe will feature in more detail in chapter 9); and second because of its ghost. It did occur to me, even given the little I knew about it, that there might be more to it than a ghost, and a late-arriving piece of material confirmed my surmise.

The Union in the name of the inn refers to the Act of Union between England and Scotland of 1707, so that seems a likely date from which the inn was active. Later in the 1700s, most of the old wooden houses in Watchouse Lane were pulled down and replaced. The three that remained were, and are, the Union Inn. My initial information referred to a sea light on a tower above the inn that would guide the 'anglers' back to shore and safety during inclement weather. The wife of the tower keeper kept this light burning when he was offshore. But one night she forgot, so that her husband and many other 'anglers' drowned. It is said that her guilty ghost haunted the steps of the long-gone warning light; she can be heard climbing. One evening I came up Watchhouse Lane, and saw a light burning in a window; I looked in vain for a shadow.

The word 'anglers' bothered me; I wondered whether, although it is often the practice for fishing boats to go out at night legitimately to catch fish, her husband and the others were smugglers. Then I came across 'Bricks and Mortar – a short walk through the history of Cowes' which gives a rather less sanitised story of the Union Inn.

[It] was a notorious haunt of the press gangs. These gangs could legally kidnap working men – usually when they were drunk – make them serve up to 15 years in the Royal Navy, leaving the men's families destitute until they returned often minus a limb or two! Also [it was] a smugglers' den, as evidenced by tunnels and secret chambers found under the building.

That the area was a haunt of smugglers, as well as at least one ghost, seems to be confirmed by the existence of a watch house in the lane since 1703 – hence the name of the lane – and the Customs house itself moved there in the 1880s.

As the introduction to this chapter suggests, the ghost of the Blue Lady of Nettlestone was used by local smugglers to facilitate their activities.

The '**Blue Lady**' at what was Nettlestone Priory (then and now a manor house, sometimes enveloped in plans, and once the reality, to make it a hotel), is much talked about. But the date for when the Blue Lady was given cause to roam is often said to be 'two centuries or so ago'. I am, therefore dating it *c*.1800. The figure dressed in blue is not in fact a grown woman, but a girl aged about 14.

At one stage in the property's chequered career it was a house owned by the Grose-Smiths, a family that lived there from the early 1700s until the last of them died in the 1920s. When Sheila White and her parents used to visit, it was owned by her paternal grandmother's branch of the family, and she was fascinated by the house; as she wrote for an *Island Eye*, Historical Buildings piece – 'Priory Bay Hotel' (2023) in which her memories are incorporated,

It had everything an old house ought [to have], tales of secret rooms, secret passages, buried treasure, smugglers and, of course, the ghost!

She, indeed, was the main attraction at the Priory for me: her portrait, full length and almost life size, hung in the dining room. It depicted a girl of about fourteen or fifteen years old with a little pointed heart shaped face, seated in a garden with a small canary fastened to one finger by a narrow satin ribbon and a king Charles Spaniel play[ing] at her feet.

Whether or not my cousin knew her real name, I never found out. I never pressed the matter, sensing somehow that that was how she herself preferred it and being perfectly happy myself always to think of her as The Blue Lady. ...

Cousin Laura said she was usually seen tripping down the main staircase or crossing the hall, at other times she was seen flitting about the gardens and quite often on especially frosty starlit nights, gliding soundlessly along the road and across the fields in the direction of the house where I now live, which was once part of The Priory Estate.

What Sheila particularly noticed as she tripped upstairs to her bedroom was a chest in the hall, because on it was a stuffed dog in a glass case by the main staircase. As she passed it she would try not to look into its baleful eye. She could not, though, resist doing so, and the flickering flame of the candle she was carrying made the dog look as though it was moving:

We used to wonder sometimes if this dog could really be the original dog belonging to The Blue Lady: he certainly looked a bit worn in parts, but could he really have survived the centuries – certainly two, but possibly three – and still be in one piece? I have no doubts now.

A sort of denouement took place when the Priory no longer belonged to Sheila White's family. She does not give the full name of the 'very wealthy and charming American woman' who bought it in the late 1920s, calling her merely Mrs S. But it is known that she was Lady St George. One day, Sheila, her mother and grandmother (who had left her card at the Priory) received an invitation and walked over to the house:

The door was opened to us by a butler who led us into what had been the dining room – where the portrait of the Blue Lady had hung – but which Mrs S had now turned into her drawing room adding to it extensively and putting some hideous new eight-sided windows that put my teeth on edge. But she herself was charming.

They were welcomed by Mrs S from her wheelchair, behind which stood her Secretary and beside which stood her magnificent Great Dane, Shadow, and it was during tea that she suddenly leant across the table and asked, 'Is this place haunted?' It turned out that her staff kept leaving, without giving her a reason.

When at last her faithful butler did the same she probed the reason and, finally he gave it to her:

'It's the noises, Madame' he told her. 'Every night, in the early hours of the morning we hear a child running through the passages crying and sobbing for her dog.' He went on to tell her that as they opened their bedroom doors and [went] out into the passages, the footsteps had actually passed them and the sobbing had been heart-rending.

We clearly heard the words, 'My dog, my dog, what have you done with my dog'. He went on, 'and it was more than flesh and blood could stand.' It was obvious that the place was haunted.

Mrs S resolved to get to the bottom of the story. She started by asking around in the village, but this enquiry was not very helpful: people talked of a Grey Lady, and weren't sure what she did. So Mrs S turned her attention to the dog. The head gardener who had been a garden boy of 13 remembered a stuffed dog in a glass case. So Mrs S got in touch with the distant cousin who had inherited the Priory and asked if he had taken the dog. He remembered it and thought that it must have been sold at auction when the house was cleared. Nothing daunted, Mrs S put an advertisement in the local papers, and the dog was traced to an antique shop in Newport where it was bought for £1. It was brought back and replaced in its old location. From that moment on all noises ceased.

When Mrs S went back to Sheila White and her family to ask who or what haunted the place, they told her what they knew about The Blue Lady or, rather, the girl who had died young. As for the portrait, Sheila, looking idly through a glossy magazine, came across an advertisement for the sale of a house; the image that graced it had the portrait hanging on the wall. But since the sale, its whereabouts is unknown, though it is possible to see the portrait above, for example, the piece 'Halloween Heritage: The Famous Blue Lady of Nettlestone Priory' (2023), posted by Warren Whitmore on the *Island Echo* website. I really do not think that should be the end of the story – it is a pity that when I saw the house, it was not fit to receive it.

Because one of my drivers in September 2022 had contacts all over the place, the gate was unlocked to allow our car into the guarded property. This enabled me to walk round what was then a rather sad deserted house in a potentially lovely garden overlooking the sea and, navigating foliage, peer through the windows imagining the painting on an empty wall. No doubt the status of the house will, and indeed should, change. Whether or not light footsteps will be heard in the small hours when the house is in some way inhabited, is an interesting question.

It should be said at the outset that the story of **Lucy Lightfoot** is not of the usual ghost, but of a supernatural happening connected to an unexplained disappearance and apparent time travelling. The most significant date is 13 June

14. Portrait of the Blue Lady of Nettlestone, from the Internet

1831, and the place St Olave's, the family chapel of Gatcombe Manor and its manor house. This manor, you may remember, was the main property of Lady Matilda de Estur who featured in chapter 3. In the church (built 1292) there was, and still is, an effigy in darkened oak, said to be that of Sir Edward Estur who had died in Palestine on one of the crusades. Lucy was a local girl from Bowcombe, near Carisbrooke, who became attached to, and then obsessed with, the real Edward Estur as she imagined him: at every opportunity she would ride the two miles from her home to St Olave's and visit his armour-clad effigy lying in a recess in the chancel, on the north side of the altar.

In 1831, Lucy, a lovely lass, tall, pale, and with long blonde hair, daughter of the local miller, was 17 (or 20) years old. In spite of being popular with her contemporaries, she was not interested in the local boys who swarmed around her: her heart belonged to Edward Estur. Her story is told in the historical novel *A Tapestry of Time: Or Effigy of Love* (2001) by Cecily Gould, a writer from Freshwater who will appear in a later chapter. To visit St Olave's and to see the effigy allows the imagination full rein, as I suspect happened for Cecily Gould. As the author weaves a slightly complicated story, pieces posted on the Internet, such as 'Notes from the Countryside blog' and 'Lucy Lightfoot & the Crusader of Gatcombe, Isle of Wight' (nd) give you the bare bones of what happened next:

On 13th June in 1831, Lucy arrived on horseback at the church at about 10.30 am, tethered her horse at the gate and went into the church as she had so often done before. Shortly afterwards, at 11am there was a total eclipse of the sun, with darkness lasting for more than half an hour, while an extraordinarily violent storm burst upon the island causing floods and great damage, and many properties were struck by lightning. Nothing to equal the ferocity of the storm, combined with the eclipse had ever happened before on the island within living memory.

It was two or three hours later that a farmer, George Brewster, came by the church and saw Lucy's horse, frightened and distressed, still tethered to the gate. He went into the church expecting to find Lucy inside, but there was no sign of her, so he looked round the churchyard and made enquiries to see if she was sheltering in one of the nearby cottages.

But Lucy was nowhere to be found, and despite widespread searches and a subsequent large reward offered by her distraught parents, no clues to her disappearance ever came to light. She had vanished without trace!

As for the effigy, upon inspection, it seemed to lack a gemstone that had been embedded in the hilt of his sword, and a metal misericord, or short steel dagger connected with mercy killing, had been torn from the hands of Edward Estur, and lay broken on the nearby altar.

This is where it gets rather complicated; briefly, in 1865, a manuscript was discovered during a search in Crusader records, confirming the name of Edward Estur on one crusade which entailed travelling first to Cyprus in 1365. What is more, 'he was accompanied by a brave and beautiful young woman, by name – Lucy Lightfoot of Carisbrooke'. In the fighting that took place in the Holy Land, Edward was fatally wounded, but survived long enough to die at Gatcombe, while Lucy waited for him in Cyprus.

Cecily Gould's novel starts with only a few pages about what happened in St Olave's churchyard, then jumps immediately to several centuries earlier when Lucy Lightfoot of Carisbrooke by chance encounters Edward Estur and they are immediately attracted to each other. But he has promised the King of Cyprus to take part in his imminent crusade and his honour does not allow him to renege on his vow. So Lucy hatches a plan and ends up accompanying him as far as Cyprus. So far, so good, but then Cecily describes a terrible crusader attack on Alexandria and the massacre that follows, with so many unpleasant details that you have to be hardy to follow it. And she ends the novel differently. I've tried not to provide a spoiler. But with what I have said about the attack on Alexandria you may feel that it's not for you. On the other hand, if you are the sort of reader who can skip pages, Cecily does show great knowledge about seafaring and everything to do with it – doubtless drawing on her own books on the subject, because of family involvement – and does evoke the times and places convincingly.

It is appropriate now to time switch again, to the 1950s, when the local rector of St Olave's, the Reverend James Evans, was increasingly anxious about low attendance at the church. He decided to write a story about Lucy Lightfoot, one of his imagination, in other words, a hoax. It did the trick, attendance rose and the love story of Lucy Lightfoot and Edward Estur became truth hither and yon. I'm sorry if this revelation spoils your visit to the church, but you will be warmly welcomed by some kindly volunteers providing refreshments. And the effigy of a crusader is certainly there, with a dog at his feet, a wooden misericord clasped in his hands replacing the steel dagger.

There is a marble statue of another warrior lying on a tall catafalque in the nave. It is a memorial to Captain Charles Grant Seely, unveiled in 1922 by HRH Princess Beatrice, governor of the Island. The inscription records that he was killed in Gaza, Palestine, in 1917. His body was buried in Gaza alongside other soldiers of the Isle of Wight Rifles whom he had led in an attack on a Turkish position. Part of his marble face was damaged when, in 1927, Nellie Kerley, incensed or in despair that her brother was not so honoured, took a hammer to it.

If you fancy visiting Gatcombe Manor, lived in, if you remember from chapter 3, by Matilda de Estur, you can only hover outside the firmly locked gate of a private property.

I find it both interesting, and sad, that the name of **Charlotte Maria Oglander** (1818–1894) is not mentioned in the very long list of Oglanders in the index of Cecil Aspinall-Oglander's family history, *Nunwell Symphony* (1945). Fortunately for this book, and this chapter, Charles Cox does include her. Charlotte was the daughter of Sir William Oglander 6th Bt and **Lady Maria Oglander** (1785–1855), daughter of George Henry Fitzroy, 4th Earl of Grafton. Maria and William divided the year between their home in London, and Nunwell on the Island which Maria loved immediately. She happily gave birth to an heir a year after marriage, and then a second son. Her birth and beauty produced a full-length and stately portrait, painted in the 1820s by Sir Thomas Lawrence. All seemed well in her world and, indeed, the letters and diary entries in *Nunwell Symphony* show that that was so.

Before her marriage, Maria Fitzroy had been lady-in-waiting to Princess Charlotte of Wales (1796–1817), daughter of George, Prince of Wales (later George IV) and Caroline of Brunswick, and heir presumptive to the throne. But Charlotte died in childbirth aged 21, after being delivered of a stillborn son. The country and Lady Maria Oglander were devastated. Pregnant at the time, she resolved to call her child, if she was a daughter, Charlotte, after both her mother and the beloved Princess. The baby was a girl. So why is she excluded from several references, particularly the long and detailed Oglander family tree? A clue is provided in the document 'Deed of Stringston manor, 21 August 1879'. Under the 'description' is this text:

Charlotte Maria Oglander of Nunwell House, Isle of Wight of unsound mind, acting through Augustus Frederick Leeds of Ryde, Isle of Wight, Esq, released Stringston Farm [Somerset] from a charge of £6,000 for Sir William and Lady Mary Oglander's younger children.

15. Lady Maria Anne Oglander,
from the Internet

Cox, publishing in 1911, introduces her, and her ghost, under the subheading 'The Island's Saddest Shade'. Charlotte was known as 'Little Missy' and a miniature of her at Nunwell shows her wearing a bonnet; he continues,

Her eyes are sea-blue and her face has a sweetness that still speaks over the one-and-a-half centuries since she was a child. She must have grown up to be a beauty, like her mother, but she was to have no suitors and no husband. She was destined to spend her long life – she was born during the regency … and did not die until not long before Queen Victoria's golden jubilee – at Nunwell; and remained, in an essential sense, a child.

At Nunwell, Charlotte would 'wander vacantly' through the rooms and gardens of the great house with her nurse at her side. And then Cox reaches the climax: 'We discovered that she still wanders there.'

Among those who reported Charlotte's continued existence was **Mrs Marjorie Monger** who lived at Nunwell for 15 years as housekeeper to **Joan Aspinall-Oglander** (1884–1961).

'We heard her and we felt her presence,' she told us. The housekeeper's room, in the Jacobean part of the house next to what is known as King Charles' room – the last free visit paid anywhere by the unhappy monarch was to his faithful Oglanders – was where the nurse attended Little Missy; and added Mrs Monger, 'we heard her crying at night and crying in the day'.

In spite of being a bit put off by the 'ghost hunters' of Northwood House, Cowes, I did have a niggle about the First World War matron whose ghost patrols a certain corridor: who was she? On 'The List of Volunteers at Northwood House Auxiliary Hospital' two matrons are named: **Ethel Mary Louisa Lowry** is listed as 'Matron & Surgical Sister'; and **Ethel Woosnam**, 'Sister, Matron & Lady Superintendent'. Frustratingly, I can find nothing more about either of them. There is a Commandant, **Eva Hermione Baring** (née Mackintosh; 1876–1934), about whom there is material; she was the wife of Sir Godfrey Baring,1st Bt, one time MP for the Isle of Wight. But the Red Cross makes clear in 'Auxiliary hospitals during the First World War' the distinction between such staff: 'a commandant, who was in charge of the hospital except for the medical and nursing services'; and 'a matron, who directed the work of the nursing staff'. It is tempting, because there is material about Eva Baring, to write about her, but she would not have been dressed as a matron; she is unlikely to be the ghost.

There is one story that Tim Wander tells about a Northwood House ghost that is charmingly enough for one, at least momentarily, to suspend disbelief. He tells how his 19-year-old daughter, Lizzie, went on her first ghost hunt joining an experienced team in the servant quarters, and continues:

I deliberately stayed on the other side of the House and drank coffee. I didn't tell her anything that had transpired before, and she had no idea what to expect or in all honesty have much clue about what was happening.

Lizzie lives in a remote Spanish village some 1,700 miles from the Isle of Wight and Spanish is really her first language. She had flown in a few days before and left a few days afterwards and although she is an excellent Chef, her grasp of 19th century history, Welsh geography and post-World War One epidemics is not so to speak … comprehensive. I think she had been to Northwood House perhaps three times and one of those was for a Wedding Fayre!

She had an 'interesting' session and was not the least fazed by it all.

When she came back to the coffee room her first question was 'Dad, what's the Spanish flu?'

I said: 'Why?'

'Because the ghost I was just ta[l]king to died of it in 1920 while working at the House as a nanny looking after the children whose parents had died here from the flu. The ghost was Welsh and from a small village that sounded like "Reedo" near Mount Snowdon. She desperately wanted to go home but died before she could leave.'

Tim goes on to explain how the House became a centre for the treatment of Spanish flu, which tended to hit those aged between 15 and 40. Many orphaned children survived and nannies were needed to look after them, some of whom, like the brave Red Cross nurses, caught the disease and died. The name of this ghost may have been Sarah, without a surname, but in any case, by then records had broken down. He concludes the account: 'But the village exists. It is actually *Rhyd-Ddu*, just 3 miles from Snowden.' Then Tim adds, 'I asked her what she thought about it all. She shrugged and said it was *interesting* and she felt sad for her.'

Just as ghost hunting at Northwood House has become an industry, so it is with what was the Ventnor Tuberculosis Hospital, more formally known as the Royal National Hospital For Diseases of the Chest, at Ventnor and, in particular its operating theatre. What was there until 1964, with the departure of the last patient, of the 100,000, who over nearly a century were treated, is now the Ventnor Botanic Gardens. Even now, the site is not neglected by ghost hunters.

The editor of the 'On the Wight' website thanks the ghost historian Gay Baldwin for the account that was published as 'Ghosts Live On At Ventnor Haunted Operating Theatre' (2008). Five years after the hospital closed, 'the eleven blocks of balconied cottages which stretched for almost half-a-mile, were demolished'. Except it was not as easy as that: the 'old hospital did not give in gracefully. Its death throes brought ghost hunters and psychic investigators from all over the world. The hospital was haunted.' It was not so much the hospital, which was fairly soon a pile of rubble, as the operating theatre: it would not demolish. The demolition contractors:

Tried to knock it down with a crane and ball, but the steel cable snapped. Then they brought in a large tracked tractor. Three huge pieces of masonry fell on it, crushing the cab, smashing the transmission and breaking the steel tracks.

And that was only the start of it: at least two caterpillar tractors suffered a similar fate. Two men told to demolish the operating theatre with sledgehammers were confronted by a ghostly figure standing in a doorway. 'A young girl looking very pale and ill, with deep sunken eyes often appeared to keep watch on workmen as they dismantled the old hospital.' One of them was John Slade of Cowes, 16 years old at the time; he remembers her well as he often saw her

standing in the corner of a ward adjoining the theatre. She was about ten years old and four feet tall. Her face and features were solid, the rest of her misty. She would appear in the early mornings or late afternoons and stand there in the ruined, roofless building, staring at the workmen. Then she would vanish.

But John remembers not only the girl but the temperature and atmosphere:

That operating theatre was the coldest place I have ever worked in. It was also the hardest to knock down. I don't know why because it was built the same as the rest. It just didn't seem to want to go.

It was not only the workmen who were affected and hurried away from the job before nightfall: 'nearby residents complained constantly – not about the noise and dust from the demolition – but about the moaning, weeping and groaning coming from the empty hospital buildings at night'.

Finally the job of demolition was done; the site was levelled and a car park was built over the top. 'But weird things continued to happen. A council surveyor peering through his theodolite saw the ghosts of two Victorian nurses pass in front of the instrument'. Few visitors are aware that there was once a hospital there, but the site of the operating theatre still exercises a 'malign and disturbing influence'. Some dogs grow agitated, refusing to walk across that area and any accident in the car park happens there.

It is likely that George Bernard Shaw's sister, **Elinor Agnes Shaw** (1856–1876), was a tubercular patient there, sent from the mainland to be treated by its famous doctor who had founded it. But she died there, and was buried in Ventnor. Her brother, only 22, and not yet a famous playwright, came over for her funeral. There is no suggestion that she is connected to any ghost story. Fast forward to 1898 and Shaw and his new wife, the political activist **Charlotte Payne-Townshend** (1857–1943), spent their honeymoon at Ocean View, Cottage Lane, Freshwater.

Smugglers and Wreckers, 1262–1836

Who would suspect that both smuggling and wrecking can be laid at the door of Isabella de Fortibus, Lady of the Isle from 1262 until her death in 1293? You may remember that in chapter 3, 'Women of Property', in which Isabella and her rule are introduced, she won a case brought against her by Edward I over 'the right of wreck'. That right had been granted by William the Conqueror when he created the first Lord of the Isle of Wight. It meant that, should a ship be wrecked around the coast of the Island and there be no survivors, any value arising from the sale of what was salvaged and, indeed, the ship itself, would provide a source of Island income. But this also meant open season by local wreckers to pre-empt salvaging by Isabella's administration.

In order to constitute a legal wreck, the goods had to come to land. If they continued at sea, the law distinguished them by the terms, 'flotsam', 'jetsam' and 'ligan'. Jetsam continues to be where goods are cast into the sea, and there sink and remain under water; flotsam is where they continue floating on the surface of the waves; ligan, even today, with the smuggling of drugs, is where they are sunk in the sea, but tied to a cork or buoy, in order to be found. In this way, smugglers historically lowered the contraband into the sea offshore; recovering sunken barrels was unlikely to arouse suspicion as crabbing and lobster fishing were major industries, and retrieving them could be passed off as the baiting of pots or checking the catch.

As for the industry of smuggling, a posting on the Red Funnel website 'Shipwrecks, Smugglers and Local Lore' (nd), explains it simply:

Much of the coastal population … was involved in smuggling goods from France, with most of the fishermen bringing it across in their boats and their families colluding in its distribution. Smuggling had taken off in a big way after the death of Isabelle De Fortibus … [she had been] taking taxes from her people. When taxes became payable to the Crown [instead,] the locals became a much more lawless lot, probably due to the excessive demands of the expensive wars that the government of the day was indulging in.

This was an interesting throwback to the place of the Island, situated as it was between the English mainland and the north of France which, as discussed in chapter 2, even in pre-Roman times facilitated trade. In view of later problems with French raids and attempted invasions, discussed in chapter 4, 'Troubled Times', there is a nice irony to the story posted on the Isle of Wight History Centre website, 'Napoleon, Josephine and the Fishermen of Cowes' (2016). It starts:

Having established a strict embargo on all British goods into France, Napoleon was horrified to discover Josephine's travelling trunks contained British clothes. According to Josephine, he had customs officers seize the goods. Details of how Josephine's attire may have been enabled by enterprising Cowes fishermen has recently been the subject of local interest

But Cowes smuggling did not need a war and embargo to facilitate it, as shown in what went on a hundred or so years earlier at the Union Inn, described above, concerning the ghost of a wife whose carelessness led to smugglers' deaths.

As for Josephine's English-made clothes, well-organised smuggling gathered pace between 1806 and 1814. It was carried out by both British and French fishing boats; for safety a transfer would be made midway from one to the other. The enterprise may also have often involved merchants who had lost legitimate trade because of the war and the embargo.

One area of British commerce Napoleon particularly intended to hit was the cotton trade, where he hoped his domestic industry would be given a chance to develop. … The British product was superior, cheaper and much coveted on the continent. The blockade resulted in plenty of demand for smuggled in material and clothes, some of which sailed from Cowes.

Not all the smuggling had a customer of such high status as Josephine, and while cotton goods may have been smuggled from British ports, and woollen ones from the Island, into France, the traffic in the other direction was most likely to be brandy, not always to the benefit of the smuggler. Sophie Dawes' father who became an alcoholic because he so freely sampled what he was smuggling, and the 'witch' Molly Downer who, having become involved in smuggling, started drinking the brandy involved, and slid further towards her end as a result are examples. Although brandy was much prized in what was also known as 'Free Trading', other substances included gin, tobacco, tea and fruit. All these goods could fetch a high price if there was no excise duty.

Many accounts of smuggling and smugglers are about men, but often family, particularly wives, were involved, just as I'm sure that Sophie's mother, Jane, was, though it doesn't sound as though she sampled the wares. The women were, unlike Molly, more involved in the distribution of the smuggled goods – including hiding them, often when the law called at the house. The men, meanwhile, were responsible for bringing the goods to the Island in their fishing boats. It was not unusual for the goods to be stacked on a raft and left to lie under the surface of the sea until the moment to bring them ashore safely was opportune. This might well be helped by spreading tales about ghosts, as the Nettlestone 'Blue Lady' was, to keep nosey parkers away in the Bembridge coastal area. The Bembridge windmill, built in 1700, and still there, served as a useful marker for incoming vessels. The fittest fisherman could row over to France, usually to Cherbourg and Harfleur, and back in one night, though it was more likely to take two dark and moonless nights. 'Brandy was brought back in small barrels named "tubs" and most of the homes, fields and even church yards along the coast would have hidey holes for stowing the contraband.'

The part involving women should not be downplayed. Typical of one of the ways was that involving the law:

> One such story recounts how Farmer Joliffe told the revenue men that they could search his house, including the room in which his wife was lying in bed, having recently given birth. Although they didn't want to disturb her, the farmer insisted and they entered to find her in bed with the nurse feeding the baby. But all was not as it seemed, as although they did not realise it at the time, the tubs were in bed with his wife and the baby was nothing but a large doll.

Fred Mew, in *Back of the Wight* (1933) tells the same story, with a little more detail, and this time it concerns Farmer Jolliffe who farmed for many years at Luccombe Farm. Farmer Joliffe (or Jolliffe) was a member of the extended Joliffe family, long settled on the Island; one of them farmed at Whitwell in the south-east. It could be that there were two farmers of that name in that area, but as the several places mentioned are very near each other, it was either an extended farm, or one in nearby parcels. A particular smuggling boat captained by a Ventnor man would land the tubs anywhere between Ventnor and Luccombe and they would be taken 'by cart to a farm near Wroxall'. I suspect that was Joliffe's farm. A list of 'Customs Prosecutions 1830–1851' names Elisha Jolliffe and his wife Mary, crime not noted, who were convicted and fined £100 which was mitigated to £25; in default of payment, the husband Elisha Joliffe was committed to the common gaol at Winchester. The census of 1881 gives their dates: Elisha Jolliffe b.1826, aged 55; **Mary Jolliffe** b.1827, aged 54. These may or may not be farmer Joliffe and his wife, or even the Jolliffes found guilty. The name 'Back of the Wight' refers to the area along the south coast of the Island that has a distinct historical and social background and is geographically isolated.

In 'The Old Smuggling Days, Shanklin fisherman relates his experiences' (1932) Derek Stephens remembered other women's smuggling subterfuges. When smuggled goods arrived on the Island, they might be re-smuggled across to Portsmouth in the ordinary packet boat:

> this work [was] carried out by the women folk and [they] concealed the tubs under their crinolines, another trick was for them to carry the tubs wrapped in shawls so to all outward appearances they were carrying infants. One of the best known at this job was a Bembridge woman rejoicing in the name of Nancy Smith, who for a great many years carried on such work under the very noses of the revenue officers, but was never once found out.

Another task that women performed was to decant the contraband into small receptacles for its onward journey. But not all the women involved were as adept, or as lucky as Nancy Smith. 'Victorian Supersleuth' Angela Buckley writes in 'Smugglers' Island', starting with Bembridge:

> Many of the village's women were tried for smuggling. On 9 February 1833, **Harriett Harbor** was caught transporting a half a gallon of brandy in to animal skins and a bladder... . She was fined £25 but was unable to pay, and so spent a month in prison. Harriett had two accomplices, **Mary Anne Fagan** and **Mary Ann Fry**, who were also found to be concealing brandy, but they managed to abscond and were never captured.

In the early decades of the nineteenth century, a number of women on the Isle of Wight were prosecuted for conveying and concealing contraband liquor, which they hid in their baskets or under their voluminous skirts. In 1830, **Mary Sweatman** of Ryde was convicted of smuggling, along with her partner John Stagg. Both were prosecuted for identical crimes, yet Mary received a fine of £50, whilst John only had to pay £25. There was no mercy for any women (or men) who defaulted on fines, and many of the female culprits ended up behind bars for a while. Another female smuggler was **Elizabeth Cooper**, who was convicted of concealing spirits. When her brother faced a similar charge, a local news reporter said, 'Although the family of Cooper is not an extensive one, our bridewell [House of Correction] is seldom without one of them'.

I hesitate to pick Angela up in a slip but, according to the Customs Prosecutions list, Mary Sweatman was not penalised more than her partner, apparently her husband, John Stagg: the fines were the other way round. Elizabeth Cooper was fined £100 for her brandy crime, several previous offences being taken into account. Many of the arrested male smugglers on the list were French, and at least one, Spanish – in one case the French and English on the same arrested boat.

Angela concludes her sleuthing account:

The female Islanders were mainly responsible for decanting liquor from barrels and casks into smaller receptacles such as bottles and pots. They removed the French identification stamps by burning and then hid the goods in places such as a chimney, under false floors, hedges and even in tombstones. Children didn't miss out on the action either, and they were used as go-betweens, passing messages from one family member to another. On the Isle of Wight, smuggling was a real family affair.

When starting the account of the life of Sophie Dawes, Baronne de Feuchères, who features in chapter 5, I was pretty sure the children as well as their mother were involved in that sort of way in the smuggling by Dickie Dawes.

Several of those named on the list were arrested and imprisoned for plundering the wreck of the *Clarendon*. This ship and its end is indeed a sorry story, given much space in reporting. One family, the Wheelers, links two aspects of wrecking: some family members benefitting from the wreck; one was bent on saving lives. The family can add making use of ghosts to their diversity. They lived in Box Cottage, Chale (Back of the Wight). 'Smugglers' Britain: Isle of Wight' shows that it wasn't just the Blue Lady of Nettlestone who performed this function: 'Chale churchyard had a reputation for other other-worldly happenings that were probably deliberate scare tactics to keep [the] nosey local away from stored tubs.'

Between them Warren Whitmore, in 'On this day: The Isle of Wight's most infamous shipwreck the Clarendon hit the rocks off Blackgang in 1836' (2022) and the article posted by Red Funnel tell the story of what happened at 6 a.m. on 11 October succinctly. The *Clarendon*, carrying a cargo of rum and molasses from St Kitts in the West Indies, sank during a howling gale and heavy seas, off Blackgang near Chale, with the loss of 10 passengers and 13 crew. The ship was 'smashed to atoms by the sea' according to James Wheeler, who continued, 'and all … aboard were drowned or killed by timbers, with the bodies being washed ashore to much dismay and sadness'.

Among the passengers was Lt Shore of the 14th Regiment, his wife and four daughters aged between 18 years and nine months; none of them survived. 'Many a tear was seen streaming down the faces of the menfolk present when they saw the bodies of the two Miss Shores washed up and mangled and nude' and in the words of an eye witness who noted the two elder sisters clinging together, 'They were lovely and pleasant in their lives, and in death they were not divided.' Perhaps the most tragic outcome was what became of the body of Miss Gourlay: it was carried away by the tide to Southsea, Portsmouth, where it came ashore opposite the garden of her father, Captain Gourlay RN. Most of the other bodies were buried in the Chale churchyard.

It was thanks to John Wheeler, who had been a Royal Navy man, and was then a fisherman, that anyone at all was saved. When locals saw a full-rigged ship battling against the wind offshore from Chale, he dashed down the Chine at Cliff's End and reached the shore before the crash. He ran into the surf attached to a rope, the other end secured by fellows onshore, and saved three sailors, carrying them ashore from the sinking ship, one of them a former shipmate who, four years previously, he had saved from drowning. If you wonder why he saved the men and not any of the women, as I did at first, I imagine that they were on deck trying vainly to avoid the catastrophe, while the passengers would probably have been below still asleep.

Timbers from the ship were used to build local houses, including the Clarendon Pub, which was renamed in its honour, but has now reclaimed its previous name: The Wight Mouse Inn. An *Island Echo* posting, 'Caulkhead Family Names' records: 'Wheelers Bay in Ventnor – that was allegedly closely associated with the looting of shipwrecks – is said to have been named after the eponymous Wheeler family.' About the Wheelers, and excepting brave John, it says, 'The name is famous (or infamous) due to its connection with a well-known South Wight smuggling or wrecking family. In the nineteenth century Robert Wheeler had logged 70 wrecks.' As so often, names can confuse: Fred Mew writes of the *Clarendon* catastrophe:

> As I write this chapter I have before me a copy of a log kept by James Wheeler from 1746 to 1808, and which in a few words describes some 60 wrecks which occurred in Chale Bay during that time, and one wonders why some effort was not made to have a light of some sort placed there so that some of that loss might be avoided. Was it because the people in the neighbourhood benefitted? Perhaps so. It was not till the wreck of the Clarendon ... that anything was done.

A lighthouse was built at St Catherine's point; it is still there. Mew gives the most detailed account of what happened, even describing John Wheeler as a 'tall, weather-beaten ex-man-o'-war man'. That may be based on fact, or it may be fanciful, though his book is not a novel, but deeply researched, often drawing on his own memories. It does, however, bring the man closer to the reader, so much so that I wanted to know more about the Wheeler family. Assuming I have found the right John Wheeler (b.1808), his mother's name was Mary Joliffe; his father's name is not given. His wife's name was **Elizabeth Wheeler** (née Groves, Mottistone; 1810–1878), they married in 1833 in Newchurch and had a son called James and one of their daughters was **Frances**, or Fanny (married Tansom; 1843–1901). I pick her out because the Peggy Nisbet Dolls website lists some of their named dolls with brief biographical details. One of them is Fanny Wheeler who was 'reputed to assist her father in gathering contraband goods. Her father was a "wrecker" who made his living plundering shipwrecks off the coast of the Isle of Wight'. I hope I am not being too fanciful in following the smuggler-wrecker family through at least one generation: from Mary Joliffe to John Wheeler to Fanny Wheeler.

Prostitutes, 1800–1853

Sophie Dawes seems to pop up everywhere. You may remember from chapter 5, 'Irregular Relations', that, as a young girl, she spent time in the Newport Workhouse, and that sources, and I, are careful not to call her at any stage a prostitute – the term 'working woman', a more modern term, might apply. That was even though, when she arrived in London, she worked as an 'actress' in the Covent Garden area and then had work of some sort in a high-class brothel and was a kept woman by at least one rich man. Eventually, she was won at cards by the Duc de Condé and was his mistress for many years in London and as Baronne de Feuchères at his properties in France until his death in 1830. But an Internet posting, 'The Legend of Sophie Dawes' taken from JR Bummell, *The Ballad of Sophie Dawes*, describes what went on in the so-called House of Industry (workhouse):

> Prostitutes scrubbed floors (hence the term 'scrubber' that has persisted into our own times). Shortly before the Dawes arrived, one prostitute was given two weeks solitary and had her hair cut off; two more were publicly whipped. By the 1830s when four prostitutes bound for transportation to Van Diemen's Land (now Tasmania) were returned to the workhouse for bad behaviour, Sophie had long gone.

Adrian Searle went into detail about what an unsavoury place that workhouse was, and it is clear now that, just as Sophie was influenced by her father's breaking the law as a celebrated smuggler, so she is likely to have been influenced by what went on around her in the workhouse. She was able to work out a way to rise through the ranks from prostitute to courtesan to long-term mistress, rich and titled, and navigate any barrier put in her way.

It was not uncommon for women or girls to become pregnant either before being sent to the workhouse or, it seems clear, while they were there, and it does not seem that there was much distinction between 'bastardy' and prostitution, as 'Workhouse Burial Ground information Panel' (nd) posted on the Isle of Wight NHS Trust website suggests: 'For unmarried mothers with responsibility arising from "Bastardy" or a reputation for prostitution supervision and training for employment was given and the fathers were instructed to make paternity payments to the Workhouse.' Alan Champion, in 'Some Facets of the Isle of Wight Medical History', writes of an 1814 Committee finding:

That Martha Macket a nurse in the House, be dismissed from her situation for having admitted soldiers into the house at night, permitting them to bring liquor and to spend the night with prostitutes under punishment. In 1826 the Committee is requested to set aside some particular room or rooms for the occupation of the loose women who may be admitted to the House.

Some public houses were prone to attract prostitutes and their clients. Newport's most notorious pub was the Tontine in South Street, located opposite the present-day bus station. In the nineteenth century it was both a slum and the red light district. As 'Isle of Wight Pubs' (2023) explains:

With a thousand-or-so soldiers at Parkhurst barracks, those engaged in the world's oldest profession were never short of clients.

The Tontine public house was at the epicentre of the then Isle of Wight sex industry. It was the 1st port of call for the police after any criminal activity. It was perhaps tolerated by the authorities to keep social problems in a single part of the County Town.

Court reports record numerous immoral activities in and around the Tontine. … For example, in 1853, prostitute Ann Baker was charged with being drunk and disorderly in the vicinity of the Tontine. The following year, Caroline and Ellen Pearce were found guilty of soliciting in the street where the Tontine was located. Also that year, 4 soldiers from Parkhurst barracks were charged with breaking into the house of a prostitute in the Tontine yard.

Newport, then, as now, the main town, seems to produce more information about prostitution than elsewhere, but there was more than one pub in Cowes, as mentioned in the 'Cowes Historic (Pub) Walk' (nd) posted by the Brewery History Society concerning the former Victoria Arms in Brunswick Road. While it was waiting to be demolished it was 'broken into at night and inhabited by women of bad character, thieves, monkeys and organ grinders.' The 'Bricks and Mortar' piece notes of the Boathouse that:

this cottage was built to accommodate servants working at Stanhope House, and a boat. It was allegedly once rented out to a lady who ran an aristocratic 'disorderly house' during Cowes week in the 19th century – the authorities approved as prostitution was contained to this house, and police ensured that nobody but the gentry were allowed in!

Stanhope House belonged to **Lady Frances Joanna Stanhope** (b.1849) and **Lady Blanche Georgina Stanhope** (1861–1939), unmarried daughters of Charles Wyndham Stanhope, 7th Earl of Harrington. Their mother, **Elizabeth**

Still Stanhope, Countess of Harrington (née de Pearsall; b.1822), eloped with their father at the age of 16, and died in Cowes in 1912. The Stanhope women are unlikely to have known what went on in their servants' quarters, though it is possible that the 'gentry' who visited the Boathouse were also entertained at Stanhope House. Don't you just love the distinction between the classes!

7 – Religion and Philanthropy, 1228–1934

Introduction

Since perhaps the mid-twentieth century, the United Kingdom has become an increasingly secular society, at least as far as mainstream Christianity is concerned. In the past philanthropy tended to be religious, and there were two main branches of Christianity, Roman Catholicism and Protestantism. The purpose of their existence, wherever they found themselves, was particular to each, sometimes it was to the glory of God; for others it was activity in their community. Henry VIII's sixteenth-century Dissolution of the Monasteries plays its part here, as do laws against, and expulsions of, the religious, both in Britain and abroad. Sometimes that meant the arrival on the Isle of Wight of established orders of nuns; sometimes it was individual women creating convents or building churches or, in one instance, both. This chapter will be only somewhat chronological, but also, where the subject or people seem to dictate, divided into sections. Typical of these are the activities of the intermarrying families of, Player, Lind and Brigstocke which made a difference to the town of Ryde. Its members, particularly its women, may have been religiously inspired, but what they achieved can also be described as philanthropy.

Mainland Abbeys and Island Manors, pre-Dissolution of the Monasteries, 1228–1539

Amice de Clare, Countess of Devon and her daughter Isabella de Fortibus were introduced in chapter 3, 'Women of Property'. As a result of their property on the Island and, indeed, Isabella's position as Lady of the Isle, they were in a position to do as they liked with their property. That is how the Island's Manor of Shorwell, part of widowed Amice's property on the Island, came to be 'given in alms' to the Augustinian nuns of Lacock Abbey in Wiltshire. The abbey was founded by Ela, daughter and sole heiress of William, Earl of Salisbury, and granted its royal charter in January 1230. The details that follow are to be found on *British History Online*, 'Houses of Augustinian canonesses: Abbey of Lacock'.

Ela assumed the nun's habit of abbess at the beginning of 1238, and she remained in this position until 1257, when she resigned the office in favour of Beatrice of Kent. It was while Beatrice was abbess that Amice's daughter, **Margaret de Redvers** (b.1240), became a nun at Lacock, prompting Amice to grant Shorwell to the abbey. There is no reason to suppose that Abbess Beatrice or other Lacock nuns ever visited Shorwell, perhaps not even Margaret after she assumed the habit; she seems then to have become a non-person to the outside world. It can be assumed that the abbey rented out the manor's farms and from that, and what the farms produced, it derived some of its income; Shorwell was not its only grant, though the only one on the Island.

When Isabella inherited the Island, as part of her administration, she confirmed her mother's grant. She may well have corresponded with Lacock's abbess. But later, particularly because of the distance between Lacock and Shorwell, there were years of legal dispute and the nuns were unable to recover possession until 1516, when Joan Temmise, the last abbess, brought a successful suit in Chancery. But Henry VIII's dissolution of the monasteries followed soon after and, in 1539, Joan officially surrendered the abbey and all its substantial possessions to the King's Commissioners. Shorwell Manor will re-enter the story of the Island's women in due course. Charles Cox, in his 1911 book on Isle of Wight churches and religious houses notes that Amice, as well as her involvement with Lacock Abbey, was said to be responsible for building St Swithin's church in Thorley. It was pulled down in 1871.

The relations between Ashey Manor and Wherwell Abbey of Benedictine nuns in Hampshire were similar to those of Lacock Abbey and Shorwell Manor, though there was less Island involvement. Once again a useful source is the *British History online* website under 'Ashey Manor'. The Island manor was granted to the abbey before 1228; included in that grant was Langbridge Manor, situated within Newchurch parish and historically linked with Ashey. In 1291 the grant 'was of the considerable annual value of £41 6s. 2d'. It is unclear who originally granted it. But the inclusion of Langbridge was confirmed to the abbess of Wherwell by Pope Gregory.

The abbey had been founded in about 986 by Ælfthryth, widow of King Edgar. She retired there to live a life of penance for her part in the murders of her first husband Æthelwald and her stepson King Edgar. By the time Ashey Manor was granted, it seems that Euphemia de Walliers, niece of Queen Matilda, was abbess and by the time she died the number of nuns had risen from 40 to 80. In 1535, when it became known that there was to be the Dissolution of the Monasteries, Morvethe (Morphita) Kingsmill (*c*.1500–1570) was elected abbess to see the convent through the process. It was she who leased Ashey Manor to Giles and **Elizabeth Worsley** in 1538. After the dissolution in 1539, Worsley continued as tenant and collector of dues until the grant of the manor to him by the Crown in 1544.

Unattached Religion and Philanthropy, 1520–1792

Should you happen to be in Carisbrooke village and planning to visit St Mary's Church, you may well note there a rather striking marble funeral monument; striking because it is not just of one woman: the central standing figure is surrounded by several others – six figures, three on each side, all disabled. It is celebrating the life and work of **Margaret Wadham** (Isabella; née Seymour; 1468–1513 or *c*.1520). As well as being the second wife (m 1501) of Sir Nicholas Wadham MP, Captain of the Island (1509–1520), and governor of Carisbrooke Castle where they lived, and where she died, she was the aunt of Jane Seymour, Henry VIII's third wife, mother of his only son. Her relatives and her husband are rather better known than Margaret is: all that remains of her is the effigy and the inscription that 'She founded a hospital for the infirm.' But the effigy speaks volumes.

16. Lady Wadham's funeral monument, St Mary's Church, Carisbrooke village, photograph by the author

If you are in Arreton, three miles to the south-east of Newport, you may be hungry or thirsty, or you may just be intrigued to come across a pub called The Dairyman's Daughter in the Craft Centre. It is named in honour of **Elizabeth Wallbridge** (*c.*1770–1801) who was religious in her own way. She would not have become known about were it not for the Revd Legh Richmond, curate of the nearby parish church of Brading and a religious writer of the period. Having interviewed her, he wrote her story as the 'Dairyman's Daughter' which appeared in tract form in 1814, issued by the Religious Tract Society.

Until she was 26, Elizabeth was a worldly young woman of Arreton, born to respectable parents who, being poor (presumably her father was a dairyman), were obliged to send their daughters into domestic service. It is not clear if Elizabeth was one of those; certainly she does not seem to have become sub-servient, as she is also said to have been wilful, proud, selfish and irreligious. But then she heard a sermon which changed her life: she became devoutly religious, showing herself to be highly intelligent, with a retentive memory that allowed her to master religious classics. As at the same time she became ill, she had the leisure to study, becoming remarkably knowledgeable about the Bible. She said of her spiritual experience, perhaps written, perhaps in her interview by Richmond:

Often I mourn over my sins and sometimes have a great conflict, through unbelief, fear, temptation, to return to my old ways – I was laughed at by some, scolded by others, scorned by my enemies and pitied by my friends, but I forgave and prayed for my persecutors, and remembered how very lately I had acted this same part toward others myself.

This seemingly complicated young woman was dead by the age of 31. She had shown a noticeable heroism during her illness, and her selfishness had become altruism in a simple way that obviously attracted Richmond to interview her. Following her burial, in the churchyard of St George's Church, Arreton, her grave became a place of pilgrimage, visited by Queen Victoria, perhaps more than once; even the chair in which she sat to be interviewed was cherished. It is fair to suggest that today the pub is more visited than Elizabeth's grave.

That church itself is the burial place of another spirited, if not spiritual, Island woman – Dowsabel Mills, who featured in chapter 5, 'Irregular Relations'. My main purpose in visiting the churchyard was to find a particular yew tree, dating back to 1740, the significance of which is that it was planted by **Gladys Jolliffe** as a memorial tree. She is said to have been buried in the shade of the tree, together with many of her descendants. Unfortunately, I was faced by many trees which seemed to be yews and no sign of Gladys. It would seem that she married William Hearn in 1751 and they had 10 daughters and 10 sons, so quite a few immediate descendants; she was left widowed in 1792. Pretty well all inscriptions in the churchyard have become unreadable. You may remember from chapter 6, 'Outsiders', that farmer Jolliffe and his wife, Mary, were a smuggler couple. In due course, Gladys of the Jolliffe cobbler family of Cowes, will appear, the Jolliffes being obviously a long-lasting, wide-spread, multi-purposed and extensive Island family.

Roman Catholic Churches and Convents, 1791–1879

The Catholic Relief Act, which came into law in 1791, allowed Roman Catholics prepared to take the oath the freedom to worship and to build churches in which to do so. **Elizabeth Heneage** (née Browne; 1734–1800) wasted no time.

She was born in Sheat (pron. Shate) Manor, Chillerton, near Gatcombe, to John and **Mary Browne** (née Urry). She was their only child and it was from her uncle, Thomas Urry, that, in 1777, she was to inherit Sheat, as well as other properties. She was educated at the famous Convent school for girls in Hammersmith, London, where the nuns were secretly disguised as lay women. In 1761 she married James Heneage, from an ancient Lincolnshire Catholic family. The couple's two daughters were to go to the same Hammersmith school, and then to a convent in Paris. When the daughters married – to two Catholic brothers – their sister-in-law was the famous Maria Fitzherbert, secret Catholic wife of the Prince Regent.

Peter Clarke, of the Isle of Wight Catholic History Society, in his article 'Elizabeth Heneage (1734–1800)' suggests that in the time of Thomas Urry, the manor house

> was reputed to have contained a secret chapel in the attic, where Mass was occasionally said during penal times. The escape routes for the priest, behind the chimney and out through a tunnel into the garden are still evident today. We have no record of the number of Masses that were said. It is unlikely to have been many, due to the Island's isolation. The family supported the local Anglican Church and they were popular in the farming community of the area so that they kept a low profile and did not draw attention to themselves. However their neighbours would have known where their sympathies [lay].

When I intruded on the family living there today, in spite of interrupting their lunch, which eight-year-old James was quick to point out, I was kindly shown the priest hole door, presumably obscured in its day.

When James Heneage died in 1786, widowed Elizabeth travelled widely in France and England. But she did return frequently to the Isle of Wight and, in due course, bought a house at 96 Pyle Street, Newport, and settled there. With the passing of the Act, Elizabeth had built St Thomas's Church in the garden. Costing £2,000, it was erected the other side of a smallish lawn from the house, which is now the presbytery, and is, outside, in the simple Methodist style. What is now the confessional was Elizabeth's private chapel which she would enter simply by crossing the garden from the house.

The complex is easy to find, entered by a wooden door in the street. When I arrived, it was just being unlocked to let a group in, but I gathered that you only have to apply to the presbytery for entry. Just inside the door of the classically simple church, to the right is where Elizabeth was buried in 1800. On the flat marble slab covering her grave is the inscription, to be found in Michael Hodges' 'An Ode to the Isle of Wight's intriguing Catholic Churches' (2021):

> Poor in Spirit amidst her Opulence From her infancy Mercy grew up with her … and she opened her hands to the indigent. Munificent in erecting and adorning Sacred Edifices And bountifully assisting others in the like works In the last Day She shall not fear the evil hearing … For alms will not suffer the Soul to go into darkness … REQUIESCAT IN PACE. Amen.

Elizabeth may have opened her hands to the indigent – she made charitable donations far and wide – but Clarke reminds us of how things were ordered in her day:

> Sunday Mass witnessed rich and poor worshipping together, but the deferential attitude prevalent in Victorian society was evident even in the churches. Seat rents were a useful source of income. There were six grades of rent at St Thomas's. The upper classes rented pews nearest to the sanctuary. Poorer

folk occupied the side aisles. The military from the barracks at Parkhurst usually went into the gallery. So everyone had their place according to their class and station.

Five years after the opening of St Thomas's in Newport, Elizabeth built a similar church in Cowes, also dedicated to St Thomas of Canterbury. 'She believed that one of the knights who were sent by Henry II in 1170 to murder the famous medieval saint, came from the Isle of Wight. Therefore this was a fitting act of reparation.' (See chapter 4, 'Troubled Times'.)

Although **Elizabeth, Countess of Clare** (1793–1879), a Catholic convert, is known for having paid for the building, 1846–1848, of 'the rogue church of great strength and originality', St Mary's, Ryde (the Church of the Sorrowful and Immaculate Heart of Hearts), she is remembered for rather more. Born Elizabeth Burrell, daughter of Peter Burrell, 1st Baron Gwydyr, and Baroness Willoughby de Eresby, daughter of the 3rd Duke of Ancaster, in 1826, when she was 23 she married John Fitzgibbon, 2nd Earl of Clare. The attraction for him may not only have been intellectual but her £30,000 fortune. It was not, however, a successful marriage and, in 1829, they parted amicably. Her husband had developed a crush on Lord Byron at Harrow, one that continued, and which seems to have been mutual if the poem 'To the Earl of Clare' is anything to go by. It certainly caused a bit of a scandal and, in 1831, he was to become governor of Bombay, dying in 1851. Following their separation, Elizabeth, for the sake of her health, no doubt a euphemism for avoiding the scandal, spent time at a hotel in the fashionable resort of Sandown, introducing her to the Isle of Wight.

For a fuller account of her life and work than what follows, a useful source is once again provided by Peter Clarke, 'Life of Elizabeth, Countess of Clare – Foundress of St Mary's Church, Ryde'.

In 1840, Elizabeth went on a Grand Tour of Europe and was converted to Catholicism in Rome in 1841; she then settled on the Island, in an apartment at 4 Brigstocke Terrace, Ryde, to engage in what was to become a life devoted to the church she had built, the foundation stone of which was laid in 1844. St Mary's Ryde included a presbytery and school and the cost to Elizabeth was £18,000. She also paid the salaries of the school teachers. That was only the start, though her work was not always appreciated by the wider, mainly Protestant, community; as Clarke writes 'The building caused some consternation among the people of Ryde when a "Roman" church of some grandeur quickly appeared in a prominent position in the centre of their town.' Undeterred, Elizabeth also gave funds for the building of a Catholic Church in Ventnor (Our Lady and St Wilfrid).

Elizabeth did not live alone but from 1839 shared her apartment with her close friend **Charlotte Elliot** (*c.*1787–1861). Jan Toms ('Janisleofwight') in the article 'Countess of Clare – Marriage, Love, Good Works' is less discreet than Clarke: she writes under the heading 'Finding Love: Meeting Miss Elliot':

Perhaps the Countess found the daughter she lacked. Perhaps she had finally found the romantic love that never blossomed inside her marriage but soon the pair became inseparable. Together they planned their lives, including a joint grave in the vault of St Mary's. This however was vetoed by the local authority for health reasons.

Clarke describes Charlotte as Elizabeth's 'lady companion' and 'an upright and distinguished looking Prussian lady'. She was also very generous towards the poor.

But she died of a heart attack while at her devotions, in 1861. She was aged 74, according to that year's census, which also give her as head of household; Elizabeth, aged 68, is called a visitor, but also as 'fundholder'. She had with her two elderly servants, joining the others of the household: lady's maid, cook, housemaid, kitchen maid, butler and page – another glimpse of a Victorian life, no matter how pious their employer.

In spite of stipulating a simple funeral, what Charlotte got was anything but and, in spite of a raging storm, many people of Ryde lined the streets along which the cortège passed on its eight-mile journey to St Mary's. Elizabeth, left distraught by her death, followed it up by petitioning for a Catholic section in Ryde cemetery. With the loss of her companion, she became something of a recluse, rarely seen in church; instead, she arrived with nieces, nephews and household and climbed the stairs to attend Mass in her private chapel above the sacristy which overlooked the sanctuary. This did not stop her donating far and wide, including to the building of a hospital in Ryde. And still her work was not done.

A convent of Dominican nuns, founded in the thirteenth century near Toulouse, had, by 1861, been invited to return to London, having been expelled from there 300 years earlier by Elizabeth I. When they decided to spread further, Countess Elizabeth stepped forward and in 1865 she invited the nuns at Stony-hurst to move to the Isle of Wight. Once again, a separate piece by Peter Clarke, 'St Dominic's Priory, Carisbrooke' is a thorough guide. Warren Whitmore's 'On this Day: Nuns Took Residence of their Carisbrooke Catholic Convent' (2022) is the livelier. Elizabeth spent £12,000 (over £1.6 million today) to have the priory built; it was completed at the end of 1866, and the nuns were invited to travel to the Island. As Whitmore tells it, The Revd Mother Prioress recorded at the time of her arrival at the Convent:

We arrived at Carisbroooke via Southampton on 10th December 1866 after some adventures on the way, not least the hoots and jeers, especially as we disembarked at Cowes. Our nuns' habits caused much amusement and laughter especially amongst the children.

The nuns were said to have responded to any hostility on their journey in a dignified manner with a simple smile.

Although the convent was a closed community, Queen Victoria, while resident at Osborne House, was invited in 1869 to visit the priory and accepted, in spite of resenting the revival of Catholicism and the influence of the Pope upon English Catholics. However she accepted, and was warmly received, causing her to mellow somewhat, although she did whisper to a lady-in-waiting, 'What a pity that these ladies have not got something useful to do'. What she did not realise was that the prioress had asked the nuns to put aside their embroidery and needlework and to listen carefully to the queen, which they did, standing completely motionless.

As it happens, those Dominican nuns were famous for their embroidery. As the text beside a photograph of it in the Carisbrooke Castle Museum, notes,

[They] not only created new vestments but their skill and care helped to preserve rare historic pieces by remounting them on new back fabrics. Often the nuns who create these sorts of garments are anonymous so it is unusual that we know the names of many of the nuns who in the early 20th century worked on specific items in the collection.

After the queen's first visit, she was to visit again, accompanied by Princess Beatrice who, when she became governor of the Island and lived in Carisbroooke Castle, visited often. Her visits helped to make the presence of the convent and nuns more acceptable to the community. The nuns' most important visitor, though, was Elizabeth who, in her later years would travel, on important feast days, the seven miles from Ryde, taking her maid and cook. She was allowed to choose the menu, cooked and served by her own staff, and to join the nuns for the meal. When she died in 1879, and was buried in the nearby cemetery, the nuns cared for her grave and prayed for the repose of her soul. Over the years that followed there were increasingly fewer nuns, and the convent closed in 1989. Of the five nuns who had remained, a ninety-year old had not been outside the convent for seventy years. The priory is now a non-denominational place of prayer and healing.

Dominican nuns on the Island were followed by Benedictines, a silent order, one devoted to divine worship and the contemplative life. In 1901, France enacted anti-clerical laws which meant that the nuns of Ste-Cécile de Solesmes (revived in 1833) had to leave France and it was to Northwood House in Cowes that they initially moved. This safe haven was thanks to Edmund Ward of the eminent Ward family who negotiated with them a five-year lease. The London merchant banker George Ward had acquired what was Bellevue House in Cowes in 1793. Six years later he demolished most of it and built Northwood House; he proceeded to buy more and more land on the Island.

By Edmund Ward's day, the family did not live in the house; it was used for soirées and other such functions. There is something delightfully contradictory about those held there before it became de facto a convent: in 1886 The Royal Yacht Squadron held its annual ball there, not for the first time, with the Hungarian band playing. Among those who attended were the Prince and Princess of Wales, the Crown Prince and Princess of Germany, Princesses Victoria, Margaret and Sophia of Germany, the Duchess of Edinburgh, Princess Louise, Prince Henry of Battenberg, Prince Albert Victor, Prince George, the Princesses Louise, Victoria and Maud of Wales, Princess Irene of Hesse and the Maharaja of Cooch Behar. In August 1889, a grand Garden Party was held to raise money for the organ and vestry fund of the Cowes Holy Trinity Church with a similar guest list. Music was provided by the band of the Oxfordshire Light Infantry, and Lord Colville's black poodle received much praise for collecting money for the appeal, by wandering among the guests with a money-box round its neck. Perhaps a more poignant contrast was between two newspaper reports. On 17 January 1891, *The Hampshire Telegraph and Sussex Chronicle* published a report of a ball at Northwood House for 180 guests, among whom was Princess Beatrice who

> wore pearl-grey satin and pearls, the Duchess of Cornwall wore a pink and white; and the Princess Louise wore a lovely yellow silk, with sprays of purple violets. Two grey gowns attracted much attention. One was figured in deeper shades, and the other was cunningly combined with pink, but a very handsome yellow brocade was, perhaps the most notable of all. The supper was most excellent and the champagne undeniable. Altogether, no pains had been spared by the Royal hosts to make the ball what it was – an unexampled success.

In August that same year, a headline in the *Isle of Wight County Press* of 24 August read 'ARRIVAL OF BENEDICTINES IN THE ISLAND'. The convent had only one nun who could compete in eminence, though perhaps not in dress. Princess **Adelaide Sofia Amelia of Löwenstein-Wertheim-Rosenberg** (1831–1909) was born in Bavaria to the hereditary Prince and Princess Agnes of Hohenlohe-Langenburg. She married Miguel de Bragança, the former occupant of the Portuguese throne, but only following his deposition. That did not prevent her, as a widow, securing advantageous marriages for their six daughters. In 1895, two years after that of her last daughter, Princess Adelaide, a devout Roman Catholic, retired to the abbey of Ste-Cécile de Solesmes in north-western France, becoming a nun in 1897. She was to be generous in financing the convent in its moves. King Edward VII and Queen Alexandra made a special visit to Northwood House and took Mass in the chapel with Adelaide, a distant relative. As **Mother Maria Benedicta**, she became prioress when the convent moved to its permanent site in Ryde, and died there in 1909, aged 78. As for dress, there is a telling contrast between a photograph of her as a young fashionably dressed and coiffed woman, and another taken in later life in a nun's habit.

While Northwood was being readied for 80 nuns, who arrived from France in batches, they stayed at the Fountain Inn, which had been established in 1793, and which was also owned by Ward. They were not simply to 'stay' in Northwood, nor only to take it over for a period, but to re-purpose it, as well as renting 40 acres of land. They organised the building of a chapel next door to the house, bringing over from France the organ, the harmonium, the grille which separated the choir from the lady chapel, the stalls, the bells and the marble altar. The whole was built of brick to a certain height, above that the walls were of wood lined with slab plaster; it was a replica of that in France, but reduced in size and, as it was only a temporary structure, it took only three months to build. It was used for the first time in April 1903.

It was a great boon to be shown round Northwood by Tim Wander (already introduced in chapter 6), to have explained, standing in the ballroom, for example, how it was remodelled as a chapel, until the building was complete, and how much of the remainder of the house was altered to cater for the nuns' particular needs. It was possible to imagine the chapel, standing where it had been; this is helped by the plans and a drawing of the impressive completed building which Tim Wander showed me. Interestingly, there seem to have been no complaints about the nuns' tenure, or even about the chapel bell being rung every seven minutes over 24 hours.

As the convent's Northwood House lease was coming to an end, the nuns made ready to move to what was to become the Abbey of St Cecilia in Ryde. Northwood House was again left empty until the First World War when it became an auxiliary hospital, perhaps sufficiently described in chapter 6 under the section on ghosts. The ownership of the house by the Ward family came to an end after nearly 150 years in 1929.

That year, the house and grounds were given to the people of Cowes (to help with substantial death duties and taxes) as a municipal property, handed over by Herbert Ward to Princess Beatrice, governor of the Island. By the early 2000s, the council had clearly lost interest in the sprawling 200-year-old mansion, which required an increasingly large amount of renovation, repair and upkeep. There was even a risk that the house would be demolished or become an 'old people's home' or a 'golf club'. But a group of dedicated local women raised the money to secure the building and estate, and set up a Charitable Trust in 2012, which has undertaken an impressive restoration programme, bringing the house back into daily use as a community, entertainment and wedding venue.

The convent, looking for a new home, had bought a large house in Appley Rise, to the far east of Ryde, formerly occupied by a notorious smuggler. The nuns' move there from Northwood House took over two months – the two places being run in tandem – and the whole venture must have been interesting to follow. Everything within the chapel and, indeed, parts of the building itself, were transported in vans pulled by little steam engines, while the nuns travelled by boat. Soon a church and cloisters were built, solemnly dedicated to St Cecilia in October 1907. Once these were established, the nuns continued their contemplative and studious life, which included working in the garden and orchard, keeping bees, producing beeswax for candles, practising specialised calligraphy and baking altar bread to raise revenue.

In 1922, the French law was changed and, after an exile of 20 years, the nuns were able to return to France; the Appley Rise convent became occupied instead by the Benedictine community known as Pax Cordis Jesu, daughter of the Liège Abbey, which was founded in Ventnor in 1882 to pre-empt an anti-clerical law in Belgium.

To visit St Cecilia Abbey today is to find a well-established convent. It is possible to sit inside the church and so see the altar brought over from France, and the grille to keep the nuns separate, allowing them to concentrate on God. Although it is a silent order, we asked a nun cleaning the floor how to find the shop and she not only replied but even, when asked, gave us her name. And in the shop, the nun in charge, as we bought several books, was prepared to answer questions. We learned, for example that no outside visits are allowed except for medical necessity.

Benefactors of Ryde: Player, Lind and Brigstocke, 1705–1934

When we turned into Lind Street in Ryde, I assumed that it was named after the renowned singer Jenny Lind, the 'Swedish Nightingale', and that she sang at the theatre in the street. Not so, though Ellen Terry is thought to have started her acting career there, and Dorothy Phillips (Mrs Jordan, the long-term mistress of the future William IV) also appeared. By coincidence, Jenny Lind did sing on the Isle of Wight, at Osborne House before Queen Victoria in 1847, 1855 and 1856, as well as possibly in both Dimbola and Farringford in Freshwater. In fact the street was named after Dr John Lind, a physician at the Royal Naval Hospital at Haslar, across the Solent in Gosport. He and his descendants were to intermarry with those of the brewer Henry Player who made his fortune in Gosport selling beer to the East India Company. In 1705, he settled on the Island, purchasing the Manor of Ryde and Ashey from the Dillington family, so becoming Lord of the Manor and, with John Lind, to create a dizzy-making family tree. But the two families were also, as owners of much land and imagination, to turn the two villages of Ryde, the lower one devoted to fishing, the upper one to farming into a prosperous and fashionable town, across the Solent from the naval town of Portsmouth, through the buildings, such as churches, for which they were responsible. The Brigstocke family joined the enterprise later. It is, of course, the women who are of particular interest here.

Before the families of Player and Lind were joined, the woman of note was **Jane Player** (1738–1826), daughter of Peter and Sarah Wynne of Orpington in Kent. She married William Player, grandson of Henry, founder of the Isle of Wight family dynasty, and they had at least seven children. When William died in 1792, Jane took over possession and administration of the Player properties, including Ashey and Ryde Manor. One of her projects was to begin to grant leases for building. These were at first granted on the new road which William had laid, joining the two villages, previously separated by 12 acres of woodland. In 1801 it became Union Street, and more development followed in the 1810s when Jane's son George Player and son-in-law John Lind settled in the town and took an active interest in its growth. Jane split her husband's legacy equally between her heirs, determining the future Player and Lind estates so fairly that some streets were split lengthways to give them one side each. You can see a pleasing portrait of Jane standing in front of a tree online; it comes from a Wynne family album,

John Lind had chosen to leave the densely populated Portsmouth to live in a quieter, more exclusive area of Ryde. In 1789 he married Jane Player's daughter **Elizabeth Lydia Player Lind** (1764–1845), thus forging the link between the two families and the land they both owned. They had one son, and five daughters. The couple built a house called Westmont which is now part of Ryde School. Elizabeth was the main benefactor, supplying both land and finance (£1,500) for the building of Holy Trinity Church, and she laid the foundation stone in 1841. Difficulties arose when the church reached street level, but the venture was saved by the intervention of the brother of Elizabeth Countess of Clare, who was visiting Ryde at the time. The church was consecrated in 1845. The first vicar, the Revd Wade, later wrote an impression of a still unfinished town: 'On the first Sunday in November 1845, I preached the first sermon. Upper Dover Street was partially formed, there was no thoroughfare to Star Street – opposite was still fields with hedgerows – cattle were feeding there.' Elizabeth was buried in the crypt. The Linds' only son, James, married but had no children, so that, with him, the Lind direct line ended. Several of this sisters, though, continued to live in Ryde after marriage.

St Thomas's Church in Lind Street was to become something of a community hub. The original simply built chapel there was erected in 1719 by Jane Player's father-in-law, Thomas. He was concerned that there was neither chapel nor church in Ryde, its inhabitants having to travel to the church in Newchurch, a difficult journey in winter. He built St Thomas's chapel, and set aside land for a churchyard for burials. George Gale, in his piece 'Churches and Chapels in Ryde' remarks that, 'The erection of the chapel so soon after the Players had acquired the Manor could be regarded as the first step by the Family towards the development of Ryde'. Jane obviously left the family's finances in good shape: a year after her death in 1826, her son, George Player, had the original chapel pulled down and a new St Thomas's built in its place at the cost of £3,500. Gale continues to explain,

> The new chapel like the old was the private property of the Lord of the Manor. [It] had a gallery for the 'lower classes' with special areas set aside for girls and boys to sit where they could be supervised by their schoolteachers. The Lord of the Manor had his own large box pew with its own entrance from the churchyard. There were other family box pews ranged along the sidewalls; these pews had high panelled sides to give protection from the draughts.

George Player and his wife **Mary Ann Player** (*c*.1763–1839) named one of their daughters Elizabeth Lydia; it was she who was to bring the Brigstocke family into the frame by, in 1822, marrying Captain Thomas Brigstocke, becoming as she did **Elizabeth Lydia Player Brigstocke** (1796–1871). The ownership of St Thomas's, which has the coat of arms of the Player family over the central door, passed then to Thomas and Elizabeth Brigstocke, and remained in the Brigstocke family until 1956. Among their children, they had a daughter also called Elizabeth Lydia, whom, to avoid further confusion, I shall ignore. But their best known daughter (who remained unmarried) was **Mary Harriette Player Brigstocke** (1824–1904).

Mary Harriette, usually known simply as Miss Brigstocke, inherited St Thomas's church, which she set about beautifying, in particular having installed three side-by-side stained glass windows. There is plaque nearby (installed later) which reads:

These windows were erected by
MARY HARRIETTE PLAYER BRIGSTOCKE
Of Stone Pitts, owner of this chapel
She was the eldest daughter of Captain T.R. Brigstocke R.N.
and Elizabeth Lydia his
Wife,
Born January 18th 1824
And died November 21st 1904
When these panels were added in memory of her

Miss Brigstocke was to become the archetypal philanthropist; some of her projects were large, some small; they were also eclectic. Was she approached or did she go round sniffing out what was needed? In 1868 Ryde became a municipal borough, at which point the corporation decided it had to have a clock tower; it was Miss Brigstocke who provided the clock itself. In 1873 it was a water trough for horses on the Esplanade (Swanmore Road) which remained in place until the restructuring of the area in the early 1960s. Was it because she loved horses? An image of it is to be found on the Internet entry 'Memorials & Monument on the Isle of Wight – Ryde – Brigstocke Trough/Fountain.' The trough bore the inscription:

PRESENTED BY
MISS BRIGSTOCKE
OF STONE PITTS
TO THE BOROUGH
ALDERMAN EDWARD MARVINE J. P.
MAYOR
1898

In 1891, Miss Brigstocke set about her most important and ambitious project, founding The Brigstocke Almshouses. They were set up in Player Street to house six 'poor aged women, either Spinsters or Widows, inhabitants of the said Parish of Ryde, who were persons of good repute and blameless poverty'. They still exist with charitable status and their website describes them. There are six self-contained flats with a communal front terrace and rear garden with lawn and flower beds. To be eligible to apply a woman must be aged 55 and over and fully capable of independent living. A person appointed as a resident is a beneficiary of the charity, not a tenant.

In 1900 Miss Brigstocke offered to find the money required to purchase the Simeon Street Recreation Ground. An illuminated address was presented to her by the Council on the occasion of the deeds of the ground being formally received by the mayor.

The quirky side of Miss Brigstocke was revealed following what happened in 1932. That December, a fire started in the Lind Street town hall which spread until it became a conflagration. Much was lost, including several valued paintings, but among those that were saved was one of Venus – the Roman goddess of love, beauty, desire, sex, fertility, prosperity and victory – which had been donated by Miss Brigstocke. As well as her particular projects and contributions, she is known to have supported various local sports and athletics clubs, as well as contributing to animal welfare. She died in 1934, aged 80, having lived a notably good life, and having made generous use of Player money. She was, of course, buried in St Thomas's Church. I cannot find any funding connection between the family and the building of Brigstocke Terrace just behind the church.

Was Miss Brigstocke inspired by another woman's almshouses built nearly half a century earlier? Ryde Social Heritage's 'Ryde Architecture' Internet posting tells of how one of the charitable works of **Augusta Wilder** (1802–1858) was the erection of almshouses in Newport Street in 1855. One, not surprisingly, was for the poor; the other was a monument to the memory of her dead husband, Francis Boyle Shannon Wilder. It bears a plaque dated 1854 with his name. Augusta managed the almshouses herself, admitting whom she pleased, 'making her selection entirely from persons who were resident in Ryde and were natives of the Isle of Wight'. They should also be 'a widow or spinster of good character and repute, and not less than 60 years of age'. They should also be a 'member of the Church of England, or a Protestant Dissenter, acknowledging the Eternal Godhead of our Blessed Saviour and Redeemer Jesus Christ'. She arranged that on her death the vicar and churchwardens of the parish should be in charge of nominations. When she died in 1858, aged 56, ' her good deeds were long to be cherished by the poor, who had lost in her a true friend'. The rest of the history of the almshouses and those who lived in them, is noted in that same posting. To the reader, or indeed, the writer, more familiar with London than the Isle of Wight, the transfer of elderly ladies in 1972 from the almshouses to the Elephant and Castle might seem confusing, but there was a place of that name in Green Street, Ryde. It was not uncommon for women with money to bequeath sums to the poor.

In 1869 construction was started on the parish church of All Saints, for which I can find no Player, Lind or Brigstocke connection either, but it was contemporaneous. Its corner-stone was laid by Princess Christian of Schleswig-Holstein, otherwise known as Queen Victoria's daughter Princess Helena. It became a landmark in 1881/2 when its spire was added, being visible from many places around the Island, and from the mainland. That it was very much a parish church is illustrated by the involvement in it of the Colyer family of three unmarried sisters who, my visit to Ryde revealed, lived a few houses away, at Cromwell Lodge, 75 West Street. When the three were introduced to me by family, it was as Dolly, Flossy and Maude. Dolly was **Alice Constance Colyer** (1870–1951); Flossie was **Florence Emma Colyer** (1874–1955); and their younger sister was **Maude Colyer** (1882–1956), and they were the daughters of Frederick Colyer and **Ann Tyser** (1843–1912). They are worth mentioning as an example of a middle-class family born in Ryde and buried in Ryde cemetery, and with a certain degree of wealth, not only shown by their house, but also by what they left at probate. Their mother left £2,022 6s 11d; Dolly £5,268 10s; and Flossie £8,832 11s 5d (about £175,000 today). Given that today the house could accommodate six people, they may well have had a couple of live-in servants. When Flossie died in 1955, the *Isle of Wight County Press* wrote of her:

> She took a keen interest in the welfare of All Saints Parish church. At one time she was a member of the Parochial Church Council, and for a quarter of a century was in charge of the distribution of the parish magazine. For about 15 years she gave valued assistance to the local branch of the Girls' Friendly Society, and also helped the Soldiers Sailors and Airmen's Families Association.

This photograph of the sisters shows how they dressed and did their hair as they aged. It was taken, at a guess, between the wars.

17. The Colyer sisters, courtesy of Penrose Halson

Foundation of Independent Schools: Blue Jenny, Countess Spencer, Elizabeth Sewell, 1761–1906

When visiting the Carisbrooke Castle Museum, which is a must, on your way upstairs, and in a niche on the left, you should look for a large figure of a girl dressed in a blue uniform. This is Blue Jenny, and it used to stand over the façade of the Blue School, which was established at 19 Lugley Street, Newport in 1761; the school moved to Crocker Street in 1886, and ran until 1907, when the charity encountered financial difficulties. When in the 1970s the statue had withstood the elements for too long, it was removed, renovated and brought inside, while a replica carved in 1980 was put over what had been the school.

18. Blue Jenny, from Carisbrooke Castle Museum, photograph by the author

The school was named after the colour of the girls' uniform; as a text near the statue explains, each girl was clothed 'in a manner suitable to her station' and they were given a new uniform by the charity every year. They were also given a Bible and prayer book which can be seen in 'Jenny's' right hand. Religious education was very important: it was believed that the lack of this was responsible for 'all kinds of vice and idleness' in poor girls. All aspects of the school were inspected by a local vicar, and church attendance was compulsory, all this in the hope of preventing 'unsuitable behaviours'. You could be expelled for offences that included theft, 'impertinence' and 'obstinacy'. The morals of the girls were well and truly safeguarded. If they got through all that, they would be found a place in domestic service, and if they stayed for a year, they would be rewarded with £1. How one would like to hear the voice of even one girl who went through the system, or even of a teacher. I have found no evidence suggesting who was behind the founding of the original charity and school, or if at any stage there were women on the charity's committee or board. Upon the school's closure the premises were purchased by the Newport District Nursing Association as a War Memorial Home as a memorial to those who fell in the First World War; the tablet to the right of the door records that.

The details behind the founding of the next school to be described were rather different. It was the project of one determined and highly intelligent woman with the ability to raise the necessary funds: **Lavinia Spencer, Countess Spencer** (née Bingham; 1762–1831). She was the eldest of five children of the Irish peer Charles Bingham, 1st Earl of Lucan, and his wife, portrait miniature painter Margaret Smyth. Lavinia herself was to become better known as an illustrator than as the founder of a school in a small but growing town on the Isle of Wight. As for her work as an illustrator, the only apparently well-known piece is 'A Pinch of Snuff', which is to be found in *Women painters of the world from the time of Caterine Vigri 1413–1462 to Rose Bonheur and the present day* (1903), edited by Walter Shaw Sparrow.

Although she lacked a dowry, George Spencer, Viscount Althorp, fell madly in love with Lavinia and they married in 1782. The following year, his father died and he inherited the title of 2nd Earl Spencer. There followed a distinguished career for him in Parliament, including as Home Secretary between 1806 and 1807. Meanwhile Lavinia, as well as having nine children, became a pre-eminent hostess in London society, important and beautiful enough to be painted by Joshua Reynolds. Of her character there are conflicting descriptions by two historians (Malcolm Lester, positive; Amanda Foreman, negative) which, as they are presumably based on gossip of the time, probably cancel each other out.

In 1810, life was to change, and perhaps to be intellectually more fulfilling for Lavinia: her husband acquired the lease of four acres of land to the west of Ryde and built a marine villa. Theirs was the first in the area and Spencer Road was named after the Earl, or perhaps even Lavinia! Although there is still a three-storey Althorp house in the road (and another called Spencer Lodge was demolished in the 1970s), their house was Westfield which, after the Spencers' time, was the home of the Spencer-Clifford family for over a hundred years; in the mid-Victorian period it was probably one of the leading houses and gardens in Europe. **Augusta Caroline Clifford** (1836–1931) – after whom Augusta Road was named – took over Westfield and lived there until her death. It was later converted into flats. These details are thanks to the posting by the Ryde Social Heritage Group, 'The Changing Face of Ryde' in their helpful 'Beyond the Graves' series.

The Spencers became worshippers at St Thomas's, where altruism was rife. Lavinia became aware of 500 children in the town under the age of 15. As the posting 'Churches and Chapels in Ryde' relates, 'She immediately set to work': she persuaded the Player family to grant a lease of land to the east of George Street – in what is now Melville Street – at a peppercorn rent for the erection of a school. A little more digging produces a sprinkle of feminine gold. It was not simply 'the Players' whom Lavinia approached, it was 'the Lady of the Manor to give a piece of land'. The Lady in question would have been Jane Player, introduced above; since 1792, she had been Lady of the Manor. The two would undoubtedly have met through St Thomas's. The land was then fields on the edge of town.

Having cleared that first hurdle, Lavinia had plans prepared, and then set about seeking assistance in raising funds to enable the first school for boys and girls to be constructed in Ryde. On 31 August 1812, she opened the school to accommodate 220 boys and 120 girls, who would previously only have had access to Dame Schools, in which often elderly women taught the young children of tradesmen the basic 'Three Rs'. Lavinia's school, known as the 'Ryde Free School', was funded by voluntary contributions and by charity sermons preached twice yearly at St Thomas's. In the church, there is a memorial, a diamond-shaped tablet, to 'Lavinia, Countess Spencer' bearing the Spencer coat of arms.

When the school ceased to be a school, it was known as the Vectis Hall, a much-loved community dance hall, but, though of great heritage, it was left empty, neglected and then became derelict. In due course something had to be done. Some of what follows was reported by the committed journalist Sally Perry, editor of *Wight News from On The Wight* and from a 2021 piece in the *Isle of Wight County Press* describing the £125,000 raised by selling the building to Ryde Town Council. This shows the aces held: 'Ryde council agrees to buy hall donated to town by Princess Diana's ancestor' which, lest there be any doubt, is spelt out in more detail: 'Lady Spencer was Princess Diana's great great grandmother.' And what is more, 'I hope that Prince William comes to open it when finished.' What was to be created in some ways harks back to Lavinia Spencer's project: 'This grant will enable us to go to the next stage and have a viable plan to seek major funding so it can be re-built with a sustainable community use for the benefit of all residents.' One of the proposals was for a young people's employment project. Sadly, the building is now in very poor condition. One of the experts involved in the process is Tim Wander, so helpful to my Northwood House (Cowes) work. He is also currently very busy as the Project Manager for the renovation and part-conversion of the nearby St Thomas's Church into a community centre for Network Ryde Youth Services. This will provide a much needed safe, secure and warm space for many disadvantaged children in the very centre of the seaside town.

The impetus behind at least one of the schools established by **Elizabeth Missing Sewell** (1815–1906) in Bonchurch, Ventnor, was deeply religious, as well as a commitment to learning. Of her earlier education, she wrote of her time at Miss Crooke's school in Newport, 'When my regular lessons for the day were over, I used to sit until bed-time with my back to the long table, on which two candles were placed, and learn by heart columns of French idioms' But she also wrote, as detailed in *The Autobiography of Elizabeth M Sewell* (1893; 1907):

> We learned Pinnock's Catechisms of History and Geography ... For Religious instruction we read portions of the Old Testament, and the Gospels, and Acts of the Apostles in a class every day, using Mrs Trimmer's Selections.

The first edition of her autobiography was printed privately by Elizabeth herself to correct some representations of her family, the second was added to and edited by her niece Eleanor Sewell. Details for Mrs Crooke elude me, but her school seems to have been active between 1819 and 1828. There is even less information about Mrs Trimmer. But it seems clear that Elizabeth's schooling contributed to her religious interest; she is better known for her prolific writing, including religious and educational texts, and religiously imbued novels, than for her schools. She was born to Thomas Sewell, solicitor of Newport, sometime mayor of the borough, steward and deputy governor of the Island, and agent for Lord Yarborough, and his wife **Jane Edwards** (1773–1848) and was the third of five daughters and seven sons. Elizabeth's unusual middle name honoured a godmother, Miss Missing. When she was 15 Elizabeth left formal education, then at a school in Bath, and she and her older sister **Ellen Sewell** (1813–1905), also at school there, home-schooled their younger sisters. Their brothers went on to have distinguished careers, one the first premier of New Zealand, another the warden of an Oxford college and, yet another, Reader in Law at the University of Melbourne. In 1840, when she was 25, Elizabeth's clergyman and author brother William introduced her to some leaders of the high-church Oxford Movement which eventually developed into Anglo-Catholicism. Her first religious publication was in 1842, in *The Cottage Monthly*: 'Stories illustrative of the Lord's Prayer'. It seems to have been the first of her religious or religion-infused publications, many of them novels. Regarding others' views of her life, Montague Charles Owen's *The Sewells of the Isle of Wight* (1906) is useful. In 1852, Elizabeth published *The Experience of Life*, a novel based on her own observations. Daisy Plant includes details of her in *A History of Women's Lives on the Isle of Wight* (2019) which focuses on women living on the Island between 1850 and 1950.

The apparently comfortably-off, educated, middle-class family, which had access to two holiday homes as well as a solid house in Newport High Street, was to experience serious money difficulties when two Newport banks failed; their father died in 1842, deeply in debt. The children, by then grown up, undertook to pay off the creditors, Elizabeth by setting aside a sum each year from her literary earnings. Jane and her daughters moved to Ventnor, and then, in 1844, to Bonchurch, a steep thickly wooded area of east Ventnor. There they were involved in charity work in the local parish, and Elizabeth continued writing, by then profitably enough to fund the furniture for a new Bonchurch church – she also played the organ there – which opened in 1848, the year of their mother's death.

During her charity work, Elizabeth noted that the only schooling available to the children of the area was Sunday School. The sale of her published stories and Ellen's sketches contributed to the establishment of the Bonchurch National School, endorsed by the Church of England's National Society for Promoting Religious Education. The sisters managed to raise about £200 (around £16,000 today) and the school, for girls up to the age of 13, opened in the late 1840s or early 1850s. It was run on similar lines to the Blue Jenny School described above, that is, poor girls being kept on the straight and narrow by being educated for domestic service. The Sewell school is described by Rosa Raine, over several pages, in the style suggested by the sub-title of her book, *The Queen's Isle, Chapters on the Isle of Wight wherein Church Truths are blended with Island Beauties* (1861) of which this is but a snippet:

> This training is far more valuable than that of an Industrial School; for it gives the girls a knowledge of the habits of the upper classes and makes them competent to enter at once upon service in gentlemen's families; besides which they are first learning to be independent; and faults, which might be ruinous in after-life, are discovered and checked by those who have an influence over them.

The Sewell sisters' work brought into operation, as Rosa quotes from a communication by Elizabeth to the Royal Commissioners on Education, 1861: 'The great element of personal influence, without which it is in the ordering of God's Providence that no lasting moral good shall ever be effected.'

The other school set up by Elizabeth was more personal, and provides some more revealing and straightforward – amusing, even – quotations. After their mother's death, Elizabeth had taken over the family's finances. Finding that her writing was insufficient to keep them, she and Ellen decided to open the school in their Bonchurch house, Seaview, which she bought and enlarged in 1854; its name was later changed to Ashcliff. Bonchurch School was to be small and select, taking in middle-class girls, not more than seven at a time (sometimes ten), and several of the girls passing through were nieces. The sisters did not see it so much as a school, more 'a family home'. Elizabeth was not interested in examinations; she had her own methods of education: her students were to read widely, and take an interest in issues of the day; she taught general history, Ellen taught music, singing and drawing – she was a pianist as well as an artist. Elizabeth's teaching was enhanced by travels within Europe, sometimes taking her students with her; she spent five months in Germany and Italy, and wrote of her impressions, and was in Germany again on the outbreak of the Franco-Prussian war. She described her teaching methods in *Principles of Education, drawn from Nature and Revelation, and applied to Female Education in the Upper Classes* (1865). The girls who passed through the school were not only made familiar with the humanities but also imbued with Elizabeth's religious teaching and example.

Two of the students, at least, wrote about their time at the school. Her niece, Mrs Hugh Frazer (**Mary Crawford**; 1851–1922), wrote *A Diplomat's Life in Many Lands* (1910) and Kate (CM) Whitehead wrote *Recollections of Miss Elizabeth Sewell and her Sisters* (1910); the latter is rather inaccessible. In spite of Elizabeth's Victorian sensibility, her entry in *The Oxford Dictionary of National Biography* says that her influence over her students was helped by a 'dry sense of humour' which was not, it would seem, always apparent. Kate Whitehead reported that evenings were devoted to reading aloud and discussing various books; sometimes arguments ensued, such as that between partisans of Queen Elizabeth and Mary Queen of Scots, but they were all Royalists when it came to Charles I. Elizabeth also read aloud to them. Mrs Frazer later wrote, calling Miss Sewell 'Aunt Elizabeth', as all the girls did:

The only unpleasant incident of my whole stay in Bonchurch was connected with the evening readings. The book in question was 'Cranford' and we were all electrified when Aunt Elizabeth came to a full stop in the beginning of the part where the nephew plays a practical joke – something connected with a baby – on the old ladies, 'I will leave this out,' said Miss Sewell, looking quite stern. Then she turned the page and took up the story further on.

Miss Sewell, by mistake, left Mrs Gaskell's novel on the table in the drawing room, with the inevitable step taken by a new girl from a rich family in business: 'Alas, poor Rosie could not resist the temptation. When I came into the room the next morning I found her devouring the forbidden page.' Poor Rosie was expelled. At least the other girls stood by her:

Oh, that was a terrible day! We all cried ourselves blind, nobody wanted any dinner, all the girls came forward to plead for the culprit, confessing that they had been 'just dying' to do the same thing. But the aunts were relentless, they said that Rosie, with her bar sinister of trade, had had no opportunity of learning what honour meant, and they should never have taken her in. They were very sorry for her, but she must leave Ashcliff.

Which she did, poor girl, and we thought the sentence terribly severe, but our respect for early Victorian principles was enormously increased, and the sense of having, in desire, at least, shared the banishment one's crime, kept us all very humble for a long time afterwards.

'Bar sinister' usually meant that her parents were not married, but I deduce that in this instance it meant that her parents were in trade rather than the professions. Oh dear! It would be good to know Rosie's last name and what happened to her in later life. A hunt for that has proved fruitless, even in Sarah Cutts Frerich's dissection, chapter by chapter, of Elizabeth and her life posted on 'Victorian Web – Literature, history, & culture in the age of Victoria' which has been helpful in providing quotations from the writing of others. To know more about Elizabeth Sewell than is provided in this chapter, this is the place to go, and it is easily accessible.

When **Emma Sewell** (1818–1897), another of Elizabeth's sisters, died in 1897, Elizabeth fell into a depression. As her health deteriorated over the years until her death, former pupils rallied round to look after her. She died in Bonchurch, aged 91, and was buried in the cemetery of the parish church. It is worth going to the slight trouble to find Ashcliff house and to see the blue plaque there.

A good photograph of the house heads Julia Courtney's piece in the magazine *Island Life*, 'Writing the Wight: Three talented women' (2018) which not only includes Elizabeth Sewell and the writer Mary Gleed Tuttiett, who will appear in chapter 10, 'Women Writers', but also, and helpfully, leads into the next chapter. The third woman is Anne Thackeray Ritchie, a denizen of the Freshwater Circle, which was dominated by Alfred Lord Tennyson, his wife Emily and the photographer Julia Margaret Cameron. Sarah Cutts Frerich's work shows the value of Elizabeth's contribution by what she wrote on this connection, drawing on Elizabeth's journal:

By her own choice she never made the most of the possibilities for literary associations that lay so close at hand. In 1857 began an acquaintance with Tennyson whom she characterised as 'almost a friend … simple and warm-hearted and unspoilt by the world.' Unfortunately what Elizabeth has chosen to preserve for the reader concerning his visits has to do with the discussion of drawings made for him by Ellen Sewell.

8 – Freshwater: Dimbola and Farringford, 1853–1928

Introduction

Anne Isabella Thackeray Ritchie (Anny; 1837–1919), mentioned at the end of the last chapter, was one of those women who straddled the two Freshwater houses – Dimbola and Farringford – the denizens of which, and the famous visitors to them, are often dubbed 'The Freshwater Circle'. Some of the characters in this chapter were attached more closely to one or other of the houses. Most typical are the servants, visitors and models of the pioneer photographer Julia Margaret Cameron who lived at Dimbola. So it makes sense, but only where appropriate, to separate the two houses, particularly as Anne, known as Anny, was close to Julia Margaret, as well as friends of the owners of Farringford. That stately house was the home of Emily Tennyson and her husband the famous poet, indeed, Poet Laureate, Alfred Lord Tennyson. Freshwater, on the far western coast of the Isle of Wight, may have been more famous because of the poet, but it was his wife who held together all aspects of the life that enabled him to write his poetry. She plays an important part in the Farringford half of this chapter; Julia Margaret Cameron rules supreme over the first part – Dimbola.

Dimbola: Julia Margaret Cameron, Relatives, Visitors and Models, 1860–1875

Julia Margaret Cameron (1815–1879) was born in Calcutta, the fourth of ten children (of whom only seven daughters survived into adulthood), of James Peter Pattle, a senior lawyer and judge in the East India Company, and his French wife Adéline Marie de l'Étang. Her grandfather looked after Louis VII's horses and riding stables, and was allegedly exiled to India for 'excessively flirting' with Marie Antoinette. At the age of three, Julia Margaret, the name by which she was known all her life, was sent to live with her maternal grandmother in Paris and Versailles where she was privately educated, and then in London. When she returned to Calcutta aged 18 she was seen as without the beauty of some of her sisters, but very clever and talented. To escape the not-always-appreciated climate in Calcutta, the family would spend some months of the year in South Africa. There, too, Julia Margaret was sent to convalesce from an illness, and there she met Charles Hay Cameron who was also there recuperating. He was a British barrister doing well in the legal community of Calcutta, and had bought land in Ceylon (Sri Lanka) to establish coffee plantations; they married in 1838. Julia Margaret was well regarded in all communities, and was known for having raised relief funds for those suffering from the 1845 Irish potato famine. When, therefore, the Governor-General's wife did not accompany him to India, she was asked to take her place as his hostess at Government House.

When Cameron retired from the Supreme Council in 1848, the couple moved to England where Julia Margaret's sisters, Sara, Maria, Louisa, Virginia and Sophia had already established themselves in society. Of those who are to reappear, Sara Pattle married Henry, known as Thoby, Prinsep, a director of the East India Company; her Little Holland House salon was where many of those who are later to be found visiting Tennyson at Freshwater gathered, and were photographed by Julia Margaret. Maria Pattle married Dr John Jackson. Their daughter **Julia Prinsep Jackson** (1846–1895) was married first to Herbert Duckworth and, following his death, to Leslie Stephen, whose wife had also died. Their daughters, were Virginia, later Woolf, and Vanessa, later Bell, the artist. **Virginia Woolf** (née Stephen; 1882–1941) was, therefore, Julia Margaret's great-niece; she is to become involved, in her own particular way, in this story. Lesley Stephen's first wife was Harriet Minny Thackeray, sister of Anny Thackeray Ritchie, daughters of William Makepeace Thackeray and Isabella Gethin Shawe.

(You may not think it but I've tried to keep things as simple as possible. As far as unpublished sources I could draw on, I'm grateful to Jane Richter for helping me to untangle the trajectory of these families; her own several sojourns in Calcutta enhanced the film she made about Julia Margaret, starting with her life in Calcutta: *Cameron, Coffee & Calcutta*. Also of help was Ian Calder's unpublished talk on Julia Margaret given at the Athenaeum Club in September 2023; it was given not only in connection with the Club's Photographical Society but also because so many of its nineteenth-century members were photographed by Julia Margaret).

The Camerons settled on the Isle of Wight in 1860, naming their house Dimbola, after one of the plantations on Ceylon. At first the house consisted of two separate parts, which Julia Margaret joined with a short tower. Charles was often absent tending his plantations, leaving Julia Margaret behind. The story is told that her daughter, thinking she needed 'an amusement' while her husband was away, gave her a camera in 1862 (when she was 48). From that sprang her increasingly accomplished photographs. But, in fact, she had become interested in photography in South Africa where she moved in rarefied circles that included not only her future husband, but also the astronomer Sir John Herschel. He had described the action of sodium hyposulphite to 'fix' silver salts (1819), a vital contribution to the chemistry of photography, and, in 1839, went on to describe a method of printing images on paper. He kept in touch with Julia Margaret during her photographic career; indeed, they were close friends. She converted a henhouse in the grounds of Dimbola into her photographic studio, and used a coal store as her dark room. She liberated the hens and hoped they weren't eaten. She wrote in 'The Annals of my Glasshouse' of her initiation into becoming a photographer:

> I did not know where to place my glass box, how to focus my sitter, and my first picture I effaced to my consternation by rubbing my hand over the filmy side of the glass

But she learned by her mistakes; indeed she was her own harshest critic and destroyed more than she kept. Yet she was adamant throughout her career that apparent imperfections, such as smudges and scratches, were integral to her work, and increased the value of the photograph. She never touched anything up, and from that developed her own unique style.

Julia Margaret was not only a pioneering photographer, she was also particularly formidable and determined. While it seems to me that most of her myriad photographs were of women and children, perhaps that is because I was writing about them. But her subjects certainly included many famous men. When Henry Wadsworth Longfellow came to visit Tennyson, as so often happened he was roped in to be photographed. As the distinguished American poet left for Dimbola, Tennyson advised him, 'You will have to do whatever she tells you. I will come back soon and see what is left of you'. Tennyson himself had been unable to resist his forceful neighbour; indeed, the story is told that when it came to being vaccinated, and he tried to avoid it, she chased him round the garden, or perhaps up the stairs where he was hiding, shouting 'coward, coward'. This was probably a game that she played with a man whom she admired and with whom she had an obviously close relationship. Other male admirers giving in to her blandishments included John Herschel, Thomas Carlyle, Charles Darwin, Robert Browning, John Ruskin, Dante Gabriel Rossetti, James Abbott McNeil Whistler, Sir Henry Taylor, GF Watts and William Makepeace Thackeray.

In 1862, when Thackeray was anxious about his daughter Anny's state of health, he sent her to stay with his long-time friend Julia Margaret, thus beginning Anny's love affair with the Island. She wrote of those first days at Dimbola, as reported by Julia Courtney:

> Cuisine was not a priority, and guests ate eggs and bacon for every meal, but I cannot tell you how much we enjoy it all. Of a morning the sun comes blazing so cheerfully, and the sea sparkles, and there is a far away hill all green, and a cottage which takes away ones breath it looks so pretty in the morning mists.

Becoming a member of the so-called 'Freshwater Circle' led Anny to pronounce, 'Everybody is either a genius, poet or painter, or peculiar in some way. Is there nobody commonplace?' Others suggest the quotation belonged to someone else, but Anny takes authorship of it in a much later letter.

When Anny's father died in 1864, Julia Margaret went to London to bring her back to Dimbola and, together with Tennyson, already also a family friend, they sought to console her. Anny was to become a well-known author, as well as custodian of her father's literary legacy. In her 1885 novel, one of several, *Mrs Dymond*, she introduced into English the proverb, 'Give a man a fish and you feed him for a day; teach a man to fish and you feed him for life'. In 1874, she bought The Porch, close to Dimbola and, in 1877, she married her second cousin, Richmond Thackeray Ritchie, an up and coming civil servant in the India Office. He was knighted in 1907, so Anny is sometimes known as Lady Ritchie, though I'm not sure that she used the title herself. They had two children. Although Richmond was 17 years her junior, he died five years before her, in 1912. The Porch, which I suspect is the cottage that had taken her fancy on her first visit, was the family home until 1919 when Anny herself died. Unfortunately, it was destroyed by bombing in the Second World War. In a 27-page paperback – *I lived in Julia's House* (2010) – Joan Brading Grayer describes how she and her sister watched in horror from the window of Dimbola as a bomb dropped yards away, destroying The Porch.

Anny's pronouncement about the 'Freshwater Circle' is repeated in a letter she wrote from The Porch in 1918, and contained in *Letters of Anne Thackeray Ritchie* (1924), edited by her daughter **Hester Ritchie** (1878–1960). Anny's step-niece, Virginia Woolf, was to write her obituary and to be her literary executor. The character Mrs Hilbery in Virginia's novel *Night and Day* is said to be based on her. And according to Henrietta Garnett's biography, *Anny: A Life of Anne Thackeray Ritchie* (2016), Virginia learned a lot from Anny. The back cover of that book shows what seems to be the most reproduced of the few photographs of Anny taken by Julia Margaret; the 1870 original is in London's Victoria & Albert Museum. She wrote of her step-aunt:

> She will be the un-acknowledged source of much of what remains in men's minds about the Victorian age. She will be the transparent medium through which we behold the dead. We shall see them lit up by her tender and radiant glow. Above all and for ever she will be the companion and interpreter of her father, whose spirit she has made to walk among us not only because she wrote of him but because even more wonderfully she lived in him.

That photograph of Anny by Julia Margaret has her sitting side on, looking into the distance and formally dressed as a Victorian woman; it seems quite unlike her usual style when photographing women and girls; men, though, are usually photographed straightforwardly. Friends, family and servants tend to be photographed as characters from biblical, historical or allegorical stories. I have found one other photograph of Anny that is more in Julia Margaret's usual style; it is entitled 'Lady Ritchie and her nieces' and has her sitting wearing a shawl from the photographer's dressing-up box. She is holding a bouquet of leaves and one of her nieces is arranging a laurel crown on her head. It, too, is in the V&A, but the girls are not named.

Going through the large, heavy, lavishly illustrated Thames & Hudson book, *Julia Margaret Cameron: The complete photographs* (2003) by Julian Cox and Colin Ford, I wrote a note to myself about those taken of the same sitter: 'How on earth did they all manage to sit through the many sessions? Where did JMC get the stamina? Why didn't they burst out laughing? There is a bit of sameness about the women; they are not themselves, but a character dictated by JMC – mostly soulful, unsmiling, usually without expression of their own'. Jane Richter, an authority with strong views on Julia Margaret, disagrees with me; of the many remarks she made on reading this chapter, she wrote:

> She was in awe of how they looked – and trying to capture their beauty – both exterior and interior. The interior beauty is as important to her as the exterior. You have used the word soul – that is exactly right – she said as much – she is trying to capture people's souls, theirs, not a reflection of her own. Smiling would have been totally out of place – isn't what she was doing. She was doing what Pre-Raphaelite painters (and others) did – you don't see many smiles there either.

19. Anne Thackeray Ritchie by Julia Margaret Cameron © National Portrait Gallery, London

In the little book, available in the bookshop at Dimbola, you can see many of the photographs that are arranged round several walls of the house, now a museum open to visitors. In *Julia Margaret Cameron* (2016) by Julia Margaret herself ('Annals of my Glass house'), there is one of Virginia Woolf and Roger Fry, taken in 1871, another of Rachel Gurney as a child, posed as an angel called 'I wait'. Rachel's sister Laura later recalled posing for their great-aunt, who photographed them several times:

> Rachel and I were pressed into the service of the camera. Our roles were no less than those of two of the angels of the Nativity, and to sustain them we were scantily clad, and each had a pair of heavy swan's wings fastened to her narrow shoulders, while Aunt Julia, with ungentle hand, tousled our hair to get rid of its prim nursery look. No wonder those old photographs of us, leaning over imaginary ramparts of heaven, look anxious and wistful. This is how we felt, for we never knew what Aunt Julia was going to do next, nor did anyone else … All we were conscious of was that once in her clutches, we were perfectly helpless.'

Laura Guerney (*c.*1867–1946) later married Sir Thomas Troubridge, and **Rachel Guerney** (1864–1920) later married the Earl of Dudley. Another child sitter was **Margie Thackeray** (b.*c*.1863) who, when her mother died, was adopted by her cousin Anny Thackeray Ritchie. Julia Margaret also photographed the children of her only and much-loved daughter, Julia Norman, who died in childbirth in 1873. Gerald du Maurier, father of another child sitter, **May du Maurier** (1868–1934), wrote of Julia Margaret,

> [She] is without exception the greatest character I ever met; I find her delightful but don't think she would suit as a permanent next door neighbour for the next 30 years or so unless one could now & then get away.

Julia Margaret started photographing Virginia Woolf's mother, Julia Stephen, when she was Julia Jackson aged 10. She was said to be her aunt's favourite niece and favourite model; she was often portrayed as herself, rather than a 'character'. As the V&A text says of one such portrait, 'This is one of a series of portraits in which the dramatically illuminated Jackson fearlessly returns the camera's gaze'. You may remember from the last paragraphs of chapter 4, 'Troubled Times', about Charles I's daughter Princess Elizabeth, that Julia was the model for the effigy commissioned by Queen Victoria in St Thomas's church. The sculptor met Julia at Little Holland House and realised she would be perfect She was also a model for the artists GF Watts, Burne-Jones and other Pre-Raphaelites who were other visitors. Watts, indeed, became a permanent fixture there, inviting himself to stay long term. He was commonly known as 'Il Signor'.

20. Julia Margaret Cameron by GF Watts,
© National Portrait Gallery, London

Although Julia Margaret was a bit of a character, being a bit over-neighbourly, even appearing to guests in her work smock, her hands stained by chemicals, it never did to underestimate her, particularly when her razor-sharp wit and ethical sensibilities were needed, as they were when dealing with Samuel Peacock. He was a *nouveau riche* printer, later newspaper proprietor, with suspect views, who could afford to bring his family to Freshwater on extended holidays every year from 1871 to 1875. Kirsty Stonell Walker went to a lot of trouble to track the family down, described in her 2017 piece 'Some Thoughts on Emily Peacock'. Was Peacock bright enough to realise what had hit him in the quotation she found in Brian Hill's 1973 biography of Julia Margaret:

> His daughters were good looking enough to sit for Julia, but their father was an affected individual who was always stressing his devotion to 'the beautiful'. He was foolhardy enough to remark one day to Mrs Cameron that really it would be a good thing if all plain people were quietly eliminated. At which I said to the man, *whom I hate*, 'Then what would become of you and me, Mr Pocock?' She was quite aware, of course, of his proper name.

Being Julia Margaret, she did not bring down the sins of the father on the daughters. **Emily Denman Peacock** (1853–1925) and her sister **Mary Peacock** (b.1851), appear in many of her photographs such as 'The Sisters', 1873. Emily, though, was a particular favourite and it must have thrilled Mr Peacock, who may well have chosen to holiday in Freshwater because the Poet Laureate lived there, when she was chosen to appear in at least three photographs, posing with Tennyson's second son, Lionel. One photograph illustrates Tennyson's poem 'The May Queen', in which she also appears alone. The third verse of a rather long poem reads:

> I sleep so sound all night, mother, that I shall never wake,
> If you do not call me loud when the day begins to break;
> But I must gather knots of flowers and buds, and garlands gay;
> For I'm to be Queen o' the May, Mother, I'm to be Queen o' the May.

In the photograph she holds the garland to her breast, but her expression suggests that her mother forgot to wake her! So well known is this photograph, that it is on a fridge magnet available at the Dimbola shop; she looks at me from my fridge whenever I'm in the kitchen. Perhaps Emily's best-known appearances were as Ophelia, in which she looks suitably fragile. During the time of the Freshwater holidays, Emily studied at Watford College of Art and Sciences, and in 1876 was married in Australia to a Cambridge graduate who was later Professor of Mathematics in New Zealand, where they both died.

However sharp she could be, however formidable she was, Julia Margaret also had a large heart; she also loved having children around her, and missed her own who, by 1866, were grown up and had fled the nest. So it is not surprising that when the plight of **Cyllena Wilson** (1851–1883) came to her notice, she adopted her and took her and her two siblings into her household, educating them and also, inevitably, using Cyllena as a model. Once again it is an exploration, told in a 2018 blog by Kirsty Stonell Walker that helps with details. Cyllena's grandfather was a missionary, minister and translator of the New Testament into Modern Greek, as well as the author of several books about his travels. His son, Cyllena's father, was Arthur Michael Wilson, born in Malta and who, in 1850, married Cyllena Butters from Devon. All started well but then, in quick succession, grandfather, father and mother died, leaving three children orphaned in 1866. But, luckily for them, their grandfather had been a friend of Julia Margaret, so their future was quickly assured.

Most of the many photographs of Cyllena – with her broad, beautiful face, well suited to close-ups – date from 1867, when she was 16; there is at least one taken in 1868. As the blog suggests, 'There is something of the impatient about her, restless and wandering', and stubborn could be added, even when posed as 'Vectis', where she personifies the spirit of the Isle of Wight. In the text under the photograph of Cyllena in 'Study After the Elgin Marbles', the blog notes,

> For Cyllena, posing was a torture, sometimes a little too literally. In order to make her model fully express despair, allegedly Mrs Cameron locked Cyllena in a cupboard for two hours. The posing and waiting was all too much for Cyllena, who obviously had some of her missionary grandfather's wanderlust in her blood. She ran away from Freshwater, getting a job as a stewardess aboard the *Parana*, sailing for New York.

On arrival, Cyllena married John Williams, probably the liner's first engineer, and returned to England, to her husband's family in Falmouth. But he was dead by 1881. Thereafter, it seems that she travelled to Argentina, and married again, perhaps more than once; she died of typhoid in 1883. By 1891 her children were in an orphanage in Surrey, but then both set off for America, the wandering spirit once again to the fore.

While some of Julia Margaret's sitters were family, some inhabitants of Freshwater, and some visitors to Dimbola or Farringford, two regulars were 'maidservants'; and it is they who feature most often among the photographs. It would please Julia Margaret to say that she had not employed **Mary Ryan** (1848–1914) and **Mary Anne Hillier** (1847–1936) for their dusting ability, but for their beauty; they were muses, not maids. That may be why it was eggs and bacon every day at Dimbola. Fanny Cornforth's blog, 'Mary, Mary, Maids of the Tennyson Isle: Julia Margaret Cameron's Marys and her Fantasy made Reality' (2015), is a good, simple introduction to this aspect. There are, of course, several biographies on Julia Margaret that provide more extensive and more serious studies of her life. But sometimes a novelist's perception provides an appealing way to look at particular facets, in this case 'servant' as 'muse', and more. As will have already become obvious, I have not hesitated to introduce novels, and even quoted from them, and sometimes a serious, factual study is not what one feels like reading. There will be readers who object, perhaps strongly, to the mingling of fact and fiction – and I know at least one!

Arresting Beauty (2023) by Heather Cooper follows the bare bones of Irish Mary Ryan's life with Julia Margaret, but fleshes them out by telling it from Mary's own point of view (not a fanciful suggestion because even when the Camerons met her begging on Putney Heath in London in 1859, she was already literate, taught by her late father).

At 10 years old, Mary was already so heart-tuggingly beautiful, and so adept at her pitiful begging, that Julia Margaret, not yet a photographer, could not resist taking her into her household to be brought up as a housemaid. But when she discovered that Mary was literate, she was allowed to join the two Cameron sons who were still of an age to be home-tutored. And when the decision was made to move to the Isle of Wight – Julia Margaret, wishing to be near her friend Alfred Tennyson – Mary was part of the train of family and baggage to travel there. When Julia Margaret started her photography, Mary was one of her first, and favourite, sitters and she photographed her with Sir Henry Taylor as 'Prospero and Miranda' in 1865. One of the problems of treating Mary as she did, as was pointed out to Julia Margaret by Taylor, is that the mismatch between her family background and her employment, with educating her, and introducing her to the famous and erudite with whom she was photographed, did not help her to understand her identity. However, she married well: Henry Cotton, a child of the East India Company, was studying to join the Indian Civil Service when he saw 'Cordelia' kneeling at the feet of 'King Lear', and fell in love. Two years after graduating, he arrived at Dimbola and requested the maid's hand in marriage. During the time of their engagement, Julia Margaret took at least one photograph of them together as Romeo and Juliet.

The couple married at All Saints Church, Freshwater in August 1867 – Mary was 17, Henry 21. Tennyson lent them his carriage, and his younger son, Lionel, was Mary's page (instead of bridesmaids). Julia Margaret and Charles Cameron were witnesses. Thus Mary became a colonial memsahib, as Julia Margaret had been, living in India for seven years and giving birth to a daughter and three sons. When Cotton was knighted in 1902 for his work campaigning for fair treatment and constitutional reforms for plantation workers in Assam where he was Chief Commissioner, she became Lady Cotton and reached towards the top of the social ladder. Back in London, they lived in St John's Wood where they mixed with artists, including Val Prinsep, known as the St John's Clique. Philip Calderon RA, a member of the group and a friend, painted Mary and her children in 1879, when she was 30. She is the height of elegance, wearing an à la mode dress and hat, holding her daughter's hand, two of her sons a little distance away, perhaps kneeling and holding staves, a bit reminiscent of a Cameron photograph. The only version of it that I can find, and a poor reproduction, is in Henry Cotton's *Indian and Home Memories* (1911; p52). Henry continued to have a distinguished career connected with India, and was also an MP. Most of the later details come from the 'Epilogue' to *Arresting Beauty*, suggesting Heather Cooper's very thorough research for her novel.

Of Julia Margaret's other favourite, Mary Hillier, she wrote:

Another little maid of my own from early girlhood has been one of the most beautiful and constant of my models, and in every manner of form has her face been reproduced, yet never has it been felt that the grace of the fashion of it has perished. This last autumn her face illustrating the exquisite Maud – 'There has fallen a splendid tear/ from the passion flower at the gate'. It is as pure and perfect in outline as were my Madonna studies ten years ago, with ten times as [much] added pathos of the expression. The very unusual attributes of her character and complexion of her mind, if I may so call it, deserve mention in due time, and are the wonder of those whose life is blended as ours as intimate friends of the house.

'Maud' was one of Tennyson's poems which he was wont to quote from, or read out loud, at any and every opportunity. The photograph of Mary Hillier which illustrates the poem was taken in 1875, and she is standing against a trellis of passion flowers. She was often photographed as the Madonna, so that sometimes she was nicknamed 'Mary Madonna'.

Mary Hillier came from a different background from that of the 'little Irish begger' Mary Ryan. She was born at Lea Cottage, Pound Green, Freshwater to John Hillier, shoemaker, and his wife Martha Ryall, both from Freshwater. Her sister worked at Farringford as a housemaid of the Tennysons. When Mary arrived at Dimbola aged 14 to deliver a message, Julia Margaret took one look at her, and her fate was sealed.

While Heather Cooper's *Arresting Beauty* is more than credibly the voice of Mary Ryan herself, Canadian Helen Humphrey's novel *Afterimage* (2000) is not so straightforward. It is supposedly, and noticeably, about Mary Hillier and her relationship with Julia Margaret and her husband Charles. But the house is in Surrey, Mary is called Annie Phelan, Julia Margaret is Isabelle Dashell and Charles Cameron is Eldon. Confusingly, when following Annie's thoughts, she is remembering the Irish background, and the grinding poverty that was Mary's Ryan's as her own. Like Mary Ryan, she was constantly preoccupied with escaping her duties and finding a place to read. That appropriation of Mary Ryan's life to superimpose on that of Mary Hillier may not matter, particularly if you do not know of the existence of Mary Ryan. It may even be that, in doing so, the author was making a point. *Afterimage*, with its interesting title, is a more ambitious book as regards style, very psychological, as both photographer and her husband become dependent on the maid who is not only a model, but also a photographic assistant. She is the only one prepared to listen to the husband, who comes to regard her as a daughter and does all he can to ascertain the details of her background. Both novels are worth reading, though of all the novels mentioned in this chapter, I enjoyed the liveliness and cleverness of *Arresting Beauty* most.

An earlier novel, her debut, by Heather Cooper, *Stealing Roses* (2019) can be seen as a preparatory sketch for her later *Arresting Beauty*. It is set in Cowes, where the author has lived since 1981, and is mainly about the life there of the comfortably-off Stanhope family of three daughters whose father has died. Their mother is old-school Victorian, determined that her daughters marry well, which two of them do, and she has her eye on a suitable husband for the third. But Eveline is a free spirit – she will choose who she will marry, if at all. It is 1862 and the first railway line on the Island, from Cowes to Newport, is just being built. The chief engineer of the project is invited to a dinner party because his boss is a family friend. Eveline, an environmentalist before her time, is against the coming of the railway, and becomes a campaigner. When she is won over by travelling in the first train to run, something happens to turn her campaigning into concern for the welfare of the workers on the line.

But all that is the subtext. A photographer has set up shop in Cowes, causing everyone who is anyone to want to have their photograph taken; the Stanhopes are no different. But when they see the family portrait, Evelyn, a bit of a hoyden, to be found climbing a tree so that she can read a book in peace, her hair awry, has spoilt the portrait. It has to be done again and she is fascinated by the process. When she goes to pick up the re-take, she asks the photographer to explain and show her how it is done. She becomes even more attracted, and finds every excuse to escape surveillance to go back and learn more. Taking the family's maid, Jenny, to act as her chaperone, she goes into town to learn all she can, becoming increasingly proficient as a photographer. When it is apparent that the family is living above its means, Jenny has to be let go. But she too has become fascinated by photography and, with the business flourishing, has been taken on as an assistant. The photographer gives Eveline his old camera set-up to take photographs at home. If that isn't a sketch for Julia Margaret and Mary Hillier, I don't know what is.

Perhaps Julia Margaret's most celebrated woman model was the up-and-coming actor **Ellen Terry** (1847–1928) who, at 16, was the same age as Cyllena had been when she arrived at Dimbola. But, by then, Ellen was already married. She and her husband, the already well-known and eccentric artist, 46-year-old George Frederic Watts, were guests either at Farringford or Dimbola in 1864. They had married, a few days earlier, following his painting of a portrait of her during which he became briefly smitten. He expected her, as his wife, to renounce her theatrical life, and instead to act as his muse, and he did, indeed, paint several fine portraits of her, including one as Joan of Arc. It was a marriage not made in heaven. They had been introduced by Julia Margaret's sister, **Sara Pattle Prinsep** (1816–1887), at her Little Holland House salon, and the marriage was destined to last barely a year, releasing Ellen to resume her career, and become famous, eventually being made a dame (DBE). Ellen's 17th birthday was on 27 February 1864, and that is the day on which Julia Margaret took the best known photograph of her. This is entitled 'Sadness', and the pose, with her hand clutching the necklace at her throat, and looking downwards, eyes closed, probably didn't require much acting ability, though she was usually a lively young woman – she often played with the Tennysons' sons, Hallam and Lionel. Julia Margaret had just been given her camera, and the photograph was apparently taken in the Tennysons' bathroom at Farringford, but it may have been taken at Dimbola.

Lynne Truss's farcical novel *Tennyson's Gift* (1996) is set in the same year and features Ellen; indeed, some editions have the 'Sadness' photograph on the cover. When on their honeymoon Ellen rows with Watts at Julia Margaret's dinner table, quoting from a Shakespeare play, a response which infuriates her husband. But the main character is Julia Margaret's visitor Lewis Carroll, under his real name Charles Dodgson, which introduces touches of *Alice's Adventures in Wonderland* into the story: it starts with Julia Margaret painting

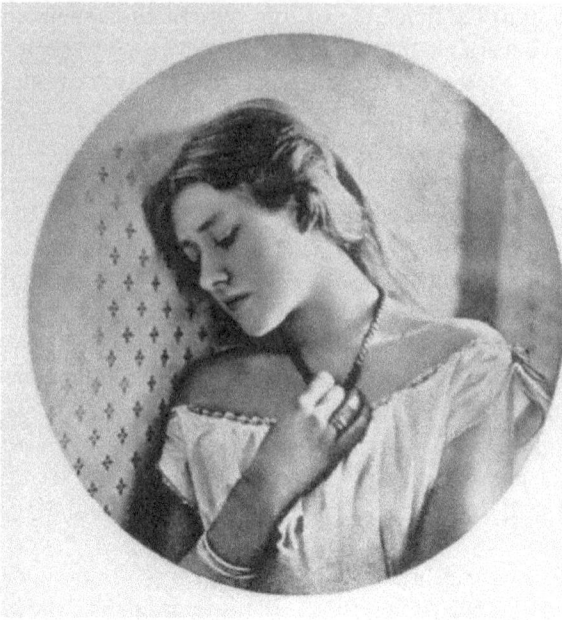

21. Ellen Terry by Julia
Margaret Cameron,
from a postcard

the roses in her garden with red paint while Dodgson watches, mouth open. He is determined to renew a brief acquaintance with Tennyson, his main reason for visiting Freshwater, staying at Holly Tree Cottage. Instead, he is sent demented after visiting the show of an American phrenologist and his precocious daughter Daisy, allowing them, against his better judgement, to read his brain and reveal the opposite of what he hoped for regarding his character. You might assume Lorenzo Fowler is a made-up character; however he did in fact exist, and toured England with his show, although there is no evidence that he visited the Isle of Wight. Daisy, meanwhile, stirs up local young girls to suggest that Dodgson has an unwholesome interest in them. If you like farce, this may well be your light reading of choice. Daisy, under her real name of **Jessie Fowler Allen** (1856–1932), became a phrenologist in her own right; she specialised in child psychology. It should be said that Dodgson was a highly regarded mathematician, and writer, not generally seen as Lynne Truss depicts him.

The usual assumption is that Lewis Carroll's Alice in *Alice's Adventures in Wonderland* (1865) was based on **Alice Liddell** (1852–1934). She was the daughter of Henry Liddell, ecclesiastical dean of Christ Church, Oxford who with his family was a friend of the author, also at Christ Church, teaching mathematics. Alice, too, was photographed by Julia Margaret a dozen times in 1872. The family visited Freshwater on holiday in August and September that year, staying at Whitecliffe House, opposite where Dodgson stayed. The photograph of the 20-year-old Alice as 'Pomona', the Roman goddess of fruitful gardens and fruit trees, the embodiment of fruitful abundance, shows her looking straight at the photographer with what can only be called a mulish expression on her face. She is photographed against the same passion flower climber, as was Emily Peacock as 'Maud'. Taken that same year, was a photograph of Alice with her two sisters, **Lorina Liddell** (1849–1930) and **Edith Liddell** (1854–1876), as King Lear's three daughters.

In much the same mocking vein as *Tennyson's Gift* is Virginia Woolf's only play, *Freshwater*, of which she wrote two versions; the first was started in 1923, but it was abandoned. She then wrote a second version which was not performed until 1935 in Vanessa's studio, directed by Virginia herself, the cast mainly members of the Bloomsbury Group. It is set soon after the death of Virginia's great-aunt Julia Margaret's only daughter when, grief-stricken, she has resolved to sell Dimbola and go with her husband to Sri Lanka. But, although all is packed up ready to go, she keeps prevaricating.

The re-writing of the play is in three acts and, although it is said to be a satire on the Victorian era, it was not performed again in Virginia's lifetime; it was found after his death among her husband Leonard Woolf's papers. It was not published until 1976 by the Hogarth Press which the two of them had set up. It features Ellen Terry resolved that she must leave her husband; what is more, she has recently met a man whom she rather fancies, and plans to run away with him. The play, the two versions sometimes combined, was later to come into its own, translated into several languages. It is now seen for more than it appears – as a study of generational change and artistic freedom. Ellen's flight is seen as symbolising freedom from patriarchy. I have to say that I read both versions one after the other; and obviously did so superficially, not appreciating any of that. I wasn't that impressed. See what you think.

In real life Ellen did leave Watts for another man, and he divorced her in 1877. He built The Briary, near Farringford, where for a while Sara Pattle Prinsep and her husband lived; later Watts himself lived there. He employed as maidservant Mary Hillier, who had faithfully remained with the Camerons until they left for Ceylon in 1875. She went on to marry Watts' gardener, John Gilbert, and have eight children. Her eldest daughter was called Julia after Julia Margaret, and her first son, George Frederick after Watts. She spent the rest of her life in Freshwater, losing two sons in the First World War, and becoming blind from cataracts and possibly the chemicals used by Julia Margaret, before her death aged 88. The Briary burned down in 1934.

Julia Margaret's concerns for the well-being of others also embraced the Freshwater community. When I was driven round Freshwater to visit places of interest on my agenda, the greengrocers at the junction of Victoria Road and Bedbury Lane (and near the thatched St Agnes Church) was pointed out to me as where Tennyson used to shop for his tobacco and, actually, everyone shopped there for everything. Of particular immediate interest, however, were the women of the Orchard family; the shop had been founded in 1865 and, since then, run by five generations of the family. The 1870 letter by Julia Margaret to the Post Office, to be found on an *Isle of Wight Beacon* posting, was about the benefits of the shop to the burgeoning Freshwater community and the need for a local post office there. She recommended William Thomas Orchard as a suitable candidate for local Postmaster and wrote,

> Mr Tennyson's correspondence is very large as you know & my correspondence averages 300 letters every month, my fortnightly correspondence to Ceylon being about 10 to 12s every month. This I tell you to convince you that it is important to us to have a central and convenient Post Office.

> Mr Orchard the other man who applies is at the very foot of Mr Tennyson's Park[,] close also to me and close also to the two large hotels[,] close also to the lodging houses at the Bay & Mr Tennyson himself & I & the landlords of the two hotels all signed a paper to request that Mr Orchard of Freshwater might be appointed Postmaster as he is a very respectable & businesslike man. He has a separate room and hall at Alexandra House fitted for the reception of letters and his locality is the most desirable.

The Post Office campaign was successful, though in 1954 the office was transferred to the stationery shop across the road. As for the Orchard women, at about that time Barbara Orchard joined her husband in running the shop. Anny Thackeray Ritchie's *From the Porch* is disappointing concerning The Porch, Dimbola, or Freshwater: it mostly consists of general articles reproduced from the various magazines for which she wrote, but there is one interesting snippet in an article about the eighteenth-century English painter Moreland: 'Mrs Orchard at the Freshwater Bay Post Office has a charming collection of Morland's sketches as well as some of those of his colleagues and imitators.' Morland, accompanied by his wife, Anne Ward, spent some time in Freshwater in 1799 sketching and painting. He was not there on holiday, though he had holidayed there before, or to paint, but was escaping from creditors and had started off in Cowes. Nevertheless, and not surprisingly, it was a fruitful time artistically. The creditors later caught up with him in Yarmouth. I still hope for further news of Orchard women.

As for Julia Margaret's touching generosity, Ian Calder tells how, in the 1940s, a German refugee researching the history of photography discovered examples of her work in the waiting room of the Brockenhurst railway station in Hampshire (where you still have to change from the London train for that to Lymington and the ferry to Yarmouth).

> It emerged that on 11 September 1871 Julia Margaret had donated prints, including portraits of Darwin, Tennyson and Lewis Carroll, to the station because staff had been kind to her when she was waiting in bad weather for her son to return after a four-year absence. Copies of the prints are still there (in the ticket office), but the originals were lost after being taken to the Southern Railways headquarters in London for safe keeping.

Although is easy to mock Julia Margaret, she is so much larger than life, and she does contribute to some images of her. This is best exemplified by her behaviour when Garibaldi, the much-feted Italian revolutionary, visited not just the Isle of Wight but, in particular, Poet Laureate Tennyson in 1864. He and Tennyson read poetry to each other, the Englishman not understanding a word of the Italian. As Garibaldi planted a tree (that still exists) in the Farringford garden, there was an intervention; what happened next is told, among other versions, in Gerhard Joseph's 'Poetic and Photographic Frames: Tennyson and Julia Margaret Cameron':

Mrs Cameron, her hands blackened with photographic chemicals, rushed up and knelt before them, imploring Garibaldi to come to the fowl-house at Dimbola to have his picture taken. For a moment there was a misunderstanding as Garibaldi took her for an overdressed beggar woman asking for charity. Mrs Cameron, realizing what was passing through his mind, waved her hands in front of him and explained 'This is not dirt but art!' even so he was not persuaded. He planted the little wellingtonia, shook hands with the Tennysons, and drove off, presumably wondering what the purpose of the visit had been.

'Exclaimed' might have been a better word to use than 'explained', such was Julia Margaret's form of communication. Others telling that story say that Garibaldi handed her a biscuit, or a sixpence. Either way, it would have been treasured.

In spite of that, and Julia Margaret often bringing to the Tennysons unwanted and strange presents which they could not refuse, she was the only person outside his family with whom Tennyson was happy to be on Christian name terms.

When the Camerons left Dimbola for good in 1875, they took their coffins with them and settled in their house on the outskirts of Kalutara, south of Colombo, on the west coast of Ceylon (Sri Lanka). Some years ago, after a lot of asking for directions, Derek and I, with a Sri Lankan colleague and friend, visited it, allowing me to imagine life there – Julia Margaret took few photographs on the island, and that was not my purpose in tracking her down. From there, she and Charles could travel up country by river to what had become tea, instead of coffee, plantations. Following her death four years later, she was taken up to be buried as planned in the churchyard of St Mary, Bogawantalawa; Charles died a year later and was buried beside her. Travelling by minibus with the wife and children of the same Sri Lankan friend, after a long drive we found the church, and I nipped into the churchyard alone. It was getting dark and misty, then starting to rain. I knew the children were tired and in danger of becoming fractious so, in spite of my usual determination, I had to give up on the frustrating search for the graves.

Farringford: Emily and Alfred Tennyson, Family, Friends and Visitors, 1853–1928

Emily Tennyson (1813–1896) and her husband Alfred rented Farringford House in Freshwater in 1853; it was to be their second home, a place where they might escape the Poet Laureate's growing fame. They bought it in 1856. On first looking out of the drawing room window on her first visit, Emily exclaimed, 'I must have that view', while Tennyson wrote of the house:

> Where, far from noise and smoke of town
> I watch the twilight falling brown,
> All round a careless-ordered garden,
> Close to the ridge of a noble down.

That 'noble down' is now called Tennyson Down and is one of the attractions of Freshwater, on the far west of the Isle of Wight.

Emily was the oldest of the three daughters of Sarah née Franklin, younger sister of the arctic explorer and governor of Tasmania, Sir John Franklin. Her father was Henry Sellwood, a successful solicitor who acted for the Tennyson family over the years; it is not surprising, therefore, that Emily and Alfred met when Emily was a girl. Sarah Sellwood died when Emily was three years old, leaving the girls' father to bring them up. A relationship developed when Emily and Alfred both attended the marriage of his brother Charles, to her sister Louisa in May 1836; Emily was 23, Alfred, four years older. He later wrote a sonnet about the occasion:

> Love Lighted down between them full of glee,
> And over his left shoulder laughed at thee,
> 'O happy bridesmaid, make a happy bride.'
> And all at once a pleasant truth I learn'd,
> For while the tender service made thee weep,
> I loved thee for the tear thou could'st not hide,
> And prest they hand, and knew the press return'd
> And thought, 'My life is sick of single sleep:
> O happy bridesmaid, make a happy bride!'

The couple became engaged in 1837, but the engagement was called off because Emily's father doubted that Alfred could keep his daughter in the life to which she was accustomed on what a poet earned. But he started earning well from his poetry in the 1840s and they were married in 1850; by then Emily was 37, and Alfred 41. Such long waits were not so rare in the Victorian period, often for financial reasons. That year was momentous for Tennyson: as well as marrying, he was made Poet Laureate by Queen Victoria. He filled the post until his death in 1892. He is always known as Alfred Lord Tennyson, as well as 'the Great Poet', but in fact the queen did not create him Baron Tennyson of Aldworth in the County of Sussex and of Freshwater in the Isle of Wight until 1884; he also took his seat in the House of Lords that year. Aldworth was in later years their main house on the mainland; there he was less pestered by the starstruck than at Farringford; they divided their time between the two places – Freshwater in the winter. I shall call him here Alfred Tennyson, or just Tennyson; Emily called him Ally in her letters when they were apart, and 'A.' in her diary. Their first son, Hallam, was born in Twickenham in 1852, Lionel at Farringford House in 1854.

After the birth of Lionel, Emily developed an incurable illness. In the years that followed, walking was increasingly difficult, and she became an invalid mostly confined to a sofa. In spite of that, from there she was remarkably active. All the attention directed towards the Tennysons was and is on Alfred, indeed Freshwater is hardly mentioned without his name being included, and even the Island, if it is not known for Queen Victoria and Osborne House, is known for Tennyson and Freshwater. But 'the Great Poet' couldn't have managed his busy, creative life, and his fame without his wife. She acted as business and financial manager, secretary, proof-reader, editor, promoter, entertainer and protector. The replies to Tennyson's fans and the famous men who wanted to visit, were written by her. *The Letters of Emily Lady Tennyson* (ed. James O Hogg, 1974) show the scope of them. Their post on return to Farringford was like an email box today, all of which Emily answered, by hand, of course. There is a quotation in the introduction to her published letters by Elizabeth Barrett Browning; she felt that Tennyson was 'too much indulged. His wife was his second self; she does not criticise enough.' *The Farringford Journal of Emily Tennyson 1853–1864* (eds Richard J Hutchings and Brian Hinton, 1986) gives an insight into their life. On 25 November 1853, when she was still hale and hearty, she wrote:

A great day for us. We reached Farringford. It was a misty morning & two of the servants on seeing it burst into tears saying they could never live in such a lonely place. We amused ourselves during the autumn and winter by sweeping up leaves for exercise and by making a muddy path thro' the plantation into a sandy one. We were delighted with the snowdrops & primroses on the plantation & by the cooing of the Stock-dove & the song of the Redwings.

As soon as Julia Margaret and Charles Cameron arrived at Dimbola in 1860, the two neighbouring households renewed their friendship. The Camerons were often included among dinner guests at Farringford, but Julia Margaret was also often there informally, playing the piano, listening to Tennyson reading his poems, and complimenting him profusely, as was her way with everything; indeed, she greatly admired him. Sources, as noted earlier, commented on her present giving. Emily usually records Julia Margaret unvarnished and, although with very different personalities, they were obviously friends, but a couple of times Emily does write of the presents: on 1 February, soon after the Camerons' arrival at Dimbola: 'Mrs Cameron arrives with two legs of Welsh mutton from Eastnor [Herefordshire]. We say that it is against our rule to receive gifts from her, dear generous creature that she is, but she persists.' And on 1 March: 'Mrs Cameron brings a vivid blue paper with a border from the Elgin Marbles. The vivid blue neither she nor we like. We as usual protest against her prodigal kindness.' On 13 May: 'Mrs Cameron wants to give us one of her lucky purchases of pictures, but we will not take it.' Has Emily got her tongue in her cheek when she writes: 'Mrs Cameron comes across the Park looking gorgeous in her violet dress and red cloak walking across the newly mown grass'? Julia Margaret was well known for her wild, mostly Indian, fashion sense, and Freshwater, with its often artistic inhabitants and visitors, was known for being somewhat Bohemian. In *Tennyson's Gift* Lynne Truss parodies the scene between Emily and Tennyson at the wallpaper's arrival; it sounds perfectly possible, if a touch cruel.

Emily was creative in her own right: she enjoyed music and wrote lyrics and music for some of Tennyson's poetry, as well as a couple of morning and evening hymns. These were for the Gordon Boys Home founded by Tennyson to educate and train boys for commissions in the army; Emily helped to plan the home. Presumably his interest in the army was connected with one of his most famous poems, 'The Charge of the Light Brigade' which most of us of a certain age will have studied at school in English Literature classes. A copy of the poem exists in Emily's hand – with corrections by Tennyson – which suggests that among her other tasks, it was she who wrote out his poems by hand, presumably dictated or, rather, recited to her. Emily wrote in her journal on 10 October 1854, 'We read full particulars of the battle of Alma and touching letters from soldiers. Great disappointment darkened England learning that the news that Sebastopol had fallen was false.' Tennyson himself was very upset about the needless loss of life and, on reading the article, dashed off the poem. A recording of him reading the poem can be heard during a visit to Farringford.

It was not surprising that Tennyson and Queen Victoria should communicate: he was *her* Poet Laureate, and he would send her his poems, as appropriate, or a book of them, and suitable commiserations when Prince Albert died in the form of his poem 'Idylls of the King', which was dedicated to Albert. The go-between was often one of the queen's ladies-in waiting – **Lady Augusta Bruce** (later Stanley; 1822–1876), daughter of the 7th Earl of Elgin.

On 14 January 1863, Emily recorded:

A beautiful day. Lady Augusta Bruce comes to luncheon & brings with her what to us is beyond price[,] *The Prince Consort* a gift from the Queen with kind words by H.M.'s own hand, also a beautiful photograph of herself & three of her children with A.'s lines under it 'May all love etc.' Also the prayers used at the Anniversary & the Sermon preached. I feel to know & to trust Lady Augusta at once. She promises to come & sleep here next week if she can.

22. Lady Augusta Bruce, courtesy of the Royal Collection
Trust, © His Majesty King Charles III 2024

A few months later, in May 1863, Emily recorded: 'A., the boys and myself
to Osborne. We lunch with Lady Augusta Bruce & afterwards drive with her
in the grounds.' Emily describes what they saw, but there was more to the visit;
I think it is worth quoting a large part of it: it says a lot about both Emily and
the queen:

Soon after we return Lady Augusta is sent for & she comes to fetch us to the
Queen. We wait in the Drawing-room & after a very little time we heard a
quiet, shy opening of the door & the Queen came in & I kissed her hand. She
shook hands with the boys & made a very low reverence to A. All the princesses came in by turns. … All shook hands very kindly with us all. We had
met Prince Alfred before in one of the corridors with Prince Louis of Hesse
& he had shaken hands with A. and talked to him.

The Queen's face was beautiful. Not the least like her portraits but small & child-like, full of intelligence & ineffably sweet & of a sad sympathy.

A. was delighted with the breadth & freedom & penetration of her mind. One felt that no false thing could stand before her. We talked of all things in heaven & earth it seemed to me. I never met a Lady with whom I could talk so easily & never felt so little shy with any stranger after the first few minutes.

She laughed so heartily at many things that were said but shades of pain & sadness passed over a face that seemed sometimes all one smile. ...

One feels that the Queen is a woman to live and die for.

I am sorry that A. might not have a warm shake of the hand such as the boys & myself had when the Queen retired. I gave Princess Beatrice A.'s poem because she had said to Lady Augusta that she wished A. would write her some 'poetries' that she might learn when she was a big girl. A. wrote his name in the back & the Princess's.

I was sorry to discover that in Augusta's memoirs the name 'Tennyson' does not appear. But Augusta does reappear in Emily's diary on 22 December 1863: 'Lady Augusta's wedding day. The boys hoist flags and fire caps in honour. From the Bradleys we have an interesting account of the wedding which was by torchlight in Westminster Abbey and very imposing.'

The Tennysons did not only have relations with one queen, and Queen Victoria also had relations with the queen who stayed at Farringford in 1865 – **Queen Emma, Dowager Queen of Hawaii** (Kalanikaumaka'amana Na'ea Rooke; 1836–1885). As seems likely from her Hawaiian name, her background is more easily simplified. She came as the very recent widow of King Kamehameha IV, and was later to put herself forward as a candidate as ruler of Hawaii against Kalakaaua; it was he who won. It is worth mentioning that this was because at this stage he was in favour of closer ties with the United States; Queen Emma was firmly in favour of the British. This preference is likely to have stemmed from the fact that her maternal grandfather was English, John Young, military adviser to the king of Hawaii; and her stepfather (in whose house she grew up) was another Englishman, Dr Thomas Rooke. Her upbringing, which included an English governess, and the run of Rooke's extensive library, produced a talented and cultured young woman, knowledgeable across cultures, Hawaiian and European. As Queen Consort, she saw to palace affairs, including the expansion of the palace library and, in 1861, she sang in the chorus of Verdi's *Il Trovatore* in Honolulu. She was known for her humanitarian activities, including setting up a hospital, and a school for girls. In 1860, she and her husband petitioned the Church of England to help establish the Church of Hawaii. He died in 1863; therefore her visit to Europe in 1865 as a recent widow was both for her health and to help the burgeoning Anglican mission in Hawaii. She wintered on the French Riviera, and visited northern Italy and southern Germany, ending in Paris, and wherever she went she was entertained by royalty. But of particular interest here are her stays in London and Farringford, where her purpose at the latter was to exchange views on literature with Tennyson.

Queen Emma and Queen Victoria had started corresponding in 1862. Rhoda EA Hackler in her "'My dear Friend": Letters of Queen Victoria and Queen Emma', in *The Hawaiian Journal of History*, relates how in 1858, the King of Hawaii wrote to tell Victoria of the birth of his son and heir, and asking her if she would be godmother, to which she agreed. So when Emma's only son died in 1862, she wrote to tell Victoria about the death of her godson, and when her husband died in 1863. The fact that Prince Albert had died in 1861 drew the two women together, in spite of their differences: Victoria was almost a generation older, ascended the throne of an important country in 1837, and had nine children; Emma became queen consort in 1856 and had one child. But when Emma's husband died in 1863, Victoria's heart went out to her. When Emma wrote to say that she was coming to Europe, particularly to England, Victoria had a problem: she would be at Osborne and had already explained to the Queen of the Netherlands that it would not be possible for her to visit her there; she could hardly then invite Emma there. And after her sojourn at Osborne, she was to travel in Europe visiting relatives.

By September 1865, however, Queen Victoria was back in town; Queen Emma was staying, meanwhile, in London with Jane Franklin, who was related to Emily Tennyson through her mother's marriage. Aunt Franklin pops up from time to time in Emily's Freshwater diary. I'm only speculating that the stay may be connected with Queen Emma's forthcoming visit to Farringford. But, before that, on 9 September, the two queens were at last to meet. Victoria wrote in her Journal:

> After luncheon I received Queen Emma, the widowed Queen of the Sandwich Islands of Hawaii. Met her in the Corridor & nothing could be nicer or more dignified than her manner. She is dark, but not more so than an Indian, with fine features & splendid soft eyes. She was dressed in just the same widow's weeds as I wear. I took her into the White Drawing room, where I asked her to sit down next to me on the sofa. She was much moved when I spoke of her great misfortune in losing her husband and only child. She was very discreet and would only remain a few minutes. She presented her lady whose husband is her Chaplain, both being Hawaiians …'.

Later that day Queen Emma wrote to her brother-in-law, who had succeeded her husband as king, 'I have this moment returned form Windsor Castle where the Queen received me most affectionately, most sincerely.'

On 26 September *The Guardian* announced:

Queen Emma of the Sandwich Islands is expected to take up her residence in the Isle of Wight at the latter end of this Week. During her residence in the island she will, it is believed, pay a visit to Mr Tennyson at Freshwater.

23. Queen Emma, courtesy of the Royal Collection Trust,
© His Majesty King Charles III 2024

Emma was to spend four days as the guest of Emily and Alfred Tennyson at Farringford. She was accompanied by her chaplain, William Hoapili, and his wife, **Mary Anne Kiliwehi Ka'aywai** (1840–1873), the queen's lady-in-waiting and a high chiefess in her own right. In an apparently anonymous and dateless article posted by the University of Lincoln's Institutional Repository the author writes,

Since the visit consisted mostly of tea and polite conversation, interspersed with the performance of Hawaiian songs and poetry, it has been dismissed by Tennyson's biographer John Batchelor as 'utterly pointless'. This was not a view held by Emma, however. Partly English, she wanted Hawaii to seek an alliance with Britain rather than America. … [Her] visit to Britain was aimed at securing the Empire's good will, and her visit to see the Poet Laureate should be seen in that context.

The visit also had an impact on Emma's British hosts. Tennyson had many books on Hawaii, procured either before or after Emma's visit, and wrote his poem *Kapiolani* following her visit. Kapiolani (*c.*1781–1841) was a high chiefess of Hawaii at the time of the founding of the Kingdom of Hawaii and the arrival of Christian missionaries. She was one of the first Hawaiians to read and write, as well as sponsor of a church. She made a dramatic display of her new faith, which is the subject of Tennyson's poem, the second verse of which reads:

Noble the Saxon who hurl'd at his Idol a valorous weapon in olden England!
Great and greater, and greatest of women, island heroine, Kapiolani
Clomb the mountain, and flung the berries, and dared the Goddess, and freed the people
Of Hawa-i-ee!

'Clomb' is an archaic past tense of to climb. The poem was published post-humously by Hallam Tennyson, though Tennyson may have sent a copy to Emma. James Rayner in his entry on Queen Emma in *The Isle of Wight's Missing Chapter* (2020) tells a charming story that sounds as if it could be apoc-ryphal, but I hope not. He writes

Queen Emma had come to the Isle of Wight specifically to see … Tennyson at Farringford because of her appreciation of literature. Unfortunately, her arrival at Freshwater caused such interest on the Island that guests kept calling in to Tennyson's home hoping to be introduced to the Queen of Hawaii. The Tennysons decided to hide Queen Emma in a summer house in the kitchen garden, so she could read her letters in peace. She later described the hiding place as being 'among the cabbages'. The Queen was taken for a walk up the Down and Mr and Mrs Hoapili sang traditional Hawaiian songs for the Tennyson family. She seemed to enjoy her time at Farringford but she had a busy few days on the Island trying to raise money to build a cathedral in Hawaii. She attended an event in the Orangery of Steephill Castle and made a brief appearance at Ryde Town Hall.

As for Tennyson, he presented Queen Emma with this chair of the ilex tree grown in the grounds of Farringford. The chair was said to be in Farringford; however, during my visit I established that that was not so. I finally tracked it down to Lincoln, home of The Tennyson Society. For some time after my request, the research centre was closed, but the first moment it opened, a very kind member of staff went and took several photographs for me to choose from, Not unnaturally, it would look better in colour. I'm sorry that by the

24. Queen Emma's chair, photograph
   by Ros Boyce, Tennyson Society

time of Queen Emma's visit, Emily Tennyson's Journal had petered out (in 1863). In a letter, published in volume III of his letters, Tennyson wrote that 'neither my wife nor myself has lost the interest in Queen Emma and that which concerns her.' And he certainly continued to read about the islands in books in his library.

It is worth adding, for those interested in the end of Queen Emma's stay in England, that two months later, following her stay at Balmoral, Queen Victoria recorded in her Journal on 27 November her gracious act towards her friend, an invitation to stay at Windsor Castle:

Went with Vicky & Fritz to see Queen Emma, who has come for the night. She is not looking well, & coughs poor thing, for which reason she is ordered to go to the south of France, to Hyeres. She, her lady, Mrs Hoopile, Lady Waterpark [Lady of the Bedchamber] and Lord Methuen [Queen's ADC] dined. The Queen sat between Vicky and me. She was amiable, clever, & nice in all she said, speaking of her own country, which she said had originally been very mountainous. There were no animals, but small dogs and pigs, and these only since they had been imported and introduced … the same with flowers. The people were now always dressed like Europeans & were all nominally Christians, but not very fervently so … Took the Queen to her room remaining a little with her.

And the following day:

Directly after breakfast, we went to wish good Queen Emma goodbye & I gave her a bracelet with my miniature and hair. She thanked me much for my kindness, & for consenting to be godmother to her poor child.

Following her time in Europe, Queen Emma visited the United States and Canada. As for her relationship with Queen Victoria, their friendship was maintained, until Queen Emma's death in 1873, by letters written from time to time, sharing news of family events, happy and tragic, exchanging photographs and small presents and enquiring after each other's health and that of their families. The interchange seems to have been a comfort to both.

As for Queen Emma's Tennyson hosts at Farringford, Emily had a collapse in her health in 1874 but recovered sufficiently to outlive Alfred by four years. He died in 1892 and is buried in Westminster Abbey. Emily is buried in the graveyard at All Saints Church, Freshwater.

Emily does not appear to have been photographed by Julia Margaret – perhaps she refused, though sitters had often refused before they had to give in; instead, this portrait painted by Helen Allingham shows her in later life. Helen will be properly introduced in chapter 9, 'Women Artists'. Emily was also painted by GF Watts in 1862, a portrait that suggests she was not comfortable with the process.

25. Emily Tennyson by Helen Allingham, from the Internet

Her grandson, Sir Charles Tennyson, wrote in the foreword to *The Letters of Emily Lady Tennyson* that Helen's portrait 'comes as near to my memory as such a work can do. It shows a face with many traces of suffering. Perhaps it misses my grandmother's strong sense of humour. I don't remember ever hearing her laugh, but she had a most engaging smile.' And further on, 'My grandmother ... had in old age at least, great beauty of feature and expression. When I think of her, I picture her in a silk dress, black or lavender voluminous and trailing, her silvery grey hair very plainly done, drawn back from a central parting and covered by a white lace shawl.'

The deaths of Emily and Alfred were not the end of the Tennyson family at Farringford. Following his father's death in 1892, Hallam became Lord Tennyson, and inherited the house. In 1884, he had married Audrey Boyle in

Westminster Abbey. Although **Audrey Georgiana Florence Tennyson** (1854–1916) had been born in England, she was brought up in Cape Town where her father, Charles Boyle, was clerk of the Legislative Council in the Cape Colony, as it was then; later the family moved to Mauritius where he was director of the railway department; the children were then sent to school in England. Audrey's mother was Jacyntha Antonia Lorenzina, née Moore. Both parents were Irish Protestants. Her mother was also said to be 'a bit difficult'. Audrey's cosmopolitan upbringing was to serve her well when Hallam's career took off, and her mother's requirement to be kept informed through letter writing was also to prove historically invaluable.

Hallam had been educated at Marlborough College and Cambridge, but when Emily could no longer act as Tennyson's secretary, and Tennyson himself was ageing, he left Cambridge and took over as his father's personal secretary, ending his aspirations of a career in politics. On his father's death, however, he inherited the role of his official biographer: his *Tennyson: A memoir* was published in 1897. The Tennyson name, the title – which Tennyson had at last accepted, partly for Hallam's sake, in the year of his marriage – and his membership of the Imperial Federation League, which lobbied the Colonial Secretary, proved helpful in what happened next: in 1899, he was offered the position of Governor of South Australia. It was with Audrey's encouragement that he accepted it. During their time in Australia, they were based at first in Adelaide and then, when the Governor-General resigned unexpectedly in 1902, he became Administrator of the Government, and later that year Governor-General. At Hallam's request, he held the post for only a year, from 1903 to 1904. He and Audrey then retired to Farringford, where he worked on upholding his father's legacy and as deputy governor of the Island.

The reason for the need to skip through Hallam's Australian careers is that Audrey, particularly with her background, took to her roles, and the colonial life, as if to the manner born, and proved immensely popular. As the *Australian Dictionary of National Biography* suggests, she was 'unremitting in carrying out, with style, the duties expected of a governor's wife'. She did more than that: for example, she encouraged charity workers and other volunteers striving to improve the pay and conditions of the seamstresses working in factories. Noting the problems of pregnant women in the outback, she was responsible for the founding of South Australia's first maternity hospital, fundraising, and overseeing the design and construction of the building; she made sure it was named after Queen Victoria. All the while, she was immersing herself in Australian life more generally, through travel around the continent. She also had three sons to look after, and the task of writing voluminous letters to her 'difficult' mother – 262 of them (an average of more than one a week) – as well as suffering from headaches. The letters, describing, from an insider's view, the excitement and anxiety surrounding the referendum in New South Wales on Federation, and then the 1901 creation of the Commonwealth of Australia itself, were donated to the National Library of Australia (Papers of Lord Tennyson). A heavily edited selection from the collection, entitled *Audrey*

Tennyson's Vice Regal Days: The Australian Letters of Audrey Lady Tennyson 1899–1903 (1968), was compiled by Dame Alexandra Hasluck.

Back in Freshwater, as a Farringford posting describes,

> She once more took on an energetic role, often writing for [Hallam] Tennyson as he was more and more frequently inflicted by gout and rheumatism. This role perhaps sums Audrey Tennyson up above all others, for her hand and help was necessary in much of the activity of the family, whilst often remaining invisible.

The charming and quirky thatched church of St Agnes in Freshwater was, in 1908, built at the instigation of Hallam on Tennyson land; it was Audrey who suggested the name St Agnes. There is a plaque on the wall there to Anny Thackeray Ritchie, friends of Audrey and Hallam, who worshipped there. Hallam devised the text:

> Her writing reveals the inheritance of Genius. Her life the inspiration of loving kindness.

In 1914, at the start of the First World War, Audrey founded a Red Cross hospital in Freshwater, and threw herself into work as its commandant. But in 1916 her youngest son, Harold Courtney, was killed in action in the Royal Navy aged only 20. That year Audrey herself died, apparently of pneumonia, but I suspect that grief played a part, and wonder about the headaches with which she was plagued in Australia. A second of the couple's sons, Alfred Aubrey, was killed in action, aged 27, two years later.

That same year, Hallam remarried, this time into the extended Pattle family of Julia Margaret Cameron. **Mary (May) Prinsep** (1853–1931) was, like so many Pattles, born in India to Charles Robert Prinsep, Advocate General of Calcutta, and Louisa White, daughter of an East India Company officer. But Mary was orphaned when she was 11. She was therefore adopted by Thoby Prinsep and his wife, Julia Margaret's sister Sara, and went to live with them at Little Holland House. Over the next ten years she tended to holiday at Dimbola with her aunt, Julia Margaret and, with her classical beauty, became a regular photographic model, for example, as 'Beatrice', and 'Elaine', the lily maid of Astelot. That continued after her marriage in 1874, to stockbroker Andrew Hitchens: there are a couple of photographs of them together, one of them as 'The Parting of Sir Lancelot and Queen Guinevere'. May posed for at least two portraits by her cousin Val Prinsep, and for GF Watts There are eight photographs of her by her aunt in London's National Portrait Gallery.

Hitchens died in 1906, and May was 65 when she married Hallam who was a year older, and went to live at Farringford. They had known each other for many years, as children and adults; one can only imagine the comfortableness of their ten years together. Hallam died in 1928; May lived for another three years.

Some sources suggest that May died and was buried in Freshwater, but I am reliably told that she was buried in Compton (Surrey). Audrey and Hallam are buried in the graveyard of All Saints Church, Freshwater, as was Emily Tennyson; so were Sara and Thoby Prinsep. Mary Hillier Gilbert is buried nearby. Inside the church is a plaque to young Harold Courtney, and another to Audrey and Hallam. It says of Audrey 'She went about doing good.'

The Tennysons left their indelible mark on Farringford, and Julia Margaret Cameron on nearby Dimbola. The two houses are very different from one another, but both reek of who lived there. Freshwater is worth visiting because of them.

9 – Women Artists, 1846–1981

Introduction

Helen Allingham's 1892 portrait of Emily Tennyson makes a neat link between chapter 8 and the other women artists whose work, in whatever medium, drew inspiration from aspects of the Isle of Wight. The women were often, but not always, inhabitants of the Island, or they were either long- or short-term visitors. While this chapter will often be chronological, that may well be within sub-headings. Helen, being a link with Freshwater, is most usefully an introduction.

Helen Allingham (née Paterson; 1848–1926) was the daughter, the eldest of seven children, of Alexander Paterson, a doctor, and Mary Herford Paterson. Her early talent for drawing seems to have been inspired by her maternal Herford grandmother and an aunt, both accomplished artists. One of her sisters also became a noted artist. Sketching and watercolouring were expected accomplishments of women of their class, but Helen studied art for three years at the Birmingham School of Design, and a year at the Royal Female School of Art; then followed her aunt to the National Art Training school; in 1867 she enrolled in the Royal Academy School. This would later become the Royal College of Art. Meanwhile she had worked as an illustrator, eventually giving up her studies for a full-time career in art. She painted for children's and adult books, as well as periodicals. The highlight of this part of her career came in 1874 when she was commissioned to provide 12 illustrations for the magazine serialisation of Thomas Hardy's *Far from the Madding Crowd*. She was now a noted artist: van Gogh, during his stay in London, is said to have been influenced by her work in *The Graphic*.

The year 1874 was an important one in Helen's life for it was then that she married William Allingham, Irish poet, diarist and editor, 24 years older than she was, and her life changed: she gave up her work as an illustrator and became well known under her married name as a watercolour painter. As they moved house around the country, she started painting scenes of the countryside about them, meanwhile giving birth to three children. At one stage, they were neighbours and friends of essayist Thomas Carlyle and his wife Jane, through them becoming acquainted with the Tennysons, and visiting them at Aldworth, their house in Surrey. That is where Helen, in 1880, at the request of Tennyson, painted the portrait of Emily, then rather frail; she also painted one of him and his dog Don. Helen wrote of painting Emily:

Lady Tennyson was never strong, and her son told me that even when he was a boy she was seldom able to walk far, and was always taken when an expedition on the Downs or to the sea was planned, in a wheeled chair, which his father pushed, and to which he and his brother Lionel were harnessed.

William Allingham was already friends with George Eliot, who, as described by Kathleen McCormack in 'George Eliot in Society', was impressed by Helen's 'delicate watercolours of country cottages, renderings that stop just this side of pastoral sentimentality'. So much so that she conceived the idea of a new set of illustrations for *Romola*. Although nothing came of that, Helen produced a frontispiece for her brother Arthur Paterson's *George Eliot's Family Life and Letters* (1928). The watercolour is of George Eliot's garden, and on a later page there is a portrait of her, possibly by Helen.

William died in 1889, leaving 41-year-old Helen to bring up their three children and to earn her living by her painting. Her happy rural scenes became very popular, and in 1890 she became the first woman to be admitted as a full member of the Royal Watercolour Society. In 1891 she arrived on the Island, staying in Freshwater in what seems to have been two cottages joined together, Hollytree Cottage and Myrtle Cottage, Victoria Road, and 100 or so yards from the Orchard family's shop, introduced in chapter 8. As Christie's catalogue noted for the sale of Helen's painting, 'Hook's Farm, Freshwater, Isle of Wight':

Helen Allingham began to paint old cottages and farms in the Surrey countryside from a desire to record their picturesque appearances before they were permanently altered by restoration or demolition. She was one of a wide circle of contemporary artists and writers, such as Thomas Hardy … and the Pre-Raphaelites, who sought to preserve scenes of simple pastoral life in their works. Her nostalgic subtly romanticised scenes of cottages and country people were already extremely sought-after in her lifetime and continue to be the most popular of her works today.

Hook's Farm was of course the home of the Hooke family who feature in chapter 5, 'Irregular Relations', and Helen was right to carry on that aspect of her work in Freshwater. Hook's Farm has since been demolished, so Helen's painting is all that remains of it, apart from some bricks used in the building of the delightfully quirky and thatched St Agnes Church.

Close to where Helen was staying were several thatched cottages. The story is told in Bonham's catalogue in connection with the auctioning of her painting, 'A cottage at Freshwater Gate', that:

Close to completing a painting of [a] thatched cottage one Saturday, Mrs Allingham planned to finish it on the Monday. On returning to the scene at the start of the week, she discovered the house had caught fire the previous night and had been reduced to a heap of rubble.

'Freshwater Gate' itself was reproduced by Marcus Huish's *Happy England* (1903), now in the Manchester Art Gallery entitled 'A Roadside Cottage'. Other paintings by Helen, not necessarily of the Isle of Wight, can be seen at Burgh House, Hampstead, London. As for any remaining thatched cottages in Freshwater, they are not easy to spot. On a hunt for thatched cottages, we found one

26. Helen Allingham's cottage, from the Internet

while driving along the little road that leads from behind and to the right, of All Saints Church down to the main road. It looked just like a Helen Allingham painting, in spite of the pouring rain. The feeling was one of soaked triumph as I photographed it.

Undoubtedly Helen's most substantial Freshwater work is contained in *Homes of Tennyson*, painted by Helen Allingham, described by Arthur Paterson, with 20 full-page illustrations in colour (1905). Although part of it concerns the Tennyson house in Surrey, it is the Freshwater section that is of particular interest.

Tennyson was a very keen and original gardener, tending a much-loved walled vegetable garden; among the vegetables grew colourful flowers. Today it is open to the public. A description in words on a Farringford posting gives an impression of the intention and the effect:

The garden slopes to the west, at the top of which is a replica of the Arbour which the poet built with rushes gathered from the withy [willow] bed, so that Emily could enjoy the afternoon sun and the view facing west. In time, the sweetly scented climbing plants will engulf this restful retreat, much as they did in Helen Allingham's portrayal of the original.

27. Thatched Cottage, Freshwater, photograph by the author

Artists' Work in Carisbrooke Castle Museum Collection, 1846–1903

While Carisbrooke Castle is an obvious place to visit, and revisit, if only to sniff the scent left behind by Isabella de Fortibus (see chapter 3, 'Women of Property'), the museum created by Princess Beatrice when she was governor of the Island, and lived in the castle some of the time (chapter 12), is also a must. Some of its objects, such as the many remnants of Charles I and his daughter Princess Elizabeth, have already been described (see chapter 4), but if you are alert, you will spot here and there as you progress upstairs to further rooms, paintings and other works of art by women depicting aspects of the Island. The order here is chronological rather than necessarily of importance.

Perhaps the most esoteric watercolour sketch was that painted in 1839 by **Harriet Darwin Fox** (née Fletcher; 1799–1842). It depicts the eggs of the Spot-flanked Gallinule (or Spotted Crake) and a Sparrow Hawk which were collected by Harriet's husband, the curate William Darwin Fox. As the museum text continues, 'It is believed that these are the only surviving studies of a collection created by the Darwin Foxes for William's second cousin, the naturalist Charles Darwin'. The cousins first met in 1828 at Cambridge, where Darwin Fox was already an entomologist and naturalist, and they remained lifelong friends, William collecting insects for his increasingly famous cousin; their correspondence contained discussions of Darwin's work and these are considered an important primary source for it.

Harriet, daughter of Sir Richard Fletcher Bt and Elizabeth Mudge, met William Darwin Fox on the Isle of Wight where he had gone to convalesce in Sandown in 1833; she was six years older than he was. They married the following year in St Thomas's Church, Ryde; and seem to have lived at Broad-lands, Sandown. As so often, and as seen most clearly in chapter 1, it was not uncommon for wives and other women to provide a pictorial record of a man's findings. The couple's marriage lasted only eight years, as Harriet died, probably from tuberculosis, having had six children. William re-married and brought his total of children to 17. He retired to Sandown and lived there until his death in 1880. During his time on the Island, he contributed to the under-standing of the geology of the Solent and how the Island became separated from the mainland.

Emma Dennett's album of botanical illustrations is dated 1846–1847, and the text continues:

> Botanical painting was a common hobby of Victorian ladies, but this album is significant and of interest to modern-day botanists. Many species no longer occur in the localities where Emma found them while others have been newly discovered in recent years, still growing in the places she recorded them.

Emma Dennett (1814–1886) was one of the five children of John Dennett and Leah Dennett (née Cave). Her father came from a well-established Caris-brooke family, and he described himself as an engineer and surveyor: he had a lifelong fascination with rockets and is believed to have been involved in manufacturing military rockets during the Napoleonic Wars. He later turned his skills to the development of a rocket that could fire a line over to a ship in distress, an invention that proved to be so effective that he became famous as 'Rocket Man'. His other interest was in history which, some years before his death in 1852, led to his appointment as custodian of Carisbrooke Castle; his family then moved there. It is apparent, from a 2016 museum note of recent acquisitions, that Emma's botanical and drawing and painting skills, as shown by the album, date from their time in the castle; many of the plants and flowers were to be found within the castle's grounds.

The illustrations are accompanied by details of the species and poems, sometimes Emma's own. Examples of the plants include the Fly Orchid, now extinct, and Wood Calamint which now grows in a single place in the United Kingdom, that being on the Isle of Wight. It was only discovered in 1846, so Emma was quick to capture it. The Rue-leaved Saxifrage which she found in the castle grounds no longer grows there, but survives (just) in the old Quarr Abbey ruins, Bilberry on St George's Down and Marvel Copse. That 2016 museum posting itemises others of her finds and paintings, and also tells readers that the album was currently being transcribed and photographed by museum volunteers. That work may now be complete as you can scroll through some of its pages on YouTube – 'Gleaning from Wood and Field'. As my notes, having watched it, record, 'One of the best YouTube I've ever looked at'. It may be aimed at children, but can be appreciated by anyone. On Emma's death aged 72, she was buried under a yew tree in the graveyard of St Mary's, Carisbrooke. Her botanical record is as important in its on way as her father's famous inventions.

The painting by **Ellen Ann Cantelo** (1825–1898) displayed in the museum when I went, is entitled 'Tower of Carisbrooke Church from the Millstream'. The museum has several of Ellen's paintings in its collection, not all of them displayed; the display may well be rotated. One of these is 'Keep, Carisbrooke Castle' (1885) and is more about a figure boating on a river, the trees along its bank bending over it. The castle keep is mistily on a hill beyond. Another in the collection is 'Old Priory Farm, Carisbrooke' painted the same year. And yet another is 'Carisbrooke Village with Miss Sanders' Great Grandparents and their water cart'. Sometimes Ellen painted away from the Carisbrooke area, one example being 'Mackerel Boat, Sandown Bay, Isle of Wight'. It is possible to bring up these paintings by scrolling down on the Internet. The importance of her watercolours is that they are a record of nineteenth-century landscapes. Details of Ellen's family background, as well as that of her sister, Elizabeth Thompson, appear in chapter 13, 'The Campaigners'.

Ellen was not only a painter (and campaigner) but, as another museum text records under the title Cantelo & Brading Photographs:

Ellen's artistic and enquiring nature led to her experimenting with photography. She went into business with Mr Brading and formed Brading and Cantelo who photographed island scenes some of which became picture postcards.

A museum posting about Island photography also records:

Many images have been taken by amateurs, but there are lots of photographs attributed to the many working photographers on the Island including Brading and Cantelo ... This visual record of the Isle of Wight and its people can allow us to see how people lived and worked, and discover forgotten buildings and events.

Watercolourist **Fanny Mary Minns** (1847–1929) was also connected with Carisbrooke; she was born at Node Hill. The watercolour displayed in the museum is of the village of Carisbrooke with a horse and cart in the foreground, signed and dated 1905 Fanny Minns. I'm assuming that the church depicted is St Mary's, though I seem to remember you have to climb some steps up to it, and this work portrays it as being at road level. Fanny was the sixth and youngest child of William Minns and his wife Mary Minns (née Bright). Together her parents ran the dry cleaning and dyeing business Bright and Minns in Newport. The fact that her mother was part of the partnership and that her former name was used, and first, perhaps suggests that her family's money may have been initially behind it. The business was to last 164 years, but working there was not the path that Fanny was to follow, though its prosperity did allow her to train as an artist. The posting giving details of Fanny, 'Suffolk Artists', suggests that she may have received painting lessons from Ellen Cantelo.

As the Royal Academy in London was closed to women until 1862, Fanny went to Dresden Art Academy and established herself as a teacher of painting, but returned to the Isle of Wight when her father died suddenly aged only 52, lived with her widowed mother, and earned her living by painting. She travelled on the Continent and made hasty sketches which she then completed in her Newport studio. She exhibited widely in galleries on the mainland, including as a member of the Royal Society of British Artists and the Society of Women Artists. She started to receive illustrating commissions, one of which was for Maxwell Gray's *The Silence of Dean Maitland*. The Isle of Wight author, whose real name was Mary Gleed Tuttiett, appears, particularly as regards that novel, in chapter 10, 'Women Writers'.

Fanny's paintings, like those of Ellen Cantelo, were reproduced on postcards. In 1899 a silver medal displayed in the museum was awarded to Fanny at the exhibition of the Island Artisans and Mechanicals Industrial Society. Her oil painting 'Under the Willow' won in the category for professional artists' drawings and paintings. She also received certificates for two other paintings. In 1911 she held an exhibition of her work at the Unity Hall, Newport, where she displayed 110 paintings. She died in Ryde aged 82, and was buried beside her mother in Mountjoy cemetery, Whitcombe Road, Carisbrooke, which was established when the cemetery at St Mary's Church became full.

The oil painting in an elaborate frame, 'The Queen at Carisbrooke Fete 1899' which is prominent is also the most ambitious and most impressive of those by women in the museum collection. **Constance Pitcairn** (1853–1916) was the daughter of James Pelham Pitcairn, a clergyman, and Emily Pitcairn (née Turner). She was born at Longsight, now a Manchester suburb. The Autumn 2019 Newsletter of the Friends of the Carisbrooke Castle Museum tells the viewer nearly all that is known about Constance by describing the painting, its acquisition and purpose:

The Museum recently acquired at auction, with the generous support of the Friends, an oil painting of Queen Victoria visiting the 1899 Carisbrooke Fete by Constance Pitcairn. Held at the Castle to raise funds for the restoration of the exterior of St Thomas' Church, the fete entertainment included a 'gypsy encampment', dances, concerts and a 'bicycle gymkhana'. In the painting (currently on display in the main museum stairwell) Queen Victoria sits in a carriage outside the Governor's House (now the museum) with her grandchildren Princess Victoria of Schleswig-Holstein and Prince Leopold of Battenberg, while her daughter, Princess Beatrice, stands beside them. Our thanks to the Friends for enabling us to secure this substantial piece.

Constance wrote at least one book, *The History of the Fife Pitcairns* (1905). Her introduction records for example, that 'Andrew Pitcairn and seven sons were killed at the battle of Flodden Field'.

By nice coincidence, the last painting in the above overview of women's paintings in the Carisbrooke Castle Museum is by Princess Beatrice while she was governor of the Island and living in the castle. Its title is 'The old gates and guardroom at Carisbrooke Castle (1903)'; the text under it reads:

> Princess Beatrice was very creative, not only painting and drawing but also designing books, medals and composing music. She was taught by William Leighton Leitch, a Scottish landscape watercolour painter and illustrator and drawing master to Queen Victoria. Beatrice was also an Honorary Member of the Royal Institute of Painters in Watercolour and President of the Isle of Wight Fine Art Society.

This painting and text show Princess Beatrice as creative in many ways, but it should also be noted that it was her idea to set up the museum, in memory of her late husband; it was funded by public subscription and endorsed by Queen Victoria. The museum, installed in the specially restored gatehouse, was opened by the princess in August 1898. The importance of her painting of the old gate and gatehouse, built originally of wood in about 1100, and then replaced by a stone one is, therefore, an important record. Before her death, she safeguarded the museum's future by setting up a charitable trust which later, when the gatehouse was no longer big enough to house its burgeoning contents, moved it to its the current location in what was the castle's Great Hall. The princess will appear again in the first section of chapter 12, 'Women in a man's world', concerning her governorship of the Island. That same chapter will note the volunteer curator Catherine Morey who took over from her husband. Princess Beatrice was not the only artist among Queen Victoria's children: Princess Louise appears later in this chapter.

A Place to Honeymoon, 1871–1889

The moment I saw the scene that Berthe Morisot painted from the sea-front in Cowes in 1875, I knew that this painting must be on the cover of this book. She had caught the colour of the sea, the blue, sometimes in a darker shade, predominant in the paintwork of that area of town. Then there are the elegant women and children in the foreground. After all, it was Cowes Week, part of the Summer Season, when British Society made its way to the Isle of Wight for the Royal Yacht Squadron Regatta, an excuse to squander and fritter their time on pleasures and follies.

Berthe Morisot (1841–1895) was born in Bourges, a city in central France. By the time of her birth, her father Edmé-Tiburce Morisot, had overcome the early setbacks to his career and was by then prefect of the Department Cher, the monarch's chief administrator of the entire province. Her mother, whom her father, 13 years older than the 16-year-old, is said to have won by good looks and charm, was Marie-Cornélie Thomas. She came from a family of high-level government officials, chief treasurers and paymasters of the province, and it was her father who made sure that his son-in-law was put on the right employment ladder, ensuring that his daughter and grandchildren – eventually four of them – would be comfortably off.

By the time Berthe was 16, the family had moved to Passy, a suburb of Paris. It was then that her mother enrolled her three daughters in private drawing classes; at the time the prestigious École des Beaux Arts was not open to female students. Their first tutor taught them the fundamentals of drawing, after which one of them dropped out. Berthe and her other sister, always known as Edma, were then enrolled to study with Joseph Guichard, a former student of Ingres, who, over three years, 1857–1860, taught them all about classical art in the academic tradition. It was under his guidance that Berthe first experimented with painting in oils, and in 1858 she registered as a copyist at the Louvre, a move that was to introduce her to artists who are still famous, and with whom she was soon to become friends. Berthe and Edma had heard about the technique of painting outdoors in natural light, *en plein air*, a technique used by the Impressionist painters. When the sisters expressed a desire to know more about it, in 1863, Guichard consulted Corot and it was arranged that they should study under the landscape painter Achille Oudinot. In the spring of 1864, after seven years of intensive artistic training, Berthe and Edma were admitted to the official salon, where Berthe would exhibit regularly. Edma would exhibit until her marriage in 1869, when she gave up her career as an artist, though thereafter she remained a constant and loyal support to Berthe, often by letter. In one she wrote:

> I am often with you in thought, dear Berthe. I'm in your studio and I like to slip away, if only for a quarter of an hour, to breathe that atmosphere that we shared for many years …

Most of the above useful information about Berthe's early life accompanies this 1865 portrait. The account is written by someone vouchsafing only the name jonathan5485, posted on the website 'mydailyartdisplay', and entitled 'Berthe Morisot by Edma Morisot'; it is one of his many such pieces. For fuller details of her life he recommends *Berthe Morisot* by Anne Higonnet (1990).

How did things stand for the artist sisters in 1868? Madison Mainwaring wrote in 'Always the Model, Never the Artist', published in *The Paris Review* in July 2019:

> Édouard Manet wrote to fellow artist Henri Fantin-Latour about the promising painters. He found them 'charming' and feared that because they were women, their accomplishments would inevitably go to waste. Manet thought the Morisot sisters should 'further the cause of painting by marrying *académiciens*, members of the jury who selected which works to display at

the Académie des Beaux-Arts annual salon'. The possibility that the Morisots might actually become artists did not seem to occur to him. Manet envisioned the Morisot sisters might make their mark in the annals of art as counsellors to men in power by influencing their tastes and sympathies and convincing them of the worth of outsider artists (such as Manet himself).

It may well be that Fantin-Latour had raised the subject of the sisters with Manet, as the three of them had met and become friends of Berthe when she was a copyist in the Louvre. In spite of Manet's opinion, Berthe's work was to be selected for exhibition in six subsequent Salons until, in 1874, she joined the 'rejected' Impressionists in the first of their own exhibi-

28. Berthe Morisot by Edma Morisot, from the Internet

tions, which included Cézanne, Degas, Monet, Pissarro, Renoir and Sisley. She went on to feature prominently in the following eight Impressionist exhibitions between 1874 and 1886. In 1894, she was described by the influential French art critic Gustave Geffroy as one of 'les trois grandes dames' of Impressionism along with Marie Bracquemond and Mary Cassat. Édouard Manet was to paint Berthe 11 times, but she never painted him; indeed, the only man she painted was her husband.

The year 1874 was important for Berthe: not only was it the first of the Impressionist exhibitions in which she was represented, but also, in December, aged 33, she married Édouard Manet's brother, Eugène. The following summer they arrived in Cowes to start their honeymoon at the Globe Hotel on the Parade which runs along the sea-front. It is from there, standing in front of where they were staying, that Berthe painted what is now the cover here. A generous and well-informed neighbour of the Globe showed me exactly where Berthe would have set up her easel. It was from there, too, that she captured a perfect image of her husband. He is wearing a boater and blazer – you have to be sharp-eyed to discern binoculars in his hand – sitting in the window of their room looking out over pots of red flowers on the window sill. He seems to be watching an elegant women and child walking past, with the sea and

yachts beyond. In reality he would also have been watching Berthe at her easel. Eugène, it has to be said, was not the most patient of models. Berthe wrote to Edma: 'I began something in the sitting room of Eugène. Poor Eugène is taking your place but he is a much less accommodating model; he quickly had enough'. He preferred to be on the move, often walking around with her, both of them carrying an easel and paints, though at first Berthe was shy to do so. She also wrote revealingly to Edma of the Island itself, artist to artist:

> It is the prettiest place for painting – if one had any talent. I have made a start, but it is difficult. People come and go on the jetty, and it is impossible to catch them. It is the same with the boats. There is extraordinary life and movement, but how is one to render it?

In another, or the same, letter to Edma, Berthe wrote, 'The view from my window is very pretty to see, very ugly to try to paint, views from above are almost always incomprehensible, the upshot is that I am not doing very much, and the little I do looks frightful …'

You can get to the Parade in two ways: if you're on foot, having reached the Union Inn (described in chapter 6, 'Outsiders') from the High Street, you turn down Watchtower Lane, and turn left at the bottom. By car you approach it from the other end of the Parade, and there is a fair amount of parking space. The Globe is now a pub serving food, from the rooftop terrace of which there is a wonderful view over the Solent, filled with various craft, including the ferry from Southampton coming in to dock, or leaving.

In 2023 the Dulwich Picture Gallery set up an exhibition, in collaboration with the Musée Marmottan Monet – 'Berthe Morisot: Shaping Impressionism' – which showed 30 of Berthe's paintings. They were, I thought, rather confusingly, interspersed with those of others – all men – Reynolds, Gainsborough and Fragonard – intended to trace the roots of her inspiration, while also highlighting the originality of her artistic vision. There was a stand-alone text, as if to explain that interspersing – a quotation by Berthe's friend Renoir which read: 'And what another anomaly to see emerge in our age of realism, a painter so imbued with the grace and finesse of the eighteenth-century. In a word, the last elegant feminine artist that we have had since Fragonard.' Elsewhere, Renoir wrote of his friendship with Berthe as 'one of the most solid of my life'.

It was disappointing for me that there was only one of Berthe's Isle of Wight paintings displayed in the exhibition, that of Eugene at the window. This was formally titled, 'Eugène Manet on the Isle of Wight'. As the date is given as 1885, that may well be when she finished it. If I remember correctly, all the exhibition paintings featured people, while others she painted on the Island, mostly, it appears, in or around Cowes, feature water vessels. It was not just a whim to honeymoon there, and they went on to visit the mainland: Berthe had long wanted to visit England. Lois Oliver, in 'Berthe Morisot: the French Impressionist's English holiday' (2023), gives a delightful explanation for the wish: 'during childhood, her English governess Louisa had introduced the family to our custom of baking birthday cakes trimmed with candles and instilled in her a precocious taste for English literature'. Berthe even thought that she might establish her career in England, like her compatriot James Tissot who had escaped to London from the Franco-Prussian War and was enjoying great success, and making a fortune there. Once in London, where the honeymoon-ers spent two weeks, and having met Tissot, Berthe wrote to her mother: 'He sells for as much as 300,000 francs at a time … He compliments me, although he has probably never seen any of my work.' And to Edma: 'Tissot tells me that during the regatta week at Cowes we saw the most fashionable society in England.'

Before the couple left the Island, they explored beyond Cowes. Though I'm not sure that she painted elsewhere, she certainly wrote about their visit to Ryde, where it was too windy for her to paint:

At Ryde there are many shops, and even a picture dealer. I went in. He showed me watercolours by a painter who, I am told is well known; they sell for no less than 400 francs apiece – and they are frightful. No feeling for nature – these people who live on the water do not even see it. That has made me give up whatever illusions I had about the possibility of success in England. In the whole shop, the only thing that was possible and even pretty was by a Frenchman; but the dealer says that sort of thing does not sell.

It was Eugène, grumbling, that led them to leave the Isle of Wight on 18 August 1875 and, once on the mainland, travel from the south by train to London. Although Berthe failed to interest any dealer there, her time was not wasted: she visited the National Gallery and other collections, which increased her enthusiasm for English painters such as Gainsborough, Romney and Reynolds, with whose works the curators of the Dulwich exhibition were to intersperse her paintings. Fragonard was, incidentally, her great-grandfather. London was not yet ready for Berthe Morisot's paintings, let alone the Isle of Wight, so after two or three weeks they returned to Paris. Since the Dulwich exhibition, Berthe Morisot, where she stayed in Cowes and from where she painted have become known on the Island; even a short video has been made, by Dr Lois Oliver, showing the exact place on the Parade.

I'll just slip in another Frenchwoman who visited the Isle of Wight, not on honeymoon, but in exile, and her visit seems to have been brief. In her day, **Élizabeth Vigée Le Brun** (1755–1842) was as famous a painter as Berthe Morisot is today, though her painting dated from a completely different era and taste. She painted portraits, most notably of women, and usually of the aristocracy and royalty of different countries, and she made them look their very best, as well as herself in self-portraits. During a long stay in England she had, in 1802, crossed the Channel to visit and paint the portrait of Eng-lishwoman, and famously notorious, **Baroness Craven, Margravine of Brandenburg-Ansbach** (1750–1828), writer and traveller. She spent three weeks enjoying Elizabeth Craven's company and hospitality. During that time, for reasons unknown, the two decided to visit the Isle of Wight. There Mme Le Brun was enchanted by the countryside and friendliness of the people. She later wrote that this, along with the island of Ischia (near Naples), was the only place where she would happily spend her entire life. The same comparison was made by Prince Albert when he first saw the bay at Osborne, which reminded him of the Bay of Naples.

Leaving aside how highly regarded Berthe is as an Impressionist painter today, one unconnected aspect of her visit to the Isle of Wight is how fashionable it was for nineteenth-century honeymooners. Some of the new wives were talented in other fields of artistic endeavour than painting, though they are ignored, and it is their husbands who are admired.

It took a while for composer Samuel Coleridge-Taylor to become part of today's composer canon, partly because of his mixed heritage. That, too, was why Sarah Fleetwood-Walmisley's parents were opposed to her becoming the wife of a 'Blackie' (as told by Samuel to a friend). Her parents did everything in their power to prevent the marriage. Samuel was the son of Dr Daniel Hughes Taylor from Sierra Leone and an English woman, Alice Hare Martin, who was to raise him alone (the Coleridge addition was in honour of the poet).

Jessie (Sarah) Fleetwood-Walmisley (1869–1962) was the niece of the composer Thomas Attwood Walmisley, Oxford professor of music, one of the finest English organists of his day, and a man best remembered for his anthems and the madrigal *Sweete Flowers*. She was one of the nine children of Major Walter Milbank Walmisley who had recently served in India, and Emma Burrows. The beginning and development of Jessie and Samuel's relationship is perhaps best told by WC Berwick Sayers' *Samuel Coleridge-Taylor Musician: His Life and Letters* (1915). Briefly, one evening, Jessie's parents gave a party to which several musicians were invited, among whom was Coleridge-Taylor, who played the violin. During the evening, he approached her to ask if she would accompany him in a composition of his own, and they played 'The Legend' from his *Concertstuck* together. They attended the same College of Music so, when she had to practise some violin and piano duets during the vacation, she approached the college for his address, and asked him if he would play with her. Jessie was six years older than Samuel, clever, quick witted, sympathetic and used at college to being taught side by side with 'coloured girls'; she was also dark, attractive and vivid, and she had a beautiful voice in singing and speech. Everything about her appealed to Samuel. She was also strong-willed, a character trait which she would need during the coming years.

When Samuel was taken up by the Anglo-German music publisher August Johannes Jaeger, he would visit the publisher at his Kensington house where the critic would listen carefully to his songs, sung by Jessie. Meanwhile, he was, between 1893 and 1897, continuing his composition studies with Charles Stanford. In December 1897 he managed to have his clarinet quintet scheduled for performance. He taught at the Croydon Conservatoire of Music, became associated with the local all-female Brahms Choir and conducted the local orchestra, which consisted mostly of women. (Membership of the orchestra was helpful to women of that era whose lives were somewhat restricted.) I pause to wonder how much Jessie influenced him in that move; she was certainly a member of the choir. Early in 1898, Edward Elgar, who had not yet achieved the height of his own fame, generously took up Samuel's need for recognition: he sent a card to a member of the Committee of the Three Choirs Festival:

> I have received a request from the secretary to write a short orchestral thing for the evening concert. I am sorry I am too busy to do so. I wish … you would ask Coleridge-Taylor to do it. He still wants recognition, and he is far and away the cleverest fellow going amongst the young men. Please don't let your committee throw away the chance of doing a good act. – Edward Elgar.

Elgar's intervention helped and it would have boosted any aspiring young composer to receive a festival commission. For it Samuel started work on his *Ballade in A minor*. Taking 15 minutes to play, its originality is described by Berwick Sayers. When in February 1898, Samuel conducted the string section from the Conservatoire Orchestra, Jessie sang songs by Schubert and Samuel. The *Musical Review* noted, 'her singing of the latter's made a deep impression.' It was soon after this that Samuel, attracted to the 1855 epic poem by Longfellow, *The Song of Hiawatha*, began working on perhaps his best-known work, *Hiawatha's Wedding Feast*. The success of his songs owed much to the support of his mentor, Jaeger. The first part of an eventual trilogy of cantatas, premiered in November 1898, became an instant success both at home and abroad, Sullivan remarking 'Much impressed by the lad's genius'.

Ever since the couple's relationship had become known, both Samuel and Jessie had been bearing the burden of her family's attempts to prevent them marrying. But with this success, and his obvious ability to support her, the family relented. The period before their wedding was happy: Jessie visited Samuel in the afternoon and, while he composed, she would read through proofs of his works, sing his new songs and enter into all aspects of his work. They appeared together at concerts and in May 1899, at the Salle Erard in London, Samuel played his *Romance for Violin*, and Jessie sang his *Three Rhapsodies for Low Voice and Pianoforte*.

The morning of their wedding on 30 December 1899, which her family attended, the bride received a telegram from her husband-to-be:

> I will never leave thee, dearest,
> I will take thee to my wigwam. – *Hiawatha.*

Immediately after the wedding, the couple set off for the Isle of Wight, staying in Shanklin for a couple of weeks. Unfortunately, in spite of digging hard, I have been unable to unearth whereabouts in the town they stayed, but it could have been the Holliers Hotel. Samuel took the score of *Hiawatha's Wedding Feast* with them to work on the scoring; while he was doing that, Jessie read novels to him. Samuel was able to make critical comments on them while he was scoring. In the years that followed, they had two children, one a son named Hiawatha, the other, born in 1903, Gwendoline Avril who started composing at an early age and later became a conductor/composer under the professional name of Avril Taylor-Coleridge. Samuel's own career continued successfully for thirteen years, and he even became known as the 'African Mahler', but he died on 1 September 1912 of pneumonia, aged only 37. In the year of his death, he wrote to a friend:

I have been very happy in my surroundings all my life, first in my mother and then in my marriage. Even without any moderate success I think I should have been one of those rare beings – a happy man. Unlike a great many painters who want to be musicians, musicians who want to be painters, and barristers who want to be journalists. I want to be nothing in the world except what I am – a musician.

It is tempting here to sketch the life of Avril Taylor-Coleridge as a successful composer/conductor, which she certainly did become, but that must be resisted. Suffice it to say that in the twenty-first century she has been 'discovered' and particularly taken up by the Chineke! Orchestra as, indeed, her father had been. I have heard them playing his music, but not yet hers; she was a prolific composer. As for Jessie, who lived for 50 years after Samuel's death, she is chiefly remembered as an appendage to her husband's life, which is a pity. She wrote *A Memory sketch or personal reminiscences of my husband, genius and musician, S Coleridge-Taylor, 1875–1912* (1943). No doubt she fostered her daughter's talent – she would have been well-equipped to do so – and enjoyed her success. A blue plaque was erected to Samuel in 1975 on the family's South Norwood house, at 30 Dagnall Park SE25 5PH. There is also one erected for Avril on Stone's House, Seaford, where she spent her last days (d.1998).

Edward Elgar, whose help was crucial in the advancement of Samuel Coleridge-Taylor's career as a composer, also spent his 1899 honeymoon on the Isle of Wight. Was there any chance that the younger man encouraged him to spend it there? Elgar and his new wife certainly started off in Shanklin, before moving to Ventnor.

Caroline Alice Elgar (née Roberts, known as Alice; 1848–1920) was born in the Residency at Booj (now Gujarat), India, the youngest of four children, and only daughter of Major-General Sir Henry Gee Roberts KCB, hero of the Sepoy Mutiny and Sikh Wars, and Julia Maria Raikes whose grandfather had founded the Summer Schools Movement. Alice's father died when she was 12, and the family returned to England. There, still a girl, she studied with the amateur geologist the Revd WS Symonds and with him and a group of friends went fossil-hunting; she later compiled the index to a book of his. Of more interest to her later life with Elgar, she studied the piano with Ferdinand Kufferath, one time student of Mendelssohn, in Brussels, and harmony with Harford Lloyd. She spoke fluent German, and conversational Italian, French and Spanish. In 1882, four years before she met Elgar, she published the novel *Marchcroft Manor* under the name Caroline Alice Roberts. The Elgar Scholar, Diana McVeagh, describes it as

> quite an accomplished, entertaining, indeed touching tale, with a control of pace and situation, and a humour that might well surprise anyone knowing Alice only from her later verses, letters and diary.

She also notes that earlier critics have drawn attention to the 'tincture of radicalism' in the book. Alice also published a long poem, *Isabel Trevithoe* (1879).

The year 1886 was noteworthy for Alice: her brothers left to join the army, leaving her to live with her elderly widowed mother in Redmarley, then in Worcestershire. That autumn she took violin accompaniment lessons from Edward Elgar, then teaching at Worcestershire High School. When her mother died the following year, Alice went abroad for a while, but then returned to settle in a house in Malvern Link (also in Worcestershire). From there, she continued her accompaniment lessons. Soon it was obvious that there was an attachment between the couple, one that was disapproved of by both families. Alice was nearly nine years older than Elgar: she was then 38, and seemed destined to remain unmarried; he was 27 and fell easily in love; she was an Anglican, he, brought up a Roman Catholic; she was a member of the gentry with an income of her own, he was a penniless would-be composer who had started composing by the age of 10, and from the age of 16 made his living as a freelance musician; his father ran a music shop in Worcester – to her family, he was in trade; Alice was firmly informed that she would be 'marrying beneath her'. What they had in common, apart from a love of music, was, underneath a Victorian reservation, a passionate soul, which they recognised in each other. What is more, Alice saw that Edward had potential brilliance that she could and would nurture.

When, against everyone's wishes, they became engaged, Alice expressed her feelings in the poem, 'Love Alone will Stay' which she gave to Elgar:

> Closely cling, for winds drive fast,
> Blossoms perish in the blast,
> Love alone will last.
>
> Closely let me hold thy hand,
> Storms are sweeping sea and land,
> Love alone will stand.
>
> Kiss my lips, and softly say,
> Joy may go and sunlit day,
> Love alone will last.

The poem is hardly the place to illustrate any of the humour Alice may have had; it says neatly and in a heartfelt manner what it means. Elgar wrote what would become world famous, a short violin and piano piece, *Liebesgruss* (Love's Greeting), in honour of Alice's fluent German. It was dedicated 'à Carice', a combination of Caroline Alice; and it was what they were to call their daughter (b.1890). The title of the piece was later changed to *Salut d'Amour* (with *Liebesgruss* as its subtitle), and was first performed as an orchestral version at a Crystal Palace concert in November 1889. It was Elgar's first composition to be published – *Salut d'Amour* (op. 12). The publisher was cannier than Elgar as regards who earned the profits from it.

Alice's family, not her parents who were both dead, did not relent: only a cousin and his wife attended the wedding which took place in a shortened Catholic ceremony on 8 May 1889 at the Brompton Oratory, Knightsbridge. On Elgar's side, his parents and a musical friend were there. To celebrate their marriage, Alice gave him her poem *Wind of Dawn* which Elgar later set to music. You can watch it being sung on YouTube with its thrilling accompaniment; the whole is a hint of the passion of both poet and composer. The wedding breakfast took place at the nearby house of a friend of Alice's; Elgar later dedicated *A Song of Autumn* to their daughter. There is not always agreement about who gave which – poem or music – and when. Let them stand in their own right to mark their love.

Following their marriage, the couple travelled from London to the Isle of Wight. Though they started their honeymoon in Shanklin, at the smart Holliers Hotel, Elgar having walked from there to Ventnor, they soon moved to that town, which is further to the south. Unlike the apparent lack of knowledge about the location of the Coleridge-Taylors' honeymoon in Shanklin, that of the Elgars in Ventnor is well documented, and the blue plaque, shown here on the outside of 3 Alexandra Gardens, is not easy to miss. It is a large house in a crescent just above the Esplanade with a wide view over the sea; it was, then, recently built (1883). On the plaque, Elgar is named as Sir Edward Elgar, although he was not knighted until 1904. He is naturally regarded in Ventnor as a celebrity, which he did not become until later, and elsewhere. If you are lucky, and if the house is empty when you're there, you can, if it is convenient to the owner, see inside. The house is often let for as many as ten people; there are five bedrooms. It is worth aspiring to: you can see exactly where the Elgars stayed, on the first floor, and an Elgar album is kept there.

29. Elgar Plaque, courtesy of John Allen

Elgar did not compose in Ventnor: there was so much else to do, quite apart from getting to know each other better, such as fishing from the pier and walking, and they had fine weather. At one stage they took a horse-drawn coach to Freshwater, at the other end of the south coast. That they much appreciated the location and their accommodation run by Mrs Horspool is expressed in a letter Elgar wrote to the friend who had attended his wedding:

> We are liking this place very much & have nice rooms over-looking the sea and shall remain here until the London house is ready ... the flowers and wild things here are marvellous, so large and forward, and the gorse, which is in fullest bloom, so abundant and large. The hills, and there are many, & dales are one mass of brilliant yellow! The weather is gorgeous & we are happy and well ...

There is an Alexandra Gardens website written and posted up by the owner of Number 3, John Allen, from which the above letter comes. In addition there is the following letter written to Carice Elgar, following her father's death in 1934, by a Mrs Richardson of Bisley; she was Mrs Horspool's daughter:

> ... The house that my mother and I occupied was too large for us, so with two maids – life was easier for people like ourselves in those days – we frequently had our friends as paying guests, who appreciated a place that was neither boarding nor lodging house yet had all the amenities of a private house ... Sir Edward and your Mother had the drawing room floor, and won all our praises for the simplicity and lack of ostentation or 'swank'. I remember they left a very appreciative and flattering account of their visit to us which I would have given a great deal to have preserved ... The recollection of your great father's visit will be green in my memory until my own call comes.

The implication that Elgar was then famous shows how difficult it can be to use oral history in trying to re-create history. He was, of course, to become famous, but that is in the future at this time and owes much to Alice. Although his successful career is well enough known for there to be no need for it to be detailed here, it is worth giving a couple of illustrations of Alice's involvement. She provided him with verse for the following works: *Scenes from the Bavarian Highlands, O Happy eyes, Fly Singing Birds*, and *The Snow* – the latter two being excerpts from her long poem *Isabel Trevithoe*. She also provided one of the poems, *In Haven (Capri)*, for Edward's orchestral song cycle, *Sea Pictures*, which was enthusiastically received at its 1899 premiere, with the soloist Clara Butt – a version that it is still possible to listen to. After 1900 Alice made only occasional literary contributions, for example the text of the carol, *A Christmas Greeting*. Even after she'd stopped writing, it was to devote herself to bolstering his resolve, both practically and emotionally. She helped him with the demanding task of copying his manuscripts and, long before he sent a manuscript off to his publishers, she had listened to it, and did not hesitate to make gentle comments that spurred him to revision – 'Don't you think dear Edward …'. Her musician's ear and brain were to remain useful. She seems to be best remembered for the comment in her diary: 'The care of a genius is enough of a life work for any woman'. It is interesting that a photograph of them has him sitting, her standing; I've noted before that this reversal of position seems also to suggest, at least to me, a reversal of role.

I toyed for a while about how to include Marie Spartali: she could so easily have fitted into chapter 8, 'Freshwater', with Julia Margaret Cameron's other models, but she was an artist in her own right, well known as a Pre-Raphaelite painter. It is not difficult to track down myriad examples of her work in that style, often of characters from classical times, but it is possible to scroll for too long (and with limited success) to find what should have been many Isle of Wight ones, though Jan Marsh describes her in 'Women Artists and the Isle of Wight' (2012). Marie's family had two properties on the Island, Rylstone Manor, Shanklin, which, though essentially Victorian, includes Gothic, Tudor and Georgian influences. It was built by Marie's father in 1863 and the family alternated between there and a house in London. The Spartalis' other Island house was Sandford, Godshill, Ventnor. Marie spent many childhood summers on the Island. Then I discovered that Marie and her husband, the American journalist William Stillman, honeymooned on the Island in 1871.

Marie Spartali Stillman (1844–1927) was the daughter of Michael (Dmitrios) Spartali, born in Smyrna (now Izmir, Turkey), the senior partner of Spartali & Lascali, bankers and grain merchants, of London, Liverpool and Marseilles, and Euphrosyne Varsamis, the daughter of a Greek merchant from Genoa. They had married in London and both eventually held British citizenship; he was Consul General of Greece in London, 1867–1881. Although the couple spoke Greek at home, the children's first language was English and Marie also spoke French, German and Italian. With two properties in England – in London and Surrey – and two on the Isle of Wight, Spartali

30. Marie Spartali by Julia Margaret Cameron,
© National Portrait Gallery, London

was obviously rich enough for their two daughters and a son to have a privileged upbringing, and to move in the sort of circles where pianist Christina could marry into the aristocracy and for an aspiring artist to meet well-known artists, including pre-Raphaelites.

By 1864, Marie was studying with Ford Madox Brown in London, and soon knew Whistler, Rosetti and Burne-Jones. The family's close Greek friends in the Holland Park area led to entrée for Marie into Sara Pattle Prinsep's Little Holland House salon. This, not surprisingly, meant that she was to meet Sara's sister Julia Margaret Cameron who started to photograph her there, and continued later on the Island, inviting her to Freshwater to pose; in all, she photographed Marie 12 or more times. From watching the photographer at work, Marie picked up tips for her own portrait painting, as well as the importance of commitment and dedication; Julia Margaret was an example of a professional woman artist. In 1870, Marie was taken to meet short-sighted Tennyson who became less grumpy when he picked up a candle and looked at her closely. Marie's father, who patronised artists, and encouraged his daughter, paid Julia Margaret good money for photographic copies of Marie. Her looks were such that other artists, such as Rossetti, also used her as a model; Whistler had already painted both her and Christina. Swinburne was reported as saying of Marie that 'She is so beautiful that I want to sit down and cry'. Marie's first exhibition as an artist came in 1867, and in 1870 she sent paintings to the Royal Academy and the Paris Salon. As Jan Marsh, author of *Pre-Raphaelite Women: Images of Femininity* (1998), writes in 'Marie Spartali 2' (2015):

> Ambition in young Victorian Women, whether of British or Greek ancestry was frowned on. Modesty, obedience and self-sacrifice were the approved virtues. Marie's demeanour was modest and retiring but her aspirations, as expressed in her picture titles were heroic.

It was at Little Holland House that Marie met William Stillman who, as well as being a journalist, was an aspiring artist; he too sat for Rossetti, featuring as his famous *Dante*. He was a widower 26 years older than Marie, whose wife had committed suicide, leaving him with three young children. They became engaged in January 1870. Her parents, as so often, were against such a union; Jan Marsh read their minds: he was doubtless 'a penniless widower wanting both a step-mother and a wealthy wife'. Marie was a loving and dutiful daughter, but she held firm, and they married in 1871; given the lack of family, that Marie was Greek Orthodox and Stillman Baptist, it was at the Chelsea Register Office. Then they set off for the Isle of Wight for their honeymoon. It did not go exactly as planned; Stillman wrote to Maddox Brown:

> We got here alright, some the worse for wear – M was excessively fatigued and feverish, but today she seems calm and stronger – the rain which considerately kept off for the wedding follows us here and shuts us indoors, while the landlord having a previous order for our room insists on turning us out. In the dilemma we go to Bournemouth by the next train.

It is not clear if most of the rest of the letter is about Bournemouth, or if it describes wherever they were first staying on the Island, but it ends, 'We shall stay at Bournemouth until the rain stops and then go over to Freshwater.' That saga makes it unlikely that Marie produced any paintings on the island then, but there were certainly other times when she could have done. Her Arreton watercolours – *The Old Church Arreton, The Farm at Arreton, The Old Barn Arreton* – date from as late as 1908. I wondered why Arreton? It turns out that Stillman's son from his first marriage, Russie, had been buried there, and obviously died thereabouts, in 1875 (Stillman, himself, died in 1901). To her three stepchildren, Marie had added two of her own. She knew what it was like to be a professional woman and a mother, particularly when it was uncommon.

31. Maria Spartali, 'Old Barn, Arreton', from the Internet

Marie's paintings of the scenes of the Isle of Wight are few, given that over her fifty years of work (1867–1919) she produced 150 paintings. She became a respected painter, praised by Rossetti and others; she was not just a model for him. Rossetti's brother, William Rossetti wrote,

Of all the women who elicited Gabriel's admiration, Marie Spartali was probably the most gifted intellectually. Of an ancient and noble race, austere, virtuous and fearless she was not lacking in a caustic wit and a sharp tongue.

Although Marie and Stillman spent much of their married life, while Stillman was a foreign correspondent for *The Times*, between London, Florence and Rome (from which Marie took inspiration), there must surely be more Spartali

Isle of Wight paintings lurking somewhere, given the number of times she would have stayed there over the years.

Marie died in London, a few days before her 83rd birthday. Her work, among that of 11 other women artists, featured in the exhibition 'Pre-Raphaelite Sisters' at the National Portrait Gallery, London (17 October 2019–26 January 2020). Unfortunately, I did not know about Marie then, and her Isle of Wight watercolours would not have featured.

The Osborne House Connection, 1848–1906

Princess Louise, Duchess of Argyll (Louisa Caroline Alberta; 1848–1939) was the sixth child, and fourth daughter of Queen Victoria and Prince Albert. She is known as the rebellious one, and rumours of potential scandal are attached to her name. The title of Lucinda Hawkesley's biography encapsulates that: *The Mystery of Princess Louise: Queen Victoria's Rebellious Daughter* (2014) and the first paragraph of the blurb on the back of my paperback copy (bought at Osborne House) reads:

> The secrets of Queen Victoria's sixth child, the artistic and tempestuous Princess Louise, have been shielded for years from public view, with rumours of her colourful life hinted at but never documented in hard fact.

I'm afraid, I'm going to ignore most of that, as well as her uneven relationship with her mother, her life as a busy royal conveniently married to the eccentric Duke of Argyll – who was Governor General of Canada 1878–1884, where

Louise accompanied him. I touch here only in passing on her 'politics': the fact that she was a proponent of higher education, a supporter of the feminist movement and women's suffrage in Britain and Canada, and corresponded with the social reformer Josephine Butler, and visited Elizabeth Garrett, the first woman doctor. In addition, she cycled, smoked and cooked, as well as danced, played the piano, acted and was considered beautiful. Instead, given the content of this chapter, I concentrate on her work as an artist, in particular a sculptor; in a way that is to sculpt her artistic life from the noise of the rest of it. Her art is well able to stand alone. And perhaps the result of her output can best and most accessibly be seen on the Isle of Wight.

32. Princess Louise, from the Internet

It is worth emphasising that both Louise's parents were artistic; Osborne House is full of paintings; Queen Victoria played the piano there and the water-colours she painted are well known about; Prince Albert, as noted, designed Osborne House, and is known for other design work, and his more general interest in the field. So it is not surprising that the children were all encour-aged in their artistic endeavours: along with her siblings, Louise had lessons in drawing and watercolour painting from the artist Edward Henry Corbould. It was a family tradition that the children would present their parents with drawings and watercolours on special occasions, as Queen Victoria did as a child, and as many children do today. Their work was kept and mounted in albums. Louise's continued to stand out: her sketches and watercolours done throughout her life are housed in the print room designed by her father.

As Louise grew older, and her skills and talent developed, she received private tuition – when she was 16 from Susana Durant in 1864, and from the sculptor Mary Thorneycroft from 1867; she later attended the National Art Training School. The training she received there, though, was intended for industrial designers and art teachers, rather than for fine artists, as it was for men. In spite of that, Louise was soon one of the first members of the royal family publicly to practise as an artist, and, as her biographer puts it concerning the Pre-Raph-aelite artists, she would come to know these young men and their circle both socially and professionally and they would have a positive impact on her life.

Louise's life-size statue of her mother in coronation robes sitting on a throne still stands outside Kensington Palace. Apparently some members of the press claimed that it was her tutor, and her mother's sculptor, Sir Edgar Boehm, who had created it. Another of the rumours was that the princess had a romance with him.

Louise's artistic interests were broad: she also involved herself in architec-tural and garden design. She was given a free hand over the Argyle family home – the castle at Rosneath where she and her husband (still the Marquis of Lorne until his father died in 1904), enjoyed working together in the garden; this was although they were said not to be a close couple. The property belonged to the Argyle family, but Louise helped with its financing. She was a friend of the famous garden designer Gertrude Jekyll who introduced her to the architect Edwin Lutyens. He not only started work on the castle, but also helped Louise with the design of the Ferry Inn (convenient for the ferries), in the Arts & Crafts style, simple and comfortable; Louise liked to think it could be a bolthole. Anne Galliard tells the story of that dream being scotched in her posted piece on the princess's forays in designs and architecture:

> Louise's dream of a simple life staying at the Inn was not to be. Queen Victoria was enraged when a cartoon appeared in Punch magazine depicting Louise as a barmaid being asked by a local drinker; 'and how's your old mother?' She forbade Louise to stay there and the princess had to stay at the Castle.

The subheading that follows that story, **Louise's finest work?** takes us to the Isle of Wight. When the family was at Osborne House, their local church was the Royal Church of St Mildred at nearby Whippingham on the Osborne estate. Although there had been a church there since Anglo-Saxon times, Prince Albert designed the one there now. Princess Louise was confirmed there, aged 17, in January 1865. In due course, the church overlooking the Medina river was to contain several of her artistic touches: the original and rather square font, given by Queen Victoria, was designed by Louise and installed in 1864; the pieces of carpet surrounding it were designed and originally worked by Louise, as well as her younger sister Beatrice (the Queen's last child) and several of their ladies-in-waiting helped her (worn bits have been restored more recently). The chair on the north side of the sanctuary dates from the time of Oliver Cromwell and was given to the church by Princess Louise.

At the back of the church, as you enter, on the left, and opposite the family pews, is the Battenberg Chapel. Princess Beatrice married Prince Henry of Battenberg in the church in 1885. Everyone in the family loved him; tittle-tattle suggested that for Louise it was more than that: and that she was jealous of Beatrice for the happiness of her marriage compared with that of her own. Queen Victoria put up much resistance to Beatrice's marriage as she was her mother's secretary and constant companion. The queen only agreed to it if they lived in a flat in Osborne House, and she made Henry governor of the Island. She did, however, allow him to sail off to the Ashanti War in 1896. He caught malaria on board ship on the way out and had to return quickly, dying before he reached home; he was only 38. He was buried in a large white marble sarcophagus in the chapel behind a wrought-iron grille, and when Beatrice died in 1945, after an initial burial in London, she joined him there. In the corner of the chapel is where you will find Louise's *pièce de résistance* – a large bronze angel incorporating Christ on the Cross.

Louise executed three similar pieces between 1896 and 1906 – one for the Argyle Mausoleum

33. Princess Louise's angel, photograph by Jane Richter

at Rosneath which went undiscovered for one hundred years but is now known to have been dedicated by Louise to her father-in-law who died in 1900 (it is now in the Visitor Area of St Munn's Church); another is displayed in St Paul's Cathedral, London, signed 1904 and installed in 1905; the third is that in St Mildred's. As Anne Galliard writes, 'The diary of Lord Ronald Sutherland Gower dates work in progress on the Whippingham statue in the early months of 1898 and there are also other records which indicate that this was the first work.'

I have only been able to find one watercolour by Louise painted on the Isle of Wight. It is housed in an album of drawings by her in the volume *Princess Louise Album 2* held in the Royal Collection, but it can be easily seen online. It is entitled 'East Cowes, Isle of Wight, Small Avenue'. You would think it was painted in the grounds of Osborne House, but it doesn't say so. This is how it is described: 'The terrace is shown in the centre, lined with flower beds. Steps leading up to the house from the terrace are shown in the foreground to the right. Trees are shown in the background.'

While in Osborne House, you will pass, in the queen and Prince Albert's quarters, a couple of marble heads sculpted by Louise. At the end of a tour, you come to the Durbar Wing which Queen Victoria had attached to the house, completed in 1891 during her phase of enthusiasm for all things Indian. The queen and Princess Louise took a keen interest in the interior design of the great hall. Louise voiced her opposition to the gallery above the fireplace and suggested a peacock instead. Her suggestion was incorporated into the final design and is what visitors will see when they step into the room.

Before Mary Thornycroft became Louise's private art tutor, and began to be a significant figure in her life, she was commissioned by the queen and Prince Albert to take casts and make models of their children. Princess Louise would have learned how to sit, measure proportion and use the appropriate tools; she would have watched Mary make plaster casts of her and her siblings and translate them into marble. An example of the process is an 1856 life-size white marble statue of Louise as *Plenty*, wearing a loose robe and holding a cornucopia in her right hand, a sheaf of corn lies beneath her right foot. Don't miss it in the drawing room at Osborne House.

When the queen died in 1901, Louise inherited Kent House on the Osborne estate, a country residence where as a widow she would spend much of her time, when she wasn't at Kensington Palace. She lived until the age of 91, dying in the year that the Second World War began.

The watercolour 'The View from the unfinished terrace, Osborne' *c.*1848 is attributed, on the original album sheet, to Leitch and Charlotte Canning, one of Queen Victoria's ladies-in-waiting. The Royal Collection details note that she was 'an extremely accomplished artist' and adds 'it is probably primarily by Canning, with Leitch assisting with elements of the composition and colouring. It was Lady Canning who recommended Leitch as a teacher to the queen'; he was to teach both the queen and her children, including Princess Louise.

34. Charlotte Canning, 'View of the Terrace, Osborne House', courtesy of
the Royal Collection Trust, © His Majesty King Charles III 2024

Charlotte Canning, Countess Canning (née Stuart; 1817–1861) was the
daughter of Charles Stuart, 1st Baron Stuart of Rothesay; her mother was
Lady Elizabeth Yorke. She was born and brought up in the British Embassy
in Paris while her father was ambassador to France. Her biographical details
describe her as a British artist and the first Vicereine of India, in that order. Her
husband, Charles Canning, whom she married in 1835, inherited his mother's
title in 1837, becoming Viscount Canning, and Charlotte Viscountess. He
served as governor-general of India from 1856 to 1858 and then Viceroy until
1862; in 1859 he was created 1st Earl Canning. Following their time in India,
during which she made four tours of the country, she was said to be one of
India's most prolific artists – two portfolios in the Victoria & Albert Museum
contain some 350 watercolours by her. Through her interest in natural history,
she collected plants and flowers, and many of her paintings are botanical illustrations. As well as keeping a journal during her time in India, Charlotte also
wrote regularly to Queen Victoria, giving detailed accounts of her life, and sent
nature samples to the royal children. She had no children of her own.

But the unfinished Osborne House terrace dates from years before, when
Charlotte served as the queen's Lady of the Bedchamber from 1845 to 1851.
Her task was simple: to be the queen's constant companion, smoothing her
way. The building works at Osborne came in the middle of that. One of the
charms of the painting is that it does not show the house, but the view of the
terrace and across the park towards the sea on which, in the distance, sails
one yacht. In the forefront are slabs of paving ready to be laid, giving only an
impression of the unfinished building behind; it is, therefore, something of
a historical record of a historical time. Charlotte also produced at least three
other Osborne watercolours: of the vinery, of Swiss Cottage, and the completed
house itself, painted from the terrace.

Looking forward to returning to England after five years in India, Charlotte Canning became ill during her last tour of India and died in Calcutta of malaria, aged 64. She was buried in Barrackpore; in 1913 her grave and memorial were located in the churchyard of St John's Church, Calcutta. Her death was widely mourned in England – it was said that she seemed to exemplify 'feminine virtue across the British Empire', Her death hit Queen Victoria in the same year that Prince Albert died.

Barbara Bodichon, Winifred Nicholson and Rebellion, 1856–1981

Although Barbara Bodichon did train as an artist, and was known as such in artistic circles, she is better known as an early feminist, campaigner and writer on the law as it affected women. But she is featured here for one particular watercolour painted in Ventnor in 1856 when she was on holiday there with her friend Anna Mary Howitt, also an artist. I wish I could show it here; it is just a cliff-scape, but its colours (which you can easily see on the Internet) are such that it is they which create its striking impression. A critic pronounced it 'a capital coast scene, full of real-pre-Raphaelitism'. The view has been identified as near Luccombe, just to the east of Ventnor, looking north-east across Shanklin Bay to Culver Cliff in the far distance; some of the forefront has been misplaced for artistic effect.

The painting is signed 'Barbara Leigh Smith' which gives an intimation of her unusual background (Florence Nightingale was a cousin). The father of **Barbara Bodichon** (née Barbara Leigh Smith, 1827–1891) was the Whig MP Benjamin 'Ben' Leigh Smith, but he was not married to her mother, Anne Longden, a milliner. What is more, he went on to live with her on and off. His main residence was in London but he also had a house on the south coast where Anne lived. He had four more children with her, without marrying her; she was known as Mrs Leigh – the surname of his well-known relatives on the Isle of Wight. Although there was a scandal when Barbara was born, Ben Smith obviously took no notice, and Anne was pregnant again within eight weeks. He was a member of the landed gentry who held radical views, a man who put his money where his mouth was in his financial help to the poor, particularly the schooling of children. He later shared financial investments giving £300 a year equally to all his own children when they reached the age of 21. No doubt some of his radicalism rubbed off on Barbara, and she was financially secure enough, unlike most women, to finance her campaigning. As far as Barbara's education was concerned, after having been sent to the local school as a child, she later studied at the Ladies College in Bedford Square where she was given instruction for work as a professional artist, which her economic independence allowed that, too, to develop.

Although Barbara married Eugène Bodichon, an eminent French physician, the year after the Ventnor watercolour was painted, he does not seem to appear in the picture of Barbara's activities. It was the same year as the Matrimonial Causes Act (1857), for which she had campaigned, was passed; it allowed women access to divorce courts. She and Anna Mary Howett were members of a group of London women, known as 'The Ladies of Langham Place', who used to meet. They are said to have been one of the first organised women's movements in Britain, pursuing vigorously, via a committee, such causes as married women's property. In 1854, she had published *Brief Summary of the Laws of England Concerning Women*, which helped to promote the passage of the Married Women's Property Act 1882. In 1858, she set up the *English Women's Journal*, a periodical which emphasised direct employment and equality issues for women. And in 1866, cooperating with Emily Davis, Barbara set up a scheme to extend university education to women; a small experiment in this idea developed into Girton College, Cambridge, to which she gave her time and money. In 1865, with others, she brought up the idea of parliamentary reform aimed at achieving women's suffrage. Chapter 12 will feature Isle of Wight women involved in the campaign for women's suffrage.

In spite of all this serious campaigning, Barbara maintained her interest in her favourite art – painting – studying under Holman Hunt. Her watercolours are described as showing originality and talent, and admired by Corot who had guided Berthe Morisot at one stage of her artistic development. Barbara exhibited at the Salon, the Royal Academy and elsewhere. She was an early member of the Society of Female Artists – as Isle of Wight artists such as Fanny Minns were – and showed 59 of her works between 1858 and 1886. She campaigned for women to have membership of the Royal Academy. Information about any other Isle of Wight watercolours signed Barbara Leigh-Smith that have eluded my attention would be gratefully received.

While Barbara Bodichon's 'rebellion' against the status quo was widespread concerning women in general, that of **Winifred Nicholson** (1893–1981) tended to be focused at first on women artists and later on the scope of art itself. The information about an exhibition at the Victoria Art Gallery in Bath notes:

> The New English Art Club was founded in 1886 by a group of rebellious young artists protesting against their repeated rejection by the Royal Academy. Their aim was to exhibit 'really good modern painting'. In 1937 the art historian and museum curator Mary Chamot described the Club as, unquestionably the most vital artistic movement in English painting of the last half century.

The exhibition of 2023 featured more than 40 works by current Club members, including Winifred Nicholson.

Winifred was born Rosa Winifred Roberts in Oxford, the eldest of three children of the Liberal Party politician Charles Henry Roberts and Lady Cecilia Howard, the daughter of another politician and the activist Rosalind Howard. Winifred started painting as a teenager with her grandfather, George Howard, 9th Earl of Carlisle, a capable amateur artist and friend of the Pre-Raphaelites William Morris and Burne-Jones, and of the Italian landscape painter Nino

Costa, founder of the Etruscan School. She attended the Byam Shaw School of Art from some time between 1910 and 1912 until the beginning of the First World War in 1914, and again from 1918 to 1919. That year she travelled with her father, who had been Under-Secretary of State for India, to Burma, Ceylon and India. A year later she married the artist Ben Nicholson.

The couple bought a villa in Switzerland on the north shore of Lake Lugano, and spent half the year there, the summers in Britain, painting still lives and landscapes. Through the 1920s they worked closely together carving out new ideas as artists and exhibiting both singly and together. Ben Nicholson had already joined and become the influential chairman of the Seven and Five Society, set up in London in 1919 as an exhibiting body for young and radical artists, by the time Winfred was elected a new member in 1925. A Howgill Tattershall fine art gallery prospectus continues about the members, who

> shared what might be described as a Neo-Romantic view of post-War Britain, being especially preoccupied by the post-War landscape and its poetic burden of local features and – beneath the skin – ancient bones. … Clearly, at this time, these artists were searching for remote parts of the country, away from metropolitan centres, where they could witness and be part of a more rustic society, a more 'authentic' people, a wider landscape.

No doubt inspired by that, at the end of 1923, they, or Winifred, bought Bankshead in Cumbria, a farmhouse built on an ancient Roman castle forming part of Hadrian's Wall. On the personal front, the couple wanted children, but Winifred took a long time to conceive. In 1924, believing that she was unable to do so, she joined the Christian Science Movement, in vogue at the time. In 1927 Winifred, hanging paintings for her first solo exhibition, fell through a trapdoor, injuring her back. Her injuries were so serious that it was thought she would not recover. However, she did so sufficiently to visit a Christian Science practitioner to help with further recovery. She was able to visit her exhibition. The following year she exhibited a painting at the Venice Biennale.

Whatever the reason for the delay in conceiving, Jake was born in 1927, the year of the accident, Kate in 1929, Andrew in July 1931, Winifred giving birth at Bankshead. But before Andrew's birth, indeed as early as before Kate's birth, there was, apparently, tension in the marriage. In the autumn of 1931, Winifred took herself off, with her three children, Andrew a babe in arms, to the Isle of Wight, renting a house in Fishbourne (a place which hasn't appeared in this book since chapter 2 when in 2016 a woman's skeleton dating from 2,000 years ago was found). Why Winifred chose the Island or Fishbourne is not revealed, but she was to stay there until February or March 1932. In 1931 Ben had met the sculptor Barbara Hepworth and started living with her just after the birth of Andrew. It is not clear if that precipitated Winifred's move to the Island, but she and Ben remained on good terms, writing to each other until the end of her life. She wrote to him from Fishbourne which, if it was as peaceful as it seemed in 2023, would have been a good place for contemplation and licking her wounds:

> I like your idea of our new relationship – clear and true in complete freedom & unexclusiveness ... The day is full of bright sunlight. The white ship in the distance came straight out of Kit's St Ives picture – moving like magic and dazzling white – serene and cold.

The letter comes from *Unknown Colour: Paintings, Letters, Writings by Winifred Nicholson*; edited by Andrew Nicholson (1987). There are other books about Winifred, or which include her. Kit was Christopher Wood, also a member of the Seven and Five Club, who often travelled and painted with the Nicholsons. Kit committed suicide in August 1930, and this tragedy apparently exacerbated the tensions in the Nicholson marriage. The ship that Winifred describes in her letter is important because it appears in one of the two very similar paintings, all that there seem to have been produced in the conservatory of the house on the Isle of Wight. They are so similar that it is a bit like those puzzles where you have to spot the difference, one is called *Kate and Jake on the Isle of Wight* which is now in the Bristol Museum and Art Gallery; the other, *Jake and Kate on the Isle of Wight*, is in the National Galleries of Scotland: Modern.

The Jake and Kate painting has the ship going either in or out behind a long narrow headland. The two children are sitting in front of a window, Kate on the left wearing a white mob cap with a ribbon around it fixed with a star and wearing a jersey with two large pale badges, one on either side; Jake is wearing a hat like a tea cosy; he is about to take a bite out of something in his hand. In front of Kate is a platter, in front of Jake a bowl, there is a striped mug or glass between them. The Kate and Jake painting is done with the children at the same table but sitting further away from the artist; the headland is shorter and thicker and the ship may be obscured by Jake's witch's hat, as if from a cracker. Kate is wearing a different jersey. In front of them both is a large plate containing two large pieces of fruit. The hands of both of them are placed differently in each.

In spring 1932, Winifred went to Cornwall, and in the autumn to Paris where she lived until 1938, spending the summers in Cumberland. In Paris she met many other artists also living there, such as Mondrian and Kandinsky. She began producing abstract paintings, and also helped at a small Montessori school for young children. More than once Ben came to visit the family in Paris. When Winifred exhibited abstract paintings at the 14th Seven and Five exhibition in 1935, Ben was anxious about any possible confusion occasioned by her using their joint name, so she exhibited under the old family name of Dacre – one she continued to use, and also in articles she wrote. Over Winifred's lifetime she showed at over 200 group exhibitions.

In 1938, with war in the air, Winifred closed the Paris flat and encouraged Mondrian to go with her to London by train. That was also the year of her divorce from Ben. After the war she travelled, painted, wrote and exhibited until her death in 1981; the details of that productive life and work can be seen most simply in the Chronology on the Internet. Apart from the books about her, there are at least two abstract paintings in the Tate, purchased in 1975. She often travelled with her daughter Kate, who is particularly worth mentioning because she, too, became an artist of note, enrolling in the Bath Academy in 1949, and studying there until 1954.

For all her travelling, there seems to be no evidence that Winifred ever visited the Isle of Wight again after 1932. As her wintry time there was probably not a happy one – it is noticeable that she produced only two paintings during her stay, and those predominantly feature her children – that is not surprising, but a pity.

10 – Women Writers, 1813–2011

Introduction

As the Preface intimated, I don't meet many people today who haven't been to the Isle of Wight. But more than one well-known, nineteenth-century British woman writer didn't even need to have visited the Island, to make use of it by name, though Jane Austen depended on a niece's visit there to prompt her. George Eliot not only visited the Island but did so at least once, and wrote letters to prove it. Many more men writers visited, but only one has managed to slip through to grace this introduction, and that's because of the possible inspiration provided by a woman Islander. Otherwise, those who appear following this introduction are either Islanders, or long-term residents. Sometimes, though, there are a writer and an artist in the same household, and one woman is a diarist who brilliantly illustrates what she writes.

It doesn't seem that Jane Austen herself visited the Island, but her brother Edward Austen Knight did, together with his daughter **Fanny Catherine Knight** (later Lady Knatchbull; 1793–1882), first-born of his 11 children. No wonder Edward's wife wasn't with the pair, as she had pretty well one child a year. Jane, who was close to her niece, only 17 years her junior, heard about her trip to the Island through her letters and made use of her visit in a snippet in *Mansfield Park* (1814). But first, extracts from Fanny's letters are worth including. Travelling in a gig, the couple, having set off at 8am on 7 June 1813, 'Breakfasted at Petersfield. Dined and Saw the Dock Yard at Portsmouth, & took a wherry [light rowing boat] over to the Isle of Wight in the evening. We slept at Ride.'

And then: 'We went on in the sociable to Newport where we dined, & then to Freshwater towards the Western Coast, & took a boat round the Needles point to Yarmouth where we slept.' A 'sociable' short for a sociable coach or a barouche-sociable, is an open, horse-drawn four-wheeled carriage with two double seats facing each other.

On another day, 'We hired a sociable and drove around the Eastern and Southern Coasts of the Island – saw the Priory a sweet place – Shanklin Chine, lovely.'

From those glimpses of the Island, Jane wrote in *Mansfield Park*, published the year after Fanny's trip, using it to display the contempt with which her character, also called Fanny (Price), is held by her cousins, Maria and Julia Bertram:

'Dear mama, only think, my cousin cannot tell the principal rivers in Russia – or she never heard of Asia Minor – or she does not know the difference between water-colour and crayons! How strange – did you ever hear anything so stupid?'

'My dear,' their considerate aunt would reply, 'It is very bad but you must not expect everybody to be as forward and quick at learning as yourself.'

'But aunt she is really so very ignorant! – Do you know, we asked her last night which way she would go to get to Ireland, and she said she should cross to the Isle of Wight. **She thinks of nothing but the Isle of Wight, and she calls it the Island, as if there were no other island in the world.** I am sure I should have been ashamed of myself, if I had not known better long before I was so old as she is.'

It may well be that Jane's niece Fanny had picked up during her visit to the Isle of Wight that, in fact, Islanders do call it 'the Island'. And Fanny, the novel's character, is its heroine, so the snide remark only shows up the character of the girls who made it, not Fanny.

Charlotte Brontë, aged 12, wrote in the introduction to her story, *The Tales of the Islanders*, written on 12 March 1829:

The play of the Islanders was formed in December 1827, in the following manner. One night, about the time when the cold sleet and dreary fogs of November are succeeded by snow-storms, and high piercing night-winds of confirmed winter, we were all sitting round the warm blazing kitchen fire, having just concluded a quarrel with Tabby concerning the propriety of lighting a candle, from which she came off victorious, no candle having been produced. A long pause succeeded, which was at last broken by Branwell saying, in a lazy manner, 'I don't know what to do.' This was echoed by Emily and Anne.
Tabby – 'wha ya may go t'bed.'
Branwell – 'I'd rather do anything than that.'
Charlotte – Why are you so glum to-night, Tabby? Oh! Suppose we had each an island of our own.
Branwell – 'If we had I would choose the Island of Man.'
Charlotte – 'And I would choose the Isle of Wight.'
Emily – 'The Isle of Arran for me.'
Anne – 'And mine should be Guernsey'
'We then chose who should be chief men in our islands ...'

Tabby (Tabitha Aykroyd) was the family's cook-housekeeper and for the first 15 of her 31 years at the Parsonage, the only servant living in, though the sisters themselves also cooked, cleaned and washed clothes.

It seems that **Elizabeth Barrett Browning** (née Moulton; 1806–1861) visited the Isle of Wight because that is where her distant cousin lived. Elizabeth's uncle Samuel Moulton Barrett MP was also a slave owner in Jamaica. John Kenyon was also known for his philanthropy towards the arts, rather than as the poet he aspired to be. He was mentor to Elizabeth and patron of Robert; indeed, it was he who induced Robert to write to Elizabeth before they met, thus bringing about their marriage. After that, he looked after their business affairs, was trustee of their wills, and after their son was born in 1849 he sent regular six-monthly sums of money. When Elizabeth and Robert were in London they lived in Kenyon's house and it was where Elizabeth finished the final sections of perhaps her best appreciated poem *Aurora Leigh: A Poem in Nine Books*. In August 1856 the fair copy was sent to the typesetter for proofs, together with its long dedication to 'John Kenyon Esquire'. It ended:

> Through my various efforts in Literature and steps in life you have believed in me, borne with me, and been generous to me far beyond the common uses of mere relationship or sympathy of mind, so you may kindly accept, in sight of the public, this poor sign of esteem, gratitude, and affection from
>
> Your unforgetting
> E.B.B.

It seems that Elizabeth and Robert had already visited Kenyon in Cowes in 1855–1856 during a tour of Paris and London but, with the completion of *Aurora Leigh*, they hastened to Cowes where Kenyon was gravely ill. While there Elizabeth worked on revisions and corrections. Kenyon was able to see the book in print, sending out numerous gift copies, but died in Cowes in December that year; he left Elizabeth £4,500 and Robert £6,500.

The verse novel *Aurora Leigh* is the story of a woman writer making her way in life, balancing work and love, and based on Elizabeth's own experiences. In praising it, the reviewer in *North American Review* wrote:

Mrs Browning's poems are, in all respects, the utterances of a woman – of a woman of great learning, rich experience, and powerful genius, uniting to her woman's nature the strength which is sometimes thought peculiar to a man.

George Eliot (1819–1880; known by her pen name) visited the Isle of Wight, with her partner George Henry Lewes; they were based in Niton, to the west of Ventnor. These extracts from a letter of 21 June 1863 to Miss Sara Hennell are taken from *The Isle of Wight Bedside Anthology* (compiled by Hugh Noyes, 1951):

> June 16 – George and I set off today to the Isle of Wight where we had a delightful holiday. On Friday 19th, we settled for a week at Niton which, I think, is the prettiest place in all the island. On the following Friday we went on to Freshwater, and failed, from threatening rain, in an attempt to walk to Alum Bay, so that we rather repented of our choice. The consolation was that we shall know better than to go to Freshwater another time. On the Saturday morning we drove to Ryde, and remained there until Monday, the 29th.

***

> Your letter was a welcome addition to our sunshine this Sabbath morning. For in this particular we seem to have been more fortunate than you[,]

having had almost constant sunshine since we arrived at Sandown, on Tuesday evening.

This place is perfect, reminding me of Jersey, in its combination of luxuriant greenth with the delights of a sandy beach.

At the *end* of our week, if the weather is warmer, we shall go on to Freshwater for our remaining few days. But the wind at present is a little colder than one desires it, when the object is to get rid of a cough, and unless it gets milder we shall go back to Shanklin. I am enjoying the hedgerow grasses and flowers with something like a released prisoner's feeling – it is so long since I had a bit of real English country.

Catherine Dickens (née Hogarth; 1815–1879; also known as Kate), visited the Isle of Wight with her husband Charles in 1838, staying, between 3rd and 8th September, at the Groves Needles Hotel, Alum Bay (now Alum House, converted into apartments, each of them named after famous authors such as Tennyson, but not Dickens). They then moved on to Ventnor, staying at the Ventnor Hotel (predecessor of what became the Royal Hotel) from 8th to 10th September. And that is all that seems to be vouchsafed regarding Kate's stay on the Island.

In 1860, Dickens returned alone to Ventnor, rather to Bonchurch alongside it, having arranged a legal separation from Kate in 1858, and having had ten children with her. When there is a mystery to solve, people often pile in to do so; thus it is with Charles Dickens' stay at the time he was writing *David Copperfield* (serialised in 1860–1861, published in three volumes in 1861). What has the mystery solvers slathering at the literary mouth concerns one of his central characters, Miss Haversham who, when jilted at the altar, confined herself to a room in her house, for ever, wearing her wedding dress. There were too many coincidences in Bonchurch that could not be resisted. The most important was that the same thing is said to have happened to **Miss Margaret Dick** when Dickens was there (staying at Winterbourne, Bonchurch), leading her to cut herself off from society. She was the daughter of Captain Samuel Dick, and the family lived at Uppermount in Bonchurch until Dick died. A 2023 article – 'What the Dickens! Was Bonchurch Women Margaret Dick the Real-Life Miss Havisham?' – was written by David Couldrey for the *Island Echo* while a television serial of the novel was being shown. This is not the only source suggesting that Margaret Dick was jilted at the altar of Holy Trinity Church on the morning of her wedding, and that she lived out the rest of her days as a recluse. What is more, there was a Haviland House in the locality where a Miss Haviland had lived. And there is another character in the novel with the surname Dick.

That's all very well, but a Ventnor & District Local History Society posting, in the form of an obituary on Margaret Dick's death in 1878 after a long illness – 'Miss Margaret Catherine Dick, Once of Madeira Hall, Bonchurch' – tells a different story, illustrated by a portrait of Miss Dick lying propped up in bed:

A Bonchurch resident of more than one hundred years ago, Mrs S Kingswell, recollected late in life that her father's youngest sister was once a companion/ nurse to Miss Dick and that the lady had taken to her bed after her father had withheld consent for her to marry a naval lieutenant. The particular pose of the photograph lends some confirmation to this account. However, not all of the information recounted ... conform[s] to Dickens's famous character, and it is likely that Miss Havisham represents a compound of people and situations with which he became acquainted, or gained a knowledge about, at different points in his life.

The Isle of Wight Women Writers

Perhaps the earliest home-grown Isle of Wight writer was **Mary Fitchett Johnson** (Mrs Moncreiff; 1779–1863) whose writing, usually in sonnet form, most easily appears in *Poets of the Wight*, compiled by Charles John Arnell (1922). She was born at St Cross, Newport to John Johnson, secretary or companion to Sir Richard Worsley of Appuldurcombe who, you may remember, appeared in chapter 5, 'Irregular Relations' – involved in the scandal with his wife, Seymour Fleming, and neighbour Bissett. Mary's father travelled with Worsley and helped him with his antique collecting. Her mother was **Elizabeth Smith of Winston** (Newchurch parish), Isle of Wight.

The family moved in Mary's youth, to Wroxall, which is due east of and very near Appuldurcombe, and both of them are just north of today's Ventnor; Wroxall is, indeed, a suburb of Ventnor. But Arnell explains what it was like then, drawing, too, on a 1790 travel writer: 'Approaching the site of what is now Ventnor, a few houses were found at the foot of a "mountain like a sugar-loaf". The road to these houses from Appuldurcombe was "dangerous in the extreme". Wroxall then consisted of a few farms and was in an area where superstition was rife; the story of the ghost was well known and appears in chapter 6, 'Outsiders'. Not surprisingly, Mary wrote a sonnet about it (him) – 'Invocation to the Spirit said to haunt Wroxall Down'. Not only that but, as an example of Mary's character, one night she armed herself with a pistol, 'scaled the hill, determined to sift the mystery to the bottom.' The man – a smuggler in a white sheet – ran away, leaving behind a keg of brandy. This, as earlier described, was a common smuggling ruse. Wroxall was, as Arnell describes it, 'one of the most wild and lonely neighbourhoods in the South of England'.

Mary wrote of her use of the sonnet form, in *Original Sonnets and Other Poems by Mary F Johnson*, dated at Wroxall Farm, Isle of Wight, March 12th, 1810, quoted here only in part:

I have taken the liberty of calling them, indiscriminately, Sonnets; rather in conformity to custom and the authority of predecessors, than to strict propriety and to the purer taste of the Italian Poets, who first invented and most excelled in this species of poetry.

She also describes her poems as 'the first attempt of a secluded, unknown and inexperienced female'. She was 31 when her volume was published.

The sonnet I have chosen to quote here – 'Wroxall' – seems the most appropriate:

Wroxall! though thou art dreary dull and cold,
   Though May, when she returns to cheer the isle,
Still finds thee numbed in Winter's icy fold
   And scarcely warms thee with her parting smile;
Though 'mid the straggling cots about thee spread,
   Nor sacred pile, nor manse, nor lordly dome,
Raises its towers, or meek, or haughty head:
   I prize thee as my rustic peaceful home.
I love to steal along thy lonely ways,
   Verg'd with wild flowers in evening dew impearl'd,
Behold no mortal in my wide-stretch'd gaze,
   And seem alone in a deserted world.
While in thy scenes I fancy charms that lie
   But in a fond possessor's partial eye.

She married George Moncrieff in 1814, when she was 35, four years after the publication of her book of sonnets and poems, and went to live with him in Perthshire. They had one daughter. Mary died there aged 84.

In the year of Mary's death, 1863, her mother Elizabeth's cousin, the archaeologist Charles Roach Smith, published a piece in the *Gentleman's Magazine*, 'Isle of Wight Vernacular' that included one of Mary's sonnets in which she used words in the Island's dialect – 'A Dream of the Isle of Wight'. Roach provided a useful and fascinating list of translations, which give an insight into both the writer and the Island.

Harriet Parr (pseudonym Holme Lee; 1828–1900) did not arrive to live on the Island until 1860, but she was resident in Shanklin for the next 40 years, and died there. Born in York, she was one of the six children of Mary and William Parr, a commercial traveller in silks, satins and coloured kidskins, who died when Harriet was about 12. In exchange for her education she became a servant at the local boarding school where she then worked as a governess. She did that until her first book – *Maude Talbot* (3 vols) – was published in 1854 when she was 26. It was successful.

Helen Thomas, who wrote a short biography of Harriet Parr in a Shanklin History update in 2020 for the Shanklin & District History Society, describes how

she sent her second novel, Gilbert Messenger, to Charles Dickens hoping it might be published in parts in his periodical Household Words. Dickens declined on the grounds that it was too long and that the subject – hereditary insanity – might awaken fear and despair in those with problems in their own families. Instead he wrote a very encouraging letter to Harriet concerning the novel's 'vigour and pathos' and saying that it had 'moved me more than I can express'.

The novel was published in a single volume in 1855 and was a great success. From then on, she wrote pretty well a novel a year until 1883, all with the same publisher. Harriet is believed to have been a favourite author of Queen Victoria who was first attracted by the story of poor Dick in 'Beguilement of the Boats' published by Dickens in his 1856 Christmas edition of *Household Words*.

Several of her later novels are set in Shanklin, to which she gave various names: in *Against Wind and Tide* (1859) it is thinly disguised as Chinelyn; in *For Richer or Poorer* (1870) it is Whitburn-on-Sea. Her novels are typically Victorian in the sense that they are usually more than one volume long and the scene-setting is very detailed; unfortunately, not only are today's readers' attention spans more limited but the re-prints, as I have discovered to my cost, are large and heavy, not user friendly, particularly for those of a certain age who might have the time and appreciation to try and hold them to read. This passage is typical:

> From the high ground, they had their first glimpse of Whitburn village. It followed the course of the brook, between two slopes of down, where the water had worn a deep chine to the shore. It appeared from the distance a pretty paradise in a hollow, with a church-spire and red-tiled roofs amongst green trees – for there were trees all about the houses, and gardens with hedges of tamarisk down to the sea. The travellers approached it from the north-east, by a long winding road, and came first to the church and the ancient manor-house, now turned into a farmstead; then to the placid parsonage and a cluster of humble straw-thatched cottages, much more than half-buried in ivy-bushes; and, at a double bend of the road, where it began to climb the opposite hill, to the village proper. Here, on an elevated lawn, stood the chief hotel and a lowlier house-of-call [a sort of public house/ labour exchange] nearly facing it, both thatched, like the cottages, as to their roofs, and as to their walls trellised with roses and myrtles, jessamine and Virginian creeper. A splendid passion-flower festooned the front of the library and bazaar which had picturesque detached lodging-houses recently built upon the heights. ...

> Mary's quick observant eyes made notes of a few gay figures pacing the green lawn of the hotel, of a group of loud-talking amphibious men in the forecourt of the 'Crab and Lobster', of a quaint old philosopher, taking in the cheap novels and newspapers which garnished a rack outside the library door; a couple of women with baskets exchanging news on the steps of the baker-and-grocer's shop, where the errand boy was putting up the shutters ...

I think that gives some idea of her style. But in some ways a recollection of Harriet, written in 1900 (at the time of her death) and published in 'Public Opinion (London)' in the *Southland Times* in New Zealand is informative. It's from a man looking back at his memory of her when he was a lad in Shanklin and it tells you something more interesting about her – again this excerpt is cut down from a long piece:

> Your few lines quoted about 'Holme Lee' interested me very much. What a flood of recollections that name calls up, after a lapse of many years; far back into the early sixties, when the home of Miss Harriet Parr was still the quiet, rural, typical English Village of Shanklin, nestling under the downs, its beach washed by the English Channel, and now known as the English Bay of Naples! Here it was that Miss Parr thought out and penned those books that, once read, leave memories behind not easily effaced; but how many of the thousands that read her books knew or thought of the quiet, simple life lived by the authoress. Only those who were privileged to be brought into contact with her in that quiet village home: and even now, as if it were but yesterday, the writer in fancy is back in the old village Sunday school, listening to that soft earnest voice reading some subject of Scripture or some story from a chosen book, holding the class of lads spellbound as they watched the small delicate hands turning over the leaves, or looked for a smile from these gentle and finely-cut features. One Sunday morning in November, 1866, at the time of the flight of the Leonids [meteor shower], Miss Parr was more than usually impressive, explaining some of the mysteries of nature, and telling her lads that such a sight would not happen again for upwards of thirty years, and it was not likely that she would be spared to see that time, but we lads might live to see it; and she expressed [the wish] that we should sometimes think of her as our teacher when she was laid to rest. But Miss Parr lived to see that time come round again, though many of the lads have long since passed away. One book especially ('For Richer for Poorer') brought out some of the most charming traits of the authoress; writing of the village life of Shanklin, she delineates her characters with a wonderful delicacy of feeling … Regarding the kind hopes in the Sphere, there can be no question as to Miss Parr having enjoyed a happy life, for such a life as hers, far from the turmoil and interludes of the busy city life, amidst the lovely surrounding of the Isle of Wight, beloved by all who were brought in contact with her – such must be the ideal of happiness. Her remains are interred in the old church-yard of St John's in the grave of her sister, Miss Fanny Parr. Her home and furniture are to be sold by her special wish, and the proceeds to go to form a cottage hospital in tribute of the happy years (upwards of forty) she spent in Shanklin.

If you go looking for St John's in Shanklin with someone who doesn't know the place, as I did, you'll be disappointed: the medieval church is now St Blasius. And Harriet was not always the gentle spinster. In the summer of

1875, she took Francis White Popham to task when he closed the lane leading near her house, past the Manor House to the Parish church. Popham was Lord of Shanklin Manor; indeed, the Pophams had been Lords of the Manor since 1710, but, following a letter from Harriet printed in the *Isle of Wight County Press*, he relented and gave her a key to the gate. In 1887 and 1889, she was still campaigning for the lane to be fully reopened to the public. Francis Popham had died in 1883 and the estate passed to his widow, **Margaret, Lady Hatherington**, then to his sister **Mary Popham White**. The Pophams, too, were buried in the St John's, now St Blasius, churchyard.

By the time Harriet died, her novels were out of fashion, but her house, Whittle Meade, presumably earned from her writing, sold at auction for £1,250 and the letter from Charles Dickens went for £14. The auction proceeds of £1,400 provided an endowment for the Arthur Webster Shanklin Cottage Hospital on Landguard Manor Road, opened in 1905. Another fitting memorial to Harriet.

The hospital came under the National Health Service on its creation in 1948 and today (at least in 2018) the building is still in use by the NHS as an outpatient clinic offering various services.

It is difficult to place the Thompson family and, in some ways, it fits awkwardly into this chapter, but fit it must: to apportion each member to a different chapter would lose the impact they make together. Their Isle of Wight connection is Ventnor, including Bonchurch; they lived in both places, 1864/5 and 1871/3. The talent of three of them spread across music, painting, autobiography, poetry and essays. The mother of two daughters was **Christiana Thompson** (née Weller; 1825–1910); she was a concert pianist, composer and amateur watercolourist; her mother, Betty Dixon Weller, was a musician. The elder of Christiana's two daughters, **Elizabeth Southerden Thompson** (1846–1933), was famous as the military painter **Lady Butler**; she wrote an autobiography which helps the story along. Her young sister **Alice Christiana Gertrude Thompson** (1847–1922) is best known as the poet and essayist **Alice Meynell**; she too wrote autobiographically about their time on the Island.

Christiana's husband, and Elizabeth and Alice's father, was Thomas James Thompson, son of an English sugar plantation owner in Jamaica and his Creole mistress. Following his father's death, Thomas became his grandfather's heir. He too, benefitted from the Slave Compensation Act of 1837 (following the Slavery Abolition Act of 1833), as did several others who spent time on the Island mentioned elsewhere, including above in this chapter. Although the family was wealthy, they were not 'landed gentry'; like many in their social class, they lived in rented properties which were cheaper in continental Europe than in England, so the Thompsons spent much of their time living there (and enjoying the climate and culture). Elizabeth was born in Lausanne, Switzerland. Though Alice was born in London, the family moved around England, Switzerland and France, and she was brought up in Italy. Today slave owner heritage matters, and Miranda Kaufmann, author of *Black Tudors* (2017), is researching those who stayed or lived on the Island. Slaves on the Island existed in the Iron Age, in the time of the Romans and were noted in the Domesday

Book of 1085 (slaves were held then at Wroxall, for example). In Victorian times, it may well not have been polite to wonder about the source of a person's wealth, let alone discuss it.

Before her marriage Christiana Weller had trained as a concert pianist and soon began receiving very good reviews. One critic wrote that she 'played charmingly ... she delighted everybody as much by her performance as her great beauty'. When she was 19, Charles Dickens saw her play in Liverpool. He immediately fell in love with her and admitted that he 'kept his eyes firmly fixed on her every movement'. So much so that he sent her a present of two volumes of Tennyson, and he told her father that she stood 'out alone from the whole crowd the instant I saw her, and will remain there always in my sight'. What he did next was to write to his friend, widower Thomas Thompson, proposing that Thompson should marry Christiana, which he did, although he had to counter resistance from Christiana's family, who did not want her to give up her career. As Clare Tomalin convincingly suggests in *Dickens: A Life* (2011), 'it allowed him to remain intimate with her, if only by proxy'. By yet another coincidence, his sister Catherine Dickens (see above) became a confidante of Christiana and a mediator during the difficulties that arose during her courtship with Thompson. The Dickens saga is told in detail in the biography Viola Meynell wrote of her mother – *Alice Meynell: A Memoir* (1929). The memoir also contains pages from the diary that Christiana kept when the family lived in Italy.

In *An autobiography by Elizabeth Butler; with illustrations and sketches by the author* (1923), Christiana's daughter Elizabeth wrote of Ventnor and Bonchurch and, particularly, of her mother's place in them:

> Our next halt was in the Isle of Wight, at Ventnor, and then at Bonchurch, and our house was 'The Dell'. Bonchurch was a beautiful dwelling-place. But, alas! For what I may call the Oxford primness of society! It took a long time to get ourselves attuned to it. However, we got to be fond of this society when the ice thawed. The Miss Sewells [see chapter 7, 'Religion and Philanthropy'] were especially charming, sisters of the then Warden of New College. Each family took a pride in the beauty of its house and gardens, the result being a rivalry in loveliness enriching Bonchurch with flowers, woods and ornamental waters that filled us with delight. Mamma had 'The Dell' further beautified to come up to the high level of the others. She made a little garden herself at the highest point of the grounds, with grass steps bordered with tall white lilies, and called it 'the Celestial Garden'. The cherry trees she planted up there for the use of the blackbirds came to nothing. The watercolours she painted at 'The Dell' are amongst her loveliest.

> Ventnor was fond of dances, At Homes, and diversions generally, but I shall never forget my poor mother's initial trials at the musical parties where the conversation raged during her playing, rising and sinking with the *crescendos* and *diminuendos* (and this after the worship of her playing in Italy!),

and once she actually stopped dead in the middle of a Mozart and silence reigned. She then tried the catching 'Saltarello' with the same result exactly. 'The English appreciate painting with their ears and music with their eyes,' said Benjamin West (if I am not mistaken), the American painter who became President of our Royal Academy. This hard saying had much truth in it, at least in his day. Even in ours they had to be *told* of the merits of a picture, and the *sight* of a pianist crossing his hands when performing was the signal for exchanges of knowing smiles and nods amongst the audience, who, talking, hadn't heard a single note. For vocal music, however, silence was the convention. How we used inwardly to laugh when, after a song piped by some timid damsel, the music was handed round so that the words and music might be seen in black and white by the guests assembled. I thankfully record the fact that as time went on, my mother's playing seemed at last to command attention, and it being whispered that silence was better suited to such music.

Christiana's version of socialising during the family's 1864/5 stay in Bonchurch provides a nice foil to her daughter's view. Her version is contained in the biography *Alice Meynell: A Memoir*:

The H.'s ball was splendid – a profusion of pink wax lights, a flow of champagne, – but poor me! About 12 I was so utterly exhausted I had to go up into the bedroom and lie covered up till 2.50 in a torpor. I seemed to be listening for a week to hideous galops, waltzes etc, drumming up thro' the floor – all of which Mimi [Elizabeth] pronounced delicious – also every now and then poor Miss Johnson was brought up to be sick by her mama. I wore my grey dove with tulle and red camelias – pretty when viewed at home but bald and poverty-stricken when contrasted with the furbelows of society. Really, what lavish absurdity to the tired looker-on the whole thing is. I am sure I should not think the same if the dances were such as peasants dance in the glorious Southern lands. At 12 Miss F. would introduce me to her papa although I told her I was too done up to open my lips – and he began a conversation upon Pre-Raphaelitism and Turner which put the finishing touch to me. And I then retired. Lovely bedroom and fire blazing and Mrs H. so kind.

While the family lived in Italy, Elizabeth started receiving art lessons. In the foreword to her autobiography she suggests that 'At seven years old little Elizabeth Thompson was already drawing miniature battles, at seventeen she was lamenting that as yet she had achieved nothing great.' In 1866 she attended the Female School of Art in South Kensington, and she began exhibiting her watercolours even as a student; in 1867 one of them, 'Bavarian Artillery Going into Action' was shown at the Dudley Gallery (founded in 1864), one of those galleries preferred by women artists, no doubt for its prime site opposite Burlington House, Piccadilly. When the family moved to Florence in 1869, she attended the Accademia di Belle Arti. While in Florence, the family became Roman Catholic and, for a while, Elizabeth painted religious subjects. But in Paris in 1860 she was exposed to battle scenes, and from then on that is where her painting was concentrated

Without knowing her earlier story it would be easy to assume that Elizabeth's military painting was prompted by her marriage in 1877 to William Francis Butler, a distinguished Irish officer in the British Army. But two points do not fit with the facts usually presented. She did travel widely round the then British Empire with her military husband, producing six children on the way. But her real fame came in 1874, that is before her marriage. Elizabeth describes the lead-up to it, showing her as a real person, a real woman, ahead of what was to come:

While at home in Ventnor I received extraordinary rumours of the stir the picture was making in London. How it was the talk of the clubs and spoken about as the coming picture of the year. Back in London to make final alterations to the picture as it hung in the Royal Academy. I returned to the boarding house to fetch a sketch of a Russian helmet I had done at Ventnor, to replace the bad one I had put in the foreground ... I could hardly do the little helmet alterations necessary, so crowded was I by congratulating and questioning artists starers.

The painting creating the stir, started in Ventnor, completed in her studio in London, was *The Roll Call* (its full title was *The Roll Call After An Engagement, Crimea*). It depicts a line of common soldiers worn out by conflict. The helmet she mentions is lying on the snow, not far from a fallen soldier, at the front of the painting. When the Summer Exhibition opened, a policeman had to stand with the painting to keep control over the crowd trying to see it. The following

35. 'Roll Call', painting by Elizabeth Thompson Butler, courtesy of the Royal Collection Trust, © His Majesty King Charles III 2024

morning, she woke up famous. Holman Hunt said that it touched the nation's heart as few pictures have ever done and Queen Victoria bought the painting. The artist who painted *The Roll Call* and her other military paintings – to name just a couple, *The 28th Regiment at Quatre Bras* (1875; Waterloo) and *Balaclava* (1876; Crimea) – is always called Lady Butler; but she did not marry William Butler until three years later, and he was not knighted until 1886.

What would today be called Elizabeth's USP (or, which I had to look up rather long after it gained common currency, Unique Selling Point) was her attitude to war; she wrote: 'I never painted to the glory of war, but to portray its pathos and heroism'. Her paintings are of the common soldier, or of a single soldier. A prime example of the latter is *Remnant of an Army* (1879; now in Tate Britain), which shows the supposed only survivor of the 1842 retreat from Kabul.

But the Isle of Wight should not be forgotten. As she was to write of that same Ventnor stay that presaged her fame, 'In 1871, we were off again. From London to Ventnor!', the place she wrote about as 'home'. She 'kept her hand in' by painting in oils life-sized portraits of relatives and friends, some ecclesiastical subjects, and two artworks relevant to the Island. But it was of that same stay that she wrote:

[It was] a return to the Isle of Wight that sent me back on the military road with ever diminishing digressions. Well perhaps my father's fear, that I was joining a 'tremendous ruck' in taking the field would have been justified had I not taken up a line of painting almost non-exploited by English artists. The statement of a French art Critic when writing of one of my war pictures, 'L'Angleterre n'a guere qu'un peintre militaire, c'est une femme,' shows the position of [military painting].

One of Elizabeth's Isle of Wight works, made on a February 1873 visit to Parkhurst, then a military establishment on the Island (later a prison) was a watercolour entitled *On Parade. Drummer of the 79th. A Sketch at Parkhurst* which she gave to the commanding officer. Just the two drummers are complete; their fellows are lightly included in pencil. The work is in the National Army Museum Study Collection; it can be seen on their website. Queen Victoria presented the 79th Regiment of Foot (the Cameron Highlanders) with new colours at Parkhurst that April. Elizabeth's Parkhurst visit had a follow-up. In May 1875, she was on a family trip to the north of England. They visited Newcastle and about that she wrote:

We did all the lions, including the garrison fortress where the Cameron Highlanders were and where Colonel Miller, of Parkhurst memory, came out, very pleased to speak to me and escort us about. He had the water colour I gave him of his charger, done at Parkhurst in the old Ventnor days ... they asked me to look at my picture by gas light. The sixpenny crowd was there, the men touching their caps as I passed. In the street they formed a lane for me to pass to the carriage. 'What nice people!' I exclaim in the Diary.

Elizabeth's other Island work during that stay was quite different: it was an altarpiece for St Wilfrid's, Ventnor's Catholic church. Chapter 7 – 'Religion and Philanthropy' – tells how Elizabeth, Countess of Clare, a Roman Catholic convert, having established a rather grand church in Ryde, causing some consternation, was undeterred and contributed to the funding of one in Ventnor. It was to be called St Wilfrid's but she insisted that it be Our Lady and St Wilfrid. It was for that church that Elizabeth Thompson provided an altarpiece. Hoping to track that down, and not finding it easy, I appealed to Lesley Telford of the Ventnor & District Local History Society who told me that the painting was destroyed in the 2007 fire that badly damaged the church itself. A photograph of it was, however, recently found.

While Elizabeth kept a diary and wrote an attractive and useful autobiography, Alice was the recognised writer of the family. She was an essayist, editor, critic and suffragist, but best known as a poet. Starting with their time living in Italy, Thomas Thompson occupied himself with making sure that these daughters of his second family were well educated. Just as Elizabeth had painting lessons when young, so both girls were taught to appreciate literature; Charlotte Brontë was a favourite, particularly after they were given *Jane Eyre* to read. Alice's daughter Viola writes in the memoir of her mother:

Their father taught the two little girls all that he would have taught them had they been sons. He was perhaps a stern task-master. Alice's first memories of the reading lessons were memories of despair, and in a later year Mimi [Elizabeth], the inferior speller, would often be saved by Alice's aid from the displeasure they dreaded.

Viola wrote about her mother's essays: 'Italy invades her essays on childhood'. These are the first two verses of one of Alice's poems – 'A Father of Women; *Ad sororem Elizabeth Butler*':

Our father works in us,
The daughters of his manhood. Not undone
Is he, not wasted, though transmuted thus,
And though he left not son.

Therefore on him I cry
To arm me: For my delicate mind is a casque,
A breastplate for my heart, courage to die
Of thee, captain, I ask.

The poem must have been written after 1877, when Elizabeth married William Butler.

Viola's fourth chapter, 'Girlhood', is about the family's 1864/5 stay on the Isle of Wight, in Bonchurch and, unfortunately is all that Alice seems to have written at about that time. This is in a diary entry which tends to be the opposite of her mother Christiana's view of a party quoted from above, though it may be another party given by the same hostess at the same house:

> Mama and I went to a ball at Mrs Hambrough's Steep Hill Castle. I wore a ravishing yellow tarlatan of the palest possible tint by night, made exquisitely, with a plaid écharpe over one shoulder, a red rose with its leaves in my hair and one at my waist. Off at 9.15 in time for the first quadrille. Glorious fun. Captain Sewell many times watched me going round and told Douglas how well I danced (who told me). I had no regular flirtations, and no particular compliments, save the truest of all, that the men quarrelled to dance with me. I would willingly have given a certain Mr Bury a dance had I been free as he very much desired it. To this dance there were *no* drawbacks.

Unlike Elizabeth, who knew very early what she wanted, Alice did not, and she was more under the influence of the Catholicism that the whole family had embraced when living in Italy. This caused a certain amount of low spirits, compounded by some family money worries resulting from a mistake made by lawyers; Alice wrote, probably not concerning Bonchurch, but meaning that travelling was curtailed: 'To-day I have shed more tears I think than I have before in all my life. I went round the garden and into every nook, and watered the grass with my tears.' Her mood was not helped by constant illness. Eventually, though, she found her métier: her first volume of poetry, *Preludes*, came out in 1875, illustrated by Elizabeth who had found fame the previous year. Her poems were well received: Ruskin, as Viola has it, 'abandoned "pretty" and left "graceful" for the critics'; 'three of its poems,' he wrote on reading the book, ' "the 'Letter from a girl," the "San Lorenzo" and the sonnet "To a Daisy", have done me more good than I can well thank you for.' He later wrote to Christiana, whom he obviously knew well, in more detail about her daughter's poems, and wrote again to Alice herself. Viola notes of a visit arranged following the publication of *Preludes*:

> a visit to Tennyson at Aldworth, Blackdown, his remote high-hilled house, was a not altogether easy experience for the two girls … on their arrival they were obliged to inform him which was poet and which was painter. A somewhat gruff demeanour intimidated them until they thought they detected in the poet something rather deliberately awe-inspiring – and immediately they feared no more.

In 1877, the same year that Elizabeth married, Alice did too. Her husband was Wilfrid Meynell, five years her junior, but very much in tune with her. They had eight children, including Viola Meynell (1885–1956), her mother's biographer; she was the penultimate child, and became a novelist. The Meynells became the proprietors of such magazines as *The Pen, the Weekly Register,* and *Mary England,* among others. Meanwhile Alice wrote regular essays, which were published in a dozen or so magazines. The Isle of Wight was not included in the subject matter, but her poems show her feminist concerns as well as her reaction to the events of the First World War. She also began to question Europe's colonial imperialism – the Meynells and others in their circle speaking out for the oppressed. It is her involvement in the women's suffrage movement that is of particular interest – not as a suffragette, but a Suffragist – particularly linked to what was happening on the Isle of Wight, discussed in chapter 13, 'The Campaigners', that ends this book. Alice was vice-president of the Women Writers' Suffrage League, and she was one of the early founders of the Catholic Women's Suffrage Society. She also established and wrote in the first edition of its newspaper the *Catholic Suffragist.*

The above are facts, and impressive, but what I like is an account of a demonstration Alice went on (accompanied by her dog, Careless), again recorded in Viola's biography; it is as if it happened just yesterday, or will happen tomorrow, so familiar does the description of the event read:

I wish you could have seen the procession. I think it must be called a great success. Lobbie and I went to the Embankment and took our places with Evelyn Sharp, May Sinclair, and the author of Diana of Dobson's around the 'Scrivener's' banner. It was a great big banner that acted like a sail in the high wind, and what Evelyn and Diana of Dobson's went through in carrying it is beyond description. The band of our 'block' was just in front of it, and the man with the drum was frequently bonneted by the sudden collapse of the banner over his head. The crowd laughed. ...

The Crowd was enormous. It reached the whole way of the march, and was generally quiet. We who marched lost the show, of course. I wish I could have seen the graduates

36. Alice Meynell, from *Alice Meynell: A Memoir* by Viola Meynell

and doctors in their robes, and all the other interesting incidents. I had a ticket for the Albert Hall. It was a wonderful gathering, but it was a cruel thing that many owners of boxes and stalls refused to let them, so there were great gaps in the audience, while hundred and hundreds of women were unable to get in.

I was so tired at night that I could not write. Yesterday I was again tired to excess. I have the Women Writers' dinner to-night. Your most loving mother, A.M.

The letter may well have been written to Viola: it is addressed to ' My Darling Dimpling'.

Both Alice Meynell and Elizabeth Barrett Browning were considered for appointment by the monarch for the post of Poet Laureate when Tennyson died; but no woman was appointed until Carol Anne Duffy, 2009–2019. Alice died in 1922, aged 75, after a series of illnesses. A posthumous collection of her *Last Poems* was published a year later. Elizabeth moved to Ireland with her husband when he retired and, when he died, she moved to Gormanston Castle, County Meath, home of the youngest of her six children, where she died just before her 87th birthday. Although in later years Elizabeth's military paintings were regarded as dated, they are still not only finely executed but valuable as a historical record. As with the by-passing of Alice for the post of Poet Laureate, in 1879, Elizabeth came within two votes of becoming the first woman to be elected as an Associate Member of the Royal Academy. The first full female member was Laura Knight in 1936. Their mother, Christiana Thompson, was widowed in 1891, thereafter living independently in Chiswick with a servant. On the Census form of 1901 she records her occupation as Composer of musical works, and Painter. She lived to the age of 85.

The novelist **Mary Charlotte Julia Leith** (née Gordon; 1840–1926) is often referred to as Mrs Disney Leith, though the stock from which she came was perhaps more noteworthy than that of the man from whom she took her married name. Her mother was **Mary Agnes Blanche Gordon** (née Ashburnham; 1816–1899), and her father, Henry Percy Gordon, was a Cambridge man, a leading mathematician during his time there, then a barrister and artist. In 1851, he inherited his father's title and became 13th Laird of Knockespock. One grandfather was Sir James Willoughby Gordon, the other George Ashburnham, the Earl of Ashburnham. Her paternal grandmother, often called **Lady Julia Gordon** (née Bennet; 1776–1867), rather than, more accurately, Lady Gordon, was one of the few known pupils of Turner – and a talented watercolourist. Turner stayed with the family at Northcourt in 1827. She painted a view of the garden there, and some of her paintings are in the Tate Gallery, London, and in the National Trust Collections.

At 25, in 1865, Mary Gordon married Colonel Robert William Disney Leith, first commander of the 106th Regiment of Foot of the Bombay Light Infantry, who had been badly injured, including losing an arm, during the Siege of

Multan in 1849. He was a neighbour of her family's estate in Scotland. They were to have six children, four daughters and two sons. Quite a burden for any writer; in addition, her name is inextricably bound to that of her first cousin, the poet Swinburne, who lived next door on the Isle of Wight.

The Gordon family seat was Northcourt Manor, Shorwell (not far from the south coast of the Island), and that is where Mary was brought up. As was usual, she was educated at home, but thanks to her father she was proficient in mathematics, as well as several languages, in addition to ancient Greek and Latin, and she was a talented pianist and organist. She illustrated some of her own books. Whereas one might bridle at her being best known as Swinburne's cousin – one source suggests that 'Her chief route into history is as the first cousin of the poet Swinburne …' – she did later write about him, and corresponded with him, and they were great childhood friends. They went riding together, though Swinburne was very frail, and they wrote Jacobean plays

37. Miss Gordon (Mrs Disney Leith),
© National Portrait Gallery, London

together in the library at Northcourt. They even collaborated on her second book, the rather cruel *Children of the Chapel*, about a 10-year-old chorister in the sixteenth century. Swinburne's involvement was not revealed until after his death. In 1917 Mary published *The Boyhood of Algernon Charles Swinburne* under the name Mrs Disney Leith. It not only drew on her childhood memories of him, but included their letters.

Mary's novel with which I'm most familiar is one I bought online as a reprint in the British Library Historical Print Collections, not realising the form in which it was to arrive – very large and very heavy, not one to read in bed. *From Over the Water: A Story of Two Promises* (1884) introduces the uninitiated to an important Island term:

Now the inhabitants of Cheveley village were no less insular than their neighbours, and one way in which their insularity manifested itself was in a strong belief in themselves, coupled with a certain implied contempt for 'over-uns' – by which title they designated those persons whose misfortune rather than their fault it was to have been born and bred on the opposite side of the Solent. When, therefore, it was known that one of their chief places of trust and responsibility on Cheveley Grange estate was to be filled by an over-un – one moreover, coming from no nearer than the north of Scotland – it might be expected that there should be a feeling not altogether favourable to the prospective bailiff.

The term Caulkhead has been introduced and explained in chapter 1, 'Dinosaur Isle'; an 'over-un' is the opposite. And, of course, the title of the novel is *Over the Water*, so you might accurately suppose that at some stage it moves from the Island to Scotland. The tenants of the 'modest cottage' in which the new bailiff is billeted are Sarah Whitmore and her brother Archelaus. The story moves at the pace and in the style you might expect of a Victorian novel. Miss Whitmore's involvement lasts until the end. It is not clear which place on the Island Cheveley represents.

Mary Leith's husband, by then a general and Companion of the Bath, died on the Island, at Northcourt, in 1892. Mary was then 52 and changed the direction of her life; this meant going to Iceland, a place she had long dreamed of visiting. During a visit when she was over 60, she rode 300 miles across the country. On a visit when she was over 70, she bathed in the Arctic Sea. She happened to be in Iceland when the First World War broke out, so that the vessel on which she returned was escorted by destroyers. In 1908 she had published a book about her exploits in Iceland, illustrating it with her own watercolours.

Mary died of pneumonia, aged 85. In the latest edition of *The Oxford Dictionary of National Biography* (DNB), thanks to the work of the University's International Centre for Victorian Women Writers, Mary Leith is among 11 until then forgotten women included. The entries are written by the Centre's staff and PhD students. This development is similar to that described in chapter 1, concerning the project set up by the Oxford University Museum of Natural History to find so far unknown women who were involved with fossils. Both projects deserve both airing and praise.

Mary died not at Northcourt but at Niton, west of Ventnor, where the family had a villa. Known as Orchard Cottage it had been bought in 1813 by Sir Willoughby Gordon, Mary's grandfather. He remodelled and rebuilt it on a grand scale into what he saw as a 'gentleman's seaside villa'. It was there that Mary's grandmother, Julia Gordon, liked to sketch, even before the rebuilding, so that she could capture its rural charm. Describing the villa in 1826, an article in *The Repository of Arts* ended: 'The drawing room contained rare and fine china with alabaster figures. There were three French windows opening onto a veranda, which formed a sitting room commanding splendid views of the undercliff.' Julia's watercolour was exhibited at the Royal Academy in 1826, under the title 'View from the Terrace of a villa at Niton, Isle of Wight'.

Should Northcourt Manor, Shorwell, be on your list of places to visit, or to stay at, it is as well to be alert to its earlier history. Just as slaves kept in Wroxall were noted in the 1085 Domesday Book, mentioned above, so they were in Northcourt Manor, Shorwell. Eventually the Manor came into the hands of Amice de Clare, and then her daughter Isabella de Fortibus (see chapter 3, 'Women of Property'). There is no need to burden this account with all the families who owned it, over the centuries – though often inheritance passed through women – until nearer the time when Mary Gordon Leith did. But what the research of the current owner, John Harrison, turned up is worth pursuing. He shared it online via the 'Isle of Wight Gardens Trust', as 'News and Views from Northcourt' (2021).

Richard Bull, from an Island family, and MP for Newport, bought North-court and the Island estates that went with it in 1795 (having rented it for 10 years before). In 1747 he had married widowed **Mary Ash** (b.1719) of Ongar (where Bull also had a property). With Mary, Bull had two daughters **Elizabeth Bull** (*c.*1749–1809) and **Catherine Susanna Bull** (?–1795). These girls were each expected to inherit £100,000 (£10 million in today's value) from the daughter, Levina, that Mary Ash had with her first husband. It is these two girls who are interesting, quite apart from their expected inheritance, though that might have been behind their father's purchase of Northcourt Manor. Unfortunately, Catherine died later in the year of the purchase; in fact, her death may have prompted it.

Jan Toms in her series of 'Brief Biographies' wrote what seems to be a speculative piece, particularly concerning Catherine – 'Elizabeth and Catherine Bull of Northcourt' (2018). She reasonably supposed that they would have had a governess and been taught the accomplishments expected of young women of their class in preparation for a suitable marriage, but it is not clear what evidence she had when she wrote, given that Bull had no sons:

Elizabeth would have been expected to marry first but she didn't, perhaps she had already decided to devote herself to the care of her father and run his household. She might have possessed that fatal flaw so dreaded by upper class men and been too clever. Given Richard's wealth, she must have been an attractive prospect but for whatever reason, she remained single.

Two points are worth making: from that it would appear that Mary

38. Elizabeth Bull, © National Portrait Gallery, London

Ash Bull, mother of Elizabeth and Catherine, was already dead, though the date of her death does not seem to have been noted. But it wasn't necessarily her father's wealth that would have been attractive, Elizabeth was potentially an heiress in her own right. Jan Toms continues to write concerning Catherine; the combination of possible fact and admitted speculation is disconcerting:

> And how about Catherine? Is it possible that in falling for the charms of a sea-going man she faced her father's absolute refusal to countenance such a union? On the other hand, if he was a young man with genuine prospects, perhaps her father decided to test the strength of their affection and sanctioned a long voyage in the secret hope that Catherine would change her mind? Richard certainly had the means to arrange such a voyage, for his own father had grown rich through trading with the Levant and across the Ottoman Empire.

Between 1783 when Richard first took the lease and 1795 when he became the outright owner, the mystery of Catherine's romance took place. Northcourt manor sits in a hollow, the estate land bisected by the highway through Shorwell village. To avoid encountering the local peasants, a bridge spanned the road allowing the sisters to cross to the south side and there gain a view out to sea. Here, allegedly Catherine kept her vigil, awaiting her lover's return. We have no dates as to when he might have been expected, or how long she continued to watch. Legend says that she continued to sew her trousseau until the day that she died.

The reader, including me, has to take that as they find it.

Elizabeth Bull, who was about 46 when her sister died, lived from 1785 in a grand Island house full of enviable objects: not only was her father a noted collector of fine prints, but he had also built up a fine library and the walls were hung with pictures. Her mother is no longer mentioned, but a date of her death eludes me. In any case, the family did not forget Catherine. Not only is there a loving plaque on the wall of the local parish church, St Peter's, but in the grounds of Northcourt a chapel was erected in her memory. Jan Toms notes:

> It is described as being of rough stone, gothic, thatched and with windows of painted glass. Beneath a very large ash tree, the light gave a dim and solemn tint to the sarcophagus within. Made of white marble, it was carved with a male and [a] female figure reclining over an urn.

There is an eighteenth century depiction of the chapel but unfortunately nothing of the building now remains. More lasting was what Elizabeth decided to do with the grounds of Northcourt; in doing so, as John Harrison notes, she was no doubt 'gaining inspiration from the many estates of the aristocracy she had visited through her half brother's marriages ...'. The landscaping she embarked on comes alive in a letter Elizabeth's father, aged 80, wrote to a friend in 1803:

My Betty is perfectly well, and regards nothing beyond her plantations. She is about some vast work in the grounds, half a mile higher than the house, and has laid an embargo on me, and my horse, so I am not allowed to visit her high places till everything is finished: All I know is that there have been half a dozen labourers employed all last winter, and all this summer.

The use of the word 'plantations' is interesting because of what John Harrison also writes, and the fact that some of the archives of the house were damaged when the army took it over in 1940, is relevant:

Researching our archives and online material has not provided any more detail as to who Elizabeth Bull consulted but the source of wealth behind the landscaping of Northcourt is better understood. Some of this wealth shows links to slavery, colonialism, rewards for political favours and more, and marriage to underage ladies to add to the collection.

There is even a posting online from the Centre for the Study of the Legacies of British Slavery concerning what happened to Richard Bull's 'Cultural Legacy details', including a collection of drawings in the British Museum.

Richard Bull died in 1805; Elizabeth, who had remained unmarried, was his heir; she stayed on at Northcourt until her death in 1809, in her 60th year. Now what links Northcourt to Mary Gordon Leith gets closer. Mary Ash Bull's first husband was Bennet Alexander Bennet; their son was Richard Henry Alexander Bennet and he was regarded as a member of the Bull family; indeed, when Elizabeth died, he put up a plaque in memory of her in St Peter's Church which noted, not only that she died 'after a long and painful illness', but ended,

R.H.A Bennet,
Her Brother,
from Affection & Gratitude
caused this Stone to be
erected.

He and his sister Levina now inherited Northcourt. Richard, from his marriage (to a girl of 15), had a son and two daughters. Emilia married Sir John Swinburne, 6th Bt, the poet's grandfather; and Julia Isabella Levina married in 1805 Willoughby Gordon. Julia was, of course, Lady Gordon, Mary Gordon Leith's artist grandmother, who also ran the households of Northcourt, Orchard Cottage in Niton, Scottish estates, and a house in Chelsea. Eventually, Mary would inherit Northcourt, bringing the story full circle.

Northcourt today, extensively renovated and modernised, provides accommodation for several families, or may be taken over for a special event. If visiting, you need to check carefully. When planning my visit, we knew that a large wedding was taking place, so could only go as far as the gate and peep in. You should note that unless you are a paying guest, you cannot enter the property.

Mary Gleed Tuttiett (1846–1923), better known as the writer Maxwell Gray, was mentioned as one of three writers at the end of chapter 7 in Julia Courtney's piece, 'Writing the Wight: Three Talented Women' (2018). She will appear under her proper name in chapter 13 – as a supporter of women's suffrage; (the topic appears in a number of her novels). A good example is *Sweethearts and Friends* (1897), described in a bibliography of her novels as 'a romance between a suffragette medical student and an otherwise perfect but sexist politician'. Her entry in 'Isle of Wight Hidden Heroes' is subtitled 'Acclaimed author and suffragist'.

Mary Gleed Tuttiett was born and brought up in Newport, first in Pyle Street, later in Castle Road, daughter of the surgeon Frank Bampfylde Tuttiett and **Elizabeth Trickett Tuttiett** (née Gleed); she had two brothers. She was largely self-educated and worked when young as a governess. In early adulthood she travelled not only to London and various other parts of England but also to Switzerland, to Yverdon-les-Bains. That last place was known for its thermal springs and it is easy to suggest that she went there for her health: she started to suffer from asthma and rheumatism. So debilitating did her illness become that she was at first confined to the house, and then, when she was able to leave her bed, to a sofa where she wrote her novels. She made occasional trips out by carriage or bath-chair. Under the circumstances, her output is extraordinary.

39. Maxwell Gray, from the Internet

Mary Tuttiett began her literary career by contributing essays, poems, articles and short stories to various periodicals. Her first novel, *The Broken Tryst* (1879), was published when she was 33 and received lukewarm reviews. Her second novel was *The Silence of Dean Maitland* (1886). For some reason its manuscript landed on the desk of Alfred Chenevix Trench of the publisher Kegan Paul, Trench and Company, best-known for its titles in economics, politics, sociology and science, but very little fiction; its authors included Walter Bagehot and Thomas Huxley. It must have taken some reading – it's one of those Victorian novels – nevertheless, he was immediately taken by its shocking content. As the introduction to one of the editions has it 'I said to myself: "It is too good to miss … I must take it." His instincts were right: it was one of the firm's great successes.

Although you may want to know what it's about I have to say that it's a real pity to know the story. I made the mistake, when I was already writing this chapter, but was not sure I had time even to finish reading volume 1 (of two), of looking up a synopsis. The suspense was broken. That allowed me to put the book aside – a pity, I'm sure. The unveiling of the story in that slow, much-landscape-described story, with just enough tension, is not unpleasing. Part of the first couple of paragraphs reads:

> The grey afternoon was wearing on to its chill close; the dark cope of immovable dun cloud overhead seemed to contract and grow closer to the silent world beneath it; and the steep, chalky hill, leading from the ancient village, with its hoary castle and church, up over the bleak, barren down, was a weary thing to climb.

> The solitary traveller along that quiet road moved her limbs more slowly, and felt her breath coming more quickly and shortly, as she moved higher and higher, and the grey Norman tower lessened and gradually sank out of sight behind her. But she toiled bravely on between the high tangled hedges, draped with great curtains of traveller's joy, now a mass of silvery seed-feathers which the country children call 'old man's beard,' and variegated with the deep-purple leaves of dogwood, the crimson of briony and roseberry ….

As regards the story when it gets going, I'll just say about humans and animals that there are two men (one of them to become a dean), each in love with the sister of the other. There are servants, tenant farm hands, a pregnant tenant farmer's daughter, horses which only one sister – the horse whisperer – can tame, and, in particular a family cat – Mark Antony – who loves only her and her twin brother; it has a big role. As it takes place over a period of about twenty years, Mark Antony may not survive; there may even be a tear-jerking death scene.

Happily, it is set on the Isle of Wight but the names of places are changed: you need to know that Malbourne is Calbourne; Barrington Row is today's Winkle Street; Chalkburne is Carisbrooke; Oldport is Newport; and Belminster is Bishop's House, Winchester Cathedral. It was speculated that the novel had been written by a well-known ecclesiastic or the daughter of the Archbishop of Canterbury. Tennyson praised the book, apparently driving to Newport to visit Mary, as her health prevented her from visiting Farringford.

In the novel that followed, *The Reproach of Annesley* (serialised 1888/9; book 1889), Arden is Arreton; Arden Cross in Arreton Cross and Medington is Newport. The clue to when it is set is given by the mention of civil war in Paris: it is, therefore, set in 1871 when the Paris Commune and its overthrow took place.

The Secret of Dean Maitland became a successful play, and was filmed three times, in 1914, 1915 and 1934. Two later novels were also filmed, *The Reproach of Annesley* in 1915, and *The Last Sentence* (1894) in 1917. The number of Mary's novels is astonishing, particularly given her ill-health.

Following her father's death in 1895, Mary moved to Richmond, remaining in London until her death in Ealing aged 76. Her obituary in *The Times* said that her body of work was 'characterised by a delicate grace and charm, and generally suggested a serious purpose, but she can never be said to have equalled her first success'.

The diary of **Maud Tomlinson** (1859–1949), published as *Maud: The Diaries of Maud Berkeley* (1985) is quite unlike any of the other books described in this chapter, and Maud herself is rather different from the other authors. The book was published in a very large, rather unwieldy format, probably to accommodate Maud's wonderfully quirky and accomplished, cartoonish illustrations; they reveal her personality as much as the diary entries do. What is more, they capture the last years of the Victorian era on the Isle of Wight – at least in the first part: after her marriage, Maud moved to London and maintained the diary for a while. So appealing did it appear in its raw form, that it was taken up and adapted by Flora Fraser with a detailed introduction by her grandmother, the historian Elizabeth Longford.

Maud's father, William Tomlinson, was 50 when she was born, and her mother was not young – Maud was the youngest daughter of four of them, and only one of the five sons was born after her. Tomlinson, 'the Great G' as Maud called him, had been a maths master at St Peter's school, York and retired when Maud was 14. In 1882, when she was 23, the family went to live on the Island, at Sandown; there her father pursued his hobby of astronomy. For some reason Maud's mother is not given the name with which she grew up; Maud calls her 'Nannie'.

Maud's diary starts when she was 29, and yet it is written in the style of a girl, perhaps because of her life style; she was the only one of her siblings not to pursue an academic career. Her sister Annie, for example, knew eight languages, and ran her own school in Ascot, which Maud attended in the later years of her schooling. Annie then went to live in Paris where she 'wrote for the papers'. Before she went blind, Emmie had taken her degree at Girton College, Cambridge, and become a medical doctor.

At 29, Maud was untrained, so she took painting lessons in order to improve the illustrations for her diary; what is more, she was unmarried. As Elizabeth Longford puts it, 'In other words she was unimportant except as a companion to her aged parents.' Her father was controlling to the extent that he 'did his best to stop her from visiting the house of shy Mr von Hacht for her painting lessons despite the fact that his sister would be present as a chaperone.' He was wary of her marrying – who would read to him when she left home? In spite of this rather dispiriting background, Maud remained unbowed; Elizabeth Longford describes how this affected her diary and illustrations:

Such were her naturally irrepressible spirits, however, that the scenes she depicted of her social life at Sandown might be concerned with young teenagers, rather than women ripe for marriage ... If Maud was not close to her own older brothers and sisters, she was totally involved with her friends on the Isle of Wight.

Maud's first diary entry, at the beginning of January 1888, reads:

Everyone very tired after the excitement of the New Year's Eve Dance at Mrs Hatchet's. What possessed that redoubtable matron to throw a dance, none of us can understand. There were rumours that a niece was expected from London, but it was only the old crew from Sandown and Shanklin who graced her conservatory. Hoggie that graceless scamp found some candles and invited us all to jump over them for luck. Mrs Hatchet was furious and declared all her domestic economy for the year ruined by this incursion into her stores. Hoggie was unrepentant and we all had a fine old time. Narrowly avoided burning the hems of our dresses and, as narrowly, avoided knocking over all the candles.

Maud does eventually marry. Colonel James Cavan Berkeley came to the Isle of Wight, following behind grown-up children from his first marriage who were already there on holiday. His first wife had died two years before Maud started her Island diary, and he was 21 years older than Maud. By this time,1892, she was 33 and, as well as a husband, she acquired six step-children, the youngest two, daughters of 17 and 19, and went to live with her new husband in London, where she had three children of her own. She started not only a new and different life, but also a new section of her diary. It is just as cleverly illustrated. I'm surprised that Maud isn't better known for this talent. The last entry in her diary, in 1901, reads:

A photograph of my three darling children marks the end of my diary writing. I am now going to turn my attention to compiling an album for each one. Devoting all my time at present to teaching Dorothy to read. Perhaps one day she, too, will write her diary. As yet, she has difficulty spelling the simplest of words.

There is a most winning sketch of Dorothy with a large wastepaper basket over her head, reaching down to her chubby little outstretched arms; it's entitled 'Where's Dodderly?'

40. Maud Berkeley, from *Maud: Diaries of Maud Berkeley* ed. Flora Fraser

Now for a complete change of mood: while I tend to use modern novels only to illustrate a historical time for which they are relevant, I'm going to slip in here Georgina Moore's *The Garnett Girls* (2023). Although its content is not remotely similar to that of Maud's diaries written at the end of the nineteenth century, it is set in the area of the Island about which Maud was writing – from Seaview to Shanklin; what is more, it does cleverly make that area come alive for the twenty-first century. It tells the story of a mother, Margo, who made the mistake of marrying the love of her life. The fallout of his leaving the family years before the story starts, without warning or explanation, infects the lives of the couple's grown-up daughters who come to visit their spirited mother still living on the Island. It is a satisfying read.

I was in a bit of a quandary about including Pearl Craigie (née Richards; 1867–1906) only because I still cannot satisfy myself that among all her writing there is anything about the Isle of Wight, let alone Ventnor. She used to visit her parents, John Morgan Richards, originally a merchant of New York, and Laura Hortense Arnold, then the owners of Undercliff Castle, in the summer holidays and eventually rented her own place nearby. Not only that, the first morning of my first research trip on the Island for this book was spent in Ventnor, with her house one of the places on the list to be visited. I was being driven from place to place by a taxi driver, Andy, from Bembridge who wasn't altogether familiar with Ventnor but, with great good humour, and almost as much determination as mine, made sure that nowhere was left unvisited, though Pearl's house was perhaps the most difficult to find. It might well have been impossible if I hadn't taken a photograph of the distinctive Tudoresque house with me; there was no one about to ask. As for Undercliff Castle, it is now a housing estate; all that remains of its glory days is a little brass plaque set low down into the remains of a stone wall, or was it the rock of the cliff face, which I photographed in the rain? Its glory days are captured in the next chapter – 11, 'Foreign Royalty and Elite Visitors' – when Elizabeth of Austria, with her suite, took it over for some months in 1874.

In 1887, aged 19, Pearl married Reginald Walpole Craigie, a handsome man seven years her senior. But he drank, womanised, and physically abused her. The marriage was so wretched that she left him in 1891, securing a divorce in 1895. As well as producing a son (born in a house near Undercliff Castle), the marriage and the divorce, which included a public trial revealing all that she had endured, left her with, as her DNB author put it, 'Emotional suffering working on a mind of a mystical cast [which] impelled her after due reflection to join the Roman catholic church'. She was admitted in 1892, adding to her Christian names 'Maria Theresa'.

But Pearl got more than a son and lasting trauma from her marriage: she was led to enrol herself into a University College, London course, studying the classics and English literature. And she started writing professionally. A seed for that had already been planted when she was nine; at that time the congregational preacher at the City Temple the family attended accepted her stories for his newspaper. Her first adult writing was for periodicals from which she progressed to her first novel. *Some Emotions and a Moral* was published in 1891 under the pseudonym John Oliver Hobbes – the surname taken in honour of the English philosopher 'whose severe dialectic she admired'. And the novel has a philosophical tinge, though, it not being about the Isle of Wight, I have read only a few pages; this gives a flavour:

'Provence,' he said, 'I have often thought – I know it is a delicate subject – that if you could meet some nice, really nice girl – women are so clever at understanding dispositions' – Here he found the subject not only delicate, but too difficult. He stopped short.

'Girls do not delight me,' said Provence; ' they appear to have no interme-diate stage between the guileless chicken and the coquettish hen. My ideal woman is a combination of the Madonna and the Wood-nymph – with the Wood-nymph element predominating. As for marriage, I fear it is a sadly overrated blessing. Wives are either too much devil or too much angel. Fancy eating bacon every morning of one's life with a blameless creature who was dangling one-quarter of the way from heaven and three-quarters from earth! I should die of respect for her.'

'And what if she were too much devil?'

'I should love her horribly,' said Provence. 'That is the worst of devils – they are so entirely adorable ...'

And so on. The novel caused a sensation, selling 89,000 in a few weeks. Living in her parents' house in London, Pearl gathered around her a circle of literary and musical figures, and moved in fashionable society. Soon after her birth, her parents had moved to London for her father's business, leading to her being educated in London and Paris, where she went to study both French and music; in 1886, she was presented at Court, but that had come to nothing (i.e., meeting an eligible young man) then. (It is assumed that this failure was because her father not only was American but also had made his money in trade.) Now, established in her own right, Pearl wrote plays, including the one-act, 'Journeys end in Lovers Meeting', which Ellen Terry (see chapter 8, 'Freshwater') produced and acted in. Did they ever discuss the Isle of Wight? Their correspondence between 1899 and 1900 is held in the New York Public Library for the Performing Arts which I have not accessed.

In London, as well as dealing with her success, Pearl attended concerts and the theatre and took an active part in philanthropic and literary movements, serving as President of the Society of Women Journalists in 1895/6; she was also a member of the Anti-suffrage League. Why she was against woman's suffrage is, at first sight, unexpected, but she was not the only woman writer to take that view. What is more, Jan Toms, in one of her 'Brief Biographies', this time of 'Pearl Craigie – Author', writes of an occasion during the author's tour of the United States:

> At one … discussion about women jurors, she made a damning condemnation of her own sex, claiming that, women did not contain a proper element of justice and that they were by nature, unfair. Cocooned in her own, privileged and liberating world, she was similarly dismissive of the Suffragette Movement, stating that I have no confidence in the honour of women or their brains. Strange that she should retain a confidence in men.

It is also said that she added a new word to the American vocabulary, that of 'blimming'. It described, perfectly, the young wives in her novels who developed the art of talking endlessly and pleasantly, without actually saying anything.

From 1900 Pearl rented her house near Steephill Castle, then named St Lawrence Lodge, where she did much of her writing. She published 14 novels, among much other writing. On 12 August 1906, recently back from that gruelling lecture tour in the United States, and on her way to a holiday in Scotland, Pearl left Ventnor for her London home. The next morning she was found dead in bed of cardiac failure. She was 39.

41. Steephill plaque, photograph by the author

Following her death, a John Oliver Hobbes scholarship for English literature was founded at University College, and her father bought and renamed her Ventnor house ' Craigie Lodge'. Her father's book, *Almost Fairyland: Personal Notes Concerning the Isle of Wight* (1914) doesn't add anything useful about Pearl or, really, about the Island where he had lived part of the time for forty years. But he also added a biographical sketch of his daughter in *The Life of John Oliver Hobbes, told in her correspondence* (1911). On Pearl's death, her parents received a letter of condolence from Queen Alexandra; why, I don't know, except that Pearl's friend, the American Lady Curzon, had helped Alexandra with her wedding dress. There is a rather washed-out plaque, not immediately apparent, on Craigie Lodge.

Somehow writer and teacher **Helen Corke** (1882–1978) has defeated me, and DH Lawrence (who used her story – see below) has annoyed me. This section about her is, therefore, unsatisfactory. *In Our Infancy: An Autobiography* (2008) tells of her childhood, apparently recalled when she was 95. She was

42. Craigie Lodge, photograph by the author

born into a middle-class, Kentish family; the names of her parents continue to elude me, but her father was a grocer and the Congregational family was interested not only in trade, but in literature too. Her father's business prospered at first, but then abruptly failed, leaving Helen, after years of poverty, becoming an elementary school teacher.

It was at that school in Croydon that she met DH Lawrence; in fact she was asked by the head teacher to befriend the new teacher, who seemed rather lost. The two used to go for walks together and discuss literature. Lawrence would read poetry to her, though not his own. As their friendship grew, and she felt she could trust him, she told him of her traumatic experience of the previous year about which she was still grieving. However short of money Helen was, she could obviously afford music lessons. She and her married teacher, Herbert Macartney, developed a close enough relationship for her to agree to spend five days with him, as it turned out, on the Isle of Wight, at Freshwater. On their return, Macartney committed suicide.

According to Jane Heath in her 1985 article, 'Helen Corke and D.H. Lawrence: Sexual Identity and Literary Relations', by coincidence Lawrence 'was on holiday with his mother and sister at Shanklin on the Isle of Wight.' That titbit of information is useful to know for what happened next.

Helen wrote a memoir of her experience in what she called her 'Freshwater Diary'. She did not intend it for publication but the whole episode intrigued Lawrence sufficiently for her to agree that he could write about it in novel form. It was published as *The Trespasser* (1912), only his second publication. I bought the book, a paperback with an introduction by Melvyn Bragg. The well-known translator of Russian literature apparently found the last fifty pages comparable in quality to the work of the best Russian school. I'm afraid I only got as far as the end of chapter 6, page 52 of 246. I'm no literary critic, but I found the self-consciously literary style impossible to cope with. Neither did I care for how he depicted the character of Helena/Helen Corke. I know it was not long after the end of the Victorians, and before the First World War, but why do you think you're going to Freshwater with a married man? I understand that she thaws out, and becomes more like the women in some of his later novels, but I couldn't wait for the passion. It was made into a film (1981) with the same title, and Alan Bates as MacNair/Macartney, just as he was to be the main male character in the film of Lawrence's *Women in Love*. I have been unable to find a copy of *The Trespasser* to watch. That would only have taken 1 hour 30 minutes.

Perhaps Helen Corke's *Neutral Ground: A Chronicle*, which she was persuaded to publish in 1933, and which would contain her 'Freshwater Diary', would tell me more of the reality. That is where my frustration was compounded: A copy was among a pile of Isle of Wight books on my desk at the British Library. I went through it and through it: I couldn't find anything resembling the event. It's bound to have been my fault: I did get a bit impatient. Should I have included Helen Corke here? Have I done her a disservice? It was not my intention, which was rather to suggest my own fallibility!

While we're in Freshwater, there's a little skip to 1960, and **Cecily Gould** (née Good; 1914–2009). Her writing, via the novel *Tapestry of Time: or Effigy of Love* (2001), briefly introduced her in Chapter 6, 'Outsiders'. There, Lucy Lightfoot became a time traveller from 1831 back to the time of the Crusaders. Just as it was a bit of a cheat to regard that as a 'ghost' story, it is a bit of cheat to put Cecily into the writers chapter – though she was a writer – when this is really about a good deed she performed in Freshwater.

Cecily was born in Freshwater, in the year that the First World War started, to Colonel Cecil Henry Brent Good and **Irene Fillingham Good** (née Saxby). She had two sisters and a brother, and was educated on the mainland, at Wycombe Abbey. Her father was a keen yachtsman, a stalwart of the Royal Solent Yacht Club, and for a time was its Commodore; Cecily caught the sailing bug from him. She wrote of when she crewed for him that he was 'a gentle master. He seldom shouted or swore at us, which is why we were happy to crew for him after 50 years together'. Her book, *Gossip: The Biography of a Yacht* (1972) tells the story of cruising in a traditional sailing boat from 1899 to 1964, with line drawings. She also published *The Living River* (1972), an illustrated children's novel about riverine wildlife; and *Island of the White-toothed Shrew* (2003) – a brave sailor on a perilous journey.

It was through sailing, and at Cowes, that Cecily met her husband. Aged 34, in 1948, soon after the end of the Second World War, she married Sir Basil Gould as his second wife. They did not only have sailing in common: Gould was 31 years older than her and his career had obviously been both distinguished and fascinating, and there is a point in sketching it here. After Winchester College and Oxford University, he joined the Indian Civil Service in 1907. He was a British Trade Agent in Gyantse, Tibet, in 1912 and 1913; in 1912 the 13th Dalai Lama asked him for help to ensure that 'energetic and clever sons of respectable families should be given "world-class educations at Oxford College, London [sic]"'. Gould was about to go home on leave, but the Indian government decided that he should guide the four young boys on their journey to England and, in 1913, assist them for the first few weeks after their arrival.

In 1926, Gould was posted to the British Legation in Kabul, and then assigned to Kurrum, Malakand and Waziristan, and, in 1933, to Baluchistan, where his first wife died. He was British Political Officer in Sikkim, Bhutan and Tibet from 1935 to 1945. In 1936, he led a delegation to Lhasa to negotiate with the Tibetan government on the possibility of the 9th Panchen Lama's return to Tibet; he also discussed British military aid to Lhasa. The Tibetan Government rejected his proposal that a British Office be created in Lhasa. In 1940 he attended the installation ceremonies of the 14th Dalai Lama in Lhasa. A year later, not surprisingly, he was knighted.

How could Cecily not become interested in Tibet as she learned about her husband's past, and probably watched the amateur films that he made while in Tibet between 1936 and 1941, and which are now preserved by the British Film Institute. He died in Yarmouth in 1956 but that made no difference to her continuing interest in Tibet when, in 1960 she was approached for help on behalf of his mother, by the Dalai Lama, in exile in India since the 1950s.

Dekyi Tsering (1900–1981, born to peasants, her birth name Sonam Tsomo, grew up, first to be the wife of a humble farmer and to have 16 children. In 1940, one of them was chosen to be Dalai Lama and she became 'the Grandmother of Tibet', or Tibet's 'Great Mother', known to Tibetans as Amala. She began having health problems not long after her arrival in India, and eventually a Delhi doctor diagnosed a throat polyp which he was sure was benign; he arranged for its removal in St Mary's Hospital, London. It was then that Cecily Gould arranged for Amala, accompanied by Rinchen Dolma Taring, to stay at a guest house in Freshwater. She received assurance that Amala could stay there incognito and the couple had the whole guest house to themselves for six weeks. Amala, safely healed, lived for another 21 years.

Cecily seems to have started her writing career after that and after the death of her husband – in her own older age. She died in Newport aged 95.

The day after the death of **Olivia Manning** (1908–1980) the local paper described her as 'The Isle of Wight novelist' in an article ending 'The Island had finally claimed her for its own.' That was only partly true: she certainly died in the Royal County Hospital in Ryde; she certainly fell unexpectedly ill at

Billingham Manor, Chillerton, where she often stayed with friends, regarding it as her second home, and her ashes were scattered in its grounds. But she wrote only one novel, *The Play Room* (1979), that almost counts: a relatively small, though important, part of it takes place on the Island. That's not to say that the Island wasn't part of her childhood. Isobel English, writing in Cowes in the introduction to the 1983 paperback copy, noted:

> When the children were young, the family used to go on day trips to the Isle of Wight. Money was fairly tight and even the fare on the ferry was a strain. Disembarking at Ryde, they would walk along the coast to Seaview and there catch the bus to Bembridge for a picnic. There was never enough time in one day to explore the interior of the Island.

Olivia was born in North End, Portsmouth. Her womanising father, Oliver Manning, whom she adored, rose from naval trainee to lieutenant commander despite his lack of formal education. While visiting Belfast, when he was 45, he met Olivia Morrow, a domineering publican's daughter 14 years his junior, and they married very soon thereafter.

Emma Garman, in a series 'Feminize Your Canon', a series to explore 'the lives of underrated and underread female authors' (2018), wrote of their daughter's childhood:

> Manning was steeped in dysfunction from an early. age … She and her younger brother were witness and referee to their parents' frequent fights, and she was routinely belittled by her mother. 'I won't say she was unbalanced,' Manning said in an interview, 'but there was something acutely psychologically wrong with her … I can remember being very surprised to find that other people were happy at home, to find that other girls confided in their mothers and were fond of them.'

Olivia wrote 18 novels before *The Play Room*, starting in 1929 with three detective stories under the name Jacob Morrow, so as not to reveal her age to posterity. She may well have transposed that family dynamic before, but she certain does in this one. The family, as hers did, live in Portsmouth, in an area which the mother would give anything to leave; the father takes her nagging and general unpleasantness about his uselessness, particularly regarding money, without rising to the bait; what little love he has to give is for his daughter and main character, Laura, who is sure there must be more to life than this.

The family used to be able to afford a cleaner, who still sends a Christmas card from the Isle of Wight in which she always invites them to visit her. One year, Laura begs her mother to let her take up the invitation. Certainly not, is the reply. But Laura has learned how to nag and eventually, if her brother Tom accompanies her, she can go. When they arrive, their hostess, all dolled up, is about to go out, and she proceeds to do the same for the rest of their stay, leaving them to their own devices – pure heaven. Needless to say, they visit places on the Island where Olivia could never go as a child. After nearly getting caught by the tide on the south coast, they clamber up a cliff and land in a private garden. There the crux of the story – the Play Room – takes place, traumatising young Tom to such an extent that they flee for their lives.

Telling this story to the most popular girl in the class – a beautiful rich girl whose parents dote on her – and her jealous side-kick, Laura begins to lead the life she longed for, until things go wrong again.

Olivia had already gone to London (as Laura longed to), been to art school, and started writing and publishing before her first serious novel was published in 1937. But life really changed for her in 1939 when she married R.D. Smith, 'Reggie', a British Council lecturer. He was posted to Bucharest (Romania) where she accompanied him as the Nazis overran Eastern Europe. Thereafter, they lived in Greece, Egypt and the British Mandate of Palestine. All this was grist to the writer's mill. I knew nothing about the Isle of Wight when, nearly 60 years ago, I read her three novels that make up *The Balkan Trilogy* (1960); I thought they were wonderful, and she was wonderful, because she'd obviously drawn, so evocatively, on her exciting experiences. The novels are not spoilt by being adapted for the television series *The Fortunes of War* (1989), starting in Romania in 1940, and starring Emma Thompson and Kenneth Branagh in the main roles (every other well-known actor of the time also stars). In real life, the couple met while making it, and married as a result.

Emma Garman starts her piece:

The British novelist Olivia Manning spent her … career longing, largely in vain, for literary glory and a secure place in the English canon. Reassurances from friends that talented writers were often rewarded by posterity cut no ice. 'I don't want fame when I'm dead,' she'd retort. 'I want it now.'

You have to feel sad for her. I suggest that you read, or even watch, her *Balkan Trilogy*, and neglect *The Play Room*.

A change of key now, for the last writer in this chapter, the poet **Mimi Khalvati** (b.1944 in Tehran); but she spent ten years, from six to 16 years old (1950–1960) being educated on the Isle of Wight, at the Upper Chine School, Shanklin. Although she did not start publishing poetry until she was 47, it is, for obvious reasons, those poems she later wrote about her time on the Island that are the most appropriate to discuss here, and they are to be found among a range of her poetry in *Child: New and Selected Poems 1991–2011* (2011).

I have confessed in this chapter to not to being a literary critic, But there is something about Mimi's poetry that wins one over, particularly once you know where she came from, how cut off from her comfortable home, her family and her country, culture and language she was (even though she wrote the poems many years later), and what, as will be revealed, a couple of her now-well-known school contemporaries felt about the school.

A *Guardian* review sets the scene for *Child*:

The book is divided into five parts, the first four ordered autobiographically (rather than by date of composition), and it is the pieces about Khalvati's childhood on the Isle of Wight that, in many ways, are the most successful – the isolation conjured up in 'Writing Home' and 'Writing Letters', the use of landscape and careful symbolism in 'The Chine', the clarity and poise of 'Rubayat', an elegy for her grandmother.

But in a way, it is a remark she made when being interviewed – a piece published in *The Poetry Magazine* – that particularly strikes home:

Many of my childhood memories revolve around learning English when I first came to England. My poem 'Dictation' comes from a memory of a dictation lesson, when I was baffled by the word 'comma' which the teacher kept repeating and I kept trying to spell.

When she left school she went on to have a life that did not focus on poetry: from the Isle of Wight, she went to Switzerland, to the University of Neuchatel, and then to London, where she enrolled at the Drama School and then the School of Oriental and African Studies (SOAS). After that she worked as a theatre director in Tehran, translating plays from English into Persian and devising new plays, as well as co-founding the Theatre in Exile Group. Poetry was, nevertheless, obviously lurking: in that same interview she confessed:

I must have been about eleven when I wrote my first book of poems. It was literally a book, with a dark blue hard cover, lined pages, and I filled it with rhyming poems and coloured ink drawings which I pasted in. It was called 'All my Own Work', and it was a birthday present for my mum. Since I was in boarding school and my mother was in Iran, I don't know if she read it, liked it, or what she thought of it. I don't remember. But I was very proud of it, and have it to this day, though the poems were embarrassing.

For a moment you wonder what Mimi's mother must have felt about her being so far away; she doesn't mention her father. The first two verses of her poem in *Child*, 'Writing Letters', read:

> After Chapel on Sundays we wrote letters
> ruling pencil lines on airmails. Addresses
> on front and back often bearing the same name,
> same initial even, for in some countries
> they don't bother to draw fine lines between
> family members with an alphabet.
> Those who remembered their first alphabet
> covered the page in reams of squiggly letters
> while those who didn't envied them. Between
> them was the fine line of having addresses

that spelt home, home having the ring of countries
still warm on the tongue, still ringing with their name.

And the second verse of the poem 'Writing Home':

Writing home meant writing in that ring, mostly
to Mummy. Mummy had a white fur coat
And framed in it her face looked tired and ghostly.
I'm very well and happy, I wrote,
meaning it. Sensing somewhere in that frame
a face too far away, too lost, to worry.
And why would I? Worry should keep, like shame,
its head down in dreams. Sorry sorry sorry
I can't write any more goodbye love Mimi
I wrote after only four lines to Mummy.

What was she really feeling, what did she really feel during those ten years as she grew up at that school in Shanklin? Two of her school contemporaries know exactly how they felt. Judith Okely (b.1941), Emeritus Professor of Anthropology, is best briefly described as 'a Pioneer of Social Research'. Following her time at Upper Chine School, Shanklin, and how she was to describe it, it is not surprising that she researched the life of the marginalised, epitomised by her 1983 book *The Traveller-Gypsies*.

She was scarred by her time at the school from the age of nine. She found it difficult to forget the day she learned there that her father had died. It was only an hour later that, as she sat on her iron bed, matron came up to her and snapped, 'Your Daddy has died. I know that. But you are to stop crying at once. You know you are not to make any noise after 7pm.'

Following a visit to Alcatraz, she described the rules there as reminiscent of those at the school:

Like Alcatraz, we were all captive on an island so there was no point trying to escape. Like Jail, every waking moment was governed by rules, only the rules were stricter. But unlike prison or Borstal, we were there because our parents loved us. ... The dorms were like cells. We had metal beds and a tiny side table. You were allowed two ornaments, perhaps a picture of home, and maybe one toy. At dinner, when we weren't eating, your hands had to rest in your lap. If you were seen resting them on the table, you would get a quick slap. In the rest period after lunch, the matron forbade us from lying on our backs with our legs up because of what she saw as sexual overtones. But we didn't even know what sex was. After that, I never cried in public again. I retreated inside myself.

Like Mimi she didn't tell her mother; later, Judith's mother asked her why she hadn't told them: 'we didn't know any different', she added.

I have to say, I never told my parents about my unpleasant time at boarding school – one didn't.

In *The Isle of Wight as a Site for English-British Identity* (2012) Judith Okely wrote:

> The Isle of Wight, though imagined isolate, has been integral to the reproduction of a specific British cultural hegemony. At the inter-flux of maritime trading, war strategies, yachting, and differentiated holiday escapes, it elaborates royal connections and class division. Two prisons once incarcerated the most dangerous and criminally insane, while idyllic locations record Queen Victoria, Tennyson, Keats and Dickens.

The late Jane Birkin (1946–2023), with her glamorous life as a singer, actor and partner of Serge Gainsbourg, was asked how she had found her time at the school; she replied that she did not enjoy it: it was 'horrid'. But, growing up on the Island, outside her school her life was rather different. She said of it:

> When people say, 'Where would you like to go in your life?' I'd like to go back to being a child again. We were allowed to be savages. We used to get up at 6 in the morning and get on our bikes, and we just went to discover things. Wrecks in the Isle of Wight – we were in a very wild part of the Island – there was black sand, and there were wrecks from the last war.

> We didn't stay on the chic side of the Island, but near Brook beach, where we would ramble and have adventures together – it was wonderful. Being a 12-year-old on a bike on the Isle of Wight with my brother and sister and Ma and Pa is for me the epitome of happiness. The bits in between, the films, my time with Serge, everybody knows about that, but they don't know about my childhood. It's a country you can never go back to.

Many years later, during my second research trip to the Island, I went to Shanklin in search of the school. I found and went up the drive leading to where it had been; it had been demolished, and a smart block of holiday apartments built in its place. But the location is the same, right up against the Chine, as it climbs down to the sea, overgrown with all sorts of foliage. A 'chine', as all Islanders and regular visitors will know, is a local word now used only on the Isle of Wight and in Dorset. It's of Saxon origin and means a deep narrow ravine, formed by water cutting through soft sandstone leading to the sea. The one that forms a boundary to what were the school grounds is still there. You can easily imagine, as the poet obviously did, the 'Shanklin Chine', the poem that opens Mimi Khalvati's *Child*; these are the first two verses:

> It surfaces at moments, unlooked-for,
> When the little crooked child appears
> to bar your way: demanding no crooked

sixpence as she stands behind the stile
in her little gingham frock and the blood
she has in mind drawn behind her gaze.

Are you the guardian of the Chine?
(Perhaps she needs some recognition.)
Of course she never talks.
She only has the one face – dark and solemn,
the one stance – blackboard-set
and a wit as nimble as the Chine.

11 – Foreign Royalty and Elite Visitors, 1854–1883

The Russian Imperial Family and Other Empresses, 1874–1884

Some members of the Russian Imperial family chose to visit the Isle of Wight, voluntarily, as part of an extended family; at least one was not so happy to do so. Of Grand Duchess Maria Alexandrovna of Russia, Duchess of Edinburgh and wife of Queen Victoria's son Alfred, Duke of Edinburgh, Stephan Roman wrote in *Isle and Empires: When Russian Royals and Radicals Came to the Island* (2021; 2nd edition, pb 2022): '[she] spent many years at Osborne House infuriating and irritating her mother-in-law, Queen Victoria'.

Marie, as she was known in her married life, was not the first Russian imperial connection with the Island: Tsar Peter the Great visited England in 1698 to pick up some shipbuilding tips to help build up his Russian naval fleet. He was not only inspired by sailing round the Isle of Wight, but he also lured an Island shipwright to join his team in Russia. And there is a monument to Tsar Alexander I on St Catherine's Down, on the south coast; he visited Britain in 1814, though did not visit the Island, only getting as far as Portsmouth. Nevertheless, the monument was erected that year by a British entrepreneur with shops in Russia, in appreciation of Alexander's part in repelling Napoleon's invasion of Russia in 1812. Marie was, however, the first imperial Russian woman not only to visit Britain, but also to live there.

Grand Duchess Maria Alexdrovna of Russia (1853–1920) was the only surviving daughter of the six children of Tsar Alexander II of Russia and his wife, Marie of Hesse and by Rhine. Like the imperial Romanovs of the time, she was brought up amid much luxury and splendour, and it is not hard to suspect, given her behaviour in England, that she was a touch spoilt by very loving parents. Maria, aged 18, and Alfred, 28, met at various European royal family gatherings, fell in love and, in 1873, decided to marry. Victoria was, as quite often, opposed to the marriage, as were Maria's parents: Tsar Alexander could not bear to lose his beloved daughter. Victoria did not trust Russia, which she considered to be unfriendly towards Britain; Marie's religion was also a problem. The royal family had never married into the imperial Russian family, and they were not going to start now. As often, too, she had to give in; the couple were not going to, and her ministers suggested that it might ease the tension between the two nations, which was live over Afghanistan at the time. Looking forward to her marriage, Maria wrote, 'How happy I am to belong to him. I feel that my love for him is growing daily. I have a feeling of peace and inexpressible happiness and a boundless impatience to be altogether his own.'

In March 1874, Maria and Alfred's marriage took place in a lavish Russian Orthodox ceremony in the imperial chapel in St Petersburg, followed by another less grand ceremony when the Dean of Westminster made them man and wife according to the rites of the Church of England. Marie's crimson velvet mantle was trimmed with a sprig of myrtle sent by Queen Victoria. (The myrtle, grown on the Isle of Wight, was worn by all brides marrying into the British royal family from 1850, starting with Victoria's children, and continuing to this day, including Meghan Markle when she married Prince Harry.) The bride arrived in England, after only a brief honeymoon in Tsarskoe Selo, with a £100,000 dowry and much splendid jewellery. Queen Victoria met them at the South-Western station, and relations started well; she wrote in her journal:

> I took dear Marie in my arms and kissed her warmly several times. I was quite nervous, so long had I been in expectation … Dear Marie has a very friendly manner, a pleasant face, a beautiful skin and fine bright eyes … she speaks English wonderfully well.

Marie's fluent English is not surprising: her nannies were English; she was also proficient in French and German. Journal entries to follow were equally favourable. The young couple moved into Clarence House, where Marie had a Russian Orthodox chapel built, and they had a country house, surrounded by 2,500 acres, in Kent.

The warm relations could not last; indeed, Marie was always too hot or too cold, particularly at Balmoral Castle. When Marie had a fire lit in her unheated bedroom, Queen Victoria would come in and order a maid to throw water on the fire and open the windows. The first open squabble between the queen and the new duchess was over her title to be used at court, and the order of precedence. As the daughter of an emperor, she was an Imperial Highness who had precedence over all the grand duchesses in Russia. On marriage to Alfred, she was only entitled to the style of Royal Highness. In the end, the queen declared that she did not mind both being used, as long as Royal Highness came first.

The next problem was Marie's magnificent jewellery, which she tended to flaunt. British princesses were envious, as was Queen Victoria. Meriel Buchanan, daughter of Britain's last ambassador to Imperial Russia, wrote,

> The Queen compared the Duchess's tiara with those of her own daughters, shrugging her shoulders like a bird whose plumage has been ruffled, her mouth drawn down at the corners, in an expression which those who knew her had learned to dread.

Soon Marie was writing to her father calling her mother-in-law a 'silly obstinate old fool'. Marie's mother wrote, 'To be frank, it is difficult to take such a mother-in-law seriously, and I am sorry on Marie's account'. The list of things that the Duchess of Edinburgh did not like about her new country and its capital was long, starting with the castles and palaces that she had to visit and stay in, none of which could compare with the splendours of the Winter

Palace. Then there were the summers spent at Osborne House on the Isle of Wight. They were tedious and Marie disliked her in-laws. The only ones of her sisters- and brothers-in law she found compatible were Victoria's two youngest, Prince Leopold and Princess Beatrice. Marie attended the latter's wedding in 1885, at St Mildred's Church on the Osborne estate, and is included in the family photograph taken outside Osborne House.

Marie was proud of her strong intellect. She considered Alexandra, Princess of Wales, married to the heir to the throne, a light-minded and foolish woman. In turn society was shocked by Marie nursing her five children herself. The British as a whole did not care for her either. Marie's daughter, later Queen Marie of Romania, was to reflect that 'My mother dearly loved her native country, and she never really felt completely happy in England.'

Marie's long life took many other turns too numerous to follow here. But concerning her visits to Osborne, I like the account of an occasion on the Island many years later when a 'Grand Russian High Tea Book Launch raised over £1,000 for Island charities'. The book concerned was Stephen Roman's new book, *Isle and the Empires*, and the charity concerned was the Mountbatten and Dementia UK Admiral Nurses Isle of Wight charity. The vodka served was Mermaid Salt, courtesy of the Isle of Wight Distillery, Rachmaninov was played, Russian tea was served from a Samovar along with Russian delicacies. The event included an unexpected skit: the established actor Helen Reading, playing Marie, 'made a surprise appearance, amusing guests with tales of her mother-in law, Queen Victoria and the dreary nature of the court at Osborne in the late 1800s...'.

By 1909, relations between Britain and Russia were much warmer, the royal and imperial families much intertwined; not only was the **Tsarina, Alexandra Feodorovna** (née Princess Alix of Hesse; 1872–1917) a favourite grand-daughter of the late Queen Victoria, but her grandson, George, Prince of Wales, and Tsar Nicholas could be mistaken for each other, so alike were they. But the 1909 family gathering in Cowes was not only that: the Solent waters outside Cowes were full of ships of the British and Russian navies.

The chapter 'The Imperial Visit to Cowes' in Alexander Spiridovitch's *The Home of the Last Tsar – Romanov and Russian History* (1928, in French; translated into American English, 2009) would be useful enough if it were just a historical reconstruction. But it is rather more than that: it is an account of the author's own experience there then: he was the head of Nicholas II's secret personal guard for 10 years from 1906. It is an eye-witness account in which he describes the 'dreary' weather as they approached Cowes. Then he wrote, and this is just one paragraph about the powerful sight of the vessels involved, and their hour-long manoeuvres, which took place after lunch:

The royal yacht Victoria & Albert came to meet the Standardt. Cannon shots came from our combat ship, and were responded to by one of the English cruisers. The King [Edward VII] came on board the Standardt, and then Their Majesties went on board the Victoria and Albert. Our Imperial Standard was hoisted up next to the English Royal flag.

Ships were not the only focus of the day:

Farther on, on the coast we could see Cowes, where they were then holding the annual Royal Yacht Club races. All the sporting members of English high-society were gathered there. The attention of yachtsmen around the world was concentrated on Cowes. The politicians, on their part, had fixed their gaze on the town with anguish where they were preparing their own equally important events at the same time.

At last the passengers could disembark. On dry land one of Spiridovitch's colleagues 'had been very embarrassed: no one in Cowes was able to understand a word of his Berlitz English. One charming English lady gave him the same response in bad French: "Pardon me, but I do not speak Russian"'. He goes on to describe the rest of the visit, but important for this chapter is his first-hand account of the escapade of the Russian Grand Duchesses, particularly that of **Olga Nikolaevna** (1895–1918) and **Tatiana Nikolaevna** (1897–1918):

The Grand Duchesses had gone down to Cowes in the morning, which had disturbed the English police. They went by car to Osborne and played there on the beach.

After lunch, the older two Grand Duchesses, Olga and Tatiana, went alone into the town, accompanied by several members of the suite. One had to see the joy and pleasure they expressed above all at being able to walk about without being recognized. Gay, hardy, they seemed quite at ease, entering into shops, buying postcards and all kinds of souvenirs. They took a ferry from one part of the town to another and were very happy that they could pay the price of the passage themselves.

However, the public soon learned who these young ladies were, happy, svelte, frolicking, in gray [gay?] dresses. They began to follow them and waited in front of the shops, and soon the crowd of the curious became quite large so that the police were then obliged to take energetic measures to cut a path through the street for the Grand Duchesses. As the crowd continued to grow, the members of the suite began to become upset.

Returning to the disembarkation quay, the Grand Duchesses looked at the time and decided that it was still too early to return to the yacht. So they hailed two carriages which took them back to town, as they wanted to visit the local church [St Mildred's, Whippingham on the Osborne estate].

The pastor was extremely happy to show them anything about the church which interested them. They visited the tomb of Henry of Battenberg and the armchair used by Queen Victoria when she went to the church [see chapter 9, 'Women Artists'].

The Grand Duchesses returned to the Standardt for tea.

There is a photograph of the two families – royal and Imperial – taken in front of Barton Manor, part of the Osborne estate, where the Imperial family was staying. The women and girls were all in white dresses and hats, Alexei, the Tsarevich, in a sailor suit, the men in white trousers, blue blazers and naval caps. It was the last time the two families were to meet.

The visit came to an end, as does the account:

The colossal fleet, stationary and sleeping, was a fairy tale vision.

When we awoke the next morning, the fleet was no longer there. Silently, without anyone having noticed, they left the harbour during the night. Only a true sailor can really appreciate the virtuosity of such a manouvre.

That same morning, our squadron left the English waters and proceeded back, with the Standardt in the lead, toward the Russian coast. The weather had again become somber. The barometer fell.

As is well known, Russia experienced two revolutions in 1917, the second, in October, that of the Bolsheviks, the result of which was to last until the Soviet Union dissolved in December 1991. This is where Stephan Roman's book comes into its own because it starts on a personal note: it recounts how, in the immediate aftermath of the October Revolution, his own family were refugees, awaiting their fate on the banks of the Dniester River, having fled Moscow through Ukraine to Moldova.

But it was rather worse for the Imperial family, the Grand Duchesses so full of *joie de vivre* in Cowes in 1909. After several months of increasingly harsh confinement, they were all shot in the basement of Ipatiev House, Tobolsk in July 1918, and their burnt bodies flung down a nearby abandoned iron mine. That is now known to be their end (whatever I wrote in the novel, *God Save the Tsar* (1978)). The Grand Duchess Elizabeth Feodorovna, Empress Alexandra's sister who had become a nun, had earlier been thrown down the mine shaft alive, and a grenade had been thrown down after her and her companions.

As you travel from Osborne House to East Cowes, you pass on your left a green sward called Jubilee Park, or Jubilee Recreation Park. There, on the edge of it facing York Road, is a very large granite monument in the shape of a cross. On one face is the inscription:

Emperor
Nicholas II
Empress Alexandra
Tsarevich
Alexis
Grand Duchesses
Olga
Tatiana
Maria
Anastasia
And
Grand Duchess
Elizabeth
Martyred
During
The Revolution
In Russia
July 1918

Above the inscription, busts of each member of the family are stamped. On the other side is the further inscription:

This Monument was created by
The Russian artist
Elena Bezborodova
And presented as a gift to the People of
East Cowes
By the Grand Duchess Elizabeth
Romanov Society, UK and private donors
07-07-2018

In 2019, on a very wet day in October, the local community came to the monument where Her Highness Princess Olga Andreevna Romanov, great-niece of Tsar Nicholas, and President of the Romanov Family Association, had travelled from her home in Kent and laid flowers at the monument.

The two empresses who follow may not have had such a tragic ending as that of Tsarina Alexandra Feodorovna, but their introductions to the Island were both under upsetting circumstances and the life of one of them did end in assassination. One short quotation from Spiridovitch's chapter about the Russian Imperial visit to Cowes in 1909 mentions one of them almost in passing; you would miss it if you weren't interested in her:

Their Majesties did not return to the Standardt until six o'clock, after which they went to visit Empress Eugenie, widow of Empress Napoleon III who was on board a private yacht. They stayed with her for about one half hour.

Maria Eugenia Ignacia Augustina de Palafox y Kirkpatrick, **Empress Eugénie of France** (1826–1920) was born into Spanish nobility. She was the youngest child of Don Cipriano de Palafox Portocarrero, three times Grandee of Spain, and Maria Manuela Enriqueth Kirkpatrick de Closbourn y de Grevigné, a daughter of the Scots-born William Kirkpatrick of Closeburn. Eugénie's ambitious mother, Manuela, was in charge of her education and sent her to several Paris institutions, and to an 'exclusive' boarding school in England where she, with her Scottish red hair and blue eyes, was teased and called 'Carrot'; she was so unhappy that her father took her away. She and her sister, who was also there, returned to Paris to be educated by a new governess, Miss Flowers (presumably British), who was to remain with the family until the 1880s. It is maintained by one writer, who was drawn on by the author of Encyclopedia.com, from whom I have drawn, that the opposing views of her parents on practically everything doomed their union from the start. A good example is that Eugénie's mother wanted her daughters to be educated in the social graces, preparing them for brilliant careers in society; their father preferred a serious education, simple clothes and a plain diet.

Eugénie had several heartbreaks before the ambitions of her mother, then a widow in Spain, indulging in what was, as one author put it, 'middle-aged lechery', were finally rewarded; and here is where this narrative moves closer to the Isle of Wight. During the early 1850s, Eugénie, with her mother, frequently attended balls at the Elysée Palace given by Napoleon III, nephew of the great French Emperor. As Prince Louis Napoleon he had been elected president of the republic, but he had recently taken power as Emperor. To describe his back-story is not appropriate here but, at one of the balls, he could not fail to notice such a beautiful young woman. On another occasion, one contemporary described Eugénie dressed for riding:

> Her dainty figure was well-defined by a closely-buttoned habit, the skirt long and wide, over grey breeches. With one of her tiny. gloved hands she held the reins, while she used the other to urge on her excited horse with the help of a little riding whip, the handle of which was set with pearls. She wore patent leather boots with high heels and spurs. She sat her horse like a knight, and despised the saddle ordinarily used by ladies.

Napoleon apparently saw her that day and, although he had planned to make a suitable royal marriage, the die was cast. On 22 January 1853 he announced his engagement to Eugénie. They were married on 30 January. The marriage was not altogether happy: the sexual escapades of her mother had put the young bride off sex, though she did eventually produce a son; her husband was something of a Lothario, and did not curb his gallivanting after their marriage. Eugénie had not been trained or educated to be an empress, and she found court life stultifying. To describe what followed in affairs of state would, again, weigh down this narrative. But it should be said that the empress played some part in what went wrong and what, therefore, happened. Three times when

Napoleon was away, she acted as regent, in 1859, 1865 and 1870. Diplomacy was not her forte, and this may have contributed to the isolation of France. Relations with Prussia suffered to such an extent that in July 1870 Napoleon reluctantly declared war. By the end of six weeks, France was defeated; on surrendering his army, Napoleon was taken to Germany, united since 1861, as a prisoner. On 4 September, a mob stormed the Tuileries.

Eugénie, now dethroned, and in fear for her life, fled with her 14-year-old son, the Prince Imperial, Lou Lou, through a side door to the Emperor's American dentist, Dr Evans. From there, the boy escaped by different means to Belgium. Arranged and accompanied by Dr Evans, Eugénie, alternately shrieking and weeping, travelled incognito for two days to Deauville where Mrs Evans was staying. Noting that she and Eugénie were much the same size, she packed some of her less obvious clothes, and some toiletries for her. The pleasure yacht, the *Gazelle*, belonging to Lord Burgoyne, was in the harbour and, by that vessel, the party travelled, surviving a violent storm, to the Isle of Wight, docking in Ryde.

Two women and a man, one of the women dishevelled and in a state of distress, all of them travel stained, made for the Royal Pier Hotel but were refused admittance; perhaps the doorman or receptionist did not believe their story. That part of the saga, though factual, is rather difficult to credit – an empress is an empress, even if she is an ex-empress, even if she was not looking like one. In any case, the party stayed instead for a few hours at the York Hotel, 21 George Street. They then travelled on to Brighton where Eugénie learned that her son had arrived at Dover the previous day They were able to meet up, to Eugénie's great relief – anxiety about him was one of the reasons for her distress.

This arrival in England was rather different from that in 1855, when Eugénie and Napoleon had arrived on a state visit to London, as Queen Victoria's guests, to cement the ties of the two allies involved, since 1854, in the Crimean War. When Victoria and Albert returned the visit, they were taken not only to Versailles, but also to the tomb of Napoleon Bonaparte, Emperor Napoleon I: 'the Great Napoleon'.

Now, safe at last, Eugénie took a lease on a house in Chislehurst and, in due course, Bismarck allowed Napoleon to join them. Eugénie discovered an affection for her husband that had hitherto been missing, but she was shocked by the state of his health. After several operations to remove a kidney stone, he died suddenly on 10 January 1873. There was now no hope of an imperial couple returning to France. The Prince Imperial was proclaimed by the Bonapartist faction as Napoleon IV.

Eugénie and Victoria were old friends. In the entry in her diary of 24 December 1857, Victoria, commenting on her Christmas presents, singled out one from 'Dearest Albert' of a 'copy of Winterhalter's picture of the Empress Eugénie in a straw hat, which I am particularly fond of, and which is charming'. And now, in 1873, they were both widows. Victoria soon visited her and her son in Kent and wrote of Eugénie that she was 'very thin and pale, but still very handsome' with 'deep sadness in her face' and frequent tears in her eyes as she spoke of her dreadful last hours in Paris as the populace stormed the Tuileries.

In her widowhood, Victoria often referred to her friend as 'dear Empress Eugénie', and sometimes as 'poor Empress Eugénie'. That was not because the former Empress was without funds: apart from any other access she had to finance, she had found time before leaving Paris in 1870 to dispatch her jewellery to a safe place. Eugénie was a frequent visitor to Windsor, Balmoral and Osborne House, the best place for the two women to discuss their widowhood. And Victoria often lent Eugénie a cottage at Osborne. In its gardens were some violets brought back from St Helena, where the first Napoleon had spent his second exile. And Victoria also visited her, and a couple of times accepted an invitation to Eugénie's Villa 'Cyrnos' in the south of France.

The queen had one regret regarding her friend: Eugénie's son, the Prince Imperial (or, as some would have it, Napoleon IV), had trained as a British Army officer; he persuaded the British Army, which the queen did nothing to stop, to allow him to take part in the Anglo-Zulu war. In 1879, serving with British forces, he was killed in a skirmish with a group of Zulus. He was 23. Victoria heard of his death before Eugénie, and felt that she bore some responsibility. She recorded that it haunted her all night 'seeing those horrid Zulus constantly before me' and 'thinking of the poor Empress who did not yet know it'. She also recorded full details of the funeral, and all those who attended.

Eugénie lived to see Victoria's son, Edward VII, ascend the throne of England on Queen Victoria's death in 1901. In the year before his death in 1910, she was visited by the Russian Imperial Family on a yacht in Cowes harbour. She lived to see Edward's son, George V, ascend the throne; she lived through the murder of the Russian Imperial family in 1918, and the end of the First World War in 1918. She died in 1920, aged 94, on a final visit to Spain. She had two funerals, one in Spain, the second in England, attended by Bonapartes, the king and queen of England and the queen of Spain. Eugénie had seen it all, or most of it.

Empress Elizabeth of Austria (1837–1898, commonly known as Sisi, born Duchess Elizabeth Amalie Eugenie in Bavaria) has probably been written about and depicted on screen more often than any other empress. She is best known for her remarkable beauty, and her care to maintain it, the suicide of her son, Rudolph, heir to the throne, and his 17-year-old mistress Marie Vetsera at Mayerling, and the manner of her death. So much has been written, and her life so picked over, that there is only space here for some bare bones leading up to her stay of at least two months in Ventnor in 1874.

Sisi was born into the Ducal royal branch of the Bavarian House of Wittelsbach, but was brought up informally, without much in the way of court protocol; she preferred riding to lessons. She was the third child and second daughter of Duke Maximilian Joseph of Bavaria and Princess Ludovika of Bavaria; the family's main home was in Munich. On her marriage to her cousin, 23-year-old Emperor Franz Joseph, at the age of 16, she became Empress of Austria and Queen of Hungary (these two countries forming the Austro-Hungarian Empire). She found life at court completely different from that of her upbringing – suffocating, and run by a domineering mother-in-law who, finding the new empress wayward, determined to tame her; in this she was unsuccessful: Sisi continued to rebel against the rigid protocols and strict etiquette.

Sisi and Franz Ferdinand had four children, the first two of whom were daughters. Following the birth of the second girl, Sisi found a pamphlet on her desk which read:

> ... The natural destiny of a Queen is to give an heir to the throne. If the Queen is so fortunate as to provide the State with a Crown Prince this should be the end of her ambition – she should by no means meddle with the government of an Empire, the care of which is not a task for women ... If the Queen bears no sons, she is merely a foreigner in the State, and a very dangerous foreigner, too. For as she can never hope to be looked on kindly here, and must always expect to be sent back whence she came, so will she always seek to win the King by other than natural means, she will struggle for position and power by intrigue and sowing of discord, to the mischief of the King, the nation, and the Empire.

Sisi's mother-in-law saw to the upbringing of the two girls. Two years later, in 1858, Rudolph, son and heir, was born. Ten years after that, Sisi gave birth to **Marie Valerie** (1868–1924). Her last daughter was born in Hungary, a country for which Sisi, as its queen, had a passion. It is perhaps not surprising, therefore, that Marie Valerie was her favourite child, and it is she who is the focus of the stay in Ventnor. When the rather delicate six-year-old suffered from a lingering illness in 1874, doctors advised that some good sea air and sea bathing would help. Ventnor and, in particular, Undercliff was recommended as a sunny spot with its own warm micro-climate, and good sea bathing in its cove. An advertisement promoting that spot, read:

> A few houses near the sea and a stretch of sand
> That will appeal to the bather
> Use of huts – 6d
> Macintosh bathing from the beach – 3d
> Undressing on the beach is not permitted.

The date of the advertisement is unknown; I suspect it was after Elizabeth's time and that when the castle was recommended to her, the beach would have been private. Her younger sister, Maria Sophie, the ex-Queen of Naples, had told Sisi that she could live in peace there and that royal privacy would be respected. Steephill Castle was built by John Hambrough in 1831–1833 in the Gothic style, with towers, turrets and extensive crenellations, but by 1860 he had gone to live on the mainland. The Austrian ambassador rented the castle for Sisi, and several alterations were set in train to make it suitable: the billiard room was turned into a gymnasium and new bathrooms were installed.

Sisi arrived at the castle on 2 August 1874. If you are imagining her wanting peace and solitude, longing to enjoy the lovely grounds and private beach with a party consisting of young Valerie and perhaps a lady-in-waiting, a maid and a cook, you are mistaken: she came with a full imperial suite. Biographies of Sisi are hardly likely to mention Ventnor, but there are a plethora of postings online about her stay; one, mkheritage, 'Steephill Isle of Wight', has it that, 'this huge foreign party descended on Ventnor, creating great astonishment among the islanders who had not seen such colourful visitors'. This was not how, at that time, they would see Queen Victoria's arrival at Osborne, particularly after 1861 and the death of Prince Albert; since then black, or at least sombre dress was de rigueur. Ventnor during the Victorian period was just turning from a village of fishing families into a town.

Soon after Sisi's arrival, the queen travelled from Osborne House to call on her, but just a few pleasantries were exchanged; the two were such different characters, and Sisi, in spite of everything, was shy and an introvert; she apparently found Victoria rather awe-inspiring. According to the same posting, 'Valerie was terrified when she first saw the Queen, who was still in widow's clothes, as she had never seen such a stout lady. Her mother regularly dieted and followed strict fitness regimes to keep her slim figure.' Sisi asked to be excused when twice invited to dinner at Osborne House; to others she said it bored her and she thought the queen's people 'stuffy'. Victoria, for her part, said that the empress might be beautiful but lacked any sense of royal duty.

David Paul in 'Forgotten Castle' posted on the Wooton Bridge website, tells the story that postings cannot get enough of: Sisi

> Would spend hours just walking silently in the grounds and during this time she would frequently visit the 'Holy Thorn' – this is a rare plant in England, coming from the East. Legend has it that soldiers used the bush to make the crown for Christ's head, the leaves being exceptionally prickly. This bush had an irresistible attraction for the Empress and she would stand silently, touching the thorny leaves.

TC Hudson, author of 'Elizabeth Slept Here' (2011) tells the same story, but starts it with more scene-setting in the castle's grounds: 'Among the beeches, chestnuts, cedars, magnolias, myrtles, rhododendrons, and other flora too numerous to catalogue which beautified the garden ...'.

Sisi did not spend all her time in the garden: she got out and about. She is said to have visited the German Crown Princess at Sandown whom she considered a friend. She was there, staying at what is now the Royal Pier Hotel with her husband Crown Prince Frederick and their children and entourage. This was surely a bit risky as this friend was Queen Victoria's eldest daughter, Victoria, who would surely report the visit to her mother whose invitations had been turned down. Victoria thought Elizabeth's lifestyle strange as she 'slept in the afternoon, dined at 4pm and rode in the evening ... but I like her and she is kind to me.' Sisi also visited Alexandra, Princess of Wales, whom she described as 'very kind, nice looking and deaf' – a different impression from that of the Russian Marie, Duchess of Edinburgh (see above). It is interesting that kindness seems to be such a well-regarded feature of royal friendships.

Sisi also went to London to walk around incognito and ride in Rotten Row with the Austrian Ambassador. Then she went on to Melton to look for hunters and to stay at Belvoir Castle with the Duke of Rutland. When 'they' (was Valerie included, or was it a Lady-in-waiting?) returned to Steephill, the Castle Club (?) had organised a race meeting for them. Sisi heard about it before she left London and sent off to a jeweller to design a cup for the winner of the main race. This was won by an Island farmer. The cup had the following inscription:

Ventnor Steeplechase Cup
Presented by Her Imperial and Royal Majesty
The Empress of Austria
Won by 'Beauty' the property of Mr Bungay of Ventnor
Ridden by Mr Weeks of Fairfields
On September 29th 1874

Local hotelier and businessman, William Judd, said that he could 'never remember seeing such a [numerous] crowd as appeared on the course that day'. He was a fine rider who had met the Empress and her party whilst out riding on the downs; she sent an equerry over to say she would like to talk to him and then suggested that he ride with them. When they rode back to Ventnor she said to him 'I have been pleased with my visit to Ventnor. I like the people and it is possible I may return'.

Sisi did, indeed, return to the Island, in 1884, making a leave-taking call at Osborne House; as Hudson put it, 'during which the old Queen, succumbing to an exercise of charm, graciously overlooked her past conduct and treated her with sympathy and friendliness'.

On 10 September 1898, Sisi, assuming her usual name on such occasions, of Countess of Hohenembs, left the Hotel Beau Rivage in Geneva, while most of the guests were at lunch, to embark on a paddle boat on Lac Leman headed for Montreux. Her servants were already on the boat, leaving only the Countess Sytáyay to escort her to the empty quay. But the anarchist Luigi Luccheni had chosen precisely that time and place at which to leap out, sharpened file in hand. It took him seconds to stab the empress in the heart; she died on the boat, aged 61.

Those visitors whose stays on the Isle of Wight followed that of the Empress Elizabeth, though revolutionaries, did not espouse such assassination. And there is no blue plaque on Steephill Castle, because it no longer exists.

The Revolutionary Émigrés, 1854–1883

The history of the Romanov Tsars may have ended tragically, but their reigns were not always benign, not even that of Nicholas II. The reign from 1825 to 1855 of Nicholas I, the younger brother of Alexander I, was particularly harsh, as seen in the way he put down the Decembrist Revolt of 1825. He was a reactionary who would not tolerate dissent. It was during his rule that Alexander Herzen, writer, thinker, and seen as the Father of Russian socialism, was forced to take his family into exile for 12 years, based mainly in England. He spent two holidays on the Isle of Wight, in Ventnor, in 1854 and 1855. Happily the blue plaque where he, as a recent widower, and his family stayed, introduces us to the woman who accompanied him to look after the children. The inscription reads:

ALEXANDER HERZEN
Russian political thinker
1812–1870
Stayed here in September 1855
With
MALWIDA
VON MEYSENBUG
German writer
1816–1903

43. Malwida von Meysenbug and Alexander Herzen
plaque, photograph by the author

Malwida von Meysenbug (1816–1903), born at Kassel, Hesse, the ninth of 10 children, was the daughter of Carl Rivalier, descended from a family of French Huguenots, and given the title of Baron of Meysenbug by William I of Hesse-Kassel. Her mother was Ernestine Hansel (1784–1861), an exceptionally well-educated woman who taught her children herself. When Malwida was 14, the revolution of 1830 made an impression on her and, she was fully supportive of the 1848 revolution. In 'Malwida Rivalier von Meysenbug', posted on the University of Ohio website, James Chastain elaborates:

Meysenbug maintained significant friendships and corresponded with ... forty-eighters. While she did not fight on the barricades ... she demonstrated her partisanship for a new society by joining the German Catholic Free Congregation of Frankfurt in 1848. The oppositional religious group was increasingly politicized, espousing social and political equality for all its members, regardless of sex; these ideals most closely mirrored Meysenbug's.

Although women were not allowed to observe the Frankfurt Pre-Parliament, Meysenbug arranged to be smuggled into St Paul's church, and secreted herself in a flag-draped balcony. When the revolution was threatened, Meysenbug's pamphlet, *Die Shwur einer Frau* (The Oath of a Woman) was published ... to hearten and encourage liberals and radicals to continue their struggle.

Susan Halstead, a specialist at the British Library, notes how Malwida explained a problem with her family, as well as adding to Chastain's account:

The tyranny of family, which in this case rests on the regrettable principle that the woman should not think for herself but remain in the place to which fate has assigned her, no matter whether her individuality is submerged or not.

At some stage (date uncertain), Malwida broke with her family because of her political convictions. I do worry about how her mother, who lived until 1861, took this. Her father died in 1847, but one of her brothers certainly took exception to her views and activities, and tried to dissuade her from them.

In 1849 Malwida travelled to Ostend, about which she wrote *Eine Reise nach Ostende* (1905). Far from being a conventional travel narrative, it presents evidence of her political convictions and her strong identification with the common people. In 1852, after a visit from her brother and a police search of her rooms, she felt forced to flee to London, where she lived by giving German lessons and doing translations. There she met and became friends with Herzen.

On the holidays in Ventnor, she was formally the governess to three of Herzen's children, but she was also a friend who offered to help Herzen cope with his children, who were recently bereft of their mother. She paid particular attention to Herzen's daughter, Olya, **Olga Alexdrovna Herzen** (1850–1953). I suspect that this was because she was determined that Olga would not be a girl straitjacketed to conform to a narrow view of the woman's place in society. There is no suggestion that Malwida's relations with Herzen were more than friendship born of similar political views.

Malwida was used to mixing among the elite, numbering Nietszche and Wagner among her friends. As the inscription suggests, she was a writer; she was also an artist of some delicacy. The title of her autobiography is variously translated: sometimes it is *Memories of an Idealist*; more like the original German: *Memoiren einer Idealisten* (1869–1876). My copy is, rather infelicitously, entitled *Rebel in Bombazine* (1936; edited by Mildred Adams from the translation of Elsa von Meysenbug Lyons).

It is not clear where Malwida and Herzen's family spent the first holiday of a week in September 1854 in Ventnor, but in the second, longer visit a year later they stayed at the St Augustine Villa, a chalet hotel, the grounds of which extended to the Esplanade, just in front of the sea, giving a wonderful view. It is of the side view of the hotel that Malwida made one of her delicate but impeccable drawings, perhaps too delicate to reproduce satisfactorily here; the sea is sketched so faintly that it is almost in the viewer's mind. Another drawing is of the coast east of the villa. A photograph of the villa in 2010 shows little physical change. These photographs may be seen on the blog: JSBlog. Journal of a Southern bookreader. They may originally have been posted by Sarah J Young, a lecturer in Russian at the UCL School of Slavonic Studies.

When that 2010 photograph was taken, St Augustine Villa seems to have been an ordinary guest house. But in July 2022, just before I visited it to see the blue plaque, it opened as a swanky boutique hotel, still called St Augustine Villa, with a restaurant ('The Terrace') and a wine-selling business run by wife and husband team, Ashley Keen and Tom Fahey. I bumped into Ashley who was, happily, interested to hear of the book I was researching. The villa is a step, and a side road, away from Alexandra Gardens where Alice and Edward Elgar spent their honeymoon (see chapter 9).

44. Malwida von Meysenbug, sketch of St Augustine Villa,
from the Internet

Sarah Young in her article, 'In Herzen's Footsteps: a visit to Ventnor' (2011), posted on her website after literally following in his footsteps on the Isle of Wight, quotes two extracts from Malwida's memoirs:

[Herzen] proposed a small trip to the sea which I had previously suggested to him and which he had turned down.

So we left. [Joseph] Domengé [a French émigré tutor] came with us, and we took the boat over to Wight Island, the natural beauty of which I had long wanted to see. On the journey across the Island to the little city of Ventnor on the southern side, Herzen, his son and Domengé sat atop the stagecoach, the children and I sat inside. Delighted by the glorious road, I called up to them 'Isn't that beautiful? Wasn't I right in suggesting this?' Laughingly, Herzen called down: 'I didn't want to tell you, but yes, you were right: It's glorious and I'm glad we came'.

We spent happy days in beautiful Ventnor. In the evenings we were usually with the Pulzkys, who were spending the summer there. Therese's mother, an educated and intelligent Viennese lady, had come with them, and this made for many a pleasant hour with her keen humour and wit. The Kossuths were also there, and he was much more pleasant in a more intimate setting than he had been in London. At the time, our thoughts were preoccupied by the war Russia had started with Turkey [the Crimean War]. Herzen, more so than the others, was very excited. He prophesied Russian defeat and wished for it, since he believed it would lead to the downfall of autocracy

Malwida also mentioned spending time in the water, presumably using a bathing machine. She and **Terézia Pulszky** (Theresa, Therese; née Walter; 1819–1866) had met by chance in 1850, but later, as émigrés in London, and then, in Ventnor, their friendship developed. Therese was an Austro-Hungarian author and translator; she also played the piano well, painted and spoke English, French and Italian. She was born in Vienna to a wealthy Viennese banker (name of her mother not noted). But she moved to Hungary, to Pest, when she married Ferene Pulszky, several months after they met in 1845. He knew at their first meeting that he wanted to marry her: she would be a political partner, not an ornament or housewife. He was elected to the Diet of Hungary and, by 1848, was appointed to a financial post in the Hungarian government. But, when that year, the 1848 Revolution reached Austria and Hungary, the couple knew they must flee, which they did, to London in 1849. In 1852, Ferene was condemned to death in his absence for being in contempt of court, having failed to attend the court. Therese wrote an autobiography which included their escape; it was translated as *Memoirs of a Hungarian Lady* (1850); its Afterword can be found online; in spite of its sometimes quirky translation, it is worth reading. Unfortunately, given the date at which the narrative stops, there is obviously nothing concerning Ventnor and Therese's friendship with Malwida.

In 1851 the Pulszkys travelled to the United States, interestingly, leaving from Cowes, so they knew the Isle of Wight before Malwida and Herzen met up with them in Ventnor. They wrote a book together about their tour of the United States. Ferene was able to return to Hungary in 1866, but Therese died in that September from cholera, the day after one of her daughters died from typhus. I have not been able to access a volume in Hungarian, *The Drawings of Terézia Pulszky and Malwida von Meysenbug Made in Emigration in England (Ventnor and surroundings, Isle of Wight, 1855–1856)*, HOM Yearbook 2019–2022.

It is much less easy to find out anything about Theresa Kossuth (née Meszlenyl; d.1863), and Malwida writes less about any friendship between them. Much is known about her husband, Lajos Kossuth: Hungarian, nobleman, lawyer, journalist, politician, statesman and governor-president of the Kingdom of Hungary during the revolution of 1848–1849. I can find no explanation for the start of Theresa's relationship with her future husband. All I can find is that he was arrested in 1837, before his appointment to his highest post, but after he had entered politics, and spent a year in Buda prison awaiting trial. How Theresa started visiting him in prison is unclear, but she knew about his politics; it is also known that her visits made prison bearable for him, particularly as she not only kept him up to date about political events, but supplied him with books as well. The Bible and Shakespeare enabled him to learn a fluent, if archaic, English. In order to be allowed to visit him, she told prison officials that she was his fiancée. In reality, he did not know her until her visits started. On the day of his release, they were married. She was a Catholic, and her church refused to bless the marriage because he was firmly Protestant, and refused to convert, and Theresa refused to become Lutheran. Their cross-denominational marriage was the first in Hungary, and caused a scandal. The couple went on to have three children. At some stage political relations between the Kossuths and the Pulszkis were established.

With the chaos of the 1848–1849 revolution, the Kossuth family escaped in disguise to the Ottoman Empire and were kept under house arrest. In October 1851, British and American intervention resulted in his release and the family sailed to Southampton. The visit of both families to the United States, where they toured, was to solicit support for Hungary's cause; though Kossuth was well received wherever he went, support was elusive. Returning to London, the Kossuths lived there for eight years, touring, again politically. The breaks both families took in Ventnor were probably important to their well-being.

Herzen wrote of his 1855 meeting Kossuth, 'Chance brought us together at one of the most exquisite spots not only in England but in Europe … I spent a month at Ventnor … '

Of that stay in Ventnor, Malwida wrote:

Herzen himself suggested that we again go to Ventnor on the Island of Wight for a few weeks. Of course, the children [Tata (Natalya), Olya and Sasha] and I welcomed this suggestion. We rented a comfortable home on the ocean, and the wonderful sea air and charmingly beautiful coast revived our good spirits. The Pulszkys were also there again. They frequently came in the evening, and I enjoyed being together with Therese, whose sensitive personality became less of a mystery to me than it had been in the political excitement of London life. News reached us there about the taking of Malakoff [a tactically important height of Sevastopol, Crimea]. This meant that Sebastopols [sic] would probably fall and the war would be over. We rejoiced at the news, not only out of consideration for human life, but especially for Russia, since it could be assumed that the new emperor would attempt domestic reforms after the close of this war he had inherited [Nicholas I died, Alexander II did institute reforms, particularly the abolition of serfdom, but was, nevertheless, some years later, assassinated].

Chastain completes his concise account of Malwida with what happened after she left Herzen. It was not all his family that she left: she took Olga Herzen to Italy with her and continued her education, while also legally adopting her. Olga married the French historian Gabriel Monod in 1873. Malwida became involved in the workers' circle movement of the revolutionary Mazzini. She never abandoned her conviction that women must be educated to independence. In 1876–1877, together with Nietzsche and Wagner, she planned to establish a school for young women in Rome. After the failure of this project, she supported herself by writing, including her memoirs, romantic novels and short stories with underlying themes of egalitarian utopian societies. She died in Rome in 1903 aged 86, and was buried there.

Jenny von Westphalen (Johanna Bertha Julie Jenny Edle von Westphalen; 1814–1881) and her husband, Karl Marx, spent two weeks in Ryde in the summer of 1874, staying at 11 Nelson Street, not far from the sea. It was primarily for Marx to convalesce following illness the year before. He mostly followed doctors' orders, reading and relaxing to a large extent, though he did interest himself in local affairs, including electioneering, and they enjoyed walking. He wrote to Engels, 'This island is a little paradise.' Even today Nelson Street is a road full of smart, white-painted houses. *The Communist Manifesto*, to be written by Marx and Engels in 1847, was published in 1848, the year of European revolutions.

Jenny was born in the small town of Salzwedel in northern Germany. Her father was Ludwig von Westphalen, a civil servant from a family recently raised to the petty nobility; her mother was Caroline Heubel from a middle-class family. One of Jenny's brothers was a schoolmate of Marx. As their fathers, too, were friends, her father befriended young Marx, so that Jenny and Marx met regularly as children. Even though she was four years older, both of them were well read and literary, so it is not surprising that they became closer as teenagers; and Marx found her the most beautiful girl in town. They were soon courting, and became engaged in 1836; they married in 1843 and moved to Paris. In the years that followed they had seven children. Their daughters all had the first name of Jenny, so it is by their second or third names that they were called, and they tended to have nicknames. In 1845, the French political police expelled Marx and pregnant Jenny, so that the birth of their second daughter took place in Brussels.

Bare bones sources sometimes leave gaps that can omit details important to a particular writer. So it is that it should be noted that their daughter Eleanor was with them in Ryde. **Eleanor Marx** (1855–1898), known in the family as 'Tussy', was later, from 1884, the partner of Edward Aveling. Eleanor was the sixth Marx child and fourth daughter. What is more, their daughter known as 'Jennychen' **Laura Marx** (1845–1911; married, in 1868 to the revolutionary writer, Paul Lafargue) joined them for a while. This becomes clear because Marx wrote to Engels on 15 July:

> When we went down to the pier to see her off we witnessed the arrival from Brighton of a temperance gang back from an excursion. Half of them were drunk. As an old Englishman next to me remarked 'it was the worst lot he had ever met in his life' and neither have I ever encountered such a mob of stunted, loutish and smutty minded idiots all at once. ... For foreigners this sample of Freeborn Britons would have been an amazing sight.

Marx extolled the beauty of the Isle of Wight, and the pleasure of walking there, to such an extent that Engels visited it in 1875 with his 'second wife'. That complicates facts, as Engels did not believe in marriage, though he did believe in having sex with any number of women in many different places, sometimes other men's wives. But he did live for 20 years with Mary Burns, a fierce young Irish woman with radical views who worked in his factory in Manchester and guided him through Manchester and Salford, showing him the worst districts for his research. That resulted in *The Condition of the Working Class in England* (1845). Mary died suddenly of heart disease in 1863, after which Engels became close to her younger sister, Lydia ('Lizzie') with whom he lived openly in London. He married her in September, hours before her death. She must be the 'second wife' who accompanied him to the Isle of Wight in 1875. In spite of that version of Engels and the Island, it may not be the whole story: there is evidence from an article in the *Morning Star* that he went to Ryde for his health, some years earlier. He complained to Marx that it was not a good start: 'finally arrived today at my new lodging in the middle of a frightful downpour'. Whether or not his 'first wife', Mary Burns, accompanied him is unclear; he does say 'my' not 'our', but that may not be definitive.

The last time Marx was on the Island, this time during the winter of 1882/3 staying at 'Chimnits', St Boniface Gardens, Ventnor, was without his wife Jenny – who had died of liver cancer in December 1881, aged 67. Marx himself was seriously ill. You would think that he would have had a daughter with him, but one, Eleanor, 'Tussy', did briefly visit him with desperate news. The story is best told in chapter 14, 'London 1883' of Mary Gabriel's *Love and Capital: Karl and Jenny Marx and the Birth of a Revolution* (2011, 2012). In receiving the news herself, Tussy left London immediately for Ventnor. She spent the time, during a frigid winter journey by train and ferry, wondering how best to break the news to her father;

> she felt that what she was bringing [him] was nothing less than his death sentence. But when she arrived she did not have to utter a word. Marx saw at a glance why she was there. 'Our Jennychen is dead,' he said. He told her to go to France at once to see to the children. She argued that it would be best for her to stay with him, but he would not hear of it. Tussy stayed in Ventnor no more than half an hour before she headed back to London and on to Argenteuil.

It is easy to confuse the Marx daughters because of their identical first names. Jennychen was Jenny Caroline (1844–1883; Jenny Marx Longuet), the eldest daughter. She died of bowel cancer, aged only 38, in January 1883. Marx was too ill to attend her funeral in France and died two months later. As for Tussy, in 1893 she died by taking prussic acid after discovering that her partner Edward Aveling had secretly married a young actress, Eva Frye, the previous year. Tussy was 43. The youngest, Laura Marx Lafargue, died in a suicide pact with her husband in 1911 at the age of 66. Jenny and Marx's daughters were all, like their parents, socialist activists. Those details about deaths are not a happy way of ending the Marx family's relations with the Isle of Wight.

12 – Women in a Man's World, 1700–2021

Introduction

There had been strong women on the Isle of Wight since at least the time of the ninth-century Queen Osburga, introduced in chapter 2. Chapter 3 described women who moved naturally in what, elsewhere, might have been considered a man's world; they were exemplified by Isabella de Fortibus, 'Lady of the Isle' in the thirteenth century. This chapter, covering the eighteenth to the twenty-first century, has two sections; it starts with women who took over, by force of circumstance, when a husband or male relative died or, in one case, was absent, and another when a dead woman, a mother, was replaced. This is followed, in the second section, by women who took the initiative to play a part in what in their day might be considered a man's world. Chapter 13 ends the story with two examples of campaigners who were determined to change the world, at least their area of it.

Women Take Over From a Dead or Absent Relative, 1839–1991

The old windmill in Bembridge, the last surviving on the Island, is not only a monument, but also a landmark, standing out against the horizon as it does, and useful, too, for mariners. It was built in the early 1700s when Bembridge was itself almost an island, cut off from the rest of the Isle of Wight, and the windmill's machinery remaining in it dates from then. For two centuries it ground flour for the local community, and provided work for generations of millers.

One of those millers was John Tull who married a lass called Frances in 1831. They had only eight years together because he died in 1839, and did so without leaving a will. **Frances Tull** inherited £300 and, with that, decided to have a go at making the venture continue to work, with herself as the miller. It took bravery to do so: it was a physically demanding job. There was a lot of heavy lifting and shifting and she took on her nephew as an apprentice to help with that. But she had to train him and doubtless she would have dragged sacks around to feed the hopper, physically positioned the sails and ensured that the whole process of turning grain into flour went smoothly. It was also a dangerous process: flour dust is flammable and work had to be carried out by lamplight. There could also be flying sparks given out by the grinding stones should they become over-heated, and windmills then were made of wood. However much heavy work her nephew took off her shoulders, Frances would surely have seen to orders and accounts, so she must have been literate and numerate. The mill remained in the family until 1841, her nephew becoming head miller. Frances remained in post, even if she was no longer actively the miller.

In the late 1800s Bembridge's isolation ended when Brading Haven was drained. The arrival of the railway, bringing cheap flour, meant that, from

1897 onwards, only cattle feed was produced at the mill. It was last operated in 1913, its activity curtailed because of the start of the First World War. In the late 1950s, restoration work was paid for by the local community before it was given to the National Trust. The Trust's website provides some historical details. Frances Tull was among the women celebrated in 2018 on the centenary of some women being given the vote.

Bembridge Mill is still worth visiting today. It is always sensible to check opening times, but it may be open 10.30am–5pm from mid-March to the end of October. I visited it on a cold, damp evening when it looked very isolated and shut, but it was still impressive, and in good condition, under which to let the imagination roam.

Princess Beatrice (1857–1944), youngest daughter and child of Queen Victoria's nine children, has already been introduced – as companion and secretary to her mother, as an artist, as the founder of the Carisbrooke Castle Museum, and as included in a work by her sister Louise in St Mildred's church. The earlier description of her work also detailed her marriage to Prince Henry of Battenberg in 1884, his appointment as governor of the Isle of Wight, his death in 1896, and the sculpture by Louise behind the sarcophagus holding them both. It was upon Henry's death that Queen Victoria appointed Beatrice governor in her late husband's place, and it was in his honour that she founded the museum. Until her mother's death she remained her secretary and, following her death, she spent 30 years transcribing her diaries, making substantial deletions.

Beatrice remained in Osborne Cottage until the death in 1913 of the deputy governor of the Island, who occupied Carisbrooke Castle. This allowed her to make the Governor's House within the Castle her summer home; she stayed there until the outbreak of the Second World War. What is now the main room of the museum was her drawing room, and she changed the functions of the various rooms that had been occupied by Charles I. She also installed a bathroom. It is difficult for us today to imagine the living quarters without one. A visit to Osborne House gives a good view of the advanced arrangements Victoria and Albert made in their day.

Princess Beatrice commissioned an altar painting in the chapel to commemorate her son Maurice's death at Ypres during

45. Princess Beatrice, from the Internet

the First World War. She also created a memorial there to honour those who fell in that war, with their names inscribed. It is likely that many would have been from the volunteer regiment which, in 1885, the year after her marriage, was redesignated the 5th (Isle of Wight, 'Princess Beatrice's,) Volunteer Battalion of the Hampshire Regiment; the Princess was appointed honorary colonel. After the Second World War, those who had been killed then were added to the monument – 2,000 Islanders in all died in both wars. On a lighter note, Beatrice created what was called a 'privy [private] garden' within the walls which, in 2009, was re-created by English Heritage in the Edwardian style, as the Princess Beatrice Garden, a pleasant place to sit and read, contemplate, or eat a sandwich, as well as stroll around. The English Heritage website details the sort of plants and flowers to be seen in it season by season. There is also a bronze statue of the war horse, Warrior, which took part in the First World War, ridden by Jack Seely from the long-established Island family; there, on Armistice Day, wreathes are laid.

The duties of the governor do not seem to have been onerous; typical of them was when in 1929 Beatrice accepted from Captain Ward the deeds to Northwood House and grounds,

On this sunny, autumnal day, under the gaze of a large gathering of towns-people, school children, representative of the civil and social life of Cowes and various Island public bodies, the Princess handed the deeds over to Mr F.W. Beken, chairman of Cowes Urban District Council.

Northwood House, you may remember, appeared in chapter 6, 'Outsiders', concerning its ghosts, and chapter 7, 'Religion and Philanthropy', harbouring the Benedictine nuns of Ste Cécile until they moved to Ryde. During her governorship, Beatrice also regularly visited the Dominican nuns at the priory near Carisbrooke; as that same chapter relates, she did much to make the priory more acceptable to the local Anglican community.

As well as the activities mentioned above, Beatrice had time for playing music at which she was more than proficient. Among the 27,000 items in the museum is the chamber organ presented to her by the people in 1937 on her 80th birthday, and her 41st year as governor. It is regarded as Flemish in origin and is even known as 'Queen Elizabeth's Organ'. It is suggested the more likely owner was Charles I's daughter, Princess Elizabeth, who died in the castle, or perhaps Queen Elizabeth of Bohemia. Princess Beatrice died aged 87 in her home on the mainland, but was first buried in Windsor. Six months later, she was transferred to be interred beside her husband in the sarcophagus in St Mildred's church where they had married.

Alderman and architect John Curtis Millgate, of 89 Castle Road, Newport, married **Grace Outridge** (*c.*1869–1903). As well as a son, they had two daughters, Grace who appeared in chapter 2, 'From Pre-history to the Coming of the Normans', concerning the excavation of the Newport Roman Villa, and **Christabella Harriet Millgate** (1899–1974). Their mother died in 1903, and as that is the probable date of her daughter Grace's birth, it seems likely that she died in childbirth, or soon after; Christabella was then four. When in 1911 their father became mayor for the first of three times, he needed a mayoress. Who should be deemed suitable but 12-year-old Christabella, who merits an entry in 'The Isle of Wight: Hidden Heroes'?

Although Christabella was the youngest mayoress in England, it was recorded that she performed acceptably the duties of the position on all possible occasions. Her public acts included:

- presentation of prizes at the Newport Council Schools to the best girls in the various departments;
- opening a branch of the Newport Literary Society with the presentation of a handsome clock; and
- helping to entertain the aged poor at a New Year tea.

At the end of her year as mayoress she was presented with a gold bracelet as a 'souvenir of her Father's Mayoralty 1911–1912'. A newspaper article reported:

The little girl Mayoress of Newport, Isle of Wight, Christabella Millgate, performed the first public function of her year of office by declaring open the ladies' branch of the Newport Literary Society. She wore her new chain of office, made a little speech, and was presented with a bouquet.

Christabella was mayoress again when her father was elected mayor in 1916 and 1926. On top of her duties as mayoress, she was also at school, and so it was on the second occasion of her father's election as mayor, which started just before the First World War that Gatcombe House was turned into a Red Cross Hospital for wounded soldiers. The *Dorking and Leatherhead Advertiser* noted that,

The young Mayoress of Newport, Isle of Wight, Miss Christobella Millgate, who is 16, and her schoolgirl friends have given up their prizes and prize-giving party in order to purchase an invalid chair for wounded soldiers at Gatcombe House, Red Cross Hospital, Isle of Wight.

Christabella died aged 75 in 1974; the report of her funeral noted that,

she was a member of the British Red Cross Society and did active work on the Island during the last war [1939–1945]. For many years she was superintendent of Carisbrooke Church Kindergarten Sunday School and a manager of Carisbrooke C. of E. Infants' School.

Her funeral was held at St Mary's Church, Carisbrooke, and she was buried in the family mausoleum.

It seems that neither Christabella nor Grace married; that may well have been because of the number of young Island men killed during the First World War.

One of the Islanders killed during that war was James Cooley, licensee of the Flowerpot pub in Newport; his wife was **Ellen Cooley**. James was 27 when he signed up in the Royal Navy, probably as soon as Britain entered the war on 4 August 1914, having only held the Flowerpot tenancy since February that year. In the short time that he was in the navy he was awarded the British War Medal and the Victory Medal. Presumably the latter was given posthumously as he was killed on 1 November 1914. It was during the Battle of Coronel when both cruisers, *HMS Good Hope* and *HMS Monmouth*, were sunk off Chile by the German fleet which is said to have been superior in both shell range and speed. James was on the *Good Hope*.

On her husband's death, Ellen was obviously faced with a dilemma: she probably served in the pub, or was involved in some other way, from the beginning, as well as helping to set it up. In any case, she decided to take over the tenancy of the Flowerpot, and ran it until 1922 when it finally closed. She died in hospital in East Cowes aged 80 and was buried in Northwood Cemetery; either that age is wrong or she was appreciably older than James. I wish there were more information about Ellen; as it is, one can only envisage what it took to wave your husband off to war, for him to be killed so soon; to be faced with a difficult decision and then to be in full charge of running a pub.

Side by side in the Carisbrooke Castle Museum are photographs of Frank and **Catherine Morey** (1856–1942) and below these is the following text:

Frank and Catherine were brother and sister, part of the timber merchant Morey family. Frank was appointed curator at the museum in 1913 and his sister helped him in its day-to-day running until his sudden death in 1925. Following this, Catherine became curator, maintaining the day-book, recording her visits to the British Museum for conservation advice, gifts made to the collection and her polite refusal of a fire-engine which, she explained, would be too big for the gatehouse rooms.

46. Catherine and Frank Morey, Carisbrooke Castle Museum,
photograph by the author

I suspect it would be too big even when the museum moved to the larger governor's quarters; it seems pretty full now. Given that those who write the captions for the museum's exhibits note all there is to know, often including material not available to the outside researcher, it is worth quoting what was recorded, particularly in the day book, which is interesting in its own right:

> Frank and Catherine kept detailed accounts of all aspects of running the museum during their curatorship. Everything from the everyday problems of damp and insect infestation in the Castle gatehouse where the museum was originally housed, to the provenance of important items, visitor comments and occasional bad behaviour are noted down. These books provide a vital source of information about the early museum and the things it collected.

Not surprisingly, more is noted about Frank, though he was the youngest of five children of a mother whose name does not seem to be recorded, and their father, Henry William Morey snr, who founded the Island timber merchants H.W. Morey; later when his sons joined the firm, including Frank who eventually became head of it, the name was changed to H.W. Morey & Sons. But Frank's real love was natural history, and that is what he is particularly known for. You may feel that, in what follows, I am giving undue space to Frank, but don't worry, Catherine will follow in his footsteps, as well as having her own interests.

Frank's natural history interest led to a life collecting specimens, and it was he who established The Isle of Wight Natural History and Archaeological Society. When space for the Society's collection was exhausted and it cost too much to run, it was sold to Frank who split it in half. He donated the geology material to Sandown Town Council and the rest of the specimens to the Carisbrooke Castle Museum. In 1913, the Museum of Isle of Wight Geology was established, for which Frank paid for a curator, as in due course did Catherine.

In a talk by Richard Smout, 'More than Catherine: The role of women in the early years of the Isle of Wight Natural History and Archaeological Society', he explained that the Society was,

> enormously male dominated ... the fields that women were involved in were limited to such specialisms as collecting seaweed and botany. In Morey's Guide of 1909, only one female author's report is included – on meteorology.

As Smout goes on to say, Catherine was not the only woman member of the Society: many others were involved, but he found them difficult to trace. One of them was artist Fanny Minns, who features in chapter 9, 'Women Artists'. Smout's talk presents a good summary of Catherine's busy life, except that he leaves out one aspect of her keen involvement – archaeology – which, fortunately the Castle Museum does not neglect. Under the heading 'Letters from the British Museum' the text tells how, in the late 1920s and early 1930s, CL Woolley of the British Museum led a dig at the site of Ur, an ancient city located between modern-day Iran and Iraq. It goes on to detail some of the finds, and the visitors, one of whom was Agatha Christie who found romance there, but it adds, 'For at least four years Catherine Morey made a financial contribution to the dig and received items excavated there as thanks. The items were two pottery vessels excavated from the Royal cemetery and beads excavated from one of the earliest graves'.

It should be added to Catherine's multiple commitments that she also supported The District Nursing Association, the Literary Society and The War Hospital Supply Depot.

Among the purchases Frank Morey had made was Borthwood Copse, on the outskirts of Newchurch, in order to preserve it for wildlife. It is part of the medieval forest, at one time a royal hunting ground, covering much of the eastern end of the Island. Under Frank's will it was to go to the National Trust, and he asked that his ashes be scattered there, which they were, in 1926. And when Catherine died in 1943, after a funeral service at St Mary's Carisbrooke, her ashes were scattered there too.

Ethel Langton (b.1911) was 15 when she was declared a heroine in March 1926; her exploit was much written about in the press, as it merited. She was the daughter of the St Helen's lighthouse keeper, Mason Charity Langton and Kate Elizabeth (née McNeil) and the family lived at the lighthouse. The first account of Frances Tull, at the beginning of this chapter, suggests that the whole extent of the east coast, of which St Helen's was a part, had only been connected to the main island by the draining of Brading Haven. In 1926, to reach the mainland to go shopping her parents had to go by boat from St Helen's Fort, of which the lighthouse was a part. It overlooked, and shone its light for, a very busy part of the Solent; one account says it was one of the busiest stretches of water in the world. On this occasion Ethel was left with her small dog Badger just for the time it would take for her parents to cross the narrow strip of water to Bembridge, the nearest town, where Mrs Langton liked to do her shopping on Saturday, do that and get home. Her parents' last words to Ethel were that they would be home by midday. Those few hours were to stretch into three days and nights.

As lighthouse keeper Mr Langton's duties were strictly regulated by routine because in that lay its efficiency. As his lighthouse was oil-burning, he had to fill the reservoir, trim and light the wick and wind the mechanism daily, and make sure that the light was burning brightly. Vessels big and small depended on it in foul weather and at night. The lamp itself was on a 20ft tower reached by a ladder on the outside.

Within hours of being left alone, Ethel heard the wind getting up; soon it was howling round the fort. Through the window she saw the waves, driven by the wind, 'leaping and tumbling on the shore'. Ethel waited. The hours ticked away. Soon it was a proper storm, the waves whipped up by a hurricane force wind. Ethel was not particularly worried, storms usually soon blew over. This one was to be extraordinary; there was no way her parents could risk the crossing to get back. But Ethel did not know that; she did however look in the larder.

There was half a loaf and an ounce or two of sugar. A slice of bread dipped in sugared water sufficed for lunch and, as Badger looked at her plaintively, she shared it with him. As darkness began to fall, she had to acknowledge that her parents wouldn't be coming back that night; she didn't even know if they were safely on dry land.

One thing Ethel did know was that the light had to be kept burning brightly if lives were to be saved. For three nights she did what was required. Fortunately she had seen her father do it often enough. She started to climb the ladder; for the first few rungs she was protected by the fort, but above that the gale whipped away her headscarf and threatened to

47. Ethel Langton, from the Internet

take her with it. Once her foot slipped and she was clinging on to the ladder, her arms taking her weight. Blinded and deafened by the storm, she climbed to the top by touch. Once there she dared not stand up but slithered on her tummy towards the hatch containing the light. For the rest of the night she periodically checked the light as she had seen her father do. She had to repeat that, chilled, wet, and desperately hungry, flopping when each routine was completed into an armchair twice more. She cuddled Badger to try and keep warm and for companionship. But even he became subdued.

After a couple of days, she saw a boat, struggling to get through the storm. The two men in it eventually got close enough to the fort to throw a sack of food for Ethel to collect. By early evening on the third day, a lifeboat took an hour and a half to struggle through; on board were her parents.

Ethel's ordeal did not go unrecognised: she was awarded the Lloyd's Medal for Meritorious Maritime Service. At 15, she was the youngest person ever to receive it. After her heroism, interest in Ethel, apart from the inclusion of her story on International Women's Day in 2022, faded from sight.

Several members of the Jolliffe family have been mentioned in the preceding chapters. The family had tentacles extending all over the Island and over the centuries. Some of its members were even disreputable, but not this one. **Gladys Hilda Jolliffe** (1899–1996), of a Cowes branch, was a daughter of H. Jolliffe and sons, the fashionable boot and shoe maker and retailer, a traditional family establishment and one of the oldest independent shops in Cowes.

Henry Jolliffe, who opened the business in 1853 was later joined by two sons, William and Harry. Gladstone, Harry's son, aged only 12, also came to work in the shop, and he was to work there for the next 60 years, and through two world wars. Gladys was 19 when she joined her father, Gladstone, in 1917, and when he died suddenly in 1954, she took over running the shop and continued until she retired in 1991; it was only then that the shop closed for the last time.

During its lifetime, when Queen Victoria was at Osborne House, the business enjoyed royal patronage, running an account to make boots and pumps for the royal staff. Princess Beatrice also bought shoes for her children there. Gladstone was not just a retailer but also a surgical shoemaker, shoe repairer and chiropodist, even going to his customers' homes. The business was also sole maker of the 'Cheapside yachting shoes', making it an integral part of the Cowes yachting world.

On New Year's Eve, 1915, two years before Gladys joined the family business, there was what seemed to be a life-changing event with adverse repercussions: the building burned down. But it turned out to be a new beginning: a new and striking building in the Art Nouveau style was designed by family member and architect, Reginald Jolliffe. It was to become a landmark in Cowes, and still is. The business closed down in 1991, when Gladys retired. When it closed its doors for the last time, it invited the Carisbrooke Castle Museum to choose items from what was left; the museum therefore acquired a collection of over 300 of them. All those not taken by the curator were left in the storeroom, together with the shop fittings. A photograph of an enviable pair of shoes can be found on the website of the Medina Bookshop with the title 'Pair of ladies' python skin shoes, from the stock of Jolliffe's shoe shop, Cowes, 1940s.' Also included in a book they published and stocked is a pair of 'Canvas bathing shoes worn by Empress Eugenie' (she appeared in chapter 11, 'Foreign Royalty and Elite Visitors').

Although the shop closed in 1991, that was not the end: around 2004, the building became a Yacht Chandlers, and some years later Jolliffe's Gallery and Coffee Shop, which also served food. As it happened we visited it on its last day: 6 September 2023; it was due to close its doors a few minutes after we arrived, hoping to have some refreshment on a very hot day. We were allowed to explore, though, and although the building was denuded of its coffee shop apparatus, there were still shoes on display and objects connected with shoe-making such as the shoemaker's

48. Empress Eugénie's beach shoes, Carisbrooke Castle Museum, photograph by author

bench at the back, I have been unable to establish what is now to become of this grade II listed building.

There was more to Gladys Jolliffe than running the shoe business, though her talents tended to be thwarted, presumably by the demands of the shop. She was a talented pianist, but did not have the opportunity to develop her skills further; she was, however, the organist at Mill Hill and later Gurnard Methodist churches. She was a qualified music instructor,

49. Jolliffe sign board, photograph by Jane Richter

though she never practised as a teacher. During the 1950s and 1960s, she was a member of S Wite's Sports Club where she was an enthusiastic tennis player.

When Gladys died in hospital in 1996, aged 77, she was buried in Northwood Cemetery, Cowes. Her occupation on her burial record is given as 'Shoe Shop Proprietor'. In 1991, when the shop closed, her occupation would not have been unusual for a woman, but she had entered the business in 1917, and worked there for over 50 years. A question it occurs to me to ask is, did she become proprietor automatically on her father's death, or was there a lot of discussion, argument even? The answer is probably that she was a shoo-in – sorry!

Women in a Man's World, 1900–1947

It is not hard to call **Blanche Coules Thornycroft** (1873–1950) a star of this chapter and, indeed, of the book; her simple designation is 'British naval architect', but there was rather more to her than that. She was, for example, one of the earliest women to have a significant role in engineering in Britain, and the first woman to be elected to Associate Membership of the Institution of Naval Architects. Her father, John Thornycroft (1843–1928; knighted in 1902), was, in 1866, the founder of the Thornycroft shipbuilding and engineering business. During the first half of the twentieth century, J.I. Thornycroft & Company designed and built some of the most significant vessels for the Royal Navy as well as for military agencies around the world. In addition, the company quickly gained a reputation for quality yachts and motor cruisers which they supplied to wealthy private customers.

Blanche's mother was **Blanche Ada Thornycroft** (née Coules; 1846–1936). To save confusion with her daughter, Blanche, Mrs Thornycroft will be left out of the picture; should she sneak in, she will be called Blanche's mother. Blanche was the second of five sisters and two brothers; her paternal grandfather and her uncle, Sir Hamo Thornycroft, were sculptors. Surrounded as she was by a family of exceptionally talented sculptors and engineers, it is not surprising that Blanche should become actively involved, when young, in the family's shipbuilding business. In 1904, her father decided to relocate the majority of the company's shipbuilding activities from a thin strip of riverside land at Chiswick, on the banks of the Thames in London, to a newly acquired shipyard at Woolston, near Southampton. He then decided to move the family home across the Solent, to Bembridge on the Isle of Wight. Blanche was then 31.

It is not known exactly when Blanche became part of the enterprise in which her brothers were also involved, but her earliest notebooks in the Thornycroft archives date from before the start of the twentieth century. In her teenage years she spent her time reading, sketching endless shapes and calculating angles. Although she never appeared officially on the company payroll, she was, in due course, trained in the way an apprentice would be, but was known as her father's assistant. There is no record that she had any formal school or university education in maths and sciences which she would have needed for her future work, yet maths is what she particularly offered to the enterprise; it seems that she simply had an extraordinary aptitude for it, self-taught on the job.

50. Blanche Thornycroft portrait, from the Internet

While her sisters enjoyed their social life associated with the family's status, Blanche stood aside from it, and was more often to be seen, notebook in hand, jotting down figures. Relations seem, however, to be warm between the sisters, as a photograph of the five of them clustered round two of them in a hammock in the garden suggests; it is noticeable, though, that four of them are in white dresses, and one, surely Blanche, wears a white blouse and charcoal-coloured skirt.

Into the landscaped garden of the family home in Bembridge, Steyne House, Thornycroft integrated a model ship test tank – a decorative water system which came to be known as the 'Lily Pond'. Once the waterfall was turned off and the water had time to settle, a model hull or vessel could be towed across the surface at a constant speed, pulled by a controlled descending weight. This wonderful photograph of Blanche, either experimenting or posing for the photographer, shows how the 'Lily Pond' is part of the landscape. The small building at one end housed the winding gear and instrumentation. Assisted by Blanche, her father spent endless hours testing, adjusting and developing hull shapes and keel designs. Test details were recorded in an accurate, scien-

51. Blanche Thornycroft and testing in the Lily Pond,
courtesy of the Classic Boat Museum Gallery

tific manner by Blanche; then significant work was involved to relate this to the design of full-sized craft.

The 'Lily Pond' is what I had the privilege of seeing when the current owner showed me round. When you sit on a bench at one end of the 'Lily Pond', you see ahead of you, in the distance, the Bembridge windmill, discussed at the beginning of this chapter, and behind you, again in the distance, the sea. Today, it is not lilies, but a yellow-flowered water plant, which I have decided, after a search, is *Iris pseudacorus*, a water flag, or yellow iris which looks like what its name suggests. What particularly pleased me was to discover how interested my host is in Blanche and her work, kindly putting up with my enthusiasm.

There came a point when the Lily Pond no longer sufficed, so Thornycroft purchased the property containing the former Steyne Woods Battery, a short distance beyond Steyne House. It was built by the Ministry of Defence between 1889 and 1894 to defend the eastern coastline of the Island and Portsmouth Harbour. But in 1909 it was used for building 'the Tank', supervised by father and daughter, and to which they then transferred their testing. That is where I went next, so that I could be shown around it by the current owner. She took me a short distance from the house, to what is a much bigger testing site, like a very large, deep swimming pool–now empty of water. Instead of being sunk into the ground, it was built above ground, and is approached by steps. As you get closer, it looks like a large liner. It was one of the first buildings ever built by pouring concrete over steel. The largest ever model tested in the Tank was of a 6,000-ton tanker. The fastest boat ever model tested there was the 400mph *Miss England III*, which achieved a world record speed of nearly 120mph on Loch Lomond in 1932.

But the facility was not used only for testing Thornycroft scale-model boats: during the First World War, in particular, other items which used Blanche's mathematical and engineering skills included moorings for explosive mines and a unique high-speed propeller, which could jump over cables. It was during the war, in 1917, that Blanche became the first woman member to be admitted to the Royal Institute of Naval Architects. She was also a member of the Women's Royal Engineering Society for 20 years.

Two of the most notable pre-First World War boats, shown in Blanche's notebooks, were the motor launches *HMS Mimi* and *HMS Toutou* (the names mean *Meow* and *Fido* in Parisian slang, and were changed from the original Cat and Dog). When war came, they travelled from Britain to Lake Tanganyika (now Tanzania), and there played an important role in the African naval struggle between Britain and Germany. It is assumed that she was present when they set off on that journey, as well as going out in one during their testing. Together with the rest of the family involved in the firm, she contributed, in 1915, to the design of the original Coastal Motor Boat (the CMB). A hundred years later, the Portsmouth Naval Base Property Trust, having spent six years creating a replica of the CMB4R launched it with a photograph of Blanche holding a recording used to test the model boats at Steyne House. Blanche's monogrammed notebooks, recording her test notes from 1907 until 1939, along with the ship tank models used in her engineering calculations for testing the models trialled in the Lily Pond, and later at the Tank, are held at the Classic Boat Museum Gallery in East Cowes. Also there are models which were the basis for the development of Skimmers (racing motor boats which later evolved into the CMBs). Other models tested ideas for Acasta and Acheron Class Destroyers, motor torpedo boats, and RAF Rescue Launches, as well as RNLI Lifeboats.

Although Blanche's father died in 1928, she continued her work for the family firm: the last date on which it was recorded that she was doing her royal naval architecture work was in 1935, on a 'special launch' for the Royal Air Force (RAF).

At the CMB4R centenary celebrations in 2023, Hamo Thornycroft, a former civil architect, marine draftsman and marine photographer, Blanche's great-nephew, and part of the CMB4R team, remarked,

It's only in the last four or five years that historians have become more interested in Blanche Thornycroft and her influence on naval engineering. I think her impact on other women working or aspiring to work in boat engineering can be considerable. The future for women working in this industry is bright. Technical development always requires good minds and in my experience women have these in abundance.

In the last four or five years Blanche has been further recognised, being chosen as 'Engineer of the Week' in the 'Magnificent Women series' at the end of December 2019. She is also included in 'Isle of Wight Hidden Heroes', submitted by the Classic Boat Museum Gallery. It would be a mistake, though, to think that Blanche had a one-track mind. Together with her mother, she helped found the Bembridge Nursing Association. She was a member of the Bembridge sailing club. She was also interested in botany and was a council member of the Isle of Wight Natural History and Archaeology Society (see also Catherine Morey in the first section of this chapter). Blanche never married.

During our conversation, as the owner of Steyne House handed me over to those responsible for the Battery and the Tank, the subject arose of whether it was Blanche or her mother, also Blanche, who passed her later years in 'a little house' in Bembridge As it happened, the CMB4R celebration was on local television, and I saw it, and Hamo Thornycroft, so I emailed him and this is the end of his so helpful reply:

> She then lived in a property in Bembridge upper High Street overlooking the harbour called the Moorings where she died in 1951. The following year I moved with my parents Peter and Pamela Thornycroft to the Moorings from London when my father took up a RNVR posting in Portsmouth. This property finally passed out of the family when it was sold in 2015 to a couple from London who lavished a great deal of attention on it.

> My father always referred to Blanche as 'Aunt Jum' (a shortening I believe of Jumbo). This was very confusing for me when latterly Blanche came to be mentioned.

Hamo also sent me photographs of the house; it is not little! Please note that both Steyne House and the Battery are private properties, as, indeed, is The Moorings.

Women During Two World Wars

Mary **Innell Jolliffe** (1882–1963) preceded Gladys Jolliffe by a couple of years in entering a man's world. There is no immediate evidence that they were closely related: Gladys being a Cowes woman, and Innell a Bonchurch (Ventnor) one. Ventnor & District Local History Society sets the scene for Innell's move into the man's world, as well as that of others who follow her in this chapter:

> During the First World War, large numbers of women were recruited into jobs vacated by men who had left for war service. There were also many women who gained occupation in jobs that came as part of the war effort, work in munitions factories affording a key example. A more singular case of women replacing men occurred in Ventnor when, in 1915, Miss Innell Jolliffe became proprietor, editor and printer of the Isle of Wight Advertiser.

Innell's father, Johnathan Jolliffe, was a well-known Bonchurch builder, her mother's name is revealed only because, on her death, Innell gave St Alban's

Church, Ventnor candlesticks in memory of **Mary Lucy Jolliffe** (d.1904). The 1911 census shows a household of widower (Innell's father), Innell, and a maid, suggesting that she may well have been an only child. She does not appear to have married, but her companion was a Miss Griffiths.

Before she took over the newspaper, Innell was one of the first Island women to take up the cause of Belgian refugees in 1914, and later dedicated a book of poems to the King of Belgium. As a newspaper proprietor, Innell was soon equipped and prepared to get her hands dirty: always arriving at 7.45am, and leaving late in the evening, she would sometimes do the typesetting herself, and was capable of working what was technically known as a 'flat bed double printing machine'. This photograph shows her at one of the machines. She also branched out into printing books and postcards; the latter could be printed at the rate of a thousand an hour. She ran the newspaper until 1923 when it was absorbed by the *Isle of Wight Mercury*, after years of newspaper rivalry.

Unlike Gladys Jolliffe in Cowes, Innell seemed to find time for a multitude of other interests – perhaps that was after she no longer had a newspaper to bring out. She had already published a book of poems – *A May Day Revel* – worked on another, and wrote articles, in later life remembering Bonchurch in the past. For two years she also edited *The Island Sunbeam*, a temperance paper for young people. She was a keen and talented photographer, and her studies of flowers won prizes. She had her own magic lantern projector and screened photographs for the public to view. She played the violin. She was secretary of various local organisations, a member of the Society of Women Journalists and The Whitwell Women's Institute, and was captain of the Ventnor Girl Guides. You could call her a busy bee, living until the age of 81.

52. Innell Jolliffe at the 'flat bed double demy printing machine' from Ventnor District Local History Society website

Just as Innell found herself taking over the running of a newspaper during the First World War, so other women were involved in different ways. As so often, the Carisbrooke Castle Museum is helpful, this time in an unusual way, with the photograph of a mob cap.

The text underneath explains its purpose under the headline, 'World War one mob cap':

Those women worked at S.E. Saunders yard, a boat building firm in East Cowes which produced its first aircraft in 1917. Women workers wore a uniform which included a fabric cap to contain and protect their hair. This cap was worn by Eva Forsdick when working on the joiners shop in 1918.

There is just a little to be found on a website featuring people connected with Southend about an **Eva Forsdick** (*c.*1901–2005); she seems to fit the bill. Her mother, Alice Bertha Rice (no father mentioned) was born in Paglesham, Essex in 1870, and Eva went to school there, leaving at 12, when she went to work as a housemaid. She later worked for a doctor's family who holidayed on the Isle of Wight. There she met Austin Guy, who worked 'in large gardens on the island'. They married, settled on the Island, and had three children, one of whom died aged two; at around that time the family moved to Southend. Just after the beginning of the First World War, their son George decided to enlist in the Isle of Wight regiment; he was killed in the Gallipoli campaign, aged 16.

What happened to Austin Guy is not recorded, but Eva was working in a parachute factory before she met and married Walter Forsdick. They were known to be very happy together until he died from a burst appendix in his 40s. S.E. Saunders is not mentioned but, as the factory made aircraft and Eva was making parachutes, it may well be there that she made them. Thereafter, all that is recorded is that Eva 'was devoutly religious, a marvellous vegetable grower and even until she was quite elderly loved to cycle around the town'. She lived to 104.

There is a photograph of **Phoebe Brannon** (1889–1959) in her Staff Nurse's uniform in the museum, and in a photograph below it, and slightly overlapping, the image of the Red Cross, which may be significant, and to the side of that there is a service tag. Although she was Island-born, Phoebe nursed elsewhere from 1917 to 1919, at military hospitals in Nottingham and then, from 1919 to 1921, in Alexandria and Kantara (El Qantara), Egypt. As the text further notes, explaining the tag:

It was compulsory for servicemen and women to wear official tags that were used to identify individuals in the case of capture, serious injury or death. As well as their name, service number and regiment or service, tags included their religion to enable an appropriate burial service to be provided. Phoebe's original red nursing ID tag is written in ink, this was common due to shortages of stamping kits during the war.

That is all that seems to be known about Phoebe, apart from her dates which were found on the Internet, but that text is interesting in highlighting an aspect of the minutiae of the First World War.

Mary Stuart Garside-Tipping (née Flynn; 1865–1917) was born in Blackburn, Lancashire, the daughter of Walter Henry Fly, an adjutant in the 5th Lancashire Artillery Volunteers, and Mary Elizabeth Pilkington. She and two sisters were cared for by servants. Her father died when she was seven and when she was about 11, her mother re-married George A. Coombs, a House Surgeon at Southport Infirmary who later changed his surname to that of his wife and, under the name Pilkington, was to become MP for Southport and was knighted in 1893.

When Mary was 25 in 1890, she married 42-year-old Henry Thomas Garside-Tipping, a naval officer, and the couple soon moved to the Isle of Wight, to Quarr Wood, Binstead, which he had inherited. They had three children, one of whom was a son who died aged 18 in 1911. When the First World War started, Garside-Tipping, who was a retired Lieutenant in the Royal Navy, rejoined the Navy and was given command of the 400-tonne armoured yacht *Sanda*. While he was away at sea Mary worked for nearly a year at the Munition Workers' Canteen, Woolwich. On 25 September 1915, while the *Sanda* was bombarding the Belgian coast, an explosive shell sank the yacht and killed everyone on board.

With her husband dead, in January 1916 Mary volunteered and was accepted for service with the Women's Emergency Canteen for Soldiers Society, she was posted to France, and there, on 6 March 1917, she was shot dead by a deranged French soldier. As she had done such valuable work among the French troops, the General Commanding in the Sector where the crime took place visited the scene of the tragedy, and laid a Croix de Guerre on Mary's coffin. She was buried with full military honours at Vauxbuin French National Cemetery, Aisne.

Baroness Patricia (Patsy) de Kerbech (née Turner; *c.*1913–1991), daughter of Archie Turner, arrived on the Island in 1926, aged 13, when her father took over the tenancy of the Commercial Inn and later the Mayflower Pub in Cowes. After attending the Denmark School, she helped her father and then entered the Cowes social scene, making useful contacts. In 1936, she passed her driving test in the year it was introduced, and on the outbreak of the Second World War she worked at the boat building firm Saunders Roe, East Cowes (mentioned in connection with Eva Forsdick above). In August 1941 she enlisted in the Women's Auxiliary Air Force (WAAF) and served in the motor transport section of Fighter Command. After the war, she married the raconteur Roland de Kerbrech, a hereditary French Baron. His past is somewhat shadowy until 1945 when he landed up in the Mayflower Pub where Patsy was to be found, and they married, after which he applied for and became a naturalised United Kingdom citizen. He became a member of the Cowes Corinthian Yacht Club and, although he was once asked to leave for 'speaking his mind' while inebriated, the trophy that he presented to the Club, the KERBRECH CUP (also known as the FROSTBITE CUP) is still presented annually to the winner during the Boxing Day races. They seem to have been a larger that life couple; I was tipped off about Patsy's existence because she was remembered elegantly enjoying the air and society on the Parade in West Cowes where the French artist Berthe Morisot used to paint during her honeymoon and the Regatta in 1875 (see chapter 9, 'Women Artists').

In 1947, they moved to Gurnard – west of Cowes – where Patsy often sang at the Gurnard Hotel; she continued doing so until 1970. Roland had died in 1965 and, remembering that he had never over-played his baron status, she offered it to her sister-in-law who then passed it on to her son, Roland's nephew. A nice touch to her life. In 1989 she received belated medals for her war service. She died in 1991 in Gurnard.

Women of Sea and Air, 1920–2021

Marion **Barbara Carstairs** (1900–1993) was known as Joe (not Jo, as a woman might be called, short for, say, Josephine). The masculine version was intentional because she was openly gay; her many lovers were said to include Greta Garbo and Marlene Dietrich, according to a Stone Crabs Theatre posting; add to that list of celebrities Tallulah Bankhead. At a time when such preference for a woman was not overt, she had short hair and tattooed arms, smoked cigars and cheroots, and usually dressed as a man. She was also known as 'the fastest woman on water' because, in the 1920s, she was the United Kingdom's most successful female motorboat racer. She lived on the Isle of Wight in those years and also, importantly here, her boats were made on the Island, in East Cowes, and it was in the Classic Boat Museum Gallery there that she was drawn to my attention. The museum holds an archive of many aspects of Joe's life, and those are available in more detail in Kate Summerscale's *The Queen of Whale Cay: The extraordinary life of 'Joe' Carstairs, the fasted woman on water* (1999).

Fortunately for Joe's passion for boat racing, her mother, Frances Evelyn Borthwick, an American beauty, was also heir to an oil fortune. Her legal father was Scottish army officer Captain Albert Carstairs, first of the Royal Irish Rifles, later of the Princess of Wales Own Regiment. But Joe's parents were divorced soon after her birth. It is suggested that her mother was an alcoholic and drug addict; she later married Captain Francis Francis and had two more children. She divorced him and

53. Joe Carstairs, © National Portrait Gallery, London

married French count Roger de Périgny in 1915, but later left him because of his infidelity. Her last husband, whom she married in 1920, when Joe would have been 20, was a French-Russian surgeon, Serge Voronoff. As a child Joe was sent to boarding school in the United States, not so much for her education, but because of her rebellious nature, surely unsurprising.

Against that background, Joe felt closest to her maternal grandmother. At the age of 18, she persuaded her grandmother to let her join the American Red Cross to drive ambulances in France in the last year of the First World War. After the armistice that year, she remained in France, recovering the bodies of fallen soldiers for identification and reburial in the war cemeteries. Still in France, she made Bohemian friends and became infatuated with Dolly Wilde, Oscar Wilde's niece, who was also a fellow ambulance driver. Joe's mother disapproved of her being an overt lesbian, and threatened to cut her off unless she married. So she did, marrying a childhood friend, the French Count Jacques de Pret, allowing her access to her trust fund. They split the dowry and, immediately after the wedding reception went their separate ways. Immediately after her mother's death, the marriage was annulled on the grounds of non-consummation and Joe reverted to her maiden name.

Joe returned to London and, as one of the texts on the wall of the Classic Boat Museum Gallery tells it:

> She returned to England, working in several jobs until she established the 'X Garage' which was a chauffeur company run entirely by women, formerly the ambulance drivers she knew in France. They took people on tours of the battlefields and war graves in France and Belgium.

You really do have to give Joe credit for great canniness, as well as her ability to turn to her spirit of adventure and recognise what she really wanted to do:

> She used her dowry and Grandmother's inheritance, as well as her own earnings, to commission her first powerboat from S.E. Saunders in Cowes. A young designer, Fred Cooper, was crucial to the creation of Carstairs' cutting edge boat. They built *Gwen* (named after Joe's variety star lover Gwen Farrar) a 17ft hydroplane at the Saunders yard in East Cowes. When it capsized on a trial run, Carstairs decided to rechristen it *NewG* and promptly won a series of races in Southampton and Cannes. By 1925 she had reached a top speed of 32.16 knots, making her the fastest on water.

Thereafter, Joe set her sights on the prestigious Harmsworth race and ordered a new boat with a more powerful engine, the *Estelle 1*, and then another, the *Estelle II*. The *Estelle II* raced in the 1928 Harmsworth Cup, in front of a crowd of 1,500,000. Joe took the lead, but the boat crashed, throwing her and her mechanic into the water. Although she lost the race she received much praise and support for her performance. That race was not between individuals, but between nations and, from 1920 to 1933, America won it. I do note that in

1903, a British woman, Dorothy Levitt, won that race, but I must resist the temptation to pursue her further; she is easily found on the Internet. Between 1925 and 1930, Joe continued to take part successfully in other races, and to win. She was also generous towards friends – she was close to several male racing drivers and land speed record competitors, using her wealth to help them; this included $10,000 towards Malcolm Campbell's *Bluebird*.

In 1934, the title of the biography about her makes sense: she spent $40,000 to buy the island of Cay in the Bahamas, constructing a grand house, a lighthouse, schools, a church and a cannery. She created an agricultural enterprise and employed hundreds of Bahamians. It may be that, as well as her generosity, her approach was paternalistic, but that was not surprising for the period. She also hosted such guests as Marlene Dietrich and the Duke and Duchess of Windsor. She sold Whale Cay in 1975, moved to Florida and started writing poetry under the pseudonym Hans Bernstein. She died in Florida in 1993, aged 93; her mascot (dog), named Lord Tod Wadley, perhaps the only creature she really loved, was cremated with her.

Dorothy Spicer should certainly be mentioned in passing because, as the *County Press* put it: 'Dorothy Spicer is important to Isle of Wight aviation history because she trained for her advance construction engineering licence at Spartan Aircraft, a subsidiary of Saunders Roe (SARO) of East Cowes.' And as the *Isle of Wight News* elaborates:

> Back in the 1930s, with the help of Saunders Roe (SARO) young Engineer Dorothy Spicer was able to break through the glass-ceiling of a ban of women engineers in aviation ... Dorothy became the first women in the world to gain all four Air Ministry licences in Aircraft Engineering.

Dorothy Norman Pearce (née Spicer; 1908–1946) was born in Middlesex, the only daughter of Hilda May Sisterson and stockbroker Norman Spicer. She studied at the Godolphin School in Salisbury, Wiltshire, and studied at University College London. In 1928, she learned to fly at the London Aeroplane Club at Stag Lane Aerodrome where she met Pauline Gower who was studying for her commercial pilots' licence. They became friends and in 1931 they started a business together. Pauline was licensed to carry passengers for 'hire or reward' and Dorothy was qualified as a ground engineer and held an 'A' (private) pilot's licence. They hired a plane, and later bought a Gipsy Moth for the business, but it was not viable enough to continue so they joined several ventures connected with circuses. During this time, Dorothy studied for the 'B' engineer's licence, ignoring the fact that institutions offering advanced courses were restricted to men. It was, indeed, Saunders Roe that facilitated her doing so. In their circus life, Dorothy and Pauline flew an Isle of Wight Spartan plane in which Dorothy persuaded its manufacturers to allow her to undertake the necessary practical and theoretical training at their workshops. She also held a 'C' (ground engineer) licence, the second British woman to achieve this (her friend and fellow pilot, Amy Johnson, was the first). In 1935, she went for the

'D' licence. Women were not usually allowed to study at such an advanced level, and it took string pulling by eminent men to enable her to do so: she did it in secret, aided by SARO owner Sir Edwin Alliott Verdon-Roe. That licence, which she qualified for, enabled her to build all elements of an aircraft, airframe and engine from scratch, and to approve the materials required for the work.

In a speech in 1937, Amy Johnson teased Dorothy: 'amidst much laughter she then called upon Miss Spicer to admit or deny the report that she held every licence that it was possible to hold'. The following year Dorothy accepted a position with the Air Registration Board in London, becoming the first woman in the British Empire to receive a technical appointment in civil aviation. Also in 1938, she and Pauline jointly wrote a book, *Women with Wings*, recounting their experiences of flying together. In that same year, there was a major change in Dorothy's personal life when she became engaged to Flight Lieutenant Richard Pearce; they married the following month, and their only child, Patricia Mary, was born a year later. Soon after Patricia was born, the Second World War broke out. In late 1940, Dorothy took on flying work as an air observer and research assistant at the Royal Aircraft Establishment, Farnborough; Richard worked there as a test pilot.

After the war, Richard became South American representative of British Aviation Services in Rio de Janeiro. On 23 December 1948 the couple caught a flight to Rio in bad weather; the plane flew into a mountainside, killing all on board. That was not the end of Dorothy's connection with the Isle of Wight. The 'Dorothy Spicer Memorial Award' was set up in recognition of the part East Cowes and Saunders Roe (SARO) played in her becoming the first woman in the world to hold all four ground engineer licences. Although the award came to an end in the 1980s, 'due to cumbersome administration', it was revived in 2015, its first student being attached to the Isle of Wight Studio School (whose partner businesses are BA Systems and GKN).

Should you decide to visit the Classic Boat Museum Gallery in East Cowes, and be taken on a tour of it, you will come to a large window from which you can look down into what was the Saunders Roe factory. The museum will come up again later in the chapter. Like Dorothy Spicer Pearce, **Mary Ellis** (née Willkins; 1917–2018) was an aviatrix, but there her similarity with Dorothy ends, both in the closeness of their relationship with the Isle of Wight, and in what they did during the Second World War.

Mary Wilkins was born in Oxfordshire, the only daughter and third of four children to Nellie, née Clarke and Charles William Wilkins. The family lived near the Royal Air Force bases at Bicester Airfield and Port Meadow (which for someone who lives a short walk away from the meadow is a surprise, but it was so). When Mary was eight, the Cobham Flying Circus visited the area and she persuaded her father to pay for a joyride in an Avro 504. That was it: she decided that she wanted to learn to fly. So, when she was 16, she started having lessons at a flying club in Witney, successfully gaining a private pilot's licence. She flew for pleasure until the start of the Second World War in 1939, when all civilian flying was banned.

In October 1941, aged 28, Mary joined the Air Transport Auxiliary (ATA). This is when the first part of her public flying life took off. She was part of a pool of women flyers based at Hamble in Hampshire. The Wight Aviation Museum tells the story in its short form, as does *The Oxford Dictionary of National Biography*; Mary's autobiography, *A Spitfire Girl: One of the World's Greatest Female ATA Ferry Pilots Tells Her Story* (2016), tells the long version. The Museum starts its entry, '1st Officer Mary Ellis ATA' with a quotation gleaned from elsewhere: 'Without the ATA's wartime efforts the RAF would not have had enough aircraft to put into the sky to counter the war in the Air.' The posting then explains the importance:

Although there were no female fighter pilots during the war, 168 women pilots took part in ATA operations flying aircraft to front line active airfields around the UK, often with only rudimentary navigation aids, no radios or any kind of defences and, in consequence, several lost their lives during operational service.

It then gives Mary's transporting statistics:

Mary flew a total of 400 Spitfires, delivering over 1000 planes to RAF stations. By the end of the war she had amassed 1100 flying hours flying on nearly 80 types of aircraft, including the Wellington heavy bomber and Britain's first jet fighter, the Gloster Meteor which could fly at speeds of up to 600 mph.

After the war, Mary moved to the Isle of Wight and began the second part of her career: in 1950, aged 37, she became Commandant of the Sandown Airport, a position which lasted until 1970. During that time, she didn't just help it develop into a thriving commercial airfield by pioneering regular air services in the 1960s from the North of England, but she also acted as air traffic controller, as well as running the airfield by installing Cathode Ray Direction Finding (CRDF) equipment. This enabled planes to fly in bad weather; I understand that the nickname for this is the pleasing 'huff duff'. And she even laid on coaches to take holiday makers to their hotels in Sandown and Shanklin. Unfortunately, these days, you cannot fly from the mainland to the Island on a commercial flight; the only way of getting there is to take a ferry across to four different places. There is a lasting memorial to Mary in the Wight Aviation Museum which she founded and chaired.

Her personal life changed in 1961 when she married fellow pilot Don Ellis and they had a house next to the runway at Sandown. Her husband died in 2009.

When Mary reached 100, she celebrated her birthday with a flight from Sandown in her favourite aircraft, the Spitfire, becoming the oldest person to do so. After a campaign, she was awarded the Freedom of the Isle of Wight in 2017; she died the following year, aged 101. John Kenyon, who had known Mary for many years, paid a tribute to her that ended:

The museum's aim is to celebrate the considerable history in aircraft design & production on the Isle of Wight, as well as those individuals on the Island who have made an outstanding contribution to aviation, of which Mary was certainly one.

The driver who, through his contacts, enabled my access through locked gates to the Nettlestone Priory to see, at least through the window, where the Blue Lady ghost haunted (chapter 6), also told me about other contacts. He told me that he'd bought Lady Beaverbrook's houseboat, and still used it, thus I was introduced to **Lady (Violet) Aitken** (née de Trafford; 1926–2021). She is sometimes known, according to the *Powerboat Racing World* posting on her death, as 'The First Lady of Offshore'. She was born the third of four daughters to Sir Humphrey de Trafford Bt, a racehorse owner, and Cynthia de Trafford (née Cadogan). She was brought up in Royston, Herefordshire, educated privately and, by the end of the Second World War, was working as a secretary in London. In 1951, she married Sir Max Aitken Bt, DSO, DFC, a former Conservative MP who succeeded to the peerage on his father's death in 1964. But three days later he disclaimed the title, insisting that 'There shall only be one Lord Beaverbrook in my time'; he did, however, retain the baronetcy. They had two children, Laura and Maxwell.

Although Violet was not strictly Lady Violet Aitken, but Lady Aitken, 'she was fondly known as "Lady Vi"', or even just Vi. Violet had already watched the Miami Nassau race in 1956 alongside her husband, so when he organised the first Cowes to Torquay race in 1961, she was already a fan when she raced in it in 1963. She did so in her own Bertram 31, *Ultra Violet*, finishing sixth (or fifth, depending on your source), ahead of her husband; she is said to have been fiercely competitive. A posting by the Classic Offshore Powerboat Club, entitled a little off-puttingly, 'Make Way for the Ladies', shows how Violet fits into the chronology of British women power boat racers that includes Joe Carstairs, calling her Betty Carstairs, a name she hated.

Over the next few years, Violet drove many boats to victory and, in 1968, Ford asked her to drive their *Fairy Huntsman 28* in the first Round Britain Powerboat Race – a gruelling two-week, 1,700-mile battle against the elements. Along with crew-mate Thelma Freeman, she won the Women's Prize and came fifth overall, with many teams not even finishing the treacherous race. I had hoped that there would be some mementoes of Violet's powerboat racing time at the Max Aitken Museum in West Cowes, but struck unlucky, though I was sent a list of her races, including in 1987 and 1988, when she raced with her daughter Laura Mallet (now Levi), winning the ladies' Prize in their boat *Sleuth*.

But powerboat racing was by no means the sum of Violet's life; she had at least one other career, apart from being on the board of the Beaverbrook Foundation. The original Lord Beaverbrook, newspaper magnate, was from Canada, and his son, Max Aitken, and later his wife Violet, had an association with the University of New Brunswick (UNB). Max Aitken took over from his father as Chancellor and, when ill-health prevented him from continuing, Violet took over from him and served as the first female Chancellor from 1982 to 1992; she was Chancellor Emeritus thereafter. Long before she became Chancellor, Violet had made numerous visits with her husband to Fredericton in the 1950s and 1960s; there, too, she was known as 'Vi'. In a UNB Alumni News posting 'Remembering Lady Violet Aitken' given by Dr Frederik Eaton, her successor, he noted how, as Chancellor, she came over

> several times a year from her home in England to participate with grace, wit and aplomb in graduation ceremonies and other special events on UNB's two campuses. In keeping with family tradition, she also took an active interest in the Beaverbrook Art Gallery and The Playhouse.

At the awarding of her honorary degree of Doctor in Law in 1990, Violet observed, 'As Chancellor I am merely the icing on top of what is a pretty large cake. I get all the glory while the president does the real work.' That false modesty may well sum up her sometimes driven, colourful and seemingly fulfilling life.

It would not be right to leave the water without bringing it more up to date, and who better to do that than **Dame Ellen Patricia MacArthur DBE** (b.1976). Unlike the two women powerboat racers, Joe Carstairs and Violent Aitken, she is, as most readers will be aware, a racing sailor. To put it more technically, she is a successful solo long-distance yachtswoman: on 7 February 2005, she broke the world record for the fastest solo circumnavigation of the globe, a feat which brought her international recognition. But there is more to her than that, and much of it has to do with the Isle of Wight, where she is a resident of Cowes.

Ellen was born in Derbyshire to parents who were both teachers; she has two brothers. Her early interest in sailing was piqued by reading Arthur Ransome's *Swallows and Amazons* (1930). Internet sources tend to follow each other like sheep in saying that another influence was someone called Sophie Burke about whom none can up come with an identity, let alone as a sailor. It seems more likely, therefore, that they mean 'Nancy Blackett', the name of the Ransome boat. (Please correct me if you know better.) Not only does that boat have a trust which owns and runs it, but Ellen is its Patron.

Ellen's first experience of sailing was on a boat owned by her aunt, Thea MacArthur, on the east coast of mainland Britain. She is said to have saved her school lunch money for three years to buy her first boat, an 8ft dinghy which, though decimalisation had taken place before she was born, she named *Threp'ny Bit*. As well as her schooling, she worked at a sailing school in Hull. Aged 17 she bought a Corribee – a model sailing yacht with good sea-keeping ability. In 1995, she circumnavigated Great Britain in *Iduna*. In 1997, she finished seventeenth in the Mini Transat solo transatlantic race; while living in a French boatyard (and picking up French), she fitted out *Le Poisson*, her 21ft (6.4m) C Class Mini yacht. And in 1998 she was named 'Yachtsman of the Year' by the British Telecom/Royal Yachting Association and, in France, 'sailing's Young Hope'. At the same time Asteroid 20043 Ellenmacarthur was named after her. Although the exploits, not the honours, might seem a bit of a list for the uninitiated, you can see that Ellen was building up her sailing muscle and experience.

It was worth it: Ellen really achieved prominence in 2001, when she finished second in the Vendée Globe solo round-the-world race in *Kingfisher*, after which she was awarded an MBE for services to sport. Then aged 24, she was the youngest competitor to complete the voyage. Two years later, in *Kingfisher 2* (a catamaran) she captained a round-the world record attempt, thwarted by a broken mast in the Southern Ocean. *B&Q/Castorama*, a 75ft (23m) trimaran, built in Australia, and designed especially to take account of Ellen's height – 5ft 2in (1.57m), was unveiled in 2004. In this, her first significant record attempt to break the seven-day west–east transatlantic crossing failed by one and three-quarter hours. Phew! Later that year she began her attempt to break the solo record for sailing non-stop around the world, breaking several records on the way. This time, she was successful: she crossed, the finishing line on 7 February 2005, beating the previous record set by a Frenchman by one day: 8 hours, 35 minutes and 49 seconds. Following her return to England, she was awarded the Dame Commander of the British Empire medal (DBE); she is believed to have been the youngest recipient of that award. She was also granted the rank of Honorary Lieutenant Commander, Royal Navy Reserve, and appointed a Knight (Chevalier) of the French Legion of Honour.

You have to stop for a moment to imagine that gruelling journey for the slip of a woman. And I'm particularly interested in it because, in the hopes of seeing an object that was most typical of Ellen, I was shown round the Classic Boat Museum Gallery in East Cowes, and allowed to photograph the model of the trimaran, larger than I had expected. It is not on public display, and there are many other objects associated with Ellen also kept in store. That was the occasion when I was also introduced to the life of Joe Carstairs, and looked through a window down into the Saunders Roe factory.

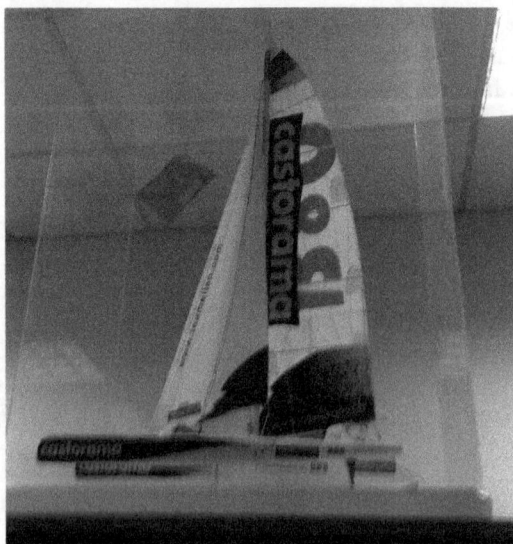

54. Model of Ellen MacArthur's *B&Q/Castorama*, photograph by the author at the Classic Boat Museum Gallery

In 2009, Ellen announced her intention to retire from competitive racing. To give more substance to my very sketchy account here of her attempts and achievements, she had already published accounts of her life and sailing: in 2002, it was her first autobiography, *Taking on the World*. In 2005, *Race Against Time*, a day-by-day account of her record journey around the world; and in September 2010, she published a second autobiography entitled *Full Circle*. But more important in some ways: in 2003, she set up the Ellen MacArthur Trust (now the Ellen MacArthur Cancer Trust) – a registered charity which supports the sailing of 8–24 year olds to help them regain their confidence while recovering from cancer, leukaemia and other such serious illnesses. And in 2008 she joined other well-known sports women and men to raise £4 million for the Rainbow children's hospice. The Ellen MacArthur Foundation (EMF), a charity inspired by Ellen's sailing experience, was founded in 2009, and publicly launched in 2010 at the Science Museum; supporting sustainability is one of its purposes. The offices of both these charities are in Cowes.

Ellen had not completely given up competitive sailing, because being involved was part of her charitable work. She is supportive and involved in the Round the Island Race, established by the Island Sailing Club in 1931. It compares with, say, the London Marathon, in that it encourages amateur sailors to take part. Although, not surprisingly, it was banned during the war, it re-emerged in 1946. Two women have won the Gold Roman Bowl Trophy – Mrs H Tobin in *Barbar* in 1954, and Julia Dane in *Glass Onion* in 1982. In 2003, Ellen took the helm for the second time of the Ellen MacArthur Cancer Trust's flagship boat *Solent Hero*, celebrating the twentieth anniversary of the Trust. She was accompanied by up to 24 young people in four boats, following their cancer treatment. As well as supporting them in this way, the race was also to raise money. Ellen had participated for the first time in 1997, but more important to her is the participation of the young people. This is a woman, aged 48 as I write, who not only makes life worthwhile for herself, through what she has achieved, but also supports countless young people to surmount their suffering. She is certainly an Island hero. This section of the chapter ends with a rather different woman.

Spy, Traitor, Saboteur or Fantasist, 1940–1950

Although **Dorothy Pamela O'Grady** (1897–1985) was rather different from all the other women in 'Women in a Man's World', she seems to qualify to be included here. There were several British women spies during the Second World War, as well as foreign women spying on behalf of the British war effort, some of whom were executed as a result, but spying is traditionally seen as being done more by men than by women. The blurb on the back of Adrian Searle's *The Spy Beside the Sea: The Extraordinary Wartime Story of Dorothy O'Grady* provides a neat introduction or, rather, ending to her occupation:

Had her appeal not saved her from the gallows, she would have been the only woman of any nationality to suffer death under the act during the Second World War – indeed, the only woman to be executed in Britain for spying in the twentieth century.

Searle, who, you may remember, was the author of the biography *The Infamous Sophie Dawes* (introduced in chapter 5), seems to like infamous women, but he introduces Dorothy gently, in a way that allows the reader to picture her:

Dorothy O'Grady has rightly been called the oddest spy of the Second World War. The 42-year-old landlady of a guest house beside the sea on the Isle of Wight, short in stature, plump, bespectacled and married to a retired fireman, she was – to put it mildly – very far removed from the archetypal 'cloak and dagger' image of an embedded enemy agent. She did not seem a woman committed to the cause of bringing the country in which she had always lived to its knees in the traumatic English summer of 1940.

Searle continues, via his usual careful research, to unravel a complicated story. To gain much more than can be given here, his book is your best source.

Dorothy's background may give some clues to her need to do something out-of-the-ordinary: she was adopted soon after birth by a British Museum official, George Squire. Her adopted mother, Pamela, died when Dorothy was 11, and her father then married his housekeeper, who treated her vindictively. Searle says that she was sent to a convent to be educated; elsewhere it is suggested that by the age of 13 she was living in a home where young girls were trained for domestic service. Searle does not mention the housekeeper, nor that training and its purpose. But by the time she was 17, both her adoptive parents were dead, and he does say that she became a domestic in the home of the Rector of Christ Church, Harrow, the Revd Ruby. Dorothy suggested under questioning that her life before the war was humdrum but, as Searle writes, that was 'at the very least economical with the truth', for she kept falling foul of the law: in 1918 she was convicting of forging bank-notes, and spent time in Borstal. In 1920, while in service in Brighton, she was found guilty of stealing clothing and was sentenced to two years' penal servitude. On release she moved back to London where she worked as a prostitute, ending up with a criminal record for forgery, theft and prostitution. You have to wonder what Vincent O'Grady, a London fireman 19 years older, knew when he married her in 1926; by then she was 29.

On Vincent O'Grady's retirement, they moved to Sandown on the Isle of Wight. There Dorothy ran a boarding house, cheekily called Osborne Villa. On the outbreak of war in 1939, O'Grady was recalled to the London Fire Brigade for wartime service; Dorothy was left behind in Sandown where she started walking her dog, Rob, a retriever, at night on the beach (a restricted area throughout the war). She was issued with a formal caution which she ignored.

It hardly needs repeating that the Island holds a very strategic position, to the south facing the English Channel; to the north commanding the Solent opposite the naval base of Portsmouth. The Island's history has shown it is a useful stepping stone for an enemy planning to invade the mainland. In August 1940 Dorothy's beach walking having aroused suspicion, her movements began to be monitored. She was arrested and charged with being in a prohibited area. When she failed to attend the court hearing at Ryde Magistrates' Court, her home was searched. She was found to be making accurate drawings and maps of the coast, perhaps not difficult for someone who had been a forger. She was tracked down under the assumed name of Pamela Arland in a boarding house in Totland Bay on the west coast of the Island. When she was caught in the act of cutting military telephone wires, she was arrested.

55. Dorothy O'Grady, from Adrian Searle, *The Spy Beside the Sea*

In December 1940 the case against her was heard in camera at the Hampshire Assizes in Winchester. There was, however, no evidence to be found of how she had passed information to the enemy, or even how she had communicated with Germany; not only had her house been searched but also her post had been intercepted. Based on her cutting of the telephone wires, she was tried not as a spy or agent but as a saboteur. She was also found guilty of two offences under the Official Secrets Act: that she had approached a prohibited place and that she had made a plan that might be useful to the enemy. On 17 December 1940, she was sentenced to death. She appealed and her appeal was heard in the Court of Appeal in London in February 1941; on the 10th, the sentence was commuted to fourteen years' penal servitude. She was moved from Holloway Prison to serve her sentence at Aylesbury Prison, Buckinghamshire. Psychological examination found her to have a high IQ, but that she was mentally disturbed, exhibiting a range of masochistic behaviour. It was more than that, in prison she was impossible to deal with, and she was shuffled between prisons as there were similar difficult women at Aylesbury and the governor feared there might be violence. Searle includes this quotation, that Dorothy had:

deteriorated rapidly in the last few days and was reported yesterday causing a disturbance and using abusive language. I remanded her for one week to give her a chance to pull herself together. This morning, however, there was a disturbance which has greatly upset the other women in D Hall. I therefore suggest that O'Grady be removed to another prison as she is unfit for the privileges of this establishment,

Perhaps today it could be suggested that Dorothy's behaviour was a form of self-harm, though apparently, after her release in the early 1950s, having served nine years of her sentence, she told a reporter for the *Sunday Express* that the whole episode was 'a huge joke and that being sentenced was the biggest thrill of her life'. But the *Daily Mail* in its article, 'Letters From Prison', told a completely different story, quoted by Searle:

O'Grady tells how she waited 16 years to wreak her revenge for the bitterness she felt about being 'wrongly' fined in the 1920s. Her anger was fuelled because her beloved puppy had died while she was on remand. She never forgave the British authorities, and Nazi Germany became the 'allied force' with which to strike back at the Establishment she hated.

Whatever the truth of her intention and motive, or motives, following her release, and the press excitement that followed, Dorothy returned to Sandown and resumed her life as a boarding house keeper. Her husband who had not only stood by her, but did all he could to get her released, died in 1953. In 1969, she went to live in a residential home at Lake, where she remained until her death in 1985, aged 88. You have to wonder what her mind was full of; if she wanted excitement, she certainly got it.

13 – The Campaigners, 1866–1946

Ferguson's Gang, 1933–1946

This bold venture started off without great fanfare at a dinner party in Freshwater in 1933. **Anne Gladstone** had moved there in 1922, following the death of her husband, John Gladstone (nephew of the former Prime Minister). She lived at the Briary, the house built in 1873 at Tennyson's suggestion for the artist GF Watts, and it is where Julia Margaret Cameron's sister Sara Prinsep and her family used to stay, as is detailed in chapter 8, 'Freshwater – Dimbola and Farringford'.

Anne was perhaps inspired by how Hallam Tennyson (Lord Tennyson by then) had, in 1927, presented 155 acres of land – now known as Tennyson Down – to the National Trust in memory of his father. She asked her guests, 'When is someone going to save the Old Town Hall at Newtown?' As it happened her daughter, Margaret **'Peggy' Pollard** (née Gladstone), was over from London staying with her at the time. Peggy was a member of a group of women who, in 1927, had established what they called Ferguson's Gang. Its main aim was campaigning to save properties for the National Trust. They had already had some success in doing so on the mainland, saving Shalford Mill, near Guildford, Surrey. In her position as leader of the Gang, the members of which not only wore masks, but further secured their anonymity by acting under somewhat bizarre pseudonyms, Peggy was called 'Bill Stickers'.

Peggy was ahead of her time in many ways: she won a scholarship to Newnham College, Cambridge in 1921, aged 17, becoming the first female student to gain a Double First in Oriental languages there. She completed further research at university in London, writing a book for which she was later awarded a PhD. In due course she became a scholar of Sanskrit, a poet and bard of the Cornish language. She was married to Captain Frank Pollard, an expert on Cornish history.

On the morning after the dinner at her mother's house, Peggy cycled the eight miles from Freshwater to Newtown to inspect the Old Town Hall. Newtown is east of Yarmouth, and north-east of Freshwater. Originally called Francheville, the town was a significant port in medieval times; there had been an official building on the site of the Town Hall since around the thirteenth century. It had not always fared well, however: it was ravaged by plague in 1349 and sacked by the French in 1377 (see chapter 4, 'Troubled Times'). It is also where, in 1664, Elizabeth, Dowager Countess of Portsmouth was granted a 34-year lease on an extensive salt marsh (see chapter 3, 'Women of Property'). In 1699 the Town Hall had been substantially rebuilt and there were further eighteenth-century alterations. Beside a photograph of one of those creeks, Polly Bagnall, in her 'Lillabullero' posting, says of the saltmarsh that it 'may look a bit dull'. It is now the Newtown National Reserve, owned and managed by the National Trust.

On inspection that day in 1933, Peggy obviously decided the Old Town Hall had campaigning potential, and it was discussed at a meeting of the Gang in

March 1933; it was positively received as their next campaign. It was bought from Sir John Simeon of Swainston (a different Sir John Simeon to the one who plays a part later in this chapter) for £5, and the neighbouring field for £100; it would take £1,000 to repair.

The Gang visited the Old Town Hall on 17 March 1934 with a typically lavish picnic. It's time now to introduce the members; as the Isle of Wight 'Hidden Heroes' neatly sums them up (there was no Ferguson):

All the members had a great sense of fun, and were quite unconventional in their time. Some were Lesbian or bisexual, some dressing in masculine outfits. They loved fine food, having Fortnum & Mason deliver hampers for meetings and excursions.

There were six core members:

Bill Stickers – Peggy Pollard

Sister Agatha – Brynhild **'Brynnie' Jervis-Read** (née Granger; 1908–2004)

Red Biddy, White Biddy – **Rachel Pinney** (1905–1995)

The Lord Beershop of the Gladstone Islands and Mercator's Projection – **Ruth Sherwood** (1907–1990)

Kate O'Brien the Nark – **Mabel Joy Gaze** (née Maw; 1907–1983)

Shot Biddy – **Eileen Souter** (née Bertram Moffat; 1910–2002)

There were also conscripted members, who included The Artichoke, an architect who acted as such on the Old Town Hall project. The other newcomers adopted suitable pseudonyms. Today the Gang would be described as 'media savvy'. While they did not initially set out to seek press attention, they attracted a lot of publicity through their unusual acts of donation. They found they could use this to their advantage to further their causes. On one headline-grabbing occasion they triggered a bomb scare, after they deposited a metal pineapple at the National Trust AGM, which in fact contained £100. That was but one example of their methods; between 1927 and 1939, the group delivered their contributions to the Trust's work with a sense of theatre and mystery; they were newsworthy. As Polly Bagnall summed it up in her Lillabullero posting, 'You could say that they anticipated both agit-prop and performance art.'

One of the Gang members penned the following 'anthem' which describes their links with the National Trust;

We ain't so many, we ain't so few;
All of us has this end in view –
National Trust, to work for you

Green grass turning to bricks and dust,
Stately homes that will soon go bust –
No defence but the National Trust.

Looking at rural England thus
George and Dragon is change for us
Into St. Clough and the Octopus.

Ferguson's Gang has paid its debt,
Ferguson's obligation, met
Ferguson's Gang has more for you yet.

Bill Stickers: Gang mastermind Peggy Gladstone
c1926. She became the first woman to gain
a double first from Cambridge in Oriental
Languages.

Red and White Biddy: Major-General's daughter
Rachel Pinney was the only Gang member to
fall foul of the law, serving a prison sentence
for kidnap.

Sister Agatha: Brynnie Granger was Peggy's right-hand
woman. She defied convention by having an affair with
her married piano teacher.

56. Bill Stickers, Red and White Biddy, and Sister Agatha,
from Polly Bagnall and Sally Beck, *Ferguson's Gang*

The National Trust posting 'Newtown Old Town Hall – Saved by Ferguson's Gang' explains the last line of verse 3: 'Their aim was to preserve examples of "traditional England" and they took inspiration from the book *England and the Octopus* by Clough Williams-Ellis. In London the group was described as an "octopus" with its tentacles spreading out across the countryside.' The 'anthem' comes from Anne Hutton North's *Ferguson's Gang: The Maidens Behind the Masks* (2013). Polly Bagnall and Sally Beck's *Ferguson's Gang: The Remarkable Story of the National Trust Gangsters* (2015) is the more obviously readable. An example of their style comes in the Foreword, elaborating on the description in 'Hidden Heroes' of the Gang's members:

> The women in Ferguson's Gang were all strong and non-conformist, as robust as the threads of their lisle stockings. From the upper, and upper-middle classes, with distinguished forebears in their family tree, they were educated, enquiring and brave. They were also inclusive and non-judge-mental and, although they shared interests, they were a diverse group … They may have been outspoken, upsetting the status quo, but together they made use of their individual differences and strengths to become a formi-dable force.

Throughout the book, Polly Bagnall, in her other life an artist, describes the women as if she really knew them. It seems likely that she had her interest in Ferguson's Gang piqued by discovering that her grandfather, John Macgregor, was The Artichoke. He was the Gang's go-to architect, though he became more to them than just an architect as his pseudonym suggests. The Society for the Protection of Ancient Buildings regularly employed him to survey proper-ties and oversee their repairs and it was through that work that he came to the attention of the National Trust. The Trust recommended him to Fergu-son's Gang and he worked with them on their first successful project, Shalford Mill, surveying and supervising the conversion of the watermill into residential quarters; that is where, in one of its rooms, the Gang set up their headquarters. Later he worked with them on Priory Cottages in Oxfordshire.

Following its repair, the Old Town Hall was to have a new life, agreed with the National Trust: it was to be used by the Youth Hostel Association (YHA), provided that the Gang should have occasional visits, without becoming members of the YHA. It was used as a hostel from 1935 to 1939, that is, until the outbreak of the Second World War, with women sleeping upstairs, and men downstairs; what had been the Council Chamber became the common room. Remnants of the old kitchen and bathroom downstairs still survive. George Macaulay Trevelyan, who had been responsible for establishing the YHA in Britain in 1931, was a member of the Gang, and known as 'Poolcat'.

Without Ferguson's Gang it is unlikely that the Old Town Hall would still be standing today. As Polly Bagnall writes at the end of her Foreword:

57. Newtown, Old Town Hall, before and after,
from Polly Bagnall and Sally Beck, *Ferguson's Gang*

Today, the generosity of Ferguson's Gang is worth tens of millions of pounds. They left another invaluable legacy too, they helped put the National Trust, a small and underfunded body in it early years, with a fraction of the four million members it has today, well and truly on the map.

Ferguson's Gang went on to campaign on behalf of other projects, including the saving of significant stretches of the Cornish coastline near to where Peggy and her husband lived. The Gang's activities and plans were recorded in their minute books, which were written in a mixture of mockney and text-speak. As well as formal meetings, they would occasionally hold what they called 'hauntings' in properties they worked to save, involving, as usual, much food and drink.

After the Second World War, the Gang's activities decreased, though they still met socially. Red Biddy had a life full of ups and downs: as a Quaker, she joined the Women's Peace Camp at Greenham common in 1981, and pioneered 'methods for conflict understanding', among other exploits; she also spent time in prison. She came out as a lesbian in 1989. Bill Stickers (Peggy Pollard), having learned Cornish, become a bard, and joined the Cornish Gorsedd. She even published *Bewnans Alysaryn*, a Cornish-language miracle play, and a book entitled *Cornwall* (1947). In 1980 Sister Agatha – Brynnie Jervis-Read – visited the Town Hall. She didn't reveal her real name but she had abandoned her mask. When asked why they had done what they did, she replied that they had been young, they wanted to help the National Trust and, above all, it had been fun. That sums it up nicely.

To visit the Old Town Hall, you will need to search the Internet beforehand, to ascertain the current state of affairs, then make arrangements to visit it and to be shown around. This is what I did in 2023, as it was kept locked; it was undergoing repairs, with scaffolding up at one end. It is worth visiting, if only to people it with Ferguson's Gang.

Women's Suffrage, 1886–1919

The campaign for women's suffrage on the mainland has been quite well covered in writing and film, mostly concentrating on the Suffragettes whose violence, imprisonment, hunger strikes and forced feeding, not to forget Emily David's death under the feet of the king's horse, make the better story than the earlier campaigning by the Suffragists. Their method was more legal, unconfrontational, and steady. Information regarding the Isle of Wight, and its women's suffrage proponents, has only been touched upon, but usefully, in for example, the last chapter of Daisy Plant's *A History of Women's Lives on The Isle of Wight* (2019), a book which concentrates on women of the nineteenth century. As she suggests, there wasn't much enthusiasm for women's suffrage on the Island:

> The prevailing view was that supporters of the movement were unhappy, unmarried, ugly old ladies, and that the majority of women were satisfied with the way things were. While there were probably a few women who did support the suffrage movement on the Island, it's likely that they were afraid to be vocal.

The nationwide campaign for women's suffrage goes back to at least as early as 1866 when Emily Davies and Elizabeth Garrett submitted a petition, signed by some 1,521 people, to John Stewart Mill, who presented it to Parliament the following year. This was the first mass Votes for Women Petition submitted to Parliament. There were many more to come and a long struggle ahead for the women (and men) involved in campaigning for women's suffrage. But among those who did sign that first petition were three women from the Isle of Wight: **Ellen Cantelo** (artist) (1825–1898) of 69 High Street, Newport, **Sarah James** (*c*.1810–1886), St James Street, Newport, and **Elizabeth Thompson** (1833–1900) of Carisbrooke. It is assumed that those signatures were collected among family and friends. Ellen Cantelo was introduced, but without family background, in chapter 9, 'Women Artists'. Elizabeth was her sister, and Sarah was either part of their extended family, or a close friend. The details of the background of Ellen and Elizabeth are to be found in what seems to be an extended newsletter about many unconnected subjects, posted in 2016 by an entity called 'Sudni Heritage Blog'. It says that what is written about the sisters came from a great-nephew, Barry Cantelo; there is also some helpful census information. Ellen and Elizabeth were the daughters of **Elizabeth Cantelo** (b.*c*.1792–1857) and William Cantelo, a publican, holding the position of landlord of the Eight Bells in Carisbrooke, and the Castle in Newport, at different times in his career; If this is the same establishment, there has been a Castle Inn in Newport since the sixteenth century. The couple had four children. Important here is that theirs was a Chartist family – the working class movement for political reform in the nineteenth century – so it is hardly surprising that they would hear about the petition and sign it.

The Island was to feature again in 1896 when a bill for women's right to vote was introduced to Parliament but failed to pass. During its passage, 76 Suffragettes were arrested when they tried to storm the Houses of Parliament. Noteworthy, as far as the Island is concerned, is the speech in the debate by Sir John Stephen Barrington Simeon, 4th Baronet of Swainston Manor (in the north of the Island, and including Calbourne and Newtown Port). He was first elected to Parliament as a Liberal Unionist in 1895, one of the two members for Southampton; he was to be re-elected in 1900; he left the House of Commons in 1906 and died in 1909.

Before I come to his speech, it is worth saying a bit more about Simeon, and what else he did in 1897; combined with the speech, it highlights the inherited privilege and sense of entitlement of some of the landowners of the Island's top echelons: the family had been on the Island since 1715. Shortly after his election, Simeon commissioned a railway station to serve his property on the line between Newport and Yarmouth; it was situated near the hamlet of Upper Watchingwell, and called Watchingwell Halt Railway Station. It would make access to Swainston Manor easier for his family and guests and also for his tenants. But there was a delightful twist, particularly in view of his speech in Parliament: the duties at the station were so light, and the receipts so small, that the stationmaster was a woman who, among her duties would signal for the train to stop; she would also work the semaphore signals provided for this purpose. (Swainston features as Swaynestone in Maxwell Gray's 1886 novel *The Silence of Dean Maitland* which was introduced in chapter 10, 'Women Writers'; see also the mention below).

Simeon spoke in Parliament in 1897, two years after his first election, and on the second day of the 1896 Parliamentary Franchise Extension Bill. This is the beginning of his speech, as recorded by Hansard:

> asked how they were to be sure that ladies would not claim to sit in the House of Commons if they once had Parliamentary votes. If once there was 'one

man one vote, and every man a vote,' how could they deny votes to women? Considering there were 1,000,000 more women than men, and every woman would have a vote if everyone got it, were they to suppose that when women could swamp the votes of men they would be content to remain outside[?] If ever they got into Parliament the end of this country would not be far off. The immediate result, however, of this Bill would be the biggest creation of faggot votes ever known. Rich men would buy votes for their wives and daughters, while the wives and daughters of artisans, who were told at every election that they were the backbone of the country, would have no votes. If the working classes were the backbone of the country, why should not the female of the country have votes[?]

(A faggot voter was a person who qualified to vote in an election with a restricted suffrage only by the exploitation of loopholes in the regulations.)

Was Simeon really calling for the woman stationmaster of the Watchingwell Station to have the vote? I don't think so. Neither do I think that he was calling for his wife, **Isabella Mary Simeon** (née Dutton; 1853–1936) to have it. The bill of 1896 was defeated.

Emily Florence Seely (née Crighton; 1870–1913) of Brook Manor must not be forgotten when it comes to Parliamentary elections. She was the wife (m 1895) of John Edward Bernard Seely, 1st Baron Mottistone. As the *Western Gazette* reported on Emily's death in 1913:

In 1900, Colonel Seely (then Captain) was serving in South Africa [during the Boer War] and was at the same time Unionist candidate for the Isle of Wight. Mrs Seely herself appealed to the voters and won the election for her husband.

Emily died on 9 August 1913, aged 42, giving birth to her seventh child.

A poll was conducted in 1911, set up by a Colonel Hamilton (I'm assuming this was Lt. Col. John Fane Hamilton), of 611 lady municipal voters of Ryde on the desirability of votes for Women. (Women were allowed to vote in local elections.) There were only 55 votes for, 191 against, and 365 undecided. Hamilton apparently asked, 'where the Suffragette assertion that wise women want to vote comes in'. You have to wonder, assuming that it was a secret ballot, how his wife, **Gertrude Catherine Mary Angela Hamilton** (née Stewart; 1870–1918) voted. I like to think that she was a secret rebel against her husband's anti-suffrage views!

Hamilton probably involved himself because, in 1910, following another petition on women's suffrage, a Conciliation Bill, the first to give the vote to one million women who owned property, was passed by the House of Commons, but it failed to become law. During its passage, 300 Suffragettes marched to Parliament, where they were beaten and arrested by police. This is known as Black Friday. It would appear that an Isle of Wight woman signed that petition; she was Mary Gleed Tuttiett who wrote as Maxwell Gray (introduced in chapter

10, 'Women Writers'). She is described as strongly interested in women's rights, as is shown in a number of her novels. Confirmation that she signed the 1910 petition is perhaps to be found in her obituary in *The Times* of 22 September 1923, which I have not yet been able to access.

The second Conciliation Bill, a Private Member's Bill, was debated in May 1911 and won by a majority of 255 to 88. The bill was promised a week of government time. But in November, Prime Minister Asquith announced that he was in favour of a manhood suffrage bill and that the Suffragists could suggest and propose an amendment that would allow some women to vote. The bill was consequently dropped.

On 2 May 1913 a police raid took place on the office of *The Suffragette*, the newspaper (edited by Christabel Pankhurst) of the Women's Social and Political Union (WSPU); it was also their headquarters. The Suffragettes there at the time were arrested, and charged with conspiracy to do wilful damage. The office was closed. Vans were filled with incriminating material providing evidence of bombings and arson and the networks and organisation behind the militant campaigns. The printers were also raided, and copy removed

Constance Chellingworth Radcliffe Cooke (1877–1963), eldest child of Charles Radcliffe Cooke and his wife Frances Parnther Broom, moved to the Isle of Wight in 1924, aged 47, because she thought it would provide a more suitable climate for her indifferent health. By then, and since 1918, women over 30 were able to vote, enabled by the passing of the Representation of the People Act. But it did not grant the vote to all women; that came in 1928 with the Representation of the People (Equal Franchise) Act, which entitled everyone over 21 to do so. This age limit was subsequently reduced to 18.

Constance had become part of the struggle for women's suffrage much earlier, challenging convention and joining the suffrage movement as an active member of the WSPU, that is, the Suffragettes (rather than the Suffragists). This was in spite of her father being an anti-suffrage MP: he publicly rejected votes for women – or perhaps it was because of that! He did, though, at one time say to her 'as a suffragette, you ought to have the vote'. Much of the information about Constance is drawn from Lisa Berry-Waite's article, '"She never let her faculties grow dull": Constance Chellingworth Radcliffe Cooke – Clare Wichbold' (2024). It was Clare Wichbold who worked to have Constance's papers housed in the Here-

58. Constance Cooke, from the Internet

fordshire Archive and Records Centre, as recorded in her 2002 posting, 'These suffrage papers are to be given to Hereford Museum and Library'.

Following her move to the Island, Constance lived at 51 Argyll Street in Ryde, a mansion in a row of grand houses, which is easy to find today. There, in 1929, she started keeping a journal, though the entries tended to be sporadic. The journal now belongs to a family member who allowed Lisa Berry-Waite to draw on it. On 3 December 1939, during the period of the Phoney War, Constance wrote: 'I as Vice Chairman of Ryde Labour Party proposed that all municipal and Parliamentary elections should be resumed in spite of the outbreak of war, difficulty in blackout of getting to the polls, evacuees, etc. Resolution carried unanimously.' Writing of the bombing of the Island, she wrote in December 1941: 'There is so much noise and bombs dropping in the near neighbourhood – the house jumps under one's feet.' And of her involvement as a fire watcher on Argyll Street, organising people to undertake their duties, she wrote:

4th March 1942: Some months ago I organised this road of 62 houses for fire-watching, a number of men having failed to do so. When asked why I should do, several said 'it'll be done if you do it'. So I just got going with Barbara Blunt to help in running about and we got 28 people to watch once a fortnight.

Before, during and after the Second World War, Constance was involved in many organisations: just one entry from her journal, that of 29 April, mentions her participation in a Workers' Educational Association (WEA) event in Newport; attending the National Labour Women's Conference at Brighton; giving a talk to the Isle of Wight Archaeological Society; and representing Binstead at the National Federation of Women's Institutes Conference in London.

Constance moved back to the village of Much Marcle, Herefordshire in 1956, her journal soon recording her involvement in local activities, speaking at the WEA classes about her suffrage experiences, joining the local branch of the Women's Institute and advocating for the Campaign for Nuclear Disarmament. She died in 1961, aged 86; her sojourn on the Isle of Wight had obviously done her good. Lisa Berry-Waite ends her posting from her position of librarian at the Herefordshire Archive and Records Centre, 'I will be fully cataloguing and researching the collection in 2024 and drawing on her journal to write a book about Constance in due course. Watch this space …'. She adds some biographical details about Clare Witchbold, including her interest in the women's suffrage movement.

The first woman to be elected to the House of Common was Constance Markievicz (Countess), in the general election of 1918. But, as a member of Sinn Fein, she did not take her seat. The first woman to take her seat was Nancy Astor (Viscountess Astor), after a by-election in December 1919.

Looking for women Parliamentary candidates on the Isle of Wight after the 1928 Representation of the People (Equal Franchise) Act is not very fruitful; I have only found one, **Helen de Guerry Simpson** (1897–1940), and her connection with the Island seems rather tangential. Born and raised in Australia, she is primarily known as a prolific writer. She arrived in England to attend St Anne's College, Oxford University, in 1914 and in 1918 joined the Women's Royal Naval Service as a chief section officer of decoding at the Admiralty. She returned to Oxford in 1919 and became involved in acting; she was sent down in 1921, without completing her degree, for breaking regulations governing women and men acting together. Thereafter she travelled between Australia and England writing, broadcasting, lecturing, getting married and producing a daughter. Suddenly however, in 1939, when her eyesight was failing, she was selected by the Isle of Wight Liberal Association to be their parliamentary candidate at the United Kingdom General Election that was expected to take place in 1939 or 1940. The seat was held by the Conservatives, but the Liberals were expected to challenge strongly to recapture the seat they had last won in 1923. She attended the Liberal Party Assembly at Scarborough in June 1939, and travelled around England speaking for the Party. There is no further mention of her being associated with the Isle of Wight. But she became ill and underwent surgery in 1940, and she died from cancer after months of suffering on 14 October that year, aged 43.

On a more cheerful note, and very much connected with the Island: for some time I've been hoarding part of a letter I copied down while working in the British Library in August 2023, from *Letters of Anne Thackeray Ritchie … edited by Hester Ritchie* (1924). It seems both funny and touching – an ideal way to end this chapter and, indeed, the main text of the book.

Hester Helena Makepeace Thackeray Ritchie (1878–1960) was the daughter of Anne, known as Anny Thackeray Ritchie, who was introduced in chapter 8, 'Freshwater'. The letter was written from The Porch, Anny's home in Freshwater, on 26 February 1919 following the General Election called immediately after the November 1918 Armistice with Germany which ended the First World War. Property-owning women over 30 had, as noted, been enabled to vote as a result of the bill that became law that year. Anny writes:

I would have taken it [a parasol received from her daughter-in-law] to vote with, but it was pouring lions and tigers. At the voting booth we displeased a clerk. I said, 'I hope I have done it all right.' He said severely, 'This is vote by ballot, you have no business to show your paper.' Why Hester and I have a vote, I do not know – anyhow we both stepped behind the screen and both voted coalition, and Hester grins and says, 'Now we counterbalance A— and Sir F— who has travelled all the way from London to give his vote to Sir Godfrey Baring' signed Votarina. [Baring lost; the Coalition won the General Election.]

Bibliography

Books by and about Women, for the General Reader

Adams, Mildred ed, *Rebel in Bombazine:Memoirs of Malwida von Meysenburg* (New York, WW Morton & Co., 1936)

Austen, Jane, *Mansfield Park* (London, Military Library, Whitehall, 1814)

Bagnall, Polly and Beck, Sally, *Ferguson's Gang: The Remarkable Story of the National Trust Gangsters* (London, National Trust Books, 2015)

Baldwin, Gay, *Ghosts of the Isle of Wight* (Isle of Wight, Gaynor Baldwin, 1977)

Barnes, Margaret Campbell, *Mary of Carisbrooke* (Philadelphia, Macrae Smith Co, 1956)

Butler, Elizabeth, *An Autobiography; with illustrations from sketches by the author* (London, Constable, 1923)

Coleridge-Taylor, Mrs JF, *A Memory sketch, or Personal reminiscences of my husband, genius and musician, S. Coleridge-Taylor, 1875–1912* (London, J Crowther, 1943)

Cooper, Heather, *Stealing Roses* (London, Allison & Busby Ltd, 2019)

Cooper, Heather, *Arresting Beauty* (West Malling, Kent, Beachy Books, 2023)

Dell, Marion, *Virginia Woolf's influential forebears: Julia Margaret Cameron, Anny Thackeray Ritchie and Julia Prinsep Stephen* (Basingstoke, Hampshire, Palgrave Macmillan, 2015)

Dunn, Jane, *Read my Heart. Dorothy Osborne and Sir William Temple: A Love Story in the Age of Revolution* (London, Harper Press, 2008)

Ellis, Mary, *A Spitfire Girl: One of the world's greatest female ATA ferry pilots tells her story* (Barnsley, Yorkshire, Frontline Books, 2016)

Fiennes, Celia, *The Journeys of Celia Fiennes* (London, Macdonald & Co (Publishers) Ltd, 1983)

Fox, John, *The King's Smuggler: Jane Whorwood, Secret Agent to Charles I* (Cheltenham, Gloucestershire, The History Press, 2022)

Fraser, Flora (adapted by) (Introduction by Elizabeth Longford), *Maud: The Diaries of Maud Berkeley* (London, Secker & Warburg, 1985)

Fraser, Mrs Hugh, *A Diplomat's Life in Many Lands* (New York, Dodd, Mead & Co., 1911)

Gabriel, Mary, *Love and Capital: Karl and Jenny Marx and the birth of a Revolution* (New York, Little, Brown, 2011)

Garnett, Henrietta, *Anny: A Life of Anne Thackeray Ritchie* (London, Pimlico, 2006)

Gould, Cecily, *A Tapestry of Time: or Effigy of Love* (Lincoln NE, USA, Writers Club Press, Universe, 2001)

Gray, Maxwell, *The Silence of Dean Maitland* (Leipzig, Bernhard Tauchnitz, 1887)

Gray, Maxwell, *The Reproach of Annesley* (Leipzig, Bernhard Tauchnitz, 1889)

Grayer, Joan Brading, *I Lived in Julia's House* (Newport, Isle of Wight, 2010)

Hannam, Vanessa, *The Hostage Prince* (Sutton, Surrey, Severn House Publishers, 2006)

Hargrove, Ethel C, *Wanderings in the Isle of Wight* (London, Andrew Melrose, 1913)

Hargrove, Ethel C, *The Garden of Desire: A Story of the Isle of Wight* (London, Grafton & Co, 1916)

Hasluck, Alexandra, *Audrey Tennyson's Vice Regal Days: The Australian Letters of Audrey Lady Tennyson 1899–1903* (Canberra, National Library of Australia, 1978)

Hawksley, Lucinda, *The Mystery of Princess Louise: Queen Victoria's Rebellious Daughter* (London, Vintage Books, 2014)

Higonnet, Anne, *Berthe Morisot* (Berkeley, University of California Press, 1995)

Hill, Brian, *Julia Margaret Cameron* (London, Owen, 1973)

Hobbes, John Oliver, *Some Emotions and a Moral* (London, T Fisher Unwin, 1893)

Huish, Marcus, *Happy England as Painted by Helen Allingham* (London, Adam and Charles Black, 1909)

Humphreys, Helen, *Afterimage* (London, Bloomsbury Publishing, 2001)

Hutchings, Richard J and Brian Hinton eds, *The Farringford Journal of Emily Tennyson 1853–1864* (Newport, Isle of Wight County Press, 1986)

Hutton-North, Anna, *Ferguson's Gang: The Maidens behind the Masks* (Great Britain, Lulu Inc, 2013)

Jardine, Lisa, *The Curious Life of Robert Hooke: The Man who Measured London* (London, Harper Perennial, 2003)

Lawrence, DL, *The Trespasser* (London, Granada, 1982)

Lee, Holme, *Against Wind and Tide* (London, Smith Elder & Co., 1859)

Lee, Holme, *For Richer for Poorer* (Leipzig, Bernhard Tauchnitz, 1870)

Leith, MCJ, *From Over the Water: A Story of Two Promises* (London, Walter Smith, 1884)

Lukitsh, Joanne, *Julia Margaret Cameron* (London, Phaidon, 2001)

MacArthur, Ellen, *Taking on the World* (London, Penguin, 2003)

MacArthur, Ellen, *Race Against Time* (London, Penguin, 2006)

MacArthur, Ellen, *Full Circle* (London, Michael Joseph, 2010)

MacEwen, Constance, *A Cavalier's Ladye* (London, Methuen, 1892)

Manning, Olivia, *The Playroom* (London, Virago Press, 1984)

Meynell, Viola, *Alice Meynell: A Memoir* (London, Jonathan Cape, 1929)

Moore, Georgina, *The Garnett Girls* (London, Harper Collins, 2023)

Parry, Robert Stephen, *The Testament of Sophie Dawes: The Queen of Chantilly and a Scandal at the Heart of Victorian Society* (publisher unknown, kindle, 2020)

Paterson, Arthur, *Homes of Tennyson, painted by Helen Allingham* (London, A & C Black, 1905)

Plant, Daisy, *A History of Women's Lives on the Isle of* Wight (Barnsley, Yorkshire, Pen & Sword Press, 2019)

Raine, Rosa, *The Queen's Isle: Chapters on the Isle of Wight wherein church truths are blended with Island beauties* (London, Joseph Masters, 1849)

Richmond, Leigh (Legh), *Annals of the Poor* (including 'The Dairyman's Daughter') (London, Griffin & Co, 1861)

Ritchie, Hester, *Letters of Anne Thackeray Ritchie* (London, John Murray, 1924)

Roberts, C[aroline] A[lice], *Marchcroft Manor*, 2 vols (London, Remington and Co., 1882)

Rubenhold, Hallie, *Lady Worsley's Whim: An Eighteenth-Century Tale of Sex, Scandal and Divorce* (London, Vintage, 2015)

Searle, Adrian, *The Spy Beside the Sea: The Extraordinary Wartime Story of Dorothy O'Grady* (Stroud, Gloucestershire, The History Press, 2012)

Searle, Adrian, *Sophie – The Infamous Sophie Dawes: New Light on the Queen of Chantilly* (Barnsley, Yorkshire, Pen and Sword History, 2020)

Sewell, Eleanor L, *The Autobiography of Elizabeth Sewell* (London, Longmans Green & Co, 1908)

Sewell, Elizabeth, ed, *Gertrude, 'Stories Illustrative of the Lord's Prayer'* (London, Longman, Brown, Green, and Longmans, 1846)

Sewell, Elizabeth, *The Experience of Life* (London, Longmans Green & Co., 1886)

Simpson, *Daisy and the Isle of Wight Dragon* (Isle of Wight, Martin Simpson, 2013)

Spicer, Dorothy and Pauline Gower, *Women With Wings* (London, John Long, 1938)

Sprules, Sarah, *Knighton Gorges: The Curse of Thomas Becket* (Createspace Independent Publishing Platform, 2014)

Sprules, Sarah, *The Last Wight Witch* (Createspace Independent Publishing Platform, 2015)

Stuart Wortley, Violet, *Sophy: The Winkle Picker* (Christchurch, Christchurch Times, 1941)
Summerscale, Kate, *The Queen of Whale Cay: The extraordinary life of 'Joe' Carstairs, the fastest woman on water* (London, Bloomsbury, 2012)
Tennyson, Emily Sellwood, *Lady Tennyson's Journal* (Charlottesville, University Press of Virginia, 1981)
Thackeray, Anne, *Mrs Dymond* (London, Smith Elder, 1890)
Thwaite, Ann, *Emily Tennyson: The Poet's Wife* (London, Faber & Faber, 1996)
Toms, Jan, *The Little Books of the Isle of Wight* (Stroud, Gloucestershsire, The History Press, 2011)
Truss, Lynn, *Tennyson's Gift* (London, Hamish Hamilton, 1996)
Whitehead, CM, *Recollections of Miss Elizabeth Sewell and her sisters* (Ventnor, Isle of Wight, Knight's Library, 1910)
Woolf, Virginia, *Night and Day* (Ware, Hertfordshire, Wordsworth Classics, 2012)

Specialist Works by or about Women (including those available on the Internet; see also 'Internet Material' below)

Anon, 'Women and Geology in the 19th Century' (2022; posting on the Geological Society of London's website
Bell, Katy, 'Isabella de Fortibus: Queen of the Isle of Wight', posting, nd
Brown, Rebecca Starr, 'Isabella of England, Countess of Bedford' (blog on her website, 16 June 2017)
Cameron, Julia Margaret, 'The Annals of My Glasshouse' in *Herself, Virginia Woolf and Roger Fry* (London, Pallas Athene, 2023)
Clarke, Peter, 'Elizabeth Heneage 1734–1800' (posted by Isle of Wight Catholic History Society, nd)
Clarke, Peter, 'Life of Elizabeth, Countess of Clare – Foundress of St Mary's Church' (posted by Isle of Wight Catholic History Society, nd)
Clarke, Peter, 'St Dominic's Priory, Carisbrooke' (posted by Isle of Wight Catholic History Society, nd)
Corke, Helen, *Neutral Ground: A Chronicle* (Bath, Cedrick Chivers, 1966)
Courtney, Julia, 'Three Talented Women' in *Island Life* (posted 2018)
Fleming Christine, 'The Lady in Red' (posted 2015)
Garman, Emma, 'Olivia Manning' (posted in 'Feminize Your Canon' by *The Paris Review* 2018)
Gould, Cecily, *Gossip: The Biography of a Yacht* (Rendlesham, Seafarer Books, 2003)
Hackler, Rhoda EA, '"My Dear Friend": Letters of Queen Victoria and Queen Emma' *Hawaiian Journal of History* Volume 22, 1988 (Honolulu, Hawaiian Historical Society, Hawaii)
Harrison, Fairfax, 'The Proprietors of the Northern Neck', chapters on Culpeper, *The Virginia Magazine of History and Biography*, vol.34, no.1 (Jan. 1926) pp 19–64 (published online by Virginia Historical Society, 2024)
Harrison, John, 'News and Views from Northcourt' posted by The Isle of Wight Gardens Trust, 2021
Hawkes, Jacquetta, 'The Longstone, Mottistone' (published online by Cambridge University Press, 2 January 2015)
Heath, Jane, 'Helen Corke and DH Lawrence: Sexual Identity and Literary Relations' in *Feminist Studies*, vol.11 No. 2 (Summer, 1985), pp 317–342
Hoe, Susanna, *God Save the Tsar* (London, Michael Joseph, 1978)
Hoe, Susanna and Derek Roebuck, *Women in Disputes: A History of European Women in Mediation and Arbitration* (Oxford, HOLO Books, 2018)

Joseph, Gerhard, 'Poetic and Photographic Frames: Tennyson and Julia Margaret Cameron', *Tennyson Research Bulletin*, Vol. 5 No. 2 (November 1988) pp 43–48 (published by the Tennyson Society)

Kellaway, Warwick, 'Sophie's Story: From Winkles to Wealth on the Isle of Wight (posted, nd)

Kolbl-Ebert, Martina, 'Barbara Marchioness of Hastings (1810–1858) – Fossil Collector and "Lady Geologist"' *Earth Sciences History* (2004), 23(1): 75–87

Kolbl-Ebert, Martina, 'Drawing as a Female Accomplishment in the Service of Geology', *Earth Sciences History* (2012), 31(2): 270–286

Kolbl-Ebert, Martina, 'Ladies with hammers – exploring a social paradox in early 19th century Britain' (June 2020, Geological Society of London Special Publications 506 (1) SP506-2029-193)

Lewis, Clarenza, 'Settlement in Hampshire and the Isle of Wight' (posted Lincoln Repository, 12.3.24)

Mainwaring, Madison, 'Always the Model, Never the Artist' (posted *Paris Review*, July 2019)

Manning, Olivia, *The Balkan Trilogy* (Harmondsworth, Penguin, 1987)

Marsh, Jan, *Pre-Raphaelite Women: Images of Femininity* (London, Weidenfeld and Nicholson, 1987)

Marsh, Jan, 'Women Artists and the Isle of Wight' (blog, posted 22 May 2012)

Morgan, Nina, 'More than Equal' (2010; blog on Trowelblazers website)

Morgan, Nina, 'Barbara Hastings' (2014; blog on Trowelblazers website)

Nicholson, Winifred, *Unknown Colour: Paintings, Letters, Writings* (London, Faber & Faber, 1987)

Okely, Judith, *Own and Other Culture* (London, Routledge, 1996)

Okely, Judith, 'The Isle of Wight as a site for English/British Identity' in *Islands and Britishness*, eds J Mathews and D Travers (Cambridge Scholars, 2012)

Okely, Judith, *The Traveller Gypsies* (Cambridge, Cambridge University Press, 1983; online, 2009)

Parry, Robert Stephen, 'Sophie Dawes (*c*.1792–1840) Her History' (posted 2020)

Poynting, Sarah, 'Deciphering the King: Charles 1's Letters to Jane Whorwood', *The Seventeenth Century*, vol 21, 2006 – Issue 1, pp 128–140 (posted online 2013)

Roman, Stephan, *Isle and Empires: When Russian Royals and Radicals Came to the Island* (Isle of Wight, Medina Publishing, 2021/2022)

Rubenstein, Hilary L, 'The Only Female Survivor of the sinking of the Royal George' (History Hits, online)

Sewell, Elizabeth, *Principles of Education, drawn from Nature and Revelation, and applied to female education in the upper classes* (London, 1865)

Shephard, Amy, 'Orchard Bros, Serving the West Wight through Five Generations' (including Julia Margaret Cameron's letter to the Post Office) (posted on *Isle of Wight Beacon*, 6 October 2020)

Shindler, Karolyn, 'Barbara Hastings: The first Lady of fossils' (2010, on the Internet)

Shindler, Karolyn '"I have found Wonders": The life, letters and passion for collecting of the fossilist, Barbara Yelverton, Marchioness of Hastings' for the Hogg Conference on Geological Collectors and Collecting' (2011, on the Internet)

Spiridovich, Alexander, 'The Imperial Visit to Cowes, 1909' in *The Home of the Last Tsar – Romanov and Russian History* (posted online 'Alexander Palace Time Machine, nd)

Steel, Lorna, 'A new pterodactyloid pterosaur from the Wessex Formation (Lower Cretaceous) of the Isle of Wight, England' in *Cretaceous Research* 26:4, August 2005

Thackeray, Anne Ritchie, *The Porch* (New York, Scribner, 1913)

Thomas, Helen, 'Harriet Parr' Shanklin History Update 2020, for the Shanklin & District History Society.

Turner, Susan et al, 'Forgotten Women in an extinct saurian (man's) world' (2010), Geological Society, London, Special Publications, vol. 343, pp 111–53

Walker, Kirsty Stonell, 'Cyllena Wilson' (posted on 'The Kissed Mouth' website, 3 December 2018)

Walker, Kirsty Stonell (Fanny Cornforth?), 'Mary Mary, Maids of Tennyson's Isle: Julia Margaret Cameron's Mary Fantasy Made Reality' (posted on 'The Kissed Mouth' website, 5 July 2015)

Walker, Kirsty Stonell, 'Some Thoughts on Emily Peacock' (posted on 'The Kissed Mouth' website, 13 August 2017)

Waller, Ruth, 'Archaeological Resource Assessment of the Isle of Wight: Early Medieval Period' (County Archaeology Service, 2006)

Welstead, Therron, 'Isabella de Fortibus', posting, nd

Whitmore, Warren, 'On this Day: Nuns took Residence of their Carisbrooke Catholic Convent' (posted 1922)

Young, Sarah, 'In Herzen's Footseps: a Visit to Ventnor' (posted on her website, 2011)

Poetry, Collections and single Odes and Lyrics by and about Women (see also on the Internet)

Arnell, Charles John, *An Anthology of Vectensian Poets* (Newport, The County Press, 1922)

Barrett Browning, Elizabeth, *Aurora Leigh: A Poem in Nine Books* (London, Smith, Elder & Co, 1890)

Elgar, Alice, 'Love Alone Will Stay' set to Music by Edward Elgar (1897)

Johnson, Mary Fitchett, *Original Sonnets and Other Poems* (London, Longman, Hurst, Rees & Orme, 1810)

Khalvati, Mimi, *Chine* (Manchester, Carcanet, 2002)

Khalvati, Mimi, *Child: News and Selected Poems* 1991–2011 (Manchester, Carcanet, 2011)

Meynell, Alice, 'A Father of Women; *Ad sororem* Elizabeth Butler' in Viola Meynell, *A Memoir*

Meynell, Alice, *Last Poems* (London, Burns, Gates and Washbourne Ltd, 1923)

Tennyson, Alfred, 'The May Queen'

Films, Plays and Operas about or featuring Women

BBC film, 'The Scandalous Lady W' (2015)

Gray, Maxwell, *The Reproach of Annesly*, filmed 1915

Gray, Maxwell, *The Secret of Dean Maitland* filmed 1914, 1915, 1934

Lawrence, DL, *The Trespasser* (film, 1981)

Manning, Olivia, *The Fortunes of War* (television Series, 1989)

Richter, Jane, 'Julia Margaret Cameron: Cameron, Coffee and Calcutta' (2023)

Woolf, Virginia, *Freshwater: A Comedy by Virginia Woolf* (the 1923 & 1935 Editions) (London, Hogarth Press, 1976)

Books, General

Albin, John, *A New, Correct, and Much-improved History of the Isle of Wight* (Newport, J Albin, 1795)

Aspinall-Oglander, Cecil, *Nunwell Symphony* (London, Hogarth Press, 1945)

Aspinall-Oglander, C. *The Roman Villa at Brading, Isle of Wight* (Newport, J Arthur Dixon c.1950)

Bamford, Francis, ed. *A Royalist's Notebook: The Commonplace book of Sir John Oglander* (London, Constable & co, 1936)

Berwick, WC, *Samuel Coleridge-Taylor Musician: His Life and Letters* (London, Forgotten Books, 1915)

Boynton, LOJ, *Appuldurcombe House, Isle of Wight* (London, Historic Buildings and Monuments Commission for England, 1986)

Bull, Andy, *Secret Isle of Wight* (Stroud, Amberley Publishing, 2022)

Cooper, Michael, 'A *More Beautiful City*': *Robert Hooke and the Rebuilding of London after the Great Fire* (Stroud, Gloucester, Sutton Publising Limited, 2003)

Cotton, Henry, *Indian and Home Memories* (London, TF Unwin, 1911)

Cox, J Charles, *County Churches – Isle of Wight* (London, George Allen and Sons, 1911)

Davies, Dorothy, *Captain of the Wight* (Ryde, Isle of Wight, Circle of Light Publications, 2008)

Englefield, Henry, *A Description of the Principal Picturesque Beauties … of the Isle of Wight* (London, William Bulmer and Co., 1816)

Hawkes, Jacquetta, *Prehistoric Britain* (London, Penguin, 1943)

James, Edward Boucher, *Letters Archaeological and Historical Relating to the Isle of Wight*, Vols.1 & 2 (Oxford, Henry Frowde, 1896)

Kaufmann, Miranda, *Black Tudors: The Untold Story* (London, OneWorld Publications, 2017)

Lockhart, Charles Stewart Montgomerie, *A General History of the Isle of Wight* (1810)

Long, WH, *The Oglander Memoirs* (London, Reeves and Turner, 1888)

Macready, Sarah, and FH Thompson, eds, *Cross-Channel Trade between Gaul and Britain in the Pre-Roman Iron Age* (London, Society of Antiquaries of London, c. 1984

Martin, Robert Bernard, *Tennyson: The Unquiet Heart* (London, Faber, 1983)

Mew, Fred, *Back of the Wight: Yarns of Wrecks and Smuggling* (Newport, County Press, 1957)

Noyes, Hugh, compiler, *The Isle of Wight Bedside Anthology* (Newport, The Isle of Wight County Press, 1951)

Owen, Montague Charles, *The Sewells of the Isle of Wight* (Manchester, Manchester Courier Ltd, 1906)

Paterson, *The Homes of Tennyson* (London, Adam and Charles Black, 1905)

Reyner, James, *The Isle of Wight's Missing Chapters* (Market Harborough, Book Guild Publishing Ltd, 2020)

Richards, John Morgan, *Almost Fairyland: Personal notes concerning the Isle of Wight* (London, John Hogg, 1914)

Rubenstein, Hilary L, *Catastrophe at Spithead: The Sinking of the Royal George* (Barnsley, Yorkshire, Seaforth Publishing, 2020)

Tennyson, Hallam, *Alfred Lord Tennyson: A Memoir* (London, Macmillan, 1897)

Tomalin, David J, Rebecca D Loader et al, *Coastal archaeology in a dynamic environment: A Solent case study* (Oxford, Archaeopress, 2012)

Wander, Tim, *The Ghosts of Northwood House* (Isle of Wight, New Generation Publishing, 2018)

Worsley, Richard, *The History of the Isle of Wight* (London, 1781)

Articles and Chapters, General

Butchart, CBR, 'Carisbrooke Castle and the Lords of the Isle of Wight' (Proceedings of the Hampshire Field Club and Archaeological Society, nd)

Harrington, Sue, 'A Well Married Landscape: Networks of Association and 6th Century Communities on the Isle of Wight' in *The land of English Kin: Studies in Wessex and Anglo-Saxon England in Honour of Professor Barbara Yorke* (Brill Online, 2020)

Jones, Randolph, 'Sir Hugh Tyrell and the French raid on the Isle of Wight August 1377' in *Hublar: Journal of the Lance and Longbow Society*, Issue no. 27, p 13 et seq

Nicholson, Cornelius, 'A Descriptive Account of the Roman Villa near Brading, Isle of Wight (London, 1880)

Redfern, Rebecca, 'Iron Age "Predatory Landscapes" a bioarchaeological and Funerary Exploration of Captivity and Enslavement', published online by Cambridge University Press: 14 April 2020

Thompson, Hugh, 'Iron Age and Roman Slave-Shackles, *Archaeological Journal*, Volume 150, issue 1, 1993, pp 57–168 (also online)

Tomalin, David and Rebecca Loader, 'An Archaeological Survey of the Wooton Quarr Coast' in *Time and Tide*, 1997; reprinted (Isle of Wight, Isle of Wight Council, 2002)

Whitehead, J 'The Priory and Manor of Appuldurcombe, Isle of Wight' (Hampshire Field Club and Archaeological Society (nd))

Whitehead, John, 'Notes of the Manor of Knighton, I of W, and the Early Manor Lords, AD 1066–1343' (Hampshire Field Club Papers, Vol. iii, pp 295–303)

Witherby, CT, 'The Battle of Bonchurch' (1962)

Newspapers, Magazines and Articles in them, and other media (also available on the Internet)

BBC posting, 'Isle of Wight "Pterosaur girl" named tourism ambassador'

The Hampshire Telegraph and Sussex Chronicle, 'Report of a Ball at Northwood House' (17 January 1891)

Island Echo, 'Largest known Eotryannus tooth discovered on the Isle of Wight' (2016)

Isle of Wight County Press 'Arrival of Benedictine Nuns on the Island' (21 August 1891)

Mael, Donald, 'Historian exposes secret sex life of Charles I' (*The Guardian*, 2007)

Manuscripts and Unpublished Documents

Calder, Ian, 'Julia Margaret Cameron', Talk at the Athenaeum, 2023

McAuley, Jenny, 'Ada Scott' (Oxford University Museum of Natural History Project 'Coming out of the Shadows', nd)

Richter, Jane, 'Chronology of the Life of Julia Margaret Cameron' (nd)

YouTube Video

Gleaning from Wood and Field Emma Dennet's plant paintings and poems

Jolliffe, Innell, 'Memories of Bonchurch' (Ventnor and District Local History Society, nd)

Reference Works (may also be online)

Armitage, Phillip, *Personnae Vectenses: Isle of Wight Notables* (Beachy Books, 2022)

The Australian Dictionary of National Biography (Australian National University, from 1966; now online)

Cox, Julian, and Colin Ford, *Julia Margaret Cameron: The Complete Photographs* (London, Thames and Hudson, 2003)

Green, Mary Anne Everett, *Lives of the Princessses of England*, vol 1 (Longman Brown Green, 1857)

Jeffares, Neil, Pastels and Pastellists. *Dictionary of Pastelists before 1800* (2006)

Long, William Henry, *A Dictionary of the Isle of Wight Dialect ... with illustrative anecdotes ...* (London, Reeves & Turner 1886)

Medland, JC, *Discovering Domesday Wight* (Newport, JC Medland, 2015)

The Oxford Dictionary of National Biography (Benjamin Piercy) (Oxford, Oxford University Press, 2004–)

Sparrow, Walter Shaw, *Women Painters of the World from the time of Caterine Vigri, 1413–1462 to Rose Bonheur and the Present Day* (London, Hodder & Stoughton, 1905) (and on the Internet)

Weir, Alison, *Britain's Royal Families: The Complete Genealogy* (London, Bodley Head, 1989)

Regular postings on different subjects (online)

Ancestry: Family Search

British History online: 'Ashey Manor'

British History online: 'Sir Thomas Kyme'

British History online: 'Nicholas de Morgan (Brook Manor)'

British History online: 'Yarmouth (King John)'

'Hidden Heroes' website: 'Arwald'

'Hidden Heroes' website: 'Isabella de Fortibus'

'Hidden Heroes' website: 'Mary Gleed Tuttiett (Maxwell Gray)'

'Hidden Heroes' website: 'Christabella Millgate'

'Hidden Heroes' website: 'Blanche Thornycroft'

'History of the Isle' website: 'Bembridge'

Island Echo website: 'Blue Lady of Nettlestone'

Island Echo website: 'Charles I and Princess Elizabeth'

Island Echo website: 'David Couldrey'

Island Echo website: 'Sophie Dawes'

Island Echo website: 'Knighton Gorges hauntings'

Island Echo website: 'What the Dickens' (2023)

Island Eye website: 'Gatcombe'

Island Eye website: 'Priory Bay Hotel'

Island Eye website: 'Manor Houses of the Isle of Wight'

Oglander, Sir John

Red Funnel website: 'Shipwrecks and Smugglers'

Toms, Jan 'Brief Biographies'

janisleofwight website: 'John Wilkes'

janisleofwight website: 'Countess of Clare – Marriage, Love, Good Works'

janisleofwight website: 'Elizabeth and Catherine Bull of Northcourt'

Wottonbridge website: 'Haseley, people of'

Wottonbridge website: 'St George's Church, Arreton'

Wottonbridge website: Paul, David, 'Forgotten Castle'

Internet Material (website not always given here; best to put name, author or title into browser; dates often missing online)

Burton, Henry Thomas, 'Descent from Edward III for Dowsabel Burton, Heiress of Kins[ley House]', (posted 2007)

Carr, Neville, posting 'The Gallus Mosaic'

'Covent Garden and Sir John Baber Physician to Charles II'

Davis, Revd RG, 'Historical Notes on the Manor of Knighton in the Isle of Wight' (posted, Hampshire Field Club & Archaeological Society, nd)

Dick, Margaret, Obituary (1878) (posted by Ventnor & District Local History Society)

'Dispatches From the Former New World' (2021)

Fox, Alex, posting, 2020, 'Hares and Chickens Were Revered as Gods – Not Food in Ancient Britain'

Gale, Tony, 'Churches and Chapels in Ryde' (posted by the Catholic History Society, nd)

'Hampshire During the Black Death and the 100 Years' War 1337–1444' (posted Wilcuma website)

Hudson, TC, 'Elizabeth [of Austria] Slept Here': An Appreciation of Steephill Castle' (posted by Northwood Village, 2011)

Isle of Wight History Centre 'Napoleon, Josephine and the Fishermen of Cowes' (2016)

Maidstone Museum, 'Staff Pick', 'Slave Chains' (2016)

Martin, Robert, 'The Scientist, the Grocer, the Governor and Grace' (posted online by Isle of Wight History Centre, 2000)

'Memorials and Monuments on the Isle of Wight' – Ryde – Brigstocke Trough Fountain (nd)

Morris, Daisy, Blog 2014

Napier, Derrick, blog, nd, 'Newport Roman Villa'

Thornton, Joanne, 'Exploring Elizabethan Newport and Historical Events Beyond' (posted County Press 2022)

University of Lincolnshire Repository, 'The Laureate and the Republic: Tennyson and the United States', 2017)

Whitmore, Warren ('Caulkhead Family Names') (posted, *Island Echo*, 2023)

Willoughby, Rupert, posting, 'Newport Roman Villa' (2018)

Index

Note: several subjects are grouped together, starting with art galleries and exhibition spaces. If you cannot immediately find a subject or person, it is worth looking for them under their grouping, which is likely to be obvious, for example, 'Artists including musicians', 'Manors houses'. Although entries of men are limited, husbands may be in brackets after their wives.